REALITY
ESCAPE FROM PLANET EARTH

REALITY- IS THE STATE OF THINGS AS THEY ACTUALLY EXIST, RATHER THAN AS THEY MAY APPEAR OR MIGHT BE IMAGINED. IN A WIDER DEFINITION, REALITY INCLUDES EVERYTHING THAT IS AND HAS BEEN, WHETHER OR NOT IT IS OBSERVABLE OR COMPREHENSIBLE. A STILL BROADER DEFINITION OF REALITY INCLUDES EVERYTHING THAT HAS EXISTED, EXISTS, OR WILL EXIST.

MIKE BRUMFIELD

WARNING: POSSIBLY THE MOST TORTUOUS EVIDENCE OF MANKIND!

Kawliga Publishing

REALITY
ESCAPE FROM PLANET EARTH
MIKE BRUMFIELD

Kawliga Publishing

© December 31, 2015 Mike Brumfield

All rights reserved. No part of this book may be reproduced or utilized in any form or by any means, electronic or mechanical, including photocopying, recording, or by any information storage and retrieval system, without permission in writing from the publisher.

ISBN-13:978-0-9908846-0-6
In Publication Data
Brumfield, Mike.
Phone: 740-993-9646
To order a signed copy send a check or money order to
1752 Wakefield Mound Road, Piketon, OH 45661

Categories:
BODY, MIND & SPIRIT / UFOs & Extraterrestrials
BISAC Code: OCC025000

Cover inking by Sarah Sents Cook
Printed in the United States

Other Books by Michael Brumfield

Is this our reality and is it happening **"EVERYWHERE"**?

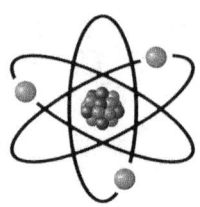 # ABOUT THE AUTHOR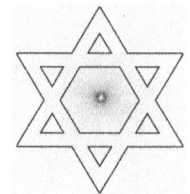

Hello everyone, I am Will, Mikes lifelong best friend. He's asked me to tell you a little about him. In his words, it just wouldn't be "RIGHT", for him to talk about himself. Well, I will give it my best shot. I will, because he begged me to. I've watched him, live a "RELATIVELY HARD LIFE" and can tell you, we are both lucky to be alive! He'll "TESTIFY" to that! He also says, that we're all lucky to be alive, after the "METEOR EVENT", in 2013. I didn't understand, then.

But, I do now. This event really changed us. He immediately contacted me and started writing this book. He told me, that after this, he is going to spend the rest of his life, educating people, about our need go "UP" and live in space. I "BELIEVED" him. I still do!

First of all, he wants everyone to know, that his life could have been worse, a lot worse. He is very grateful, because of this "FACT" and wants, no pity, only forgiveness, for hurting people. He makes it "PAINFULLY" clear, that he hurts alot of people, telling his story and needs all the forgiveness, he can get. He is most apologetic, to his sons and is spilling his guts, to stop the further mistreatment of children, everywhere! He says kids lives are shattered daily, at the hands of their "POWER" hungry parents, like him and he doesn't want them to suffer, any longer. He is writing this story for them! He says kids, are the future! They deserve better.

Mike wants all children, cherished and protected, more than anything else. He believes, we should give our lives, for the "GOOD" of our children. I "BELIEVE" him. I have kids!

I'll start at the beginning and give you a brief over-view, of who Mike is and how this book, came to be. Mike was born in Portsmouth, Ohio on 9-29-1961. As he was growing up, I saw his dad, constantly bounce him back and forth, from there to Marion, Ohio. His mother's concerns, over their unhappiness, never seemed to matter. He was the boss and they all knew it! He made sure of it, by beating it into them. Mike's mother included! He did have a good side, though. He loved them all deeply. He was, "MENTALLY SICK".

Mike tortuously, attended 10 different schools in 12 years and was bullied, at every turn. However, he "SUFFERED" through it all and still managed to graduate, in 1979!

Unfortunately, less than a year later, he was arrested for D.U.I. and forced to enroll in college, join the military, or go to jail! He chose the Marine Corps. He thought it would give him the best chance to pursue higher education and not burden himself, nor his parents, with any future debt. He said he done this, because it the "RIGHT" thing, to do. Mike came from a hardworking, lower middle class, blue collar family, who definitely couldn't afford it. Not to mention, the fact, that he was raised by a dad, who strictly enforced everyone pulling their weight. I know he was raised hard! I was also afraid of his dad! Sadly enough, several of his family members had already died. Mike knows, that he could be next. He said he's been dead, since his little sister "PASSED" on. She was only three days old. He shared his guilt of not being able to take her place. He doesn't want to live, without her!

In 1980, he shipped out to boot camp. It didn't go well. He "SURVIVED", being "LIED TO BY RECRUITERS", a vengeful drill instructor, and then sixteen long hard months, trying to change his M.O.S./job.

The one he was given, prevented him from going to college. This devastated him, because it was the only reason he joined. This, was his goal! He tried to remedy the situation, failing time and time, again. Mike, wouldn't get the chance, to fulfill his dream of higher education, until, after he got out of the military.

Finally, in 1982, after, going a.w.o.l., and having to accept a discharge, called a G.O.S./" good of the service", he made it home. The next day he started college. But, not before "HELL" would pay him a visit, one more time, on his way home! Well, he actually said "AGAIN", not one more time. That's my "MISTAKE". Why again, though? Well, because, he said he already served his time, in hell and could prove it! He saw a sign, saying this very thing, as he crossed a bridge, going to boot camp. It read plain as day! Welcome to hell, boot camp in Paris island, S.C.!!! He recalled painfully, how he said "NOT AGAIN", as he passed under the sign. "Sadly" after that, he said. "It would never stop!"

Well, Mike said, that it surely was hell, alright. But, it was nothing compared to what was coming his way. It was far worse! He describes it as the most "EVIL" hell, in the universe.

His descriptions, of the torturous pain it causes him, are bone chilling. I don't think I was prepared, for what I was about to hear, let alone see. He would breakdown many times and yes, I would even break, with him. Let me, tell you, his story was very hard, for me to endure. With every agonizing memory, came a flood of emotion. I could truly feel the fear and resentment, that he had of his father, when he was a child. I could also feel his remorse and shame, which he still carries, for "UNINTENTIONALLY" doing the same, to his own sons. I have it, as well. I'm so happy, that he is breaking this vicious cycle. He now understands why and how, this happened. It wasn't his dad, nor him, that done these things. It was their "EGO". I can relate. I think we all can. We all have the "DAMN" thing!

He firmly states, that our egotistical sexual nature is the "DEVIL" of our species! He understands why his parents religion didn't help him or his dad, in curing it. He says religion's devil story is ridiculous. To him, it's isn't a person, it's our "EGO" and he still fights his everyday. Unfortunately, "IT" still wants him to live, for himself, though! He says he can't, it's illogical. He knows, that it's sexually driven and has taken the intellectual path! He told me, that he lives for his family and made a vow, to never hurt them or anyone else, again. The last thing he said, made me cry.

He spoke softly and with tears in his eyes, said "children are looking into the eyes of devils, everywhere, even as I speak." He paused and then said, "the sad thing is, that most of them are sexually addicted parents, like Tammy and I "WERE"! I knew this, all too well! I shook, as I remembered too many bad experiences, with my kids. Anyway, Mike told me about one of his. He got so angry at Matt being jealous of him and his mother, getting ready to have sex, that he spanked him!!! He said he felt like, he became possessed! Matt was only seven at the time. He said he was so ashamed! He cried out, that he didn't mean to "GET ANGRY" and tried to hug him. But, Matt still drew away from him, like he'd seen a monster. Mike says, that moment killed him. Matt did see a monster and he wasn't in his "RIGHT MIND". I quickly told him, he was right! I also know, what wanting sex, can turn people into. I became a devil, to my own son, because of it and I am also ashamed, for it. We both hugged and cried tears of shame.

As, he slowly began telling his story, you could see this, anguishing torturous mental pain, building up inside of him, with every word he spoke. It really was, as if, he was fighting, a "DEMON, TRYING TO DEFEND ITSELF"! Thank god, Mike was winning. However, it became very apparent, that he certainly had experienced a nightmare of hellish proportions. He had experienced things, that I never knew about. But, I did know, one thing for certain. What he was recalling must've been very traumatic and I felt like, if I didn't stop him, it would just hurt him, all over "AGAIN"! I didn't want to do that and started to stop the interview. But, he suddenly choked, struggled and continued telling his story.

"The worst kind of hell", he said barely able to hold back the wave of emotions, building inside him. "Happens when parents lose it and become monsters at each other, in front of their children. It destroys their trust, just when they need it most!" He spoke with so much sadness, that we both broke. "I know", he said sobbing. "Because I've done it and am still doing it. Even though feel I have to do this, it is still my greatest regret. I thought I could "CONTROL" the situation. I tried my best, to help my son's sexually addicted mother, get help. But, it always made a monster of me, too! I couldn't save them, I can't save shit.", he wailed. I got up and hugged him. We took a break.

After a breather and some much needed beers, to calm our nerves, we got back at it. He started by saying, again. That he was telling his story, so other kids wouldn't have to suffer, at he hands of sexually addicted parents, any longer! He was determined to make amends, for what he had done, to his own. I really didn't know the extent of what had happened. Just, that it was bad and he desperately needed to do this. So, I'm his best friend and that's what I'm here for. Who am I to judge him. Besides, everyone will need a friend, sooner or later. I need him. I've done some pretty bad things, myself.

We picked up where he left off, boot camp hell! He said, crossing that bridge, was just the beginning of "IT". His world would soon become a "SEXUAL HELL"! It would never stop, ever. He broke again and said, he is still living it today! I'll never forget that moment. It felt, like I could've ripped the air "OPEN", with a knife. But, even if I could, I knew I still couldn't escape his "REALITY". The "SEXUAL TORTURE" he was revealing in his life, ravages the entire species of mankind. Sadly, "IT" has always "RULED" our world. At that moment, we could've heard a pin drop. The silence was deafening. I didn't think he could continue. Then suddenly, he came apart and really broke down.

"It still doesn't stop", he screamed out, grabbing his head and shaking it. The tears, again, came streaming down his face. He began shaking uncontrollably and involuntarily, spewing out all the painful memories, of his past. His body heaved with convulsions, as he recalled each one. He carried so much guilt, for not being able to stop his anger! He went on and on, about how he failed to protect his son, from his wife's affairs and his outburst. He said she became a man-eater and "DIDN'T CARE", about him, her family or anyone else around! His marriage was spinning out of control and he couldn't stop it or leave. She made sure of that, he said. Many times, he left and filled his son with fear, from his own anger. He cried for mercy and begged for his "FORGIVENESS", over and over, again. I hesitated a minute, but had to ask him, why he couldn't forgive himself. I knew, that he would never hurt his sons, intentionally. He turned his face toward me and with a look of sadness, that I hadn't never seen before, said bluntly.

"Because, I became an angry monster, in front of my kids and there's no excuse for that. None, goddamn it!" he screamed. "I'm their dad. I scared the hell out of them! That's, not what a dad is supposed to do. I could've just put up with her bullshit, instead of trying to stop it. Instead, I broke! It happened, way too many times. I let my ego get the best of me and I hurt them!" He ended harshly and directed all his anger toward himself. I let him. I knew he didn't want my pity.

He dropped his head, as the tears flowed and he looked away. At this point, I stopped the interview, if you want to call it that. I didn't, I'm his best friend. I was just trying to help him. I didn't want to do this. I could hardly bear his pain, myself. I tried to get out of doing this. But, he begged me and said he had to tell his story. He felt it best, for me to tell you, instead of him. Again, he said it just wouldn't be right. He says he was wrong for getting angry, period! Logically and scientifically, he knows that he is still way too angry, to tell anything. But, he said he has too! I can see, that he doesn't hurt, anymore. When, all is said and done, he says he only wants to be, "FORGIVEN". He said he would want the same. "This book is for Tammy's forgiveness" he told me bluntly. If I can forgive her, then her son and everyone else can too!" He always cited the golden Rule and says he has to live it, no matter what. He said we all have to be perfect, if we want to make the world perfect, for our children. I'm not surprised, by his "LOGIC". He says it is his goal, at this point, in life. Wow, he wasn't talking, like a man living for himself, anymore. He was obviously living for his kids. No, all kids. Slowly, he began to finish telling his story. Before he did, though. He looked me square in my eyes and said the most beautiful thing.

"You want to know, why I have to do this? I do, because it's only logical, that in an "INFINITE UNIVERSE", only the good guys would finish last. Well, I don't mind being last." he said with a slight smile. "I'm "GRATEFUL" to be alive and I sure don't mind being last as long as I finish. Hell, I just hope there will be a "LAST to die! I don't want my kids to die or anyone else, for that matter. I'd "GIVE EVERYTHING" if I could bring my family back. I'm lost without them. I'm lost! I would give my life, to cure death for everyone and end this first/last bullshit. I would, because I'm a dad and... I want "FORGIVENESS"! I grabbed him. We hugged, long and hard. I loved him, like my brother. I knew he was still grieving over his niece Linda and nephew Danny's, recent death's. This was the moment, I needed. After we separated, I asked him to just try and focus on, finishing this bio. His memories caused him, too much pain. He nodded his head and picked up, where he left off. I was sickened, by what happened next.

He said, another bus ride from "HELL", was about to, roll into his life. Again! "But", he puffed up and defiantly blurted out. "At least this time, though. I was going to college and nothing was going to stop me!" "Well, you sure did, do that, bud!" I instantly replied in admiration. I watched him do it, on his own and take care of his son, on the weekends. He said it wasn't a big deal. But, I knew it was. However, he always reminded me, of all the help he got, along the way. "Anybody can sign-up. The hard part is doing it. I done it with help, from my family and Sam! I was lucky and I'll forever be in their debt." He never "FORGOT" them. I know that! He continued to tell me his story.

It was summertime in 1982. Immediately, upon receiving his discharge, from Camp Lejune, North Carolina, he headed back to his parents house, in Ohio. Like I said earlier, on a greyhound bus, from "HELL". I asked him why he called it that. He quickly replied, "bus stations are hell! They're full of sexual predators, just waiting to prey on green scared kids, like me." I knew what he meant. I've been to some scary bus stations! Anyway, he began to tell me, that he had left his car there, but would find out, it was now up north, in Marion. His dad let his brother Steve, who lived there and had gone home with mom and dad, drive it home. He said, that this one "TWIST OF FATE" would change his life, forever. It gave him "SAM"!

Anyway, before this would happen, he first, had to get back "HOME". Here's where you better get ready and brace yourself. It gets bad. "REAL BAD"! His trip back, included a three hour layover, in Winston Salem, N.C.. As he patiently waited, a man approached and asked, to sat beside him. Mike immediately said o.k.. He said he "LOOKED NORMAL"! The stranger began telling Mike, that he was also waiting, on the same bus. He said, that his nephew was coming home, from the military. Right! He talked Mike, into going "SOMEWHERE", having a beer and shooting some pool. He said it was close by.

"Everything seemed so legitat first", Mike said disgusted like. "But, it didn't turn out to be the case." He said they drove away from the city and soon, pulled into a city park! He then revealed, that he was a deputy sheriff and just needed to stop for a minute! Mike said he couldn't believe what was happening and knew what was "COMING". He said the guy reached over and opened the glove box. Mike's said his heart began to beat his brains out and it took everything he had to keep from hyper-ventilating, when he saw "THE GUN"! Immediately, he raised up, with the gun in his hand and asked to give Mike oral sex! Mike suddenly felt helpless. He had no choice and told him, that he would, but only if they went back to the bus station, first!

The man quickly agreed. He laid the gun between them, on the seat. Mike said, that he suddenly felt like, he was just given a "MIRACLE". The man said he was doing this, to prove he wasn't going to hurt him. Mike, breathed a sigh of relief and immediately, came up with a plan. He said, he still can't believe, to this day, that he didn't panic and grab the gun. "SOMEHOW" and for some "REASON", he said with utter relief, in his voice. He just knew, it would've been the worse thing, he could've done. Instead, gripped with fear, he just kept praying, that this "NEW PLAN", would work. It had, too! He trembled with fear, at the worst case scenario. It kept raping his mind, mile after mile, as the ride back, dragged tortuously by. Was he going to get framed, if he had to pull the gun on the guy, to try and get away? Even worse, was his vision of having the guy, pull the gun on him and make him do things, that he couldn't even think about, let alone do! His body convulsed, at the thought of it! But, he had to stop it. He knew he had to make a decision, fast. Little did he know, the new plan was about to "UNFOLD"! He described the next ten minutes, as the most torturous of his life!

He said it seemed like an eternity, but soon they pulled back, into the bus station parking lot. The encounter started, immediately. Mike said he was frantically trying to decide what to do, but the sheriff caught him off guard and grabbed his belt to undo it. He still couldn't believe, what was happening. He just knew, that he had to make his move and he had to make it, fast. Suddenly, he felt the stranger "GROWING" oblivious, to his surroundings. At this point, he just wanted "SEX"! This, was the moment, Mike was "PLANNING", for. Suddenly, just as he "FELT" the opportunity "ARISE", he started to pull the gun on the guy. He was going to try and turn him in. But, much to his surprise, something entirely different happened, instead. He suddenly saw his bus pull in and start loading up. Wow! He couldn't believe his eyes. Without hesitation, he grabbed the keys and pulled the man's head up, by his hair. He jumped out of the car and told the begging cop, just how lucky he was, to be alive. The cop knew it and begged him, for the keys. Mike said he made the guy give him all his money and then threw the keys, as hard as he could. He said he cussed him good, turned and ran onto the bus. He made it, just as it was getting ready to shut it's doors and pull out. Instantly, he knew that he made the right decision. This, was his only way out, without repercussion! Who would believe him? I immediately asked him about taking the money. He said it somewhat, vindicated his actions. He, at least got paid, for the acting. He said, unfortunately, from then on he knew he could sell himself! He saw the "POWER OF SEX" and it's hold on humans. "Wow, poor Mike!", I said to myself.

He continued his story. Luckily, as he got to the bus door, he saw an empty seat and it was right behind the driver! He said, that he shook with relief and quickly collapsed, into it. He described numbly, how he sat there in disbelief, as he watched the sheriff, frantically climb out of the car and began searching, for his keys. He sat there watching, as the bus pulled away. For one second, their eyes met. Mike, could see in the man's eyes, that his "ESCAPE" worked. He knew he couldn't do anything, about it. Sadly, though, Mike did, too!!!

Mike finished the story and turned away. He had tears in his eyes. I heard him say, how lucky he was, to have gotten away. I hugged him and agreed. He told me, that he wants everyone to forgive the man. He said, that even though he didn't want to, then. In hindsight, he's glad he did. He said he is, because he knows first-hand, how sexual torture can drive a person to do terrible things. He saw it his whole life, starting with his grandfather. Then, with his brothers and best friends. He finally, revealed his own shameful, torturous memories. He cried mercilessly and begged for forgiveness, after he told me about them. He ultimately recalled the most horrible moment of his life, when he almost did something sexual, to his one-year-old niece. It happened while she lay asleep, nursing her bottle. He was 11. He heard his dad come in, just as he was getting ready. He thanks his "DAD" for stopping. He said he was more afraid of him, than god! It was then, and only then, that his "RIGHT MIND", took over! He immediately "SNAPPED BACK TO REALITY" and put his 'LITTLE PRIVATE PART", away. It was just inches, from her face! Right then, he cried out, that he felt like a sex crazed monster and immediately ran to the bathroom. He quickly relieved himself. He knew how. He watched his grandpa do it. From then on, when he felt this way, he masturbated. Just like, his "MENTALLY SICK" grandfather, did. He said he had, too. It kept him from doing more crazy stuff, like masturbating his grand........no, read on. He does talk about it. Again, he says he has, too! "We all do.", he ended disgustedly. Mike said he continued doing it, like a "MAD DOG". His brothers "DIRTY MAGAZINES" made sure of that. They tortured his mind. He knew where they were. He "FOUND" and "LOOKED" at them, everyday.

His dad beat his grandfather several times, in front of the family and it still didn't cure him. He said it was terrible and the first time it happened, he saw "SEX", as our biggest problem! It could make people become evil monsters! But, he knew it was, when it almost made him one. He vowed it would never happen, again. He said it was ironic, that through his grandfather's illness, he inadvertantly learned how to relieve, his own sexual torture! How sad, that at such a fragile age, he had to "ACCIDENTALLY" discover sex. Even worse, he couldn't talk about it, with his family. "Shame on society", He blurted out. "How can we let this keep happening, to our children. Why do we have to hide, from such a "SIMPLE TRUTH", about ourselves? Why do we make "SEX", so taboo?"

Shameful, as all this was and is for Mike, he still claims, that he has to tell his story! He says he has to, because he finally films flying saucer and to him, their obvious technological superiority proves, "NOTHING IS HIDDEN, THAT WON'T BE REVEALED" To him, our minds will be "READ"! He says, the future isn't coming. It's here "NOW". He "SEES", that it is just a "MATTER OF TIME", before "TIME'S" not relative, anymore!" This was deep for me. You will soon read why, as you discover his "INFINITE ASTRONAUT THEORY"! Beware, it challenges everyone to logically "RE- EXAMINE THE SPIRIT STORIES

AND IMAGINE THE FUTURE, EXISTING NOW"! Anyway, he wants everybody to know, that he is so ashamed and sorry, for what he "ALMOST" done, to his precious little niece. I know Mike would never hurt her, another child or anyone, in a million years. Now, I know why he has to do this, I suddenly realized, this was for her!!! He began crying and begging, for her forgiveness. He jumped up and screamed, "GOD-DAMN our sexual nature! How can I not, "CONFESS"?" I am guilty", he screamed in disgust, as he started pulling his hair. I started toward him. He began to slap himself, in the face. I finally grabbed him, but not before he managed to punch himself, in the face. He tried to do it again. We fell to the floor, as I struggled to stop him. He continued to flail at himself and begged me, to let him be. I tightened my grip and just held him. He finally collapsed in my arms and hollered, "THE TRUTH SHALL SET US FREE, GODDAMN IT! THE SAUCERS HAVE ALWAYS EXISTED AND SO HAS MANKIND'S SEXUAL NATURE. THIS IS HELL AND SADLY, WE LOVE IT!!!" The last thing he done, was beg me for forgiveness. I forgave him. After that, I was the one who needed the break.

    I smoked a cigarette or two and got some fresh air. I didn't want to go back inside and finish the interview. But, I did. Mike begged me. He, slowly continued his story and you could see his pain. I couldn't imagine experiencing, what happened to him, in Winston Salem, N.C.. But, as bad as that was, he told me things were about to get, even worse. I didn't see how they could. But, they did! He explained how he tried to relax, for the next three hours and couldn't. He was having a hard time, dealing with it. Again, little did he know, "SEXUAL HELL" was about to torture him, "AGAIN". I really didn't think, that things could get any worse. But, believe me, they do! As he continued his story, I began to wonder, how he ever made it "HOME". Unfortunately, Mike had another layover in Charleston, W. Va.. It was a Saturday night, in the worst part of town and about midnight, when he got there. The bus station was filled with shady looking people and smelled terrible. He immediately, saw a fellow service member and grabbed the empty seat, beside him. They introduced themselves and started to talk. Mike said, that all of a sudden, the man abruptly gets up and starts toward a man, coming through the door. Mike knew a drug deal was happening. The men exchanged money and left. Twenty minutes later, he returned. He confided in Mike and told him, the deal had gone bad! He asked Mike, to walk with him and help look for the guy. Mike hesitated, but the man started begging. Reluctantly, he "GAVE IN" and followed the man. He stopped at this point and abruptly told me, he was lucky to return!

No sooner, than they got outside and started down the street, a carload of party goers, shouted "QUEER" at them. Mike, immediately told the guy, to keep silent and move away. He didn't. Less than thirty seconds later, he was being sucker-punched, knocked down, kicked and beat repeatedly, while he rolled on the ground. He said he desperately tried to get away, but It wasn't working! He finally, grabbed the guys leg and pulled him off balance. He quickly jumped to his feet, only to face a girl, swinging a tire iron at him! He said he'd been hit enough. So, he turned, caught it and acted like, he was going to hit her, with it. She stopped, for a split second. He knew better, than to stay and fight or try talking his way, out of it. Logic already proved, that. He should've run in the first place, instead of talking. He said he looked over and saw the other guy getting beat, pretty bad. He wanted to help, but this was his chance.

Instead of repeating history, he said he just turned and began running for his life. After he got away, he stopped and turned toward them. He screamed for the guy to run, but he didn't. He just kept fighting back. He wanted to help, but realized, that this guy caused all of this. How could he "TRUST" him? Somebody could get killed! No, not again. Mike said he was lucky enough, already. He just escaped one possible murderous outcome and said he wasn't taking a chance, on another. Instead, he ran back to the bus station, as hard as he could and notified the police. Thank God he didn't stay and fight, everyone. My "BROTHER" survived! Mike added, that the stranger was alright. He came back to the station, before Mike left. Mike, said he wasn't alright, though. His world radically changed, from that day, forward! He said he wanted revenge, but knew "BETTER". He knew he could have died, that day! He raged, that it could've happened at the hands of these "CRAZY SEXUAL HUMANS" or his own ego. He ended by sayin he's just lucky to be alive. In fact, he added, that a part of him, did die though! His ego! But, he didn't care. Like he said, at least, he finally made it home and "SURVIVED"! From then on, he said he became suspicious of everybody. His innocence was gone. To him, "CRAZY HUMANS" shattered and killed "IT". He said they still do, everywhere he goes!

He went straight to college the next day, after telling his parents, what happened. He had to tell them, he couldn't hide it. His mom saw his busted lip immediately, when they picked him up. He lied about it. But, he couldn't lie any longer, after they got home. She saw his bruises, when he took off his clothes to bathe and cried uncontrollably. He had to confide in her, to calm her down. However, he never told anyone about the sheriff, until... "SOMETHING MYSTERIOUS HAPPENED"! Read on! One morning after college, he headed north, hitch-hiking to get his car. He made it to Columbus, when a stranger, who "JUST SO HAPPENED TO BE" a lawyer in his hometown, "MYSTERIOUSLY" picked him up. His name was Sam Frowine and he had just finished his first visit to see the doctor, after recently having a lung removed. He asked Mike where he was headed and said he was going south. Mike said he told Sam, that he was headed north and it was o.k.. They were both surprised , when Sam asked Mike where he was from. Much to their surprise, they both lived in Portsmouth, Ohio! Well, this man, not only went out of his way, to take Mike to Marion, which is fifty miles north of Columbus. He even did it, with his eyelids taped in place. He couldn't shut them and had to constantly put drops in them, to keep them from drying out. If this wasn't enough, he also helped Mike financially, when Mike returned home! Sam, soon, would even steer him toward a law degree! Mike said, Sam was an "ANGEL"! He became his mentor and confidante. Sam was the first, to ever hear of Mike's sexual molestation, by the sheriff. Mike said he will forever be indebted to him, for listening!

According to Mike, because of Sam's help, he graduated from Shawnee State Community College, in 1986, with an Associate of Applied Sciences and History. Sam, not only helped Mike nurture his thirst for knowledge, he kept insisting, that he continue pursuing a higher degree. Mike, more than gladly cooperated. He said he excelled and for the next three years, pursued a History degree through Ohio University's partnership, at his home school. Sam, successfully talked him into, becoming a lawyer. But, it wouldn't happen, before Sam died. It still hasn't, "YET". They did have a good run together, though. He would soon, even get to see Mike make wooden indian's! But first, Mike worked as a social worker, for three years and then one year as a general manager of a brand new assisted living center. All, while attending college full time and raising his son. Sam was so proud of him. Everything was going great. Then, he started chasing women and getting deeper into drugs. He was trying to get rich, so he could help, "EVERYONE". His grades started failing. He tried to be a "ROBIN HOOD" and it was getting the best of him!

Sadly enough, his pursuit of a law degree, ended abruptly. Not because of the grade problem or the finances. But, because of a surprising and unusual phone call, from his "FAMOUS UNCLE BRICE", who was an artist/woodcarver, living in Phoenix, Arizona. He "DESPERATELY" needed Mike's help, on a legal matter. His step-sons were filing a lawsuit against him, over his wealthy wife's estate and had seized his bank accounts. Mike was only in his fifth year of college. He wasn't a lawyer. He couldn't pass calculus the previous year and it kept him, from getting a bachelor's in Business. Without it, he couldn't get into law school. He wanted to help Brice, but said he really didn't want to stop school. When, all was said and done, he went with Sam's blessing! Sam loved Brice and his art! He even offered to help Mike, act as a paralegal, for Brice's attorney. He, also promised to help him finish school, when he got back, no matter what. Sam died two years later and Mike never returned to school. He says he still, very much wants and plans to finish! He wants to do it for Sam, Brice and himself! Well, Like I said earlier, in 1987, Mike followed his heart and Sam's advice. He made the trek west. "How could he not", he boldly stated, and then cited "GOLDEN RULE"! He said that he had to help him, because he would've wanted the same, for himself. Besides, he was the only artist in the family and Brice had no biological children! Mike lived with Brice for the next two years, off and on. Brice had to eventually settle, for less than he expected and Mike ended up back in Ohio. Damn lawyers sucked him dry, Mike said! Even though, things didn't "COMPLETELY" work out. Another mysterious "PHONE CALL/INVITATION" would, yet again, "CHANGE" his life. And strangely enough, it would involve Brice! Wow, crazy huh! Meeting Sam was weird enough. But man, could this really be a "COINCIDENCE", too!

Well, this "TIME", it was 1989 and the next "PHONE CALL" brought him to Nashville, Tennessee. It was here, that he would re-discover his true passion of music. But, thankfully enough though, not before he learned to carve wooden Indian's, with his Uncle Brice. Especially, since it paid the bills then and still does, now! He says, he can't ever thank him enough and will always be grateful, till the day he dies. He treasures, the memories of painting his Indians and carving with him. According to Mike, he is the one who made him, the artist he is today! However, he's also quick to thank, his entire family, for their support. He says they all helped him, even the little ones. They all love to paint his indians. He loves being "UNCLE MIKE", just like uncle Brice did! This is where he starts to tear up. I asked him why. He said he cherishes kids, because they are everything. "Brice did too", he quickly added. He revealed, that his nieces and nephews, show him more love, than his own kids. I felt sad for him. He told me, not to and feel sorry for them. He said they didn't have a mom and dad who stayed together, just like Brice. He did. He said he was lucky and knew, that his boys loved him. He also knows he isn't alone in this sad, world-wide epidemic. He finished by saying,"unfortunately, hell is a broken family and they're everywhere!" I sure agreed. My own was broken!

Remarkable, as it is, Mike's life, was indeed forever changed, by "NASHVILLE" and Brice's art had everything, to do with it! He had made a wooden Indian, for the Country Music star, John Schneider, back in the seventies and it was used on "The Dukes of Hazard" television show. It became his signature piece of artwork and like Mike, everybody loved it! He also made them for Waylon Jennings, Loretta Lynn, and many other, famous country music stars. Wow, was this "DESTINY" or what? Had "FATE" taken over or did it just "SEEMINGLY" guide Mike's "FUTURE"? What are the odds, that of all this groundwork had been laid decades earlier, by Brice and now was paving the way, for Mike's instant success! Well, Mike said he wouldn't call it instant success, but he surely was welcomed into their homes and musical lives, because of it. I saw that, with my own eyes.

He began selling art, to all these celebrities and his future seemed to be unfolding, right before our very eyes. He said it all started, with a daily carving exhibition, at his friend's satellite business, in Nashville. It was here, that he met and married the grand-daughter, of the late Lester Flatt, Tammy. Her papa was half of the famous country music duo "Flatt and Scruggs", best known for their number one hit, "The Ballad of Jed Clampett". Mike didn't know them, just the song, from the Beverly Hillbillies. Little, did he know, just how famous, they really were. Well, he was about to find out. She had a brother and mother, but was the majority owner, of his estate. She lived with him, till she was 12 and stayed under his control, for the next three years. He died in 1979. He couldn't believe it and didn't know, until after they married, the full extent of her "POWER". His buddy did, though! He begged Mike to marry her. It turned out, that she got royalties, from "The Beverly Hillbillies"!!!

Wow! Great, right? Well, not so fast. Things were about to turn bad, for Mike, again. Why? Well, if this tells you anything, he said it took two years, but he eventually married her. She was married twice before and spent her inreitance. He said she was viciously mean and spoiled, but has a beautiful side, as well. She was raised by a very "MATERIALISTIC" family and her mother was threatening to sue her, within a month of them getting together! He said like Tammy, she also has a beautiful side, to her personality. But, when it was bad, it was bad! The same applied to her famous mother Gladys. None of them, were always this way. They all had a good side. However, the bad would ultimately destroy our relationships. Sadly, this wasn't the worst thing to deal with. Mike's wife wasn't just spoiled and materialistic. She also had an addiction to sex and power! In hindsight, Mike says, the only "REAL" bright side in all of this, was his "SONS" birth! I know another one, though. He's alive! You'll soon see why, as you read on.

It wasn't long, before Mike tried becoming an aspiring country duo act, with his friend. Unfortunately, his friend had another agenda, as well. He had an O.B.E (out of body experience) and quickly, got Mike "CAUGHT UP", in his "SEARCH FOR SPIRITS". Their search lasted, for about three years and Mike's conversion to vegetarianism, nearly destroyed his marriage. Ultimately, only Mike ever entertained the idea of spirits, either not existing or being real flesh and blood E.T.'s, with advanced technologies. His buddy stopped searching and began looking at Tammy! He finally went back to Ohio, in Mike's truck! Mike, stayed in Nashvilee and continued to hunt them. He still does, everywhere he goes.

Mike wrote 7 books, as a result of this whole ordeal, with his "SPIRIT BUDDY"! Strangely enough, they "BECAME" a continuous storyline. He wrote furiously, one after another. He said, it felt like, he was living a "REVELATION" of knowledge, through his books. At times, it even felt like, he's done this, before. He continued to find, ancient evidence of "PEOPLE IN THE SKY"! I was blown away, by his stuff. The last book, climaxed with his "ANSWER" or theory, about our mystery and why they don't co-habitate, with us. It is titled; "Infinite Astronauts: The Theory of everything". I couldn't put it down, what a book!

In it, he relentlessly searches for the "TRUTH" and takes the Scientific road, while his buddy, stays on the "SPIRITUAL" one. Sadly, they never got their break in the music business, nor found anything "TOGETHER". But again, there was a "BRIGHT" side, in their time together. It is Mike's son and he named him, after his buddy! He would later, take it away! Read on!!!!!

After many failed attempts, to break into the music business and find "SPIRITS/E.T.'s. He and his buddy, just agreed to disagree and go their separate ways! By this time, Mike was on his fourth book tour and trying to book the Jeff Rense radio show. Finally, he "THOUGHT" he found the " SMOKING GUN EVIDENCE", that would prove, flying saucers created religion. He found a picture of Johnny cash, looking up at a flying saucer and shockingly, it looked "JUST" like a seventeen thousand year old cave drawing! Wow! He just knew it would give him the break, he needed. He put it on the front cover, of the next book. It didn't! But, fate seemingly intervened, again, when Mr. Rense's representative, turned him down. He said, it could possibly be slanderous, to Johnny Cash and he couldn't take that chance. He added, that it could also be criminally slanderous, to Johnny's ex son-in-law, Marty Stuart. The picture was taken by Marty Stuart. Mike tried to explain, that he had asked him for permission, but ultimately was "IGNORED". You'll read about this, later in the story. Mike said Marty wasn't happy about it and never gave him permission. However, he still hasn't sued him, either. Go figure, huh? Mike says this will be the biggest story, of all time. It will, because the picture proves E.T. has "ALWAYS EXISTED"!

Well, even though, Mike didn't do the radio show, he did get introduced to Jeff Willes. He is the world's most famous U.F.O. hunter! Mr. Rense's representative, told him about Jeff's flying saucer evidence and recommended, following up on it. He said it was, very similar to Johnny's. Mike, jumped at the chance. Unbelievable, as it is, they looked, just alike! Mike used the picture, on the next book's, front cover, as well. Mike said he didn't care, about the contraversy. Kid's are dying. E.T contact is the biggest thing we can hope for, whether Marty wants it or not. This picture was and still is, a "CRYSTAL" clear picture of Johnny, looking up at a flying saucer! Wow, it truly matches a seventeen thousand year old cave drawing of one, as well as, Jeffs and finally, Mike's, too!!!!! Man, was I ever blown away, when he found one. But, I can't begin to imagine, being Mike. He still can't believe, that this evidence is not being taken, seriously. He adamantly and firmly says, it is the smoking gun, for proof of E.T.'s.!!!!! Mike says he's is passionate, because "ALL SCIENTISTS" clearly see contact, as the most important event, in human history and he agrees! He asked Marty to respond. Marty called Tammy, not Mike! He was angry. Read on.

Mike still hasn't gotten a response, and thinks it is simply, because he's rich! Mike's, story is simple and Marty know's it. He's giving everything to space exploration and he's calling Marty out, to do the same, like the rest of us! I couldn't believe, what I was hearing. But, it even gets better. Get this, Marty "COINCIDENTALLY" grew up, with Mike's wife, in Lester Flatt's home and Johnny only lived, a couple blocks away! Come on. What are the chances? This may not seem, that incredible, but the resulting mysterious introduction to Jeff Willes, was! It would turn Mike's life upside down, yet again! Mike said he watched his video footage of flying saucers and couldn't believe his eyes. He immediately called Jeff and they begin planning, to get together. Again, how could he not! After-all, this was what he and his "SPIRIT" buddy were supposedly "LOOKING" for, right? Well, think again. Mike said, that his buddy was and still is religiously brain-washed, like the rest of the religious world. They won't budge, when it comes to challenging religion's spirit traditions or God's ability to make the world perfect and not doing so, now! Mike always told them, kids are dying, hoping they'd "WAKE-UP"! They didn't.

Mike, soon flew out to Phoenix and had his first meeting, with Jeff Willes. It produced "AMAZING" results and changed his life forever! It's on youtube and is incredible! Mike told me he saw and filmed the same saucer, as Marty's. He had just seen one in Sparta, before he left!!!!!

(you will read about it, later) Anyway, Their footage was aired on Fox News, in Phoenix, on March 6th, of 2006. They became a team! "LUCKILY", Jeff's famous footage of a flying saucer, in 2003, was subsequently purchased, by Walt Disney World and used on the movie "Return to Witch Mountain"! These guys continues to film "THEM" to this day and are currently pitching a "REALITY SHOW", called "UFOFINDERSLIVE: The Jeff and Mike Show"! Their motto is "We don't hunt them, we find them and you can, too"! Wow, now I'm going to find them! How, can I not?

Mike continues to live with Tammy, now his ex-wife, in Sparta, TN., part time. He moved to Michigan three years ago, after the Meteor event in Russia on Feb. 15th, 2013. Like I said, it forever changed his, life. To him there's "NO TURNING BACK"! He has to hire scientists, now! He recently bought his deceased brothers place, in Ohio and named it 'Brumfield Station'. Terry is buried on the property and Mike has built a store there. He named it Tim and Terry's Place. He is currently building his mother a restaurant, as well. His brother Tim, who "ALSO" lives there, is appropriately naming it; 'Memaw's Whistlestop Cafe'. We all love Memaw! His son Josh, wife Melanie and grandchildren also, live in Ohio. His son Matthew and girlfriend Jessica, live with Tammy, in Sparta. Besides, filming Flying Saucers, Mike continues to pursue his dream of music. He is currently working with Tammy's nieces Alex, Maddy and best friend Mykenzie, on their first single, "That's His-Story(history)". Oddly enough, he recently re-wrote it, with his "Spirit Buddy's" nephew, this past year! His name is Brandon and yes, their story is also, full of wierd coincidences! Primarily, he says because, this kid is a musical "PRODIGY". Mike says he's a genius! Mike says, the wierdest thing of all is, that Brandon's daddy, Scotty introduced Mike to his Uncle Dewey, thirty five years ago and none of this would've happened without him. Remember, Dewey lived in Nashville, at the time and as you've read, eventually asked Mike, to move there. He was trying to get a break in the Music business! None of this would've happened, without this small, but unbelievably, life altering detail. "COINCIDENCE"? Or was it a twist of fate? You decide, like I had, too! Enjoy the mystery. The rest is "HIS"-story and you are about to read it!

The song Mike and Brandon wrote is a breakup song for every girl in the world, who had one. Especially the ones, who have had a bad boy and don't want to talk, about him. Now, with this song, they can simply play it and people will get the point! Mike says this song, could be a "HIS-TORY CHANGER" for women! He's betting on it and thinks it could possibly become, a very fitting national anthem, for the pursuit of women's rights, everywhere. He says, that like the confederate flag and all equal rights issues, some things in history, have to "CHANGE". "HIS-STORY" has to be re-written. Logic dictates it! "EQUALITY FOR ALL" does as well. With this song, maybe, "HISTORY" itself, will change for the better.

He hopes, for girl's sake everywhere, that "HER-STORY" will become a new word and women all over the world, will "FINALLY" get "EQUAL" billing, with men! Please enjoy Mike's incredible story of "POSSIBLE, LIFE CHANGING DISCOVERIES". Also, please check out his songs, books and videos on you tube, under Mike Brumfield! He is giving all proceeds to Science, for the purpose of stopping Meteors, conquering death and making a perfect world for our children. "SPACE" is his goal. He says, "IMMORTALITY" requires it! Enjoy.

I can promise you one thing, with certainty. Mike's "RELIGIOUS REDNECK BRAIN- WASHING SURVEY VIDEO" will not only, have you busting a gut laughing, but it will leave you with a smile on your face, as well. Mike says, that "NOTHING" speaks louder, than a big smile. "Well, except for a good joke and I'm it", he remarked laughing at himself.

He came up with two, to put in this story. Here's the one, that he wants to start with. He admits it isn't very good, because of it's sponge-like nature. But he says it's "EXTREMELY RELEVANT", to his story and we will "ALL" get it, at the end.

He's saving his best for last, as usual and is going to put it, at the end. However, he wants me to warn you, of it's adult content, beforehand. Beware, it clearly drives his "POINT"/theory home. Here's the first one; "Do you know how to tell the difference between a religious person and a non-religious person? "SIMPLE", the way they "LOOK"! LOL!! This is one of those jokes, that was born, out of a real experience. He said it was funny, when he made it. One of those, had to be there things, I guess. He said it just came to him, "OUT OF THE BLUE". He and Brandon were writing recently and decided to take a break. Mike headed to the bedroom and saw the pope on t.v., telling everyone, that even though we're all different, we should honour our "INDIVIDUALITY"! What! He added, that it does not take away from, what we truly, "SPIRIT"! Wow, what a contradiction to "COMING TOGETHER" and then he tells children we're "SPIRITS? What! Who does he think he is?

Anyway, when this happened Mike said, he hollered at Brandon and asked him to come see it. The pope was addressing the United Nations, with a group of religious leaders and they were all dressed up, in their proper religious attire. You know, the "SUNDAY BEST", fancy stuff! This is when Mike, "CAME UP WITH" his joke, about them. Mike said Brandon came into the room and he re-winded the clip. He played it, again. Then, he told Brandon his joke. He loved it! Mike said they both just laughed and shook their heads. They couldn't believe how "ILLOGICAL" the pope is. Mike was so disgusted, at how they dress up, to kneel down and "HUMBLE" themselves!!! He told Brandon that being naked and "UNDRESSING" ourselves, defines humility. He said they couldn't believe the Pope was telling people to celebrate their differences and yet seek heaven, where they're all "EQUAL"! What a joke! I understood.

Mike couldn't stand people worshipping him. It is something "JESUS" preached against! Neither of them, could believe what they just saw.

"Don't they know, that Jesus would never do that?", Brandon asked. "Yes", Mike said he replied quickly. "The whole world does, but they love tradition, power and money, more than the "TRUTH", little buddy! Just like Marty, obviously does." Brandon agreed. Mike said, he quickly thought about his own life, for a moment. He was a walking contradiction, himself. Mike said he had to laugh. He was seeking fame with Brandon, in the country music business and yet, he was always reminding him to never forget, that their "TRUE REALITY, IS TO CONQUER DEATH". Mike said Brandon always agreed and didn't want to die, either. He even said he was ready to help Mike, find flying saucers and give up his dream of fame, as long as, he gets to play music, "FOR PEOPLE"! Mike told me he was a little surprised, by this. He knew how much Brandon wanted his music to be recognized, so he could get the girls, that goes with it. He didn't think Brandon would ever give it up for anything. He breathed, ate and slept with, that guitar. It was, at this moment, that Mike felt a "SPECIAL" connection, to him. Right then, they weren't Mike Breezy and Brandon Eezy, anymore. They were, "IMMORTALISTS" and their goal was to conquer "DEATH"! Mike said he even felt like, he could be Brandon's Sam, a "GUARDIAN ANGEL", too! However he felt, though. "DIVINE INTERVENTION" still hasn't given them, their break! So, in his mind, that rules out the "DESTINY", thing. "Sure" he said, "I still get those feelings. But, I don't accept, that any "INDIVIDUAL'S" future, has already happened. Only Mankind's inevitable self destruction!" However, he said he did feel like, he was playing a role in Brandon's life, that was "ALREADY WRITTEN" and even if it wasn't, he was going to help him, get his break, anyway.

 He said he had to laugh again, at the thought of Brandon's mis-fortune, if it does come true. Mike laughs, because Brandon is very aware of his anti- wealth/beauty, "INFINITE ASTRONAUT THEORY". Brandon "SEES" our sexual problem and of course, he knows he has it, too, just like we all do. Right? So, Mike asked him, if he was "REALLY" ready? Would he devote his life to finding flying saucers and give up his dream, of "STARDOM". Naturally, he freaked and said, yes but not now! Mike said he just laughed and already knew, that he wouldn't. He told me, they'd just had a meeting, with the president of the Nashville Song Writers Association Bart Herbison and he loved Brandon's stuff! Mike said he was adorned by young beautiful girls, everywhere and Brandon definitely took notice! Mike says this is America's favorite perk of fame and Brandon absolutely wants to experience it. Hell, what young man wouldn't. Mike admitted, his ego wants it, too. Needless to say, they immediately went home and wrote a song, about a girl, that Bart said is a future star. Her name is Lillian and Mike says he's right, she's a "SUPER" talented girl from Alabama.

Mike helped Brandon re-write an old song and named it; "Alabama Girl"! He gave a nod to Muscle Shoals and Alabama, on the way home, and created a new bridge. Brandon made it short and climactically sweet, just like Bart wanted it. Since then, she made it to American Idol! They've rewritten it and called it; "I'm just an Alabama girl"! This was their moment and they both, just knew it. Well, they hoped anyway. They felt destined! Then they shrugged it off, talked, laughed and drank another beer, to the most important thing of all. They both saw a flying saucer! Wow, how could they not entertain "DESTINY"?

Especially, since Brandon's uncle, used to be Mike's "SPIRIT/E.T." seeking partner!!! Well, again ,that was before he started "SEEKING", Mike's ex-wife! How they got here is weird. Really weird!I don't want to spoil the ending, but I will tell you this. Brandon becomes Mike's new partner, along with Jeff Willes and they find U.F.O.'s! Mike vows to never stop! His goal is to help everyone find them and end the "SPIRIT/DIMENSION DISEASE", that rules the "EARTH"! It's time to find them or "NOT"! Yes, keep reading and hang on! You're, about to take, the ride of your "LIFE"! Mike's story and the "EVIDENCE" he presents is mind-blowing. I am truly blown away! He, wants you all to know, that he "LOVES" you and wishes you the best. He ask each of you, to please try and enjoy his story. He says he always "TRIED" to enjoy it, even during the hard times, when he had to accept the "UGLY" truths, he found. He says, solving "THE MYSTERY", of mankind, is like getting old. It aint for sissy's!!! To him the truth is "HARD"! He said it is because the evidence has to dictate the answers. What we "THINK" about it, shouldn't matter, if we are truly looking! I think we can all agree, on this simple fact of life.

Beware! At times, this "EVIDENCE" tortures Mike and he is confident it will do the same, to everyone. Well, at least, anyone who is addicted to "VANITY", like him, he says. It was and still is, hard for him, to "ACCEPT". The "REALITY" he envisions, makes mankind a choice of these "ALIENS", that are addicted to "THE POWER OF BEAUTY". His story paints a matching scenario, to the angels/devil of the "JESUS" story. They are equal and one wants "POWER OVER OTHERS"! He said, that the story of "Jesus saving us", sounds like our current Meteor problem! We need "SAVED"! Wow, I've got to read, this again! The "TRUTH" he finds is bittersweet, depending on how you "LOOK" at it! It's hardest to do, with "SCIENTIFIC EYES", if you're vain, like him. But, he wants you, to please try? Please, he asked me to beg you? If people get angry at you, for agreeing with this evidence, then Mike wants you to forgive them, for they "KNOW NOT WHAT THEY DO". If you get angry, when they attack you, like he did. Well then, you don't know what you're doing and "VANITY, has you, too! Admit it and "GET OVER IT"! Mike admit's he's got the "DISEASE". He's vane!

He wants us all to keep looking for u.f.o.'s and promises, that anyone can "find" them, if they're truly "LOOKING". He proved it to me. I've seen his footage and it's as plain, as the nose on our, face! He's convinced me, that if we exist, then it's certainly possible life exist everywhere "ELSE", too? How advanced is the question, he ask of us all? He says it is only logical, that in an "INFINITE" universe, they would be "INFINITELY ADAVNCED"! He says it time to solve this "TIME" thing and realize, that what we call "THE FUTURE" has already happened!!! He boldly states, that our purpose is "SIMPLE"! We should "MULTIPLY" and seek "IMMORTALITY". According to him, our first priority should be, to get; "REALITY ESCAPE FROM PLANET EARTH" and choose

"IMMORTAL LIFE"! Second, join him, Jeff and Brandon in the search, for Flying saucers! Third, "CONQUER DEATH"! I'm with him, on that one, for sure. I'm 54 as well. Lol. Come on everyone, let's "FACE", this shit "HEAD" on, shall we? Kids are dying, as we speak! In the words of Mike's brother, Terry. Let's do this! Life aint "NO-THING", just same shit, different day!!! Love and miss you Brother! Sincerely, Mike's best friend, Will Powers.

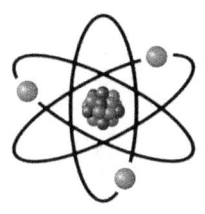 # TABLE OF CONTENTS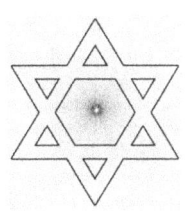

Preface	3
My Introduction	39
Chapter 1: The Past	55
Chapter 2: The Present	119
Chapter 3: The Future	221
Author's Thoughts	229
Photographic Evidence and Illustrations	250

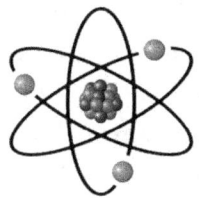 # PREFACE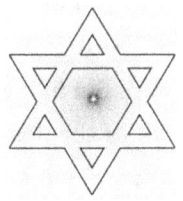

Hello everyone, I'm Mike Brumfield. I want to thank Will, for his "MOVING" account of my life. I want to tell you myself, what this book is about and how it got started. It was a beautiful morning, Feb. 16th, 2013 and let me tell you. I felt so lucky, to be alive. I had recently turned 52 and just "SURVIVED A BIG METEOR EVENT, IN RUSSIA THAT COULD'VE BEEN,....... THE BIG ONE"! Wow! It happened the day before and today was the world's, "WAKE-UP CALL"! When I saw the "BREAKING NEWS", yesterday, I had an "EPIPHANY". It was then, that I began to write, like there was no tomorrow. I immediately headed toward the computer and came up, with the title. I typed feverishly as I wondered if we would get to see another day. Woo hoo, we did! I knew then, how "LUCKY", we all were, just to be alive! I wasn't about to waste another minute. I had to stop "METEORS"!

Well, this is my eighth and final book. It has been and still is, the most difficult one I've written, so far. Let alone, finish! It has now "CONSUMED", nearly two years of my life and I can't tell you enough, how I struggled mercilessly, to complete it. It absolutely "TORTURED" me, everyday. Whether, it was, what I was writing or not writing. Either way, I couldn't get it done, "FAST ENOUGH"! Not one day, was easy.

I know why. I've been living in re-write hell, since I started. I don't care me. I just don't want to hurt anybody, especially my family. But, I do and I know, that it does. This story involves them. Actually, it already has and I can't change that. It's my story. I can't erase my past and ignore the flying saucer I saw, in2006. I saw it and it changed my thinking, about the possible existence of E.T.s! I don't want to offend anyone. But, I saw them and then, went on to find them. I, even, filmed them! I also saw, something else! I saw the possibility of "NUCLEAR DESTRUCTION, METEOR EXTINCTION AND E.T CONTACT", in our future! I had to stop them. This is my "REALITY"! Again, I hope you enjoy it and imagine the possibilty of this happening to you. Please read my story, with "EMPATHY"! Please?

My story, chronicles a project, that I've been researching and working on, for the last 25 years. It is a continuation of the previous seven books and tells the story, of my many attempts, to solve the "MYSTERY OF MANKIND". I'm wrote them as a mystery, for everyone to solve, just as I had to. I am quoting and capitalizing words, that I think will help you figure out, what "MY ANSWER" will be, at this books end. I am calling it a theory, for science and "SAFETY REASONS"! LOL. However, it's up to you, as to "WHAT" it is or not. Fortunately, "RIGHTEOUSNESS", rules the world of religion, not science. I want to be a scientist, that's not "RIGHT", about anything and only present s a theory. But yes, I "FINALLY" do have an answer, to our mystery and yes, I've discovered, that everyone does love a good mystery. I do too! I guess, it's just the "NATURE OF THE BEAST", in us all! Anyway, this is my reasoning for writing my books, as a mystery. I want everyone to try and solve it! I hope to entice everyone's "SEEMINGLY UNSTOPPABLE BEAST-LIKE COMPETITIVE NATURE", with "MONEY". We "ALL WANT MONEY"! Whoever find's the answer gets the "CASH"! I want to "INCITE" people, to hopefully, "FIND THE ANSWER ON THEIR OWN". Boy, I sure "HOPE" this works. It could make, the "JOB OF SEARCHING KNOWLEDGE", competitive, "FUN" and lucrative! So, without further adieu. Here's, goes nothing. Let's all hope this works, for our kids sake!!! Please enjoy it and have fun solving my "MYSTERY"!

Ultimately, I am "CHALLENGING EVERYONE", to put their money where their mouth is and give it all to science. In doing so, they will prove their "TRUE INTENTIONS", regarding humanity. I want them to "PROVE", that they want a "PERFECT WORLD"! I'm doing it first and I yes, know how dangerous, this is. I know why money is the root of all evil, believe me! That's why I have to do this. We all have to do this! If this book, becomes successful, everyone will have to prove their "INTEGRITY", once and for all. We will be required to give "ALL" of our money to science, for the prevention of a "METEOR EXTINCTION EVENT"! Here's, why! Unbelievably enough, today is June 30th, 2015 and it "JUST NOW", marks the beginning of "ASTEROID/METEOR PREVENTION DAY"! Come on, people. Please tell me this can't be true, is it? It should've started the day the Russian meteor struck, if not way before. Wow! That is so bizarre! Why hasn't this happened already? Man, these last two years, sure went fast! How can we, still be so primitive? I was stunned, by this "REALITY". I felt like, I must be, from the future or something. And maybe, just maybe, I was having a nightmare. Well, I checked and....no, I wasn't! LOL! Damn, that hurt. Man, this is so, "REAL". OMG, NO!!!

People, I'm making my story a mystery and a challenge, for one "REASON"! Because "GREED", drives people and that drives capitalism! This is real! We need all the "MONEY" we can get, to stop meteors. Besides, "I HAVE TO MAKE THIS BOOK SUCCESSFUL AND WIN THIS FIGHT"! It is already written in "MY HEAD MOVIE". LOL. Thanks, Lon for sharing the movie moment, with me! I needed a good laugh. Hell, I think the whole world does. Lonnie could sure make them laugh. He's a great comedian/actor/dancer/SINGER! Go, bud!

He's also my best friend, who made the drawing, at the end of this book. He drew a "FLYING SAUCER", when he was, only 8 years old!

Cool, huh! Anyway, yes, I have to win and make this book a success. I do, because it becomes and is, an integral part of my story- line. Heck, what am I talking about? It is my story! Ironically, the success of this book is the only thing, that I ever pre-"DICKED" in it and it still hasn't come true. Again,"YET"! Lol. Please pardon the sexual pun. I promise, it is relevant, in solving our "MYSTERY" or I wouldn't use it. You will read more. Believe me, I'm a "LOGICAL" person and I'm not doing it, to be mean. I don't like mean behavior, either. Nobody does! Wow, I just thought of something, funny. Not, even mean people, like it. But, in all seriousness folks. It's "URGENT", that I "WIN", this "FIGHT AGAINST METEORS"! Not, only for my kids. But, for all of our kids sake, for everyone. Now, good luck and read on.

In this story, I make a "LIFE CHANGING/SAVING" scientific discovery! At least, in my mind, anyway. When, it happened. I immediately became obssessed, with it and began showing the evidence to "EVERYONE". It didn't work out, so well, as you've already read. Hardly anybody, took me or my findings seriously. I knew why. I chose the intellectual path, while my "TROPHY" wife and mostly everyone around me, chose the sexual. As a result, I felt, they were mean to me. Go figure, huh! I know they weren't in their "RIGHT MIND", when it happened! I wasn't either, when I got mad. My ex-wife isn't a "HORRIFYINGLY VICIOUS SEXUAL PREDATOR", either. No matter, how many times I say she is, in this story! I was angry. Her disease, embarrassed her and hurt us, over and over, again. My anger done the same. Many times, our "DISEASE" would come close to killing, us all. We're lucky to be alive. My "ego" wants her to go on the Maury Povich show and take a "LIE DETECTOR TEST"! The golden rule won't let me. I have to let this all go. My freedom lies just ahead, in the distance. This burden is temporary. My "PLAN IS ALREADY WRITTEN"! I just hope, that I live long enough to see it, come to fruition!

Man, it's hard for me to wrap my mind around, what she's done? Her "NARCISSISM" totally destroyed her compassion and ability to be empathetic. Again, in my "WRONG MIND", Tammy rarely ever cared more for us, than herself. I tried to leave and yet, she wouldn't let me go. I tried many times, but we caused my son so much pain, that I always stayed. Hell, I'm still here!

I was and still am tortured, with my desire, for a "LOYAL" lifetime mate. You'll read about it, throughout this entire story. I wanted it "BAD" and it is, what drove my anger. She didn't want to be it and yet, didn't want me to have it, either. She became my "DEVIL". I became trapped and helpless. Again, I still am! Hang on and beware, everyone. What I'm about to tell you, is truly sad. My story is "FULL OF SEX", betrayal, heartbreak and worst of all tragedy! But, I have hope. Like I said, in 2006 I saw and filmed a flying saucer!

I constantly struggled and still do, to do the "RIGHT THING", for my children's sake. But, man it's tough, when it comes to being, sexually happy. Damn this sex thing! Life is short enough, without us having to rage "WAR" against it, our whole life. I often wonder, if I'll ever win. I want to! But, this " SEXUAL BATTLE", continues to rage, inside of me. It does, to this day and I can't seem to stop it. I have to win, though! I have to, for the "GOOD" of my children's future and "MY OWN SAFETY'S SAKE"! I will win, even if I have to give up my dream of having "ONE FAITHFUL WOMAN" ! I have a plan. Read on and find out, what it is! I haven't ruled becoming a Monk, though! Lol!

Well, struggle as I might. I failed constantly, when it came to losing my temper, during this journey. But, I have "LEARNED" one thing. If I/we don't win this "SEXUAL WAR", within ourselves, most of us won't live long enough, to know what "WISDOM" is. Let alone experience it and stop this war! My ex-wife and I are lucky. We are, because I am still surviving "OUR" war. And as a result, she is too. I have become wise to her sex addiction and finally realize, that I am only a "TEMPORARY" prisoner, of it. No-body's winning. Unfortunately, nobody will. The winners are the kids who survive, if you want to call them that. But, it's true. If you don't believe me, just watch the news. A lot of kids die, because of

"MARITAL PROBLEMS/DOMESTIC VIOLENCE". Fortunately, ours didn't and I don't plan on letting it happen, now or in the future!

My ex-wife and I are sorry. We are the "BIGGEST LOSERS", of all! "I/WE" have begged our sons and all those who we have hurt, along the way, for their forgiveness. You are getting ready to read, about our troubles and what caused our marriage, to go "HELL IN A HAND BASKET"! It started, when I began trying to get "RIGHT" and find "HEAVEN"! Ironic, huh? Isn't that what every young couple wants, for themselves? Well, if you think that's crazy, wait til you read my story. From the beginning of my "SPIRITUAL JOURNEY", she became bored and began lying to me, about where she was going. She still lies to me everyday and I film Flying saucers! She's still bored with me, too! I obviously stopped impressing her a long time ago and now, it's too late. I don't care, if I ever do again. I want her to get help! She became a sex addict and still is!!! Hell, I am to! I confess. I don't want to be ugly and I still want a "GOOD" woman! I want to get cured. Well, no matter how many times, I try to talk to her, she refuses to acknowledge it and throws a temper tantrum. When she does admit it, she does so, sarcastically. When I start to leave she starts pleading, for me to stay and begs. She blames all of this, on her uncle Gillis and has a hard time, "OWNING" it herself. He molested her, when she was 10. She said it went on for years! This was not her fault!!! I felt sorry for her, but never saw her, get help. That enraged me. She hurt a lot of people with her insatiable appetite, for sex. She even had multiple relationships at once. I screamed many times, that this was not normal and now, it was all on her.

People, we all want answers for our "MYSTERIOUS SPECIES". But, I ask you. Will we want it, at "ANY AND ALL" cost. What if it means giving up sex and money? Well, if this scares you, like it does my ex-wife, then stop reading. I'm sorry. But, in my theory, these "TWO THINGS", turn out to be the reason why "E.T's/SPIRITS", stay away from us. They can't make us choose life, over "DEATH/POWER"! People, in Heaven don't marry and don't have money!!!!!

These two powerful forces of mankind, are the "SIMPLE" and yet, hard choices we may have to sacrifice, if we want to survive. Why, is simple. Because, we can "SCIENTIFICALLY" stop "METEORS" and cure the ills of "MANKIND", if we do give them up. I want to fight fire with fire. "MONEY" can definitely cure the sexual torture, of our species. So, let's get rid of it! It's a no-brainer. We should've never started marriage in the first place. It's just a "MONEY THING"! I will make, the invention of a new lie detector, the best selling technology in the world. It will be called the "DEAL-BREAKER", for marriages! Unfortunately, somewhere along the way, my ex began thinking she's prettier, than I am. We all know how "PRETTY POWER WORKS HERE", let's not kid ourselves! We can't anyway, if we watch t.v or mingle, with the public. Sex sells everything and she sold her soul to the "DEVIL", for it. It's just "UP" to us, whether we want to accept, this "REALITY" or not. People, the "CHOICE" is ours and our children's lives depend on it. Meteors will not stop. Money can prevent them form taking us out! They are coming, even as I type. It's "NOW" or never and it's up to everyone, to make this happen!

My family hates my open-ness, about our sexuality and I "SOMEWHAT" understand. I do know, where they're coming from. But, I can't avoid being sexually explicit, any longer. Every child, should be taught about, "THE AMBER ALERT". It can't any longer, just be ignored. It's still happening and your child, could be next. In my theory, "SEX" has everything, to do with our mystery and my answer! I'm not wanting to be vulgar, just completely open and scientific. We must talk about and "REVEAL", this "TORTUROUS EVIDENCE", of our species. I want all children to see "IT", for what it is, "SEXUAL AD-DICK-TION". My hope is that they will see it scientifically, without the moral scrutiny of any religious parent, making it a "RIGHT OR WRONG" issue. For Christ sake, we are the only species, who commits criminal sexual acts, against each other. We are, also the only species, that doesn't go naked or have sex, in front of our children! Why can't we talk about this? These are provable facts.

People, it is 2015, not 1914. It is "TIME" to address this "SEXUAL PROBLEM", openly! Children deserve it, even it offends their parents. I apologize to them and my families, if it does. But, it has to be done. It's simple logic! Every child, can become, another Amber alert. Even our own! This is our "WAKE- UP CALL", people!!! Please don't let this opportunity pass you or your child by. They deserve it!

This book is about to reveal, some "UGLY" truths about "MANKIND". But, they will also "GIVE" children, the tools to protect themselves, from "SEXUAL PREDATORS". I don't think we can ask, for anymore than that, can we? What a wonderful gift, this would be, to our children. No more amber alerts! So, again, I'm sorry if my story offends you. But, no I'm not holding back, anymore. Unfortunately, you'll soon see, that I never did and yes, it has cost me dearly. My ex-wife, always lets me know that, everyday. She gets to have the last word.

People, I have kids and there are children all over the earth, that need our help. If we want a "BETTER" world, then we must ensure their safety, by giving them the best future possible. This "TRANSPARENT WAY OF LIFE", will provide a better future, for all children! The whole world knows, that "KNOWLEDGE IS POWER"! As parents, we must make this our goal and a "LIFE-TIME" commitment! If we want to make a "PERFECT WORLD", then we must expect, nothing less of ourselves. This is simple logic. Please everyone, let's all "BE PERFECT" and "GIVE EVERYTHING WE HAVE, TO MAKE THIS HAPPEN"!!! It would truly, be a "DREAM COME TRUE"! I have no greater love, than the love, I have for my children and all children. I am the lucky one! Now, "PLEASE EVERYONE", enjoy yourself and charge headlong, into my world of discoveries. By all means, challenge "EVERYONE OF THEM"! I'd love to hear, from you. Please, though, first and foremost, "DON'T FORGET THE METEOR THREAT". We can always talk, later. Again, here's my story. Well, here's at least the short of it, anyway. I've got, to get this damn preface, done.

I was 52 years "OLD", when this meteor event happened. And "I MAY BE CRAZY"! But, I never gave it much thought, til then. I know why. I see a "POSSIBILITY", that I can't ignore any longer. I've always been "a-DICK-ted TO BEAUTY INSTEAD OF KNOWLEDGE" and don't know why. Well I mean, other than the fact, that I'm a sexual being. Right? Of course, "WE" all know that, right? Well no, fortunately children don't. Most, don't know about the amber alert, either! Most of my family, don't want to talk to them, about it. They don't want them to "KNOW", yet. People, we can prevent this tragedy, from happening. Who are we kidding? They will only be ignorant about their sexuality, until "PUBERTY" comes calling. Unfortunately, "IT" will teach them the hard way, if we don't! We aren't helping them, by hiding it. Really people, shouldn't we all be past that "STUFF", by now? I don't want them to learn from a "CRAZY GRANDPA", like me and Shawna did! I saw dad put a knife to his throat over her!

Well, I'll be the first to admit. This sexual stuff, still scares the "SHIT" out of me, too. It has to stop. After all, I am now, 54! We all "LEARN", that "TRUE BEAUTY IS ON THE INSIDE", but do we live it? My addiction to outward beauty really and truly, bothers me. No, it tortures me! Again, it does, because I want a "FAITHFUL" and yet, "BEAUTIFUL" woman. Why can't I be happy, without one? I know why, "TEMPORARY SEXUAL INSANITY". Also, another thing bothers me. I know this goes, without saying, but getting older and uglier, scares the living shit out of me, too! Not to mention dying! Shit when I think about that, I just shake all over. When this happens, sex is definitely the last thing I think about. All I can think about, then. Are my kids!!! Wow, obviously, this explains why a "N.D.E.", (near death experience) has, such a profound effect, on adults. It is our ticket to reality! Could realizing our death, be the key to solving "OUR MYSTERY"? I think it could. Man, what a change it would make, if we could all live like we were dying, "NOW". Telling my children, about sexual predators is, bad enough. But, I can't even begin to tell them, they're going to die. Hell, I can't handle it, when my sons thinks about their death, now. My youngest son, freaks out over it, to the point, he scares the living shit, out of us. I have to deal, with it. I can't stand the thought of my kids dying and he is worrying me. Suicide is real. I have to stop this. I am trying! Read on.

No!!! It happened again, today. I can't even get this goddamn book done, without another child dying. (who am I kidding, their dying everywhere, while adults build mansions!) One of my friends children, died today. It is terrible and my heart is breaking, for his parents. His name is Stacey Howard and he was the finest young man, a father could ask for. I am lucky to have been his friend and am saddened deeply, by his death. I want to call his dad and console him. I want to let him know, that I continue to see flying saucers. I want to let him know, that there is "REAL" hope, of seeing his son, again. But, I can't. I will, just give George a copy of this book, when I'm done. I hope he understands, my reasoning. My words won't cure his pain. It hasn't cured my brothers and I understand why. Words can't. I love them all and can only hope, that I've showed them as much, during our time together!

Suddenly, I had dejavu! Wow, what a terrible moment, to live through, once. Let alone, "TWICE". I tried hard to continue writing. But, I just couldn't shrug off, this nagging idea, in my head. I've had it, since I was a kid. Maybe, just maybe, the future has already happened. Why do I feel this way? I guess its because, we all have "DEJAVU" and it's "FREAKY"!!! Hell, I've never gotten over it, from the first one, I had as a kid. And now, if the universe is infinite, I "SEE" this "POSSIBILITY", as a "LOGICAL REALITY"! Wouldn't these people, be living everywhere, in space and not on planets recycling intelligence? People, we're surrounded, by this "SCIENTIFIC REALITY" and yet, "BELIEVING IT", is still a choice!

Well, if so here's the next obvious "LOGICAL QUESTION", we should be asking ourselves. "WOULDN'T THE SMARTEST PEOPLE OF THE UNIVERSE RULE EVERYWHERE, LIKE WE DO AND SEPARATE THEMSELVES FROM THE BAD GUYS, IN

ORDER TO MAINTAIN, A PEACEFUL EXISTENCE AND MULTIPLY. AGAIN, LIKE WE DO HERE?". People, this is what all ancient religion's say, has already happened. "BECAUSE THE UNIVERSE IS INFINITE, THIS IS LOGICAL"! Science and common sense dictates, this same "REALITY EVERYWHERE", as well. Why? Because bad guys don't cooperate with the good guys! They don't let them exist, if they can stop them. Also, they don't last long enough themselves, to rule anywhere, alone. Why? Because, they "EVENTUALLY" kill each other off! So, people. "GOOD E.T.s EXISTENCE is logical"! This has finally led me, to ask myself, "TWO FINAL QUESTIONS"; "WHY DO THEY STAY AWAY?" and "WHERE DO THEY COME FROM?". My answer/theory is based on the universe being infinite and that premise is based on the definition of energy.

Well, guess what? Stephen Hawking's, the leading astrophysicist of today, says that "THE UNIVERSE IS INFINITE" and that's good enough, for me! If so, then we have to "IMAGINE" life existing "EVERYWHERE" and with a level of knowledge, that would also be infinite! Surely, these "PEOPLE", would be capable of doing all the things, religion says, wouldn't they? I don't think so. We have to challenge, one thing. "AN OMNIPOTENT GOD MAKING THE UNIVERSE PERFECT"! We do because it isn't. Come on. It never was. Look at the moon. "METEORS/ASTEROIDS"!

Anyway, I started asking everyone, "THE QUESTION", that helped me see the "PHYSICAL REALITY" of achieving "IMMORTALITY". You will read about it, at the end of this book. I discovered, that someone else, already has a "PHYSICAL REALITY THEORY"! Wow! It blew me away. How could they not see religion as proof of E.T. having "AN INFINITE LEVEL OF KNOWLEDGE" and existing now, in space? Surely, they can see it would be easy to hide from us, while we slowly "LEARN", about them. Well, I see this possibility and it "BECOMES MY OBSESSION". It also destroy's my marriage and is the reason I scared my son to "DEATH", too many times. Crazy, huh!

I love him. This disease, like all the other, that are sexually based, only have one cure; "THE MYSTERY"! I tried sharing this ancient school of thought and my "THEORY", or better said, "POSSIBLE ANSWER TO OUR MYSTERY", with others. It didn't go over well, either. Well, that's my story. Sad as it is to say, it "BECAME MY CURSE" and still is! Well, let's just say, it's been and still is, tough to keep doing it! Let alone get anybody else to do it. I'd like to leave it, at that. But, I can't. There's more. I still can't shrug off this bizarre universal phenomenon of DE JA VU". What a "STRANGE" world, I'm in. I can't stop feeling, like I've been sent back in time. Logically, this tortures me. I can't stop thinking, that I must have done something, really bad, to be here. Because, this isn't a "GOOD" place. I tried hard, everyday, to imagine the capabilities of these "PEOPLE UP IN THE HEAVENS/SKY". Recently, I read a quote from Albert Einstein, that helps explains my dilemma, to a tee. He said "THE TRUE TEST OF INTELLIGENCE ISN'T KNOWLEDGE, BUT THE IMAGINATION"! Wow! I rarely talk to anyone, that is "IMAGINING THE FUTURE", let alone, thinking it could' have already happened! Man, what a conundrum. This was and still is my biggest curse. It is, because what I'm about to propose is "TRULY INCREDIBLE", if it's true. I hope, that it will challenge your imagination, to be "LIMITLESS", in it's thinking. Here's "THE QUESTION"; "HOW ADVANCE COULD LIFE BE IN AN INFINITE UNIVERSE"?

I have to tell you, that one question, continues to plague me. I finally figured it out! I relentlessly pursued "MORE EVIDENCE", in support of my theory/answer to the "MYSTERY OF MANKIND" and kept sharing it, with everyone. I'm a glutton for punishment, I know. Every time, I ask "THE QUESTION", all hell still breaks, loose. Why do I keep experiencing, this problem? It continues to happen, about ninety percent of the time, when I try to share my logic/"IT", with others. Here's another question, that usually makes them angry, too: "If these "PEOPLE UP IN THE SKY" do exist and have advanced technologies, then why would religious people or anyone be angry, at such a wonderful possibility?"! Why wouldn't we all, "SEE' the beauty of such a thing? Could a person's allegiance and desire to protect their religion, really cause them, to be so "BLIND". Unfortunately, it does. I don't "SEE" any other reason. You are about to "SEE", how this can be the case, in your family or anyone else's. People, I've never had any "AGENDA TO BUILD WEALTH" and only do so now, to "STOP METEORS"! I think I finally figured it out. I know why "WE" all get angry, about anything. It threatens our "TRADITIONS" and then, mankind's "PRIDE" raises it's ugly head. It defends them! If not controlled people, it becomes an inherent and uncontrollable "LEARNING DISEASE". Pride is a killer of knowledge! By and large, most people don't like the idea of someone saying, they are smarter, than them. I don't either and I am trying to get over my disease. We all have "PRIDE"!!! Unfortunately, some of "THESE PEOPLE" in my story, who's "BELIEF" keeps them from "IMAGINING" my "INFINITE THINKING POSSIBILITY", have threatened to kill me, over it! They not only, can't think infinitely or logically, about technological scientific advances, existing now or, in the future! But most, like my family and the majority of Earth's "RELIGIOUS FOLLOWERS", have fallen prey to the world- wide mental disease, of following religion's "SPIRIT TRADITIONS". If that's not bad enough, the others fall into a "DIMENSIONAL OR ATHEISTIC/AGNOSTIC THINKING" category! They also, think their right or just don't care, wheter they are or not. Either way, this scientific complacency/laziness ravages the planet and I am sad! People, why doesn't science rule the earth? "METEORS ARE COMING"! We all have to give everything, "IF WE WANT TO LIVE FOREVER".

Man, sometimes I just feel so frustrated, about this "REALITY", I live in. It's 2015 and people actually believe in "SPIRITS OR "NOTHING", but can't imagine E.T.? I can't beg everyone, enough. Please try and imagine or find, "FUTURE" technologies! If you do, you may find them existing, in our ancient past! When you dig further, you may find they came from other people, "THROUGHOUT" the universe. People, this is what I found and it should be our "REALITY, EVERYWHERE NOW", not tomorrow. This is only logical, because we exist, now! If we can do this, then we will "IMAGINE" technologies, that could give us the ability to "SCIENTIFICALLY CREATE A NEW SPECIES", like I'm alleging and then have to live apart from them. This is the simple story of what religion's god or these god's have done! Wow, what is going on? How can everyone, not see this, "REALITY"? Especially, "SCIENTIST"! This is a logical reality, for an advanced flesh and blood, being who conquered death/"ALWAYS EXIST"! Always existing, being the key words here, to figure out. The art of thinking infinitely among humans is and always has been rare. Even worse,"VERY FEW ARE FIGURING OUT HOW TO BECOME INFINITE/IMMORTAL, NOW"!

Well, throughout this story, it seems like everyone refutes anything I show them, as possible E.T. evidence. Nothings changed and I've been doing this, for well over fifteen years. Why would they do this? Sadly, I "THINK" I know why!!! I have the same "MENTAL DISEASE"! We all do, it's "PRIDE"! I must cure myself and "FIND THE MYSTERY", again!

Alright, already. Enough is enough! I'm finishing this damn preface. "EVERYONE", I film "FLYING SAUCERS". They look the same as they did, thousands of years ago! This made a light-bulb goe off in my head and I can't make it turn on, in my families. My story may be painful, but it is also, joyfully exhilarating, because of this evidence. To me, it is "OFFERING" us proof of "INFINITE KNOWLEDGE" and the possibility of "IMMORTALITY"! I am trying to get people to "SEE", this wonderful possibility. I don't think I can win. But, I think the evidence can, it always wins.

"I KEPT TELLING EVERYONE", that this evidence should make the "LIGHT-BULB TURN ON IN EVERY-ONE'S HEAD". But, it didn't and I know why. Religion and apathy/scientific laziness. I was so frustrated. People, this proves E.T.'s/god's have achieved omnipotence, in space travel. It does, because "THEY AREN'T MAKING A NEW MODEL AND THEIR EVERYWHERE"!!! I've got to stop here. You'll soon see the pictures, in the back of the book. People, I will keep "FINDING AND FILMING FLYING SAUCERS/ U.F.O.s EVERYDAY", as long as, I can. I won't stop, until my "REALITY" show is the "BIGGEST HIT", of all! Surely, everyone will "BELIEVE IT" then, won't they? Hang on, you're about to find out.

We can all agree, that science is "TRULY" wonderful and amazing. Please everyone, we can't keep allowing religion, to ignore it. We can't, for our children's sake. It could save thousands of children, from the hands of their "INNOCENTLY BRAIN-WASHED" religious parents, like mine and many others. How can any government, continue to allow the option of choice, when it comes to a medical treatment, for children. Whether, it be a life or death situation or not. Especially, knowing it is based on religious doctrines, that defy common sense. We all know of one, like "GOD COULD MAKE THE WORLD PERFECT, IF HE WANTS, TOO"! Come on, people. Here's another, "GOD KILLING EVERYONE", in the flood story and he "FORESAW IT"! What the hell, he sets around and watches "RE-RUNS" all the time! LOL! Even worse, he murders innocent children! Let's get real here, everyone. THIS IS CRAZY, SHIT! God is most famous mass murderer in history!

Shouldn't "RELIGIOUS PARENTS", at the very least, have to take a religious brain-washing exam or something, before they have kids. At least, a history lesson, "SCIENCE EXAM", or something for "GOD'S SAKE"! You want to know, what's really crazy. There are people, who will argue, that god killed everyone "FOR A REASON". Obviously, they are still not "SEEING", the conflicting logic of it. This "REASON" is the disease of Religion, everywhere. "ALLEGIANCE TO RELIGIOUS TRADITION'S REJECTS LOGIC"! It is rampant everywhere! It is called a universal disease called, "PRIDE"!

People, I'm not trying to be mean. It's just ridiculously obvious, that religion's depiction of an "ALMIGHTY/OMNIPOTENT GOD OR GOD'S", defies common sense. Heck, why would they live in the sky, "LIKE WE NEED TO", if they're "SPIRITS"? I personally know, that most religious parents are extremely ignorant of science, like mine. Sadly, I also know, that most aren't very knowledgeable of their religion's history, either. Hell, history period. But, come on. It's got to stop! It does, because it gets sadder, than that. Most, even "FOLLOW" dead people, that were filthy rich! Again, just like mine do! Come on people, let's get real here, please. If rich people want the best for everyone, why are they rich? We can't allow them to preach, that everyone should be "EQUAL" and continue to be rich! I'm sorry, but "RICH PEOPLE ARE SPIRITUAL AND SCIENTIFIC HYPOCRITES"! O.k. now, that I've got that off my chest and out of the way. What does this say, about the world leaders of today? Aren't they rich?

Well, don't worry. I won't keep ranting and spewing this "VILE ANTI-WEALTH LOGIC", anymore. I know, that " everyone" wants to be rich! Wow, no wonder, just a "FEW" go to heaven, huh. Thank god for "MEMAW"! I know I'm raising a stink and I also know, that I'm putting my "LIFE ON THE LINE", in doing so. But, I'm not worried. I "FIND AND FILM FLYING SAUCERS"! I know they don't play this, "BELIEVING" game, that "MANKIND" plays! People, I want no followers and I will give everything, to help people see this "METEOR REALITY".

In this book, I have put together a body of evidence, that suggests "PEOPLE, LIVING UP IN THE SKY" exist and I can't emphasize "UP", enough. I am still profoundly moved by it and find it only logical, to "CONSIDER THIS POSSIBILITY", since we ourselves are destined, to do the same. Shouldn't we challenge them, being "SPIRITS"? I can "SEE", that the ancient and modern evidence matches, yet most of my family, see "NOTHING". I never could change this, but I never stop trying. I can't. I have children and "METEORS", will not go away!

People, my story isn't about converting anyone or gaining followers. This is for "ME", my sons, and all the children of the world, who have had their civil rights violated by religion. This is still happening, as I type. Especially, in respect to the teachings of science and evolution. Religion is keeping us scientifically ignorant! We have to stop it. People, "CONTACT IS THE MOST IMPORTANT THING, THAT CAN HAPPEN TO THE HUMAN RACE"! Again, I film flying saucers. Please give my footage a chance?

The time has come to break this vicious cycle of religious ignorance. Children should not have to suffer, at the hands of their parents, cruel and "DEADLY" traditions, anymore. Today, like in our courtrooms, matching scientific evidence, must be, the judge and jury, in deciding our children's fate.

With this book, I am presenting my new "A.S.K. DISCOVERY" (advanced scientific knowledge / evidence) and attempting to start a new, "SCIENTIFIC EVOLUTION REVOLUTION"! My children will not be taught, that I am "RIGHT", anymore. I have to stop this vicious cycle and apologize. I done this. I can only hope, that I always told them I could be wrong. I want them to learn about "EVOLUTION" and to prove or dis-prove it, on their own. I want them to use "SCIENTIFIC METHODS", to do so. Most importantly, I want them to learn about the "WORLD-WIDE DEBATE, EVOLUTION VS. CREATION" and "SEE" that it still exist! It does because religion rules the earth with "IGNORANCE"!.

This is just the beginning of my struggle. I hope to "FREE" the world, from Ancient Religious traditions and help everyone overcome, the challenges of global scientific learning. Again, I was once, "IGNORANT OF SCIENCE", too. But, not anymore. I've buried my "SHAME" and see, that we must, all do the same. We must conquer it, once and for all. "EVOLUTION IS PROVABLE" and I will "PROVE" children of the world deserve nothing less. I hope to give them a simple and quick understanding, of it. From it's, "SINGULARITY POINT BEGIN-

NING TO THE 14.5 BILLIONS YEARS OF AGE", that it is today. I want everyone to ask questions. The biggest is "WHERE DID EVERYTHING COME FROM"? I want them to see how, all "LIFE", like everything else in the universe, had a single source and yet evolved, by multiplying itself! This can be seen in all living things, like cell growth, as well as, the big bang!!! People, "THE FACTS MUST SCIENTIFICALLY SPEAK FOR THEMSELVES"! And when they do, "BELIEVING THEM SHOULD NO LONGER BE A CHOICE PARENTS CAN MAKE FOR THEIR CHILDREN", only themselves.

That day is here, people. It is here, "NOW"! Only science can save us. We just got hit by a "METEOR" and this one, on the front cover is coming in 2029! Good luck, to us all. We will need it. Especially, since we face, such a "VICIOUSLY PROUD AND SELF-RIGHTEOUS" sea of religious rulers, all around the globe. Oh yeah, let's not kid ourselves here either, "GREEDY HYPOCRITES", too! This is sad, but true. Unfortunately, I've found that "THE MAJORITY OF ADULTS ON EARTH DON'T BELIEVE IN EVOLUTION". Bummer. Unbelievably, it gets worse. They don't know what it is and say it isn't true! How can they do this? Is it, just because, their religion tells them so? No, this can't be!!! It isn't logical. Would they want their children to follow science, just because the scientist, tell them to? No, the scientific world doesn't allow that and neither should they. This can't be happening to me. But, it is. My parents said and still say the same thing, that evolution isn't true. It is time to start my "EVOLUTION REVOLUTION"!

Wow! I suddenly realized something ironic and sad at the same time. I'm still trying to prove that "RELIGIOUS CHILDREN AREN'T BELIEVERS OF EVOLUTION, SIMPLY BECAUSE THEIR PARENTS SAY IT ISN'T TRUE! PEOPLE, IT IS TIME TO WAKE-UP. THIS HAPPENED TO ME! WE KNOW, THIS IS MESSED UP! WHY DO WE ALLOW THIS? WE HAVE METEORS COMING AT US AND WE WILL NOT PRAY THEM AWAY"! How do I know? Because, I pray everyday and "ASK GOD/

E.T. TO MAKE IT PERFECT". Nothing happens. It isn't perfect! Again, UNFORTUNATELY", this is my "NEW REALITY". Unlike, religion's "ALLEGEDLY OMNIPOTENT GOD", I would make the world perfect if I could. Accepting, that anyone can is ridiculous. We can't keep ignoring this fact!

People, babies are dying everyday. Who wouldn't want to pray this away, if they could?"REALLY", this is the only question, we should be asking ourselves. We can deal with evolution and all the other "STUFF", later.

The thought of a perfect world is huge. But, the "METEOR" on the front cover, poses the most relevant question, now and forever! It will, as long as, we live on a planet. That question is simple."HOW CAN WE ESCAPE, PLANET EARTH", before it becomes "PLANET DEATH"? If we don't escape, the perfect world won't matter, anyway. However, the fact remains, that "METEORS" will "ALWAYS" be "LIFE'S BIGGEST THREAT"! These quoted and capitalized words are clues, to my answer. I have been searching for "IT", a "LONG TIME"! This is my story.

"EVERYTHING" you are about to read is "REAL"! The "METEOR," on the front cover, is coming at us! I'm not trying to sell books, by preying upon, anyone's fear of "DEATH", as some of my harshest critics, claim! This is our "REALITY". It is happening "NOW"! If you don't think it is or that, your god will save you, get over your-"SELF" and find "SCIENTIFIC INTELLIGENCE"! God isn't helping us. I don't "CARE" if you "THINK" he is! Well, of course I do "CARE", but you know, what I mean. "FOR OUR CHILDREN'S SAKE", there is no "TIME", to argue! Get over it! It is "COMING" and God isn't stopping it.

Wow, my mind never seems to stop. I can't stop wondering, if we will be able, to "SAVE" our-"SELVES", from this "METEOR". Could these people "UP" in the sky, really be capable of stopping this or helping us, like religion and my parents say. Even more importantly, why wouldn't they, "NOW," if they could? Why would they let this mystery continue? I had to find out! They may be the "ONLY REASON" we exist! We still can't stop meteors!

These are just, some of the questions I've had to ask myself, in order to solve this mystery. Why in the hell, wouldn't they just "OPENLY" live in the sky and not let this mystery exist, in the first place, "IF THEY COULD"? Damn this question. It tortured me, "UNTIL I BEGAN ASKING MYSELF, MORE QUESTIONS". Is it "POSSIBLE," that "THEY CAN'T" change us and this has already happened "BEFORE," like all religion's say? Are we "IMMINENTLY DOOMED", to repeat history again? What is time and does it really exist? And last, but certainly not least, why do we all have déjà vu? Can time travel, in any "FORM," be possible? I just can't "BUY IT". Two reasons, "LOTTERY AND DEATH"! It defies logic and the evidence.

People, I can accept the idea of these people, "THAT LIVE IN THE SKY", making an artificial "HEAVEN", in space. However, I can't buy, the perfect world story. Again, I can't, because babies are dying! Like, Stephen Hawking challenging and questioning "NOTHINGNESS", in his examination of the "BIG BANG" theory. I must also question time travel, with the same logic. Why wouldn't it exist now, if it were possible? Who wouldn't make the world perfect, if they could? Well, be careful, that's a loaded question!

You are about to "SEE", that the question; "WHAT IS PERFECT", is also loaded! With me, it's simple! I'm a parent. I want a world, where children don't die. Hell, anyone for that matter! I don't want to die, either. Call it fear or whatever, you want. But, to me. Again, it's simple "LOGIC". None of us would be here, if we weren't, all "AFRAID" of dying!!! "THE FEAR OF DEATH IS JUST A NATURAL BEHAVIOR, SHARED BY EVERY LIVING THING"! Try and kill a fly, if you don't believe me. It's just, the "NATURE" of all life! Heck people, we all know that it's just "NATURE ITSELF", to "NOT THINK" about dying and only react, when it faces us! Well, that reaction is called "FEAR OF DYING"!!! It is nothing to be ashamed of. I want you, to "THINK HARD", about this simple evidence. Please, let humility guide your "RATIONALIZATION", in dealing with it. This is how "LOGIC" works.

Well, again here, I'm not sold on God or any-ones time travel idea. It still hasn't been proven. However, I am intrigued by it. Albert Einstein and another "WORLD FAMOUS MAN" named Jesus/"YESHUA", do talk about time, being "RELATIVE". Does that mean it's conquerable? In times case, we have this thing called, "TIME DILATION". It happens in space and it is truly weird. The faster we go away from earth, in a space-craft, the slower time goes! Essentially, it "THEORETICALLY" proves, that if we reach the speed of light, "TIME WOULD STOP"! It wouldn't exist. Bizarre, huh? Well, hang on, it gets weirder. Really weird, like everything, being made of moving parts, that makes it appear as a stationary solid object! When in reality, the image is really an illusion of the past and never solid! Sunlight itself, proves this amazing fact of "RELATIVITY". Check out a quasar! We can see it and take a picture of them, but they are already gone! Believe me, by the end of this book, I'd like us all to "KNOW" what "TIME" is and be a relative of it. LOL! Just, without the "GROWING OLD" part or at least, looking it anyway. That's my goal. LOL! Uh, oh! My "KARMA," just ran over my "DOG-ma"!!! People, I admit it. I'm guilty. I just revealed my "VANITY DISEASE"!

Boy, being "SCIENTIFICALLY INTELLECTUAL" and vain at the same time, is "REALLY, NO DIFFERENT" than being a vain religious person. It's contradictory and hypocritical! Wow! I am literally, a walking contradiction! I'm that person. Isn't it, just human nature, to want youth and beauty, forever? How can this be so "BAD"? It wouldn't be, if we all looked the same! Eureka!

Wow, this is such a "DARK" subject matter, I hope you don't "MIND," if I try and keep things "LIGHT"-hearted. Life's, too hard, to always be, so "SIRIUS"! Well, I'm over "MY- self ", now. Like I said before, I'm not wanting to hurt people or be a smart-ass. It's just, that his subject matter is so sacrilegious, it begs for humor. So, I promise to give you, all that I can. However, "BELIEVE ME," there's nothing funny, in what you're about to read. I must warn you now. It is horrible.

Children die, we die, everything living, will die!! But, wait a minute, does that mean we have to "STOP EXISTING"? Religion and science both, say it doesn't! Thank God and and, oh yeah Albert, too! Eienstein, that is!

Well, now that I've gotten, that out of the way. I hope it's alright, to be a little "FUNNY". Because, I truly want to be a genius. Well no, my "EGO" does. I just keep "FORGETTING" to "CURE" the damn thing! I guess I need to, let go of my ego! I laughed as I remembered, the old commercial. LOL. Wow, am I ever "GETTING" old! It's happening people, and there aint a damn thing funny about that!!!

Seriously, though folks. I do hope to provide simple answers, for these complicated questions, I've just talked about. However, I won't succeed "UNTIL CHILDREN ARE COMPLETELY FREE TO READ, THIS SCIENTIFIC EVIDENCE"! Parents should not be allowed to keep them, from it. I've always started my "BOOKS," the same way life works, from the beginning to end and guess what? There is a little light, at the end of the tunnel, just like, when we were born!

Fortunately enough for children, the historical "KNOWLEDGE" of mankind's origins is universal and preserved, for everyone to see. And even though, the world is full of constant "CONTENTION," about it. We've finally discovered and accepted, that the "EVIDENCE DOESN'T LIE, MAN DOES"! We are not only, rewriting history, as we speak. We are also, making "NEW DISCOVERIES OF OUR PAST", everyday.

However, change is slow. "MANKIND'S RELIGIOUS DISEASE" continues it's rule, to this day and it isn't our parent's or anyones, fault. It's just "TRADITION" and human nature! Everybody, wants to be "RIGHT"! Ironically though, their is a bright spot, in all this. Adults agree, that time is "PRECIOUS" and we shouldn't be wasting anymore, period! The problem is, that we're still "WASTING TIME", arguing about it. People, come on. Don't we all agree, that time is "MOST PRECIOUS, WHEN WE'RE DYING"? Well, we are all dying!!! This "METEOR COULD'VE BEEN THE BIG ONE"!

"TIME", unfortunately "BECOMES," even more precious, as it flies by. It seems to go faster and faster, each passing day. In fact, I think anyone over 40 can agree, on another thing. It "TRULY IS THE MOST VALUABLE THING OF ALL", as we get older! I can tell you, that by the time you reach fifty, it becomes "PRICELESS"! I'll buy all I can get!

It is my "HOPE," with this book, that we can "ALL AGREE," it's "TIME TO QUIT ARGUING", about "WHO'S RIGHT OR WRONG" and do something. I hope we can talk "PEACEFULLY," about "ANSWERS"! Please? "THIS METEOR IS COMING"!

Common sense should compel us, to act 'RATIONALLY AND IMMEDIATELY". We should give everything, to prevent the death of our children.

This story is dedicated, to everyone who's time in life was "SHORT", like my friend Stacie. He suffered terribly, from the moment he was born, with sugar diabetes. He joins a list, that tragically keeps growing and is way too long for me, to mention. However, I have to mention a few. My friend and former co-worker Betty Gronna, my nephew Danny, my little sister Nancy Gail and my niece Linda Joe. Betty died at 29 of cancer. Danny died at 22, in a head on collision. My little sister died, before she even left the hospital and Linda died at 30 of suicide. They are all tragic deaths. I miss and love them all, dearly. Their lives gave and still give mine, a "NEW MEANING, A NEW PURPOSE", everyday. They do, simply because I'm still alive! Pardon me, here, for saying this. But, I don't feel lucky. I feel sad and yet, "FORTUNATE" at the same time. I have a "REASON" to live, now. I am sad, without them here. But, I am able and driven like never before, to do something about it. I can't just sit idly by and watch everyone, "DIE". My goal is to "CONQUER DEATH"!

I hope these beloved lives and the "COUNTLESS" others, who died "EARLY", impacts us all, in such a way, that it emboldens us to seek the "IMPOSSIBLE". It has done, just that very thing, to me. Sadly, they had very little "TIME", but we're still living! Again, to me, this should give our lives, "PURPOSE". I hope, that it makes life more "VALUABLE THAN EVER"! We are "STILL ALIVE"! It's up to us, to do something about our deaths.. Let's all start doing something to "ACHIEVE THE IMMORTALITY OF OUR SPECIES"!

What do we have to lose, but ourselves? "TEAM" may not have an "I" in it, but family certainly does and it will take every "I" in the bunch, to do this. We must keep our eyes on the prize, of "IMMORTALITY". We can achieve this, seemingly impossible dream, if we do so! Maybe, we will even eventually, bring our loved one back? If it happens, would we want to be the person who helped or who didn't? No-brainer, huh? People, we will never run from the law of physics. These possibilities aren't going to be easy, I assure you. But, I do "BELIEVE" it is possible with science, in an "INFINITE UNIVERSE". Great news, at least, the "ODDS" are in our favor and we still exist!

Stephen Hawking's says this very thing himself, in the movie, "THE THEORY OF EVERYTHING"!!! He says, "WHERE THERE IS LIFE THERE IS HOPE"! However, there is no truer saying than: "ALL IT TAKES IS ONE BAD APPLE TO SPOIL THE WHOLE BUSHEL"! People, I will give my life, for the sake of family. "MY GREATEST WISH IS THAT WE WILL ALL DO THE SAME"! Today, "ALL LIFE", should be "SACRED"! Logic dictates this simple and yet, torturous truth. How is my life, anymore valuable than a sparrow or my loved ones, whom have already died. It isn't and I don't want to live without them. Hell, I want snowball, back! Death may be a certainty, "NOW". But, that doesn't mean, it will be tomorrow. To me, life is an adventure! I am going to spend every waking moment trying to achieve, the "IMPOSSIBLE". Call me crazy if you want. But, I think we can eventually, conquer disease, aging and most of all, "DEATH"! Now, enough! I've got to keep finding flying saucers, too! They obviously have the answers!

I bet you're thinking, that I'm crazy, right about now and I don't blame you, if you are. But, I've also been thinking about something else, just as crazy. Maybe, we should be asking ourselves the ultimate "SACRILEGIOUS QUESTION". Can "RESURRECTING THE DEAD" really be possible and would we want to bring everybody back? Science is "AGAIN" saying it is, just like religion. People, can this really be true? Can we "POSSIBLY" bring our loved ones back? Wow, reincarnation is about to be scientifically "BORN "AGAIN"!

I "THINK", that this is not only possible, in the "NEAR FUTURE". But, I also "THINK" it's been done before, by these "PEOPLE IN THE SKY". Their is ancient evidence of mummification is on every continent of earth! Wow!!!

Boy, have I ever "LEARNED" a lot, about the "MYSTERY OF MANKIND", in the last 20 years. I've been so overwhelmed, by it all. I can't believe it, but I keep discovering amazing advanced scientific knowledge, from our ancient past. Sometimes, I think I've learned more, than what I bargained for. I do, because, now, I can't even ignore "THE EVIDENCE", you're about to see. "IT IS WHAT IT IS" and it has definitely, forever changed me! "HOPEFULLY" it will challenge and "AWAKEN EVERY-ONE'S SCIENTIFIC IMAGINATION OF REALITY"! It has mine. Regardless, we still can't stop "METEORS", yet!!! "YET", being the key word here. Gotta go! This is the single most important achievement to make happen. I will do it!

People, we can't turn back the hands of time and make this "HISTORICAL EVIDENCE" go away. It will "CLEARLY" speak for itself. It will show, that the true nature of "INTELLIGENCE IN AN INFINITE UNIVERSE" is not about our own survival, but "LEARNING TO SURVIVE ASASPECIES, FOREVER"! We can only do this, as a family, not "ALONE". Again, to do so, every eye must stay "FOCUSED", on the prize of "IMMORTALITY"! DISCOVERY" haunts me and yet, fills me with hope, that this is possible. Like Stephen Hawking, Albert Einstein and "JESUS"(yeshua is his real name). I too, think that; "Where there is life, there is hope"! This evidence, keeps me going, even in the face of anyone debating or "NOT BELIEVING" it.

We don't get over, "DEATH". "UNFORTUNATELY", we just stop talking about it and go on with our lives. Tragically, the "PERSPECTIVE" thing, just seems to get lost, in the shuffle. Wow! This one word best describes, what my story is all about! "PERSPECTIVE"! People, I don't want my family to hurt, because of this book. I just want to talk to them and share this, "WONDERFUL EVIDENCE OF FLYING SAUCERS". But, I can't! Most of the time, it becomes a heated debate. Most are religious and we all know better, than to talk about religion. The others are "AG-NOSTIC" and don't want tot talk about it!

Well, again, I'm just a glutton for punishment or a dreamer, at best. I'll take the latter and just keep "SCIENTIFICALLY" trying! Beware! Some say, my "BELIEF IN FLYING SAUCERS AND ALIENS", has become a religion to me, too! Yeah, not a bad thing, right! I know I've always had to quickly reel in, my own "ZEALOUSNESS", during this journey. I still do if I want to be successful and continue on. I realize, that just because I see this "MATCHING EVIDENCE", doesn't mean, that everyone else, will! You will see, I tried many times and failed. But I never stopped. I never gave up! I guess I'm crazy for trying, huh! Well, I can't just do nothing and let my kids die. I've got to do something about it!!! People, I film flying saucers! I have a picture of it. If you don't believe it, then here's an "IRREFUTABLE" piece of evidence, to support the reality of it. We have scientists, that "LIVE UP IN THE SKY, JUST LIKE THE ANCIENT UNIVERSAL RELIGIOUS STORIES, SAY THEIR CREATORS DO"! Well, if this meteor would have been the "BIG ONE", scientists would've been the only ones, to survive!!! Scientists could be the ancient god's/creators of primitive man! We also have ancient universal stories of "RESURRECTING" the dead, mummification on every continent, and today's scientist's saying this is theoretically possible, as well! The fact that these pieces of evidence match thousands of years apart, can't be a coincidence. How could primitive man have known this "ADVANCED SCIENTIFIC KNOWLEDGE" when "SCIENCE JUST RECENTLY HELPED US ACHIEVE THIS GOAL", ourselves. Why don't we all "KNOW AND SEE" this, "MATCHING EVIDENCE"? Television tells us "SPACE IS THE FINAL FRONTIER", but do we all "SEE" it, that way? My parents don't and I know why. Religion uses science when they want and in this case, when they don't. My parents still want to "LIVE ON EARTH, FOREVER"! No!!!

I am truly sorry if this hurts my family. Their feelings certainly matter. It just doesn't change things! I want my loved ones back and I'm willing to do "WHATEVER IT TAKES", to achieve this goal. Even, to the point of begging my family, for forgiveness and begging everyone to "GIVE THIS THEORY A CHANCE"! Please, I'm begging all of you, to just give this a chance?

I want "OUR LOVED ONES" back, people! I don't want my kids to die, for "GOD"S SAKE". That's "ALL"! To hell with the glory of being "RIGHT ABOUT US" and our mystery. I'm not afraid to be "WRONG". Again, I just can't stand the thought of my children dying!!!

To prove my sincerity, I will give everything to guys like Michael Hall. He is a "SCIENTIST" who is also proposing "IMMORTALITY" and "RESURRECTION", to be possible! Yes, "RESURRECTION", just like the "JESUS"/Yeshua story and movie Jurassic Park!

Wouldn't that be wonderful?

I think we all know the simple answer, to this question. Yes, but as rosy as this seems, I have found, that my perspective tortures most people. Primarily the ones, that are "RELIGIOUS, AGNOSTIC, ATHEIST, SCIENTIST, UFOLOGIST, CARNIVORES, SPORTS-MANS, POLITICIANS AND ANYONE WANTING TO BE WEALTHY OR WHO ALREADY ARE"! Wow, what a list, huh! This is just about everybody, including me! As far as wealth goes, people. I only want to get rich, so I can give it all away and challenge everyone to do the same. I want to be the first "SCIENTIST", to use money as a weapon, against itself. "WEALTH/GREED" are the "DOWN- FALL" of all, that is good.

I will give all I have, for "METEOR PREVENTION" and the abolishment of "WEALTH." I will fight fire with fire! The "METEOR" can be put out with money. But, we need "EVERYONE'S MONEY"! Remember, life is all about "PERSPECTIVE". You can't take it with you! I know my "PERSPECTIVE"! I'm dying fast and have very little "TIME" to cure death or stop this meteor. I need to make money, as fast as I can. I have to hire scientists, doctors, and who knows, what else! Well, duh! Rocket-scientists, of course! Wow, everyone. This time, life is all about "ROCKET SCIENCE"!!!

Man, my life is hard enough, without taking on anymore projects. But, I have too, for mom. My mother has suffered the most. She saw the death of my beautiful and precious newborn baby sister, her only daughter. We only got to see her picture, from atop a cake, the day she was supposed to come home, from the hospital. It was awaiting her arrival, along with the rest of us.

Mom's, best friend Maureen, had placed it beautifully, on the center of the dining room table, surrounded by gifts, cards and flowers. It was so beautiful! We all chipped in and helped decorate the entire house, while dad went to bring them home. It was the least, we could do, for Mom. She was the best! She finally had a girl, after giving birth to six straight boys! We were all so excited, to see our "NEW" little sister. At first, we all stayed busy cleaning and preparing our "SURPRISE", for her. Agonizingly enough, as it was for us kids to wait, time began dragging by, slower and slower. We got fidgety! It was taking longer than it should have. Something was wrong. Suddenly, the phone rang. We all danced with excitement and begged to talk, to whoever was on the phone. We wanted to know, where they were and why they weren't here, already. Maureen held the phone away from us, as soon as, she answered. Our excitement quickly turned to fear and then.... our world was shattered!

It was dad and whatever he told Maureen, was bad, because she started crying. She barely manged to hang up the phone and then tried to tell us the horrible news. She didn't have to say a word, we just knew. We knew, that Nancy Gail had died!!! We all broke down and cried mercilessly. All the babies, died from a staph infection, brought in by a nurse, the night before. Mom and Dad were crushed! This one event, not only "KILLED" my parents, but it took away our innocence, as well. That fateful day changed my life. Little did I know, how much this would impact me and my search for answers, to life's mysteries, later on. For one split second in life, everything changed. We all got more than, we bargained for, that day. We saw "DEATH" and it's powerful effect, even our religious parents. When they got home, mom went straight to her room. She was devastated, like the rest of us. We never saw her or talked about our little sister, for a week. She was so beautiful. No, she "IS" beautiful! Mom, didn't deserve this. No one does! My dad tried to "RE- ASSURE" us, that we would see her again. But we could clearly see his doubt, as well.

Why did she have to die? Why? Why did any of them, have to? Life, is too short, as it is! I'm angry and I'm hurt. Life isn't "FAIR." No parent should have to bury their child and we can't begin, to imagine their pain! I don't want too! I'm a parent!!! I'm sorry. But these "PAINFUL" memories still haunt me. I'll try and keep it together, for "EVERY-ones" sake, "JUST LIKE MY DAD", did. I'll always be thankful to him, for that.

Again, I know I may sound crazy! But, when Nancy Gail died, I knew right then and there, why I was "GOING TO GET RICH"! Even though, I already was and didn't know it! I was and still am because I "HAVE," a beautiful family!!! That, is the true wealth of life. "WE WOULDN'T EXIST WITHOUT FAMILY"! Think about it. We're nothing without family and mine "MEAN EVERYTHING", to me. I think I had my first epiphany, then. From that moment on, I had a vendetta to fulfill with life and death. I was going to invent immortality and conquer death! I was going to "MAKE LIFE BETTER", for Mom and Dad! Heck, "FOR US ALL"! I was going to "BRING NANCY GAIL

BACK", even if I had to die, to do it! Why did she die and not me? I've never been o.k. with it and I'm still not. When and "IF" I die, I will think of her, to calm my fear and use it to help me "REALIZE", just how "LUCKY I AM TO HAVE LIVED LONGER"! Wow, that sounds so sick and "SELFISH" doesn't it? But, we all know it's "STATISTI-CALLY TRUE". I do, like all of us, still have a chance, to achieve the "IMPOSSIBLE". We can bring them back!

People, sadness about death, depends on our "REALITY"? Religion doesn't see death, that way. Most people have heard the old biblical quote on t.v., from the book of "Ecclesiastes": "Rejoice for the end of man, not his beginning"! Well, I don't care, what the hell it says. I don't blame mom, I couldn't do it, either!!! I still can't be happy about someone's death, unless they're in pain. If they are, then I am, only because they're pain-"FREE". But, I'll still be sad and miss them. I never trusted mom and dads religion, after this. I would later, discover "JESUS" saying mankind is evil and that only those in Heaven are good. What? My parents religion, say we are good! Wow! Suddenly, I "SAW" where their lack of faith, came from. A cover-up of information, in their own religion! Sadly, I tried to share this with them, thirty years later. I am sorry for this, as you will soon read. This preface is about complete.

If it's the last thing I do, I'm going to "HELP" everyone be "HAP-PY". I couldn't help, but to immediately think of a current pop song and started singing. I love it! Go Pharrel, thanks for the "HAPPY SONG"! We need it. It makes us happy and now I hope this book, makes everyone happy, too!

People, this book is my "LIFE'S WORK", about "THE MYSTERY OF LIFE". And yes, it's a damn shame I started so late, in trying to figure it "ALL" out. I admit, that I was too goddamn selfish, "SEXUALLY" motivated and ignorant, for my own damn good. I was in love with myself, for too damn long! I wasted a lot of money in doing so—relatively speaking of course, chasing a beautiful woman! I could have put it to better use, that's for sure. But, the question of just how much money is too much, continues to divide families and people all over the earth, to this day. It's been that way, since the beginning of "TIME". Wealth, has become "RELATIVE, JUST LIKE TIME"! But, let's not kid ourselves, here. We all know the truth, when it comes to money and dying. We'd all give everything we have, for one more day, "WHEN IT'S HAPPENING"! Sad, huh? Don't worry, I think we're all guilty, at least us adults anyway. If you're not, then great. But, what we do "NOW", is "ALL THAT REALLY MATTERS"! Right now, we have "METEORS" coming at us.

People, it's "PAYBACK TIME"! I know this is a ridiculously long preface, but I had to set the stage, for what my book is really, all about. The "END/BOTTOM LINE"! It's time to put our money where our mouth is and make a "BETTER WORLD", for "OUR CHILDREN". Shouldn't we all be living for them, anyway? We've all had a relatively "GOOD" existence and they deserve one to. I'm grateful to be alive and "HOPE", that we can all learn, from our "PAST". I want to, in order to make a better "FUTURE", for my children's sake. Kid's "DESERVE" it. They're the "INNOCENT" ones! We wanted them. They, not only didn't ask to be here, but, "THEY DIDN'T ASK FOR A DEATH SENTENCE, EITHER"! We may have given it to them, innocently enough. But, we've grown "UP" and we're not innocent, anymore! We're the "GUILTY" ones, because of it! We owe them back, nothing short of, "IMMORTAL LIFE". It is time, to "INTENTIONALLY", do something about it. Please, join me? Let's give all we have to science and challenge everyone else, to do the same? Please? I'm begging you. Please, for our children's sake?

I have two boys, Josh and Matt. I "DESPERATELY" want to give them, a "PERFECT WORLD"! It's my duty, as their father, to try and make that happen. It's what I live for. I owe them that. I owe them, because I can't live without them. I need them, in order to make my world, "COMPLETE", family and all. I never knew "TRUE LOVE", until I had them! Now, I know how my parents feel about me! Because of them, I exist and now my "GREATEST WISH", also came true. I "CREATED" a family, too. I see them and my family, as the greatest gift in the world. I must find "THE PERFECT WORLD—HEAVEN", for them and all of us! But first, I have to do one more thing. Stop "METEORS"! Please let's begin! We can "ALWAYS" conquer space and make "HEAVEN" artificially, "LATER". LOL!!! But, "REMEMBER" and "NEVER FORGET", we can't, if a "METEOR" hits us, "NOW", can we? Wow, "DEJAVU"? LOL! Don't be so serious here. Watch "RIDICULOUSNESS" or some A.F.V.!!!

O.k. enough already. I hope you get the "BIG PICTURE", by now. With all that, said and out of the way. I want to end this preface, with this "METEOR REALITY". Would you please help me help "EVERYONE", learn this "NEW OLD REALITY". It is here now and always has been. It doesn't matter, that "THE ANCIENTS FORGOT WHERE HEAVEN" is! It only matters, that we know. It is "HIGH"-time, to cure mankind's amnesia, about "IT" and get on, with the "SPACE" program! "UP", is where we must go and live to survive. Survival is the true nature of intelligence. "UP is not only, where we must live if we want to survive, but "LIVE FOREVER" as a species! People, space should be called heaven and it is, where we must live, just like the god's!!! Earth's should be called, hell. Mother nature will kill us here, eventually. It will do it, with father time's, help! Our mother is the growing sun and we can't escape her, "STAYING HERE"! To live forever, we must seek "REALITY" and escape, "PLANET DEATH"! Wow! I almost changed the title. All planets die. I've discovered, that the universe we live in is conquerable, because it doesn't think. "THINK ABOUT IT". Ironically, it's the only reason, that we can do this! It's a "REALITY", simply, because we aren't "COMPETING AGAINST" it. It isn't trying to out-smart us, we just have to out-smart it. If we don't, we won't exist.

I "LOOKED" everywhere, in the ground or on rocks, to tell me, what was here in the past. I was astounded and blown away, by alien looking art universally displayed all over the earth, on every continent. I found "REAL PHYSICAL EVIDENCE" of an "ANCIENT HU-

MAN SPECIES", that all look the same. Finally, it hit me like a ton of bricks!!! Every species of life looks the same, except us humans. A Light bulb went off, in my head and my mind turned on. I was no longer in the "DARK". I was 33 years old. Here's what happened next. I stumbled upon, this amazing piece of "SIMPLE EVIDENCE" and had another epiphany. It was my first, as an adult. I saw a medical show, about stem cell, viruses and bacteria. I saw, how one cell, became two, in a petrie dish and they were identical! Suddenly, I realized, that this is how evolution worked. Only then, did I somewhat understood, the "BIG BANG THEORY". I didn't know everything, but I finally had something, that I could sink my teeth into. I felt like I knew something, that was real and provable, for the first time in my life. It proved "AGAIN, TO ME" that all species of life and the big bang share a singular origin. I soon discovered, that life can multiply asexually, too.

The "SINGULARITY POINT", as science calls it, is simple and yet, amazingly complex. It begs us to ask, where it came from and what is around it. I did and still do study this "GREAT QUESTION OF SCIENCE". Scientist, are divided about it, always existing or not. I say, like STEPHEN HAWKING" if it didn't, then what is "NOTHING" and why doesn't it exist now? I have a simple answer, later.

Well, I can't spoil the ending, now, can I. But here's a hint, $E=MC2$. This equation tells us matter is always changing form and it never stop's existing! Anyway, my parents angel story, has a lot to do with my findings. So does the singularity point and discovering, how life "EVOLVED", from it. All life, but humans, looks the same. The angel story, led me to theorize, that they are all possibly, equal in looks. Looks are what gives us "POWER OVER EACH OTHER". I found supporting evidence, in the "HEADS OF EASTER ISLAND AND THE OLMEC GODS LOOKING THE SAME". People, could these gods have evolved and created us, for the power we possess, through our unique beauty of flesh? Furthermore, could they be so advanced, that they can live through us, by memory transplantation or some other actual "ADVANCED SCI-

ENTIFIC KNOWLEDGE" we just don't have yet? Couldn't this be what we have always called a soul or spirit? Isn't "MEMORY" really just, all we are?

People, if this doesn't spark your scientific interest, we do have ancient surgical proof of brain surgeries, on every continent, as well! We have called it brain-trepannation and it is still done today, even after being, a lost art for thousands of years!! This evidence supports my theory/ this possibility as well as, universal reincarnation, mummification, etc. and so on.. I even found ancient writing, that do the same. It is from, the bible in the book of Jude. This text supports, just that possibility. Here's the quote: "Though you once knew this, I will tell you again. The angels which kept not their first estate, left it for a "STRANGE FLESH" and for them is reserved a lake of fire chained in eternal darkness". People this is earth! Are we this strange flesh?

Could these angels be primitive man's ancient alien looking "HUMANOID ART"? Could they be" MAKING HUMANS" and down-loading, their "MEMORY/SPIRIT/SOUL", into them for the "UNIQUE POWER", we would give them? Could earth be religion's "HELL"? It is a lake of fire? Could mankind be "RELIGION"S DEVIL"! My brain is in and surrounded by a lake of fire. People, it is our prison! Oh my god, no! I remembered my best friend Dwayne and his book called "COME UP OUT OF HER MY PEOPLE"! We differed in our opinion of what was coming out. To me it's memory, Dwayne was open to it, but called it a spirit. He accepted my questioning of it's existence, graciously. He knew I questioned his spirit existence. But, he had no answers, for my "CRAZY QUESTIONS". He didn't know they live or why they would want to have sex, with "US"! He didn't know if they watch t.v. play sports or what. Most importantly, where did they come from? I propose to have answers and questions, to get people thinking "INFINITELY"! Could we be living an A.S.K. (advanced scientific knowledge)"REALITY", that is happening "NOW" and "JUST NOT KNOW IT." Could we be them, addicted to a beautiful scientifically created species, that only exist because, "THEY CREATED" us? Before, you say no. Ask yourself; Do you want to be ugly?

People, I am addicted to "BEAUTY"!!! My wife makes it painfully clear, that we all are. You are about to read a lot of things, that "MAY SEEM CRAZY", like my pictures of flying saucers, on the front cover. But, don't kid yourself, here. This isn't, as scientifically far fetched, as people think and I did find "FLYING" saucers, with Jeff Willes. I filmed them with Jeff. They are real and it doesn't change anything, if you don't believe me. It only matters, if you "BELIEVE" the evidence. We, all may not know what they are, but we can learn and "FIND", out. If we don't, I think it's safe to say, that it won't matter if we want to find "IT" or not, when it comes! It is "ADVANCED SCIENTIFIC KNOWLEDGE" and it will find us, even if we, don't want it, too. Let's be real, again here, people. We all know we can't stop "PROGRESS"! Now, I will give you the "THE MOST IMPORTANT CLUE" I have, before I end this preface. I want to continue on with my story.

Here it is: Please "THINK INFINITELY", please? I fear a president, who thinks like RONALD REAGAN and wants to create a "STAR WARS DEFENSE" system! If that's not bad enough, he's doing it just in case, "MORE ADVANCED ALIENS ATTACK US"! Do we really think, that they wouldn't be attacking us, now? Duh, they're "MORE ADVANCED"! One word, "HITLER"! People, this reflects a primitive scientific "FINITE" thinking, even from a president, about possible E.T. intelligent life, that is very easy to "SEE". We all know, that good guys, always finish last! Not by aggression, but by "OUT- SMARTING" their "ENEMIES"! If an "INTELLIGENT SPECIES" is "ANYWHERE", to be found in this "GOD-FORSAKEN" universe. They would be "EV-ERYWHERE", here now, and watching us, like we do with our threats. It's only Logical, that they would just keep staying away, until they have to save us, from "EXTINCTION". But, it would only be, for the good of what we "COULD BE" and that is surely, "INTELLIGENCE"!!! My answer/theory is just, like "JESUS"/YESHUAS, they won't be "COM-

ING" here, from "SOMEWHERE ELSE". Not, in an infinite universe or one that's fourteen and a half billion years old, either! Maybe, the existence of our species, in the face of, this "INFINITE METEOR THREAT TO ALL LIFE ON EARTH" isn't such a coincidence, after-all? Huh? Maybe, our memories can be "BORN AGAIN"? People, atoms will always exist, in the birth/re-birth of every "SUN/SON". As far as, their minds/memory/soul/spirit or whatever you want to call, goes. Maybe, it "CAN", too?

Well, I will leave that up to you. Now, I am going to finish this preface and let you get on, with reading my book. That is, if you want to? I don't want to keep you any longer. But, I have to tell you one more thing. The smallest piece of matter, that we have seen in science is called coincidently enough, "THE HIGGS BOSOM/GOD PARTICLE". We see it "FOR JUST A SPLIT SECOND", against the blackness of space. Then, like lightning, it's gone. It flashes, from one place to another and it doesn't stop! Sounds like, looking at suns in fast forward, huh? Even more spectacular than that, it sounds like our lives! Wow, that's the simple point of the bible story. Possible Immortality? That's up to us. Will we find it and possibly preserve our memory? Regardless, of whether "WE, IT, OR ADAM/ATOM" lives forever or not. We all must give everything we have, to stop "METEORS" and we must do it "NOW"! We don't "NEED" to worry, about Adam, though. Atoms always exist, whether Adam "KNEW" this, or not. "WE" will, too. However, the question is obvious and still remains, there's only one; "WHAT WILL WE BE, IF AND WHEN WE DO?"!!! I know one thing, whatever it is. I just don't want to be ugly! I'll admit it. I ain't a fool. It's the truth and I want it to set me free! Before you "LIE" and say it doesn't matter to you, ask yourself one question; "Do you want to be ugly?" P.S. Better be careful, the aliens may have a lie detector test, that can kill us if we lie!!!

Funny thing is, we'd actually be killing ourselves!!!!! LOL. Please keep reading. Here's, the rest of my story. Peace, love, and harmony to all. Intelligence always forgives! Revenge is evil. Love always, Michael

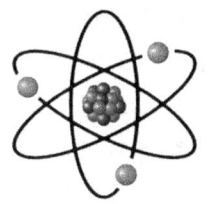 # MY INTRODUCTION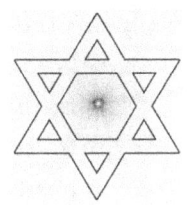

THE PAST
"DEJAVU"

September 29th 1961: This is my birth date. "WHEN I WAS BORN" I heard a famous quote, from a TV show called STAR TREK. Here it is; "Space, The Final Frontier", I breathed a sigh of relief. Then, a little later, again on the TV news; "The first man goes to space." What? No way! This can't be true! Then, much later, these horrific words at my college graduation commencement speech; "When we finally "CONQUER SPACE" and aren't any longer "PRISONERS" of earth." No... no it can't be! "WE" haven't conquered space? "WHO" am I? "WHAT" is happening to me? "WHERE" am I? "WHY" am I here? Is this "REALLY HAPPENING"? My "REALITY" began to unfold. I was afraid and scared to think about what could happen next.

But it didn't matter. I couldn't stop it!

Soon, I would make a life changing "A.S.K. "DISCOVERY" and "BECOME" an author. It happened because a friend of mine "PERSUADED" me to look for "SPIRITS". He had a powerful O.B.E.. Well, I didn't find any. Instead, I found "ANCIENT EVIDENCE OF PEO-

PLE LIVING UP IN SPACE"! "THANK GOD"! People "MUST" have "FINALLY LIVED LONG ENOUGH" to do this.

I immediately tried to figure out "WHAT GAVE THEM THIS ABILITY" to do so, but I didn't have to. Instantly, I knew when I saw "IT" and had an epiphany. The heads of Easter Island all look the same! How did this help them? My story reveals why. I didn't care why. I was just relieved! Thank God "SOMEONE ELSE" sees this "ADVANCED SCIENTIFIC KNOWLEDGE." They must've known this!

Why am I the only one to see this "HEAVEN/SPACE REALITY" and not my buddy? Could I be the "FIRST"? I found out that I wasn't. I was glad! Wow, maybe there's "HOPE" after all! "MAYBE" we aren't "ALONE"! I began telling everyone, that this knowledge is "TO SCIENTIFICALLY ADVANCED", to be a coincidence. Most didn't get it. Why is simple.

We're just now "LIVING UP IN SPACE" ourselves! Wow, another thing hit me. "WHERE THEY LIVE." Living "UP" in space proved they evolved, from nothing! It does so, because "NOTHING"/space is where we "ALSO" must live, to achieve immortality, like them. We are "EVOLVING IN THAT DIRECTION" and didn't have E.T.s or gods helping us either, just like "THEM"! They made it from nothing and we can too! We must go "UP"! "EVERYONE KNOWS" planets die, "right"? Wow! Wow! Wow! WRONG! Everyone doesn't know! Man, I couldn't believe what was happening to me.

In 2000, I released my first book and began to share this "EVIDENCE" with everyone.

Much to my horror, I quickly saw that most of the "WORLD" didn't "REALLY BELIEVE" it. Even worse, they didn't "SEE" or "KNOW" how "IT" was possible and most of them were "RELIGIOUS"! I was blown away. Of all the people in the world, they're the ones who are supposed to "BELIEVE" it! Well, I saw how this is possible and I wasn't "RELIGIOUS"! Bingo, another epiphany! This was the key! I didn't go to church or follow anyone! I "CONTINUED TO STUDY EVERYTHING MYSELF"!

Needless to say, I became a weirdo! I seemed to be the only one, other than a few scientists, who saw this "REALITY." However, it gets weirder than that. I could "SEE", that even though were on the same page, there is a "BIG" difference between, them and me. I think I see something "BIGGER." Something so advanced, that just maybe they don't see it.

I saw that an evolving intelligent "SPECIES" wanting "IMMORTALITY" would learn to get off a planet, as quickly as they could. I also saw, that this is religion's past and our future. They matched! This isn't possible unless it's already happened before!

I tried explaining this, but it is "DEEP." Not too many people followed me. Hardly anyone "UNDERSTOOD" it, let alone "BELIEVED" me. One did, well two, maybe even three. It was slowly happening. I knew why. It was because, I wasn't a "BONAFIED SCIENTIST"! Heck, I wanted to be. I just couldn't afford to become one. I had a family to feed. Instead, I opted, to relentlessly pursue more "EVIDENCE" and continue researching my theory! I wrote six more books, none of which were successful and my life became a "LIVING HELL"! THEN ALL OF A SUDDEN... 52 years and 7 books later,

"THE INEVITABLE HAPPENS"!

THE PRESENT
"The scariest day of my life!"

FEBRUARY 15th, 2013: CNN BREAKING NEWS: METEOR EXPLODES OVER RUSSIAN CITY WOUNDING 1,600 PEOPLE AND LEAVING MASS DESTRUCTION IN ITS WAKE. SCIENTIST EVERYWHERE, SAY, WE MUST GO "UP" TO SURVIVE. WORLD LEADERS IGNORE INCIDENT. "NO"! I screamed in disbelief. "WHY," why are they ignoring it! Why haven't we "CONQUERED SPACE" yet? OMG! We need to do this now!

I couldn't believe what was happening. Why aren't we uniting to stop meteors? Surely to God, everyone "MUST" know, that we can achieve this goal! We just have to start, "NOW"!

"NO"! I screamed louder! Someone, please tell me, this isn't "REAL." Please, don't tell me, that we haven't already come together, to solve this problem. Can this really be "HAPPENING"? Is this "REALLY TRUE"? Can we "ACTUALLY" not have, a worldwide "METEOR PREVENTION" plan in place? I quickly headed to the computer and couldn't believe what I was seeing and hearing. We didn't! My worst fears were coming true. Our future is in the hands of bickering power hungry "RULERS" that can't get along and we don't even have a "GLOBAL METEOR PREVENTION PLAN"!!! No, I screamed and cried. I felt so helpless.

All I could think about, at that moment, was my kids. I was thinking, about their future and the question, all adults were asking themselves about right now; "Will we have enough time to, "SAVE OUR KIDS", from these "METEORS"? Knowing, that this dilemma is all about the money, I didn't think so. I couldn't help, but to think of how money had destroyed my own family. I asked myself another question, but I already knew the answer: "Could our "THIRST FOR POWER AND A-DICK-TION TO MONEY," be what destroys us?" Well, one thing's for sure! It will if we "ALL" don't act "NOW"! Inevitably, "METEORS" will happen again and again. It will not stop. We need, not only global unity, but we also "NEED ALL THE MONEY WE CAN GET TO STOP IT"!

For me, this event finally confirmed and simplified my theory of religion. Its view toward good and evil "IS very "SIMPLE." We have to give to be good and live to "GIVE"! All I had to do, was look at my own family to see the disparity of it "ALL." I have a wealthy religous brother and nephew. I just sat there stunned and petrified. I was gripped with fear, for the future of my children and all children. We're all spoiling ourselves with being served and calling it "THE GOOD LIFE"! Damn the American dream of wealth.

Even in the face of such tragedy, I couldn't help but to be amazed, by it. This meteor event and our ignoring it, mirrored the ancient story of Atlantis. The similarities are way too eerie, to ignore. It is more matching proof of the "GODS/ALIENS", existence! Could they be "RESPONSIBLE" for keeping us from being hit? Is it really just a coincidence, that we only have 6,000 years of recorded history and it all stems, from these gods, who gave us this knowledge? Right down to "PREDICTING" our end? You may want to think INFINITELY, before you say no. This is a logical scenario.

Wow, obviously "MATERIALISM" is our incurable disease, no matter where we are in the universe! Instantly, I had to accept the harshest reality of "LIFE". It really is, "ALL" about the money, just like all religions say. This "METEOR" proved it! We've known about them "FOREVER" and we're still doing nothing "COLLECTIVELY" to stop them! I suddenly realized this won't change.

I cried and screamed, at the horrible thoughts going through my head. "FOR SOME REASON", I just couldn't hide from them! I couldn't stop the visions. "SOMEHOW", I knew the outcome of "MANKIND" and it TORTURED ME".

People, "WHAT ARE THE LIVES OF OUR CHILDREN WORTH OR OUR OWN"?

I'll let you be the judge of that and decide for yourself. I'd rather, just share my amazing story with you, the world and let the chips, fall where they may! I calling it amazing because I am amazed at "MY" discovery. Yes I am "OVERLY" excited about it, as I hope you will be, when you're done reading! I'm guilty of pride ! I "ADMIT" it and I'm ashamed of it.

I promise, this story isn't about bragging on "MY" discovery, though. A lot of people might think so and "HATE ME", for it. I say this because my "CRITICS" have relentlessly accused me of this, in the past. I can't change it. My story is about an unbelievable "LIFE CHANGING SCIENTIFIC DISCOVERY", that I made some 20 "ODD" years ago! I learned it from "OTHERS" before me! I give them the credit. I don't claim to be special. Anyone can find it.

But people, this discovery is my story! Look, I do apologize if I offend anyone, I'm not special and I'll be the first to say that anyone, could have made it as well. I say this with the utmost "HUMILITY," because a "FEW" already have! In fact, "MORE AND MORE are "SEEING" it every day. "HOPEFULLY," it will be "MANY," soon! "WE NEED TO STOP METEORS, NOW"! Let's do this thing!

Please, kick back, relax and "ENJOY" yourself. The adventure you are about to go on, really was an "UNBELIEVABLY," "HAIR-RAISING," "MIND-BENDING," "REALITY-WARPING," "HELLACIOUS" roller coaster of a ride, for me and guess what? It still is! WOO-HOO!

All jokes aside, I hope, this story leaves you as emotionally drained and yet full of "HOPE" as I was, at its end. Be careful though, emotions are dangerous. I am still reeling from it all, as I write. I know promises are made to be broken. But I promise you, this story will not let you "DOWN." The urgency of this "METEOR EVENT" won't let it! It is, after all, what made me get busy and start writing this book. Our very existence depends on it.

You are about to embark, on a "TRULY" marvelous journey of "MIRACULOUS DISCOVERY" and exciting challenges, as you continue to read my story! Sure, you will have to face bitter truths and entertain some very harsh realities of life. But, there is hope and you can't get any worse, than what you've already heard— children are dying! So, please give it a chance. Because there's "NOTHING" more wonderful, than the thought of stopping it and bringing them back.

Don't worry, believe me the mystique of mankind and our stories of "RESURRECTION" will draw you in, just like it did me. It won't, or may not, let you go if you continue to read on, but don't be afraid! The outcome could be "GLORIOUS." "DON'T FORGET," fear is a curable disease! Imagination and seeking knowledge is the treatment!

I must warn you, one last time, before you continue reading. The "ENDLESS" and wonderful possibilities, in this book can absolutely, turn into a nightmare. It did for me!! Please be careful of what you wish for and follow along "CARE-FULLY"! You're going to enter a harrowing world of "SUPERNATURAL AND OTHER-WORLDLY" encounters where "TRUTH" really is stranger than fiction. Some truths will torture you, just like they did me. They still do!

You can take solace, in one "BITTERSWEET" fact of life, that I found, as well. As painful as these "COLD HARD TRUTHS" are, they are truths of epic proportions. Like bad tasting medicine, they will "CHANGE" children's lives, for the better. They will give us a world where "OUTWARD BEAUTY" is an illusion and "EQUALITY" becomes our foundation. "INNER STRENGTH AND LOGIC" will rule as the cornerstone of our society! Nature will become your new love. It will give you "HOPE", that anything is possible and the commonsense to know that, only we can make the "WORLD PERFECT." The possibly of creating, our own "HEAVEN" lies, "WITHIN US ALL"! But, don't ever forget. It is "ONLY POSSIBLE, IF WE GET OFF THIS PLANET". Maybe, just maybe, someone already has. Religion says so and the ancient artifacts confirm it. See the back cover. This became my obsession and it still is. I film flying saucers! I "KNOW" they have.

I want to share one last thing, that dawned on me, because of this meteor. Like a moth drawn to a flame, I became mesmerized by the magnificent wonderment and sheer splendor of "OUR MYSTERY." But, I soon found, that it precariously hinges on a constant door of heart wrenching emotion. Sadly, it swings both way. One direction constantly intoxicates us, with the love of life and hope of immortality; while the other saddens us, with the cold hard "REALITY" of death. It's always just a phone call away! Unfortunately, I live in "ANXIETY HELL"!

Throughout my journey, I kept clinging to the latter. It is, this hatred of death, that fuels my search for "HOPE"! Things changed today. I "KNOW" how lucky I am! My children didn't get killed. Thank God they're "ALIVE"! I will not waste another minute "HATING" anything! I "LOVE" life! I'm even studying this hatred thing! It's not "NATURAL". Animals don't have it.

I "NOW" have a new motto. We may be just a phone call away from death, but we're also just an invention away, from immortal life. So don't ever give "UP" and always remember one thing. "DON'T FORGET", ever "AGAIN", about :METEORS"!

I have to "CONFESS" one last thing before I continue writing. The "COLD HARD TRUTHS" and "BEAUTIFUL BREAKTHROUGHS", in this story, depending on how you view "LIFE," has taken its toll on me. Several of my family committed suicide and I couldn't stop them. Mental pain can be a torture.

Isn't "PLEASURE" really, just the absence of pain? I guess though, this is the same as some- one's view toward life. After all, it does depend on how we look at it and adults know, that "PLEASURE" is "SUBJECTIVE"! We can create our own Hell! I'll never understand "HOW" my family could have committed suicide, having children. But, I do understand "WHY." The dreaded "MENTAL DISEASE". People, we have to see our children's lives, or others, as more important than our own. If not it will "KILL" us all!

Wow, I'm so nervous. I began to write. I am attempting to solve "MANKIND'S MYSTERY." I know what you might be thinking, about now. That's pretty big... right? You probably even think, it can't get any "BIGGER" than that, either. Right? Well, actually it can and it is. It's not all about us. It's about "OUR KIDS SURVIVAL"!

"FIRST," we need to "FIX" our "METEOR EXTINCTION" dilemma! It is the most serious threat facing humankind, "TODAY"! Everyone, that is successful, knows "TIMING IS EVERYTHING!!! Well we just pushed our luck "AGAIN"! We all have to give "NOW"!

It "TRULY IS" time for me to get this book done and the ball rollin' on the "METEOR PREVENTION PLAN"! It seems like science can't make it happen because of religion and religious people "REALLY," don't believe it or worse yet, want to live on the Earth. My family wants to live on earth forever, just like their religion tells them they can!!! Sadly, most just want to "RULE" this Earth. Besides that irony, I've discovered a funny thing about, "HEAVEN." "MOST PEOPLE" want to go heaven. They just don't want to go right now! LOL!

For shits and giggles, I kicked on the song "Everybody Wants to Go to Heaven" and focused on the line "but nobody wants to go now"! "Wow, I said out loud as I laughed to myself and at my new-found "PERSPECTIVE." "NOW," really, is everything!" Because of this "METEOR," "NOW," became my "PERSPECTIVE FOR LIFE! I'm hoping it always was when I watch my own movie back!

I sat there, at that computer and typed and typed, like "THERE WAS NO TOMORROW." I never left it from the moment I proved there wasn't a global meteor prevention plan. How could I?

Before I knew it, the house was dark and silent. Everybody must have gone to bed and I didn't even notice it! Wow, was I ever on a roll. Eventually, I slipped into the bedroom and fell asleep, exhausted at the thought of it, "ALL." I marveled at the beauty of the sunrise and I was surprised, at the same time. I got to see the sun "RISE"! I hadn't done that in a long time (that I welcomed, anyway)! Today is a gift a "BEAUTIFUL GIFT"! I'm giving away everything and to everyone, that is poor. I could hardly believe it, but I had been typing, since 3 o'clock yesterday afternoon! Wow, I suddenly realized something. Yesterday will always be remembered as our wake-up call from now on. It is another day that will live in "INFAMY." That day will forever be the day the "METEOR," hit and hurt a lot of people. "IT COULD HAVE KILLED US ALL, IF IT WOULD HAVE BEEN BIGGER"! That day was FEBRUARY 15th, 2013

The next few months flew by. I wrote and rewrote. I became obsessed, with the desire, to make this book, "PERFECT." I wanted it to be perfect and, "SIMPLE ENOUGH FOR ALL CHILDREN TO UNDERSTAND IT"! Also, I wanted it to be my last. The reason why is about to become clear. "PAINFULLY CLEAR"!

December 31st, 2013: Woo-hoo! Today is my oldest brother's birthday! I dearly miss him am I am officially postponing the "PREPLANNED" release, of this book! His name is Terry. I tried desperately to get this book done and release it on the anniversary of his death September the 22nd. He's been "DEAD" over a year now! I was working on my last book with him, right before he died. Sadly, like this book, I didn't get it into his hands before it happened. Instead, I rushed to finish it after he died and screwed it up! I really wanted to finish this book, on his birthday and I tried. But I can't, though! I have to do better for him and all the kids in the world.

His birthday is special because he's "SPECIAL" and it is relevant to me and my story! You'll see why. He was my biggest supporter in this adventure and completely "UNDERSTOOD" my "DISCOVERY"! We were going to rock the scientific "WORLD" with my new book! Again sadly we didn't and the book didn't, either. It hasn't been successful, "YET"!

Terry, my oldest brother, was anything, but typical. I dearly loved him for that. He epitomized the role of "JOHN BOY" as our guardian angel and protector, just like the television show: "The Waltons. He was that and a whole lot more, to all of us younger brothers. He was the best "OLDER BROTHER" you could ask for! Really, he was all this and much, much more, rolled into one! He was a blast and bigger than life, just like Gomer Pyle!!! God, how I miss him.

I think our whole family died with him, that year. I'll "NEVER FORGET" it and I'm sure, none of them will, either. The only good thing, about his death, is that it "MADE" us forgiving and it brought us together. NOT! Our family still needs a lot of forgiveness, because Terry's death didn't bring us together. Instead, it tore us apart! It was like a second death! It still is a nightmare, to me!

Terry died suddenly and tragically. Of all things, he was killed in a freak train accident at his house. He lived by those tracks for 17 years and was crossing them to buy supplies, for my book's billboard! I was "FORTUNATE" enough to buy his place and keep his grave-site, in our family. His wife buried him on the property, alongside his beloved lion. Told you he was a character. I bought his place because we shared the dream of having a family business. "WE" were on our way to make it happen when the accident occurred.

Now that he's "GONE," I am going to carry his torch and make our dream come true! The entire family is welcome! I hope we all want to honor his dream and be a part of it. It is, what he and I wanted, most. We want the "FAMILY," back! My brother Tim wants to be buried beside Terry. So, in a way we're getting there. Just not the way I'd like!

It still hurts so bad!

I am happy to say "BRUMIELD'S STATION" will have its official grand opening, on the anniversary of his death, this year! It will include a huge free play area for kids, appropriately called "Terry's Place"! I have so many mixed emotions, right now.

A part of me has to go on for my kids, for his kids, and for all our kids. He would want that. He loved kids! Hell, what am I saying, we're all still kids at heart, ourselves! So this is for the "KID" in us all!!!

People, this book isn't finished. So, I have to get on with the "PROGRAM"! I have to get it right, for him and them. I can't screw this up, "AGAIN"! The last one was bad enough. This will be my eighth and "FINAL" book, on this subject matter. It is the "LAST" word, on "LIFE AND OUR MYSTERY," for me.

The "EVIDENCE SPEAKS FOR ITSELF" and has given me, a very clear picture of an "INFINITE UNIVERSE", filled with life, that evolved and all looks the same. I shared my knowledge of it and the "EVOLUTION VERSUS CREATION" debate with Terry. He lit up, with the same excitement, that I had when my light bulb went off. When I explained it to him, he instantly understood. We both cried at this "WONDERFUL REALIZATION OF INFINITE POSSIBILITIES" and couldn't wait to tell Mom. To us, Nancy Gail could possibly be alive "SOMEWHERE." Sadly, we didn't get much "TIME" to convince her, or anybody else, of this "FACT", before tragedy struck! I feel so lucky to be writing this for Terry and his children, and "ALL CHILDREN"! What father wouldn't want to share "LIFE'S ANSWERS" with their children, before they die. Terry did! We know that most parents won't get the time.

Again, this book is not about right or wrong, truth or falsehood. It really isn't even about E.T.s or God. It's about "LIFE" and our intentions, toward it! Are we truly sacrificial and "GOOD" or selfish and "EVIL," when it comes, to our children. Will "EVERYONE" give, all they have, to prevent "METEOR EXTINCTION"? Terry would! I know, because I will, too! We made this pact, while I was working, on my last book. I know he would have loved to experience, all this with me. Especially the "METEOR." He got it, like I do and Neil DeGrasse Tyson (see back cover).

I began to write, feverishly. I had a new sense of purpose and passion, "NOW"! Terry, children, "LOVE of LIFE," and the "FAMILY DREAM", were all well worth "FIGHTING" for!!! I reached up and wiped the tears out of my eyes. My body heaved with emotion as I convulsed and I let all pain out. I tried, but I couldn't stop it. I didn't want to cry. I've cried enough. I had to get this book done. It was "LONG OVERDUE, NOW"! I kept writing. I was shaking. My heart ached. I hurt so bad, but I kept on writing.

THE FUTURE
"Same shit different day"

2029: METEOR COMING!!! My books have failed to make a difference, since their "BIRTH" in 2000. Will they become a success? I don't know? I don't profess to "KNOW THE FUTURE." I don't think anybody else does either, with the exception of astronomers and scientists, who predict "PHYSICAL" celestial events. It's common sense. I'm not going to make a prediction. Instead, I want to end this book with a hypothetical prediction, about my own future and I want it to be funny!.

I shared this "HYPOTHETICAL FUTURE" with my granddaughters and their friends. They thought it was hilarious and "ABSOLUTELY" wanted me to use it, at the "END" of this story. I told them I was worried about "IT" being, too sensitive for kids. I didn't want to use it and hadn't used it in, any of my other books. But, they said it was such an obvious "no brain-er" that I had to! I agreed. We all laughed and laughed about it. It was a "KODAK" moment! I love them so much! They weren't afraid of the "MY REALITY," even though it was theirs, too! They don't want to be ugly, or have their minds read either!

Unlike "MOST" adults, kids are glad, that we won't out run technology. Even if the "TRUTH" hurts! My granddaughters agreed it's going to hurt, but at least in a "GOOD" way. We laughed until we cried, because it is "SUBJECTIVE"! They finally said I had to use it and I agreed! You'll see why!

Here's a clue. As a kid, I was such a chicken shit, when it came to "UGLINESS," OK! So whatever happens, if I wake as an ugly alien, I'll still be scared! But I'll deal with it. You can't get any scarier, than this meteor and death. It's our "REALITY." The ending chapter is not a prediction, just possibly my "HYPOTHETICAL FUTURE." If you "RELATE" and don't like it, don't feel lonely or freaked out. I haven't found anyone who does like it! Nobody wants to be "UGLY"!

Please keep reading and share it, when your done. Even if you don't like it, please. Does this book "FINALLY" change things? No again, that's "SUBJECTIVE" or personal. I can't make anyone see "MY REALITY"! No one can. Is it possible, that the recent "METEOR EVENT" and this newly discovered one, will make a difference in "PEOPLE'S MINDS"? Could my "A.S.K. (ADVANCED SCIENTIFIC KNOWLEDGE) DISCOVERY" evidence, solve our "MYSTERY" and help "SAVE" us "ALL" from extinction? Will anyone "BELIEVE" it, even if science, says it could? Well people, I guess that remains tobe "SEEN"!

I can't tell the future of a human and logic tells me, that no one else can, either. The world would be perfect, if we could. Logic assures me of that! People, a father's "LOVE" is the strongest emotion, that I have! I would die to make the world perfect for my sons. But, I can't. It just isn't. I live to make that happen. The universe is conquerable, not perfect. It never will be, because it isn't now! Only us humans can be perfect. Logic dictates that we have to serve others and give away all our money.

Thank you for "GIVING" my story a chance, so far. I "HOPE" you are enjoying it. As you can tell, by now, I do believe that "PEOPLE, LIVE UP IN THE SKY"! To me they are E.T's,n that are omnipresent! "NAYSAYERS" can say all they want, that I can't prove it, and "hope is all I have." They can even deny my "FLYING SAUCER EVIDENCE"! But, it still won't bother me. I'd take "HOPE" any day of the week, over "NOTHING." They can't take this "EVIDENCE" away from me or hide, from it. It does exist! The "FACT," that we have these universal ancient religious stories mirroring today's reality, is "SOMETHING." Science already "ACKNOWLEDGES" it. Whether they agree with it or anyone else does, is irrelevant. I do have "HOPE"! One day we will "PROGRESS/ EVOLVE" and live in the sky like they do!.

"HOPE" puts a twinkle in my eye and a smile on my face. So here's to you, eternal "HOPE." I wish you luck. Na Nu Na Nu, May the Force be with you, live long and prosper, all together now, Let us be "BECOME ONE" with the universe! "NOW GOD- SPEED EVERYONE" and would you please give all you "CAN" to help stop "METEORS"? We can save our children from "METEOR EXTINCTION"! "SURELY" we all want this—don't we? Please enjoy the rest of my story. (again quoted capitalized words are clues, to help you solve our mystery.)

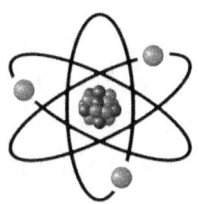 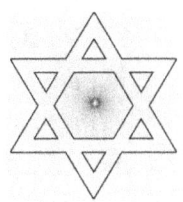

CHAPTER 1
MY PAST

Hello, everyone! I want to give you a little more background, about myself and this "LIFE CHANGING" A.S.K. discovery, I made approximately 20 years ago. I hope this will better help you understand "WHERE I CAME FROM" and "WHERE I'M GOING", in this story. Again, I also hope that you and I, can meet one day. I would love to hear "YOUR STORY", as well. Thank you so much for reading mine. I do appreciate it "DEEPLY". It's true, everyone does have a story.

Most of my friends call me Mikie, but my family, has always called me Mike. Well, unless they are mad, then they call me MICHAEL DUANE! LOL!!! It's true for all of us, huh? Dreaded middle name syndrome! Well, once they get over it they call me Michael doodle, doodle bug, and yes even, Mikie too! It doesn't bother me. To the contrary, I love it! Again, it's just like the "MIKIE" thing from the 1970s TV commercial! I've had to eat a lot of things, just like he did! Mostly humble pie. LOL.

In all seriousness I'm grateful to be so loved, though. I'm the youngest of six boys! Thank you big brothers, Mom, Dad—and oh yeah—a little sister, who, who...!!! LOL, just kidding! Love you, little sister!

Anyway, I like plain and simple, Mike. But, any of these names, work for me. I'm a "SIMPLE" guy, for the most part. I had a pretty normal childhood growing up, other than the grandpa thing and a violent dad. We went to church and still saw violence. God killed the most people of all! Wow, it seemed like the whole world was at war. However, nothing "EXCEPTIONAL", happened to me, other than that. LOL! But, things did happen, eventually. It began, when I "FINALLY" started "LOOKING" for answers about, life's origins. I also started remembering what happened to me, when I was six. I'm forewarning you, now. It gets weird, really weird!

I'm by no means "SPECIAL", because of my research. I don't profess divine intervention, either. But, there were definitely weird and traumatic things, that happened, after my little sister died. I met and discovered many other people, who also had "PHENOMENAL" encounters, as a child, too. Like, my best friend Lonnie and Jeff. More on them, later. I know looking is not a pre-requisite for "FINDING". Discoveries can happen by chance, to anyone. Like , what you're about to read, with my experience as a kid. It wasn't until, much later on, that I just became more open and "AWARE" of it, being real. I finally, "STARTED LOOKING". That's all.

I do feel "LUCKY" it happened, though! Everybody wants to see a "GHOST OR AN ALIEN AND A FLYING SAUCER"! "DON'T THEY? Well, hang on! you're about to hear of one. I also "FEEL" lucky, that I was damn near 33 when "IT" happened, again! I don't know, if I would've been able to deal with, it otherwise. When I was young, I was terrorized, by my parent's "RELIGION." It "REALLY", had me freaked out, "BELIEVING IN THE DEVIL"!

The last encounters, all took place, when I began searching, with a buddy of mine, for "SPIRITS! Surprisingly, it didn't take long for us, to find them! Well at least one. It was a voice out of thin air, while three of us were doing "THE MYSTERY". Later, we would saw my name, written on a foggy mirror at a motel. It happened, while I was taking the shower. There's more! After awhile, I wondered if they could be E.T.s, but my buddy thought, that was crazy! What? I was surprised then, but not now. He's a hardcore "SPIRIT BELIEVER"!

He was incapable of entertaining a flesh and blood hypothesis, which we "KNOW" exists, over spirits, which we don't know exist. LOL! I told him, that was crazy, because spirits aren't proven and our "FLESH AND BLOOD REALITY IS". Heck, just pinch yourself, I told him a thousand times. He didn't get it. His understanding of the universe is "FINITE". I showed him, that with technology, we can now replicate spirits, with a hologram. He didn't "BUY" it. I did everything I could. I shared the "ETs HISTORY" with him, but he still believes in "SPIRIT'S. I don't get it! Wait a minute, I do. One word, "RELIGION." I quickly saw its universal symptom, that it's "DISEASE", causes. It's "DENIAL"! No matter, what you show them.

Anyway, our disagreement continues to this day, as does our search for "SPIRITS OR ETs"! We heard "ONE". We saw writing on my motel mirror, but we never saw them! Both cases involved multiple eye-witnesses of these accounts. What they are, is up to you. You be the judge. My buddy, he's hooked on spirits. For me, the ancient art points to E.T.s and the ability to remain invisible to us, through advanced scientific technologies. Now, I film flying saucers, that look just like they did thousands of year ago and he still doesn't get it. It doesn't matter to him. He will only believe it when he sees it and he doesn't look! What a paradox, huh? I understand why he doesn't. Mirrors! He's so vain!

If you disagree with my hypothesis, at the end, it's OK! The evidence still remains the same. We "DO" have an ancient universal history of "PEOPLE LIVING 'UP' IN THE SKY"! According to these legends/writings they, "CREATED US AND PROVIDED ADVANCED SCIENTIFIC KNOWLEDGE" to help us survive, "MULTIPLY" and "WORSHIP? SERVE" them!

Why? The reason is clear! "MULTIPLY"! They made our species to serve their needs, even sexual ones. These are "PROVABLE FACTS." I agree with my buddy and religion, that they exist! But, isn't our search all about "WHAT THEY LOOK LIKE"? Not, who's right or wrong. For God's sake, remember the "METEOR", I still tell him! If that doesn't do it, nothing will. "HE DOESN'T LOOK"! I told him, that I will be happy, when the evidence speaks for itself.

Please, I got to where I didn't want to argue or debate anyone, anymore. Because, here's why. This is more serious food for thought. Science says, we're the rarest form of life to be found in the universe, so far. Even, to this very day! Look, again, I don't care if my buddy is right and I'm wrong. It's o.k. to disagree. We're still close, even though we've gone our separate ways. I'm just glad there's hope after all! To me, I'm just thankful we have these stories! It's better than not! I'll let everyone else argue, whether it's just a coincidence or not. To me, this was too advanced scientifically, not to be true. This gave me hope. Finally, real scientific HOPE!

Before, I go on with my story. I want to stop here and you to just look at "THIS EVIDENCE", please. The scientific implications of it alone, "SHOULD" give words like "RELIGION AND GOD" a new meaning. It's 2014 and we have a "SPACE STATION"! Just "IMAGINE, THE FUTURE" ramifications of this wonderful news, if it is in fact "REAL"? People, this gives us "HOPE" of survival! Especially in light of the slim odds and rarity of our existence. Oh yeah, and "DON'T FORGET" the "METEOR", that just happened! Again, coincidence or not! Heck, we're "LUCKY" to be "ALIVE", now! This stuff, blew me away!

Needless to say, this evidence "COMPELLED ME" to ask myself one "FUNDAMENTAL AND VERY IMPORTANT QUESTION"! "WHAT IS EVOLUTION VERSUS CREATION?" I continued to search for the evidence of it, in our history! I couldn't believe what I found!

OMG! I suddenly saw the whole problem, with religion's "UNIVERSAL CREATION STORY", right then and there. I found that all matter is energy and it "ALWAYS" exist! The ancient stories have "GODS," not only creating it, but as a "PERFECT" universe, too. This is impossible, since it always exists. And it's not perfect! One word "METEORS"!

The "EVIDENCE", that I showed him and most "RELIGIOUS PEOPLE", didn't change a thing. Neither, did this "METEOR" or even the craters on the moon, that we see every night! "TO ME", it's "PERFECTLY CLEAR, METEORS WILL ALWAYS EXIST" and the universe can never be perfect!

My struggle is painful. It was just "MY EVIDENCE", they'd say, with complete contempt for "MY THEORY." "TO THEM" it didn't mean squat and they could sure be mean about it. They always got the last word in by "PROCLAIMING! science is wrong and God not only created it. But he created it perfect, too. They would always say we screwed it up. Come on, we caused the meteors to hit the moon? I tried to tell him how ridiculous that sounds, but he didn't get it, either. I explained one last time, that meteors have always existed He challenged me to prove it. I couldn't.

It is a "FACT", torturous and undeniable, as it is. But, I can't prove, that it was never perfect and they are right! I can't disprove what hasn't been proven, yet! I can't get them to see, that I'm not the one "CLAIMING" it was "PERFECT" either. They are! They bear the burden of "PROOF"! I always ended, by saying I would make it so, if I could, but I can't. That's enough logic for me. It isn't perfect, now. Ironically enough, most said they would, too. Even my buddy! Why can't they see this irony! I begin to see why quickly. They really don't believe Einstein and his energy theory $E=MC2$! I know why. They don't study it.

Eventually, I got, so tired of "TRYING" to get "EVERYONE" to challenge "RELIGION'S LOGIC", that I quit. I just asked them one thing from then on. Can we "ALL" just agree that we want a perfect world and it isn't? Shouldn't we challenge religion? This is "LOGICAL" isn't it?

My family's anger and resentment toward, my new-found "ZEALOUSNESS", hurt! It still does. I've stopped asking them, about "GOD" or "PEOPLE 'UP' IN THE SKY"! I'm sure they're glad, too. "I" can't seem to control my temper, when I do! I know my ex-wife is!

Sadly, I'm sorry for getting so angry. I was just frustrated and always felt, that they were cruel to me. I could understand it though. Religious people follow, such a "PROVABLY CRUEL GOD." But, I didn't understand it, from my own sons! You'll read about this tragedy soon. I'm saddened by it. I became an asshole to the ones I loved the "MOST"! Wow, all this, because I want us all, to "LIVE FOREVER"!

I told my boys, that sometimes it seems as if they don't want these "PEOPLE" to exist and I know why. I could see how it's easier not to "BELIEVE" the evidence, or care about it, than to say you do and do nothing about it. If you believe it and didn't live it, you'd be a hypocrite! Pursuing it is the real proof and I told them I was doing it! I'm an idiot! I offended them and hurt them, way too many times. I'm so sorry for it. I didn't want to argue with anyone.

I'm sorry if I seem "ARGUMENTATIVE." I don't mean to be! What the "GODS" look like and what they are... is the focus of my story! The evidence is still "SUBJECTIVE" to most people, unfortunately. My story will show that people "CAN" say what they want and refuse to "SEE", what they don't! Nothing will matter whether, there is evidence to "SUPPORT IT OR NOT"! Again, to them if there is, it's wrong. They have the bible and "FAITH"! I finally realize I can't "WIN" and give up! However, I don't give up on finding and filming Flying saucers. Read on!

I want to start by saying, that you can check me out everywhere. I am not afraid of scrutiny and by all means welcome it. Please challenge everything, "ESPECIALLY ME." Remember though, I want a perfect world ! We'll never get it arguing, about who's right or wrong. We can only get it, by "GIVING ALL WE HAVE TO SCIENCE"!

I don't care about being wrong. I just don't want my kids to die! I want to conquer death, if I can. "I'M SCARED OF DYING"! I don't want anyone else, to die "EITHER"! I "HATE" death! I'm "GRATEFUL" to be alive! Why are any of us building wealth, instead of giving all we can, to cure death? Before this, I didn't even give meteors a thought! Like everyone else. But, "NOW". I can't stop thinking about them, "EVER"! I'm a "FATHER". I have no choice.

As the chapter heading implies, I am about to take you back in "TIME" when all this "BEGAN." Two decades have passed since I made this "DISCOVERY" and my "WORLD" has become a far different place, than what it was "BEFORE"! When I started searching, my future seemed pretty dismal. Now, it's bright! All this happened "THANKS" to my "SPIRIT" buddy, for inviting me to Nashville in 1989! Wow, what a ride I've been on!

I hope the evidence, that you are about to "SEE" will "TEST THE LIMITS OF YOUR IMAGINATION" and leave you asking your-"SELF," could this "A.S.K. DISCOVERY" be real? Could more advanced people have been here in the past and are they here, now?

You are about to see for yourself and it is my hope, that you will decide to learn about "METEORS." It won't hurt my feelings anymore, if you think I'm wrong. Please before you judge me to be crazy or not at the end, ask yourself one question: "WHAT IS YOUR CHILD'S OR ANY CHILD'S LIFE WORTH"? Maybe then, you will empathize with me, for being so passionate, about "MY DISCOVERY"!Please, I'm a "FATHER"!

Yes I am "PASSIONATE" about it, as any dad would be. I am because "CONTACT, WILL BE THE MOST IMPORTANT EVENT IN HUMAN HISTORY, WHETHER IT IS AN EXTINCTION METEOR OR E.T."! That's the consensus of science and not just my opinion. I won't argue, anymore! I'll just keep looking. I might dis-"CUSS" it, later. But I won't argue "ANYMORE"! I'll leave that up to "THE ANGRY PEOPLE." Oh, I forgot that's me. LOL! Oh well, I will cure that, too. But, right now, I want to continue on with my "PAST"!

After searching all religion's, I began "THEORIZING", that we can't make "E.T.'s or SPIRITS" coexist or communicate, with us. Obviously, because they're smarter than us. But, we can still learn about them, from "HISTORY AND ANCIENT ARTIFACTS"! Their stories reveal future scientific technologies and their space craft show they aren't changing over tens of thousands of years. This speaks volumes. They must be "ALL KNOWING" or "OMNISCIENT"!

Wow, they must be able to read our minds. Man, would that ever eliminate all our problems. People couldn't hide their "INTENTIONS," anymore. Thank God! Then we could really get on with avoiding "METEOR EXTINCTION", people.

I continued to propose, that even though these capabilities, and much more, might lay in the hands of "E.T.s or GOD". It may be possible, that we could also, achieve them! During, the course of this life changing journey, I began sharing these similarities, between the "SUPER-NATURAL POWERS OF RELIGION AND POSSIBLE ADVANCED TECHNOLOGIES" with "MANKIND."

Ironically, I found that most humans "FEAR" them, especially mind reading! Some even revile them! "WHY"? Why would anybody not want them? You'll soon see "WHY." However, I think we all know, that the answer is as simple as asking ourselves: "DO WE WANT OUR MINDS READ AND OUR PAST TO BE REVEALED"? I don't. I'm ashamed and embarrassed, by most of it. I want to be forgiven

I can't lie. I "BELIEVE" this technology exist! I know I will be ashamed and embarrassed, by my past. Sex has tortured me! All my "MISTAKES" were driven by it and stemmed from it! I'll also admit, that I always wanted the "MOST BEAUTIFUL" girl in the world! I "BECAME" a "BEAUTY ADDICT"! "LUCKY ME", I "FOUND" her and along the way of my making the "BEST" of it, "ALL HELL BROKE LOOSE". She taught me the most "VALUABLE LESSON" of my life! Because of her, I finally saw inner-beauty, "AGAIN". Like I did, when I was a kid. Oh, how blissfully ignorant I was, then! Not now, though!

It all started happening, when I went to Nashville. Actually, she was the one who thought she was the most beautiful girl in the world and that's when things, went "BAD". That was the point, my "HELL" began. "SEXUAL POWER"! From that point on, I damn sure knew "SEX" had everything to do, with our mystery. Well, here's what started it all. I let a women hit on me, at a songwriter's night! My "NEW" wife found her card, in my pocket, after I got home. It was 5:00 am! I apologized and promised nothing happened. I told her I had been doing "THE MYSTERY". But it didn't help. She was going to get revenge.

My life became a nightmare. She was the only grand-daughter of a famous country music legend and boy "WAS" she ever spoiled. I know now, in the "ADDICT WORLD", that sex and money are one and the same! Nothing can stop either, from causing us to be evil to one another. "MURDER" was even a possibility! Sadly, some people can't even be stopped at that! They end up committing murder and suicide, if they don't get their way! I was about to "SEE", this "UGLY" fact of selfish angry humans, firsthand and it would almost kill me!

I will tell you, that no one was murdered though! I didn't let that happen. It could have! I just wanted out, of my relationship, with her. But, when I tried to leave she threatened to commit suicide. She didn't care about using me or my son, then. It was "HELL"! I stayed and endured her wrath and eventual "SEX ADDICTION"! She became a "MAN-EATER"! I couldn't let anything happen. Instead, I "SACRIFICED MY TIME", for the greater good of "MY SON"! We're "ALL" lucky, to have survived, her disease! "POWER FROM BEAUTY OF THE FLESH"! She was drunk with it! Everyone told her she was "BEAUTIFUL" and she "ATE" it up. She became the biggest and most vicious Narcissist I ever knew!

I wish, that I could have predicted all this, from the beginning. I wouldn't have stayed! But, I couldn't and I don't think anyone can. Maybe, "PREDICTING" what we will do "NEXT", is "THE REASON", these beings stay away from us. Well, that and them "OBVIOUSLY BEING REAL PEOPLE, LIKE US"! It's the only thing that makes sense of them not coexisting with us. It's easy to read the stars in the skies, because they don't "THINK". But reading our minds is a "DIFFERENT DUCK", all together. It won't help, if someone reacts out of "INSTANTANEOUS IRRATIONAL" anger and attempts, to kill you. Just imagine "MIND READING REALITY", happening right now! It would be instant chaos, for everyone who wasn't "ALONE"! Nobody wants someone to be prettier or smarter, than themselves. Well, except for kids. They aren't sexual!

I've tried to rationalize this problem and it is logically, the only "REASON WHY" they wouldn't coexist with us. They don't want to die, either! All the stories, say they are flesh and blood people, just like us! What if they have the same scientific and physical limitations in nature, as we do? I mean this is possible, right? We have physical limitations, too. Right? So, couldn't they?

Some people want to theorize, that these "PEOPLE 'UP' IN THE SKY," may be time travelers. Science sees a problem with this. It's called the "GRANDFATHER PARADOX," check it out! I think it can be dis- proven, with simpler evidence, though. I've mentioned it already. We don't have a perfect world! Besides that, we wouldn't have the lottery and babies dying, everywhere.

The reality is, that "HUMAN TIME TRAVEL HASN'T BEEN PROVEN," yet. And "IN MY OPINION" it "DEFIES LOGIC"! Who wouldn't prevent our current "CONDITION" "IF" they could, right! I'm a "FATHER" and "I WOULD." So it can't exist! Heck if anyone could predict the future (besides celestial events), we'd all be lottery winners! Look, again, I don't want to offend anyone here. I just want, "COMMON SENSE" answers, for my kids. I don't want them to "HAVE TO DIE"! People this is a no brain-er! "TIME TRAVEL" doesn't exist! "TIME DILATION" does. Check it out!

Anyway, this is my "LOGIC" and it is the "FOUNDATION" of my story. I would die to make the world perfect, for all children! I have, "TWO"! If you wouldn't then you might as well stop reading. You will soon see, that I push the envelope in my "MAD RACE AGAINST TIME", to save "US." I must save my kids. I can't worry about offending anyone, anymore.

As a matter of fact, I want everyone, to "THINK" about something else. When God wants to be worshipped, it's called "RELIGION." When we want worshipped, it's called a "MENTAL SICKNESS". People this logic, or lack thereof, dictates wanting to be worshipped or special is "A SICKNESS"! Please, if you have it, get over it! Denial is the symptom, owning it is the cure"

Well, now that I've added more unnecessary fuel to the "FIRE". I want to also let the "CAT" out of the bag, about how I really feel toward religion and it's perpetuation of illogical ideas! It should be banned, because it creates killers! But believe me again, I don't want to offend anyone. I was religiously brainwashed when I was a kid and it wasn't my parents fault. They were too! I want to do this, in a nice respectful way and give everyone something funny, to end with. This isn't about blame. I just want to reveal the depth of religion's hold on people, when it comes to logic. Like, it has on my family. Here it is and I hope you enjoy it as much as I did and still do! This is so illogical, it's hilarious!

I saw a billboard, in Toledo Ohio, that proves my "LOGIC POINT" beautifully and it is funny. Thankfully, even to religious people! I love it. Maybe humor is the key, to "SEEING" it. Someone had advertised this want ad: "HIRING PSYCHICS," one million dollars. Want to know where to apply? Thought you were a psychic! LOL! I just about died. I almost wrecked from laughing my ass off! I love this. With all the hell, I've gone through I don't know how I kept from crying. What am I saying, I did. I was overwhelmed, that I wasn't the only one "SEEING LOGIC," here! This became my new approach!

How can anyone get angry, at this? This proves, we all "KNOW PSYCHIC ABILITIES" haven't been proven or this ad wouldn't exist! That's what so funny!!! LOL!!! "BUSTED"!

If this is you, it's OK. Please don't be mad. I understand. Like I said, I had this disease. My parents "GAVE" it to me, "WHEN I WAS A KID"! It isn't their fault. This is just a product, of passing on a tradition and they were "VICTIMS," as well! I then became like them and done it to my children, too! This has to stop. Psychics prey on people who have lost loved ones and this is wrong! I've lost loved ones and no amount of money, will bring them back! "OR WILL IT"? Please give my story a chance and let's ban religion. We have the law and science to make us "GOOD" citizens, don't we? Religion creates hatred intolerance and ignorance. I promise it could happen to anyone. Maybe even......?

Finally, "ALMOST" all scientists are theorizing, that E.T.s should exist. They are also asking one very important and logical question: "How can they exist in our skies and we not know it?" Well first of all, who says "WE" don't. We all know this. History is religion. It's just a matter of whether you "BELIEVE" it or not. Fermi's paradox is the next question. (look it up)

Even if you don't believe this is possible, the evidence "REMAINS THE SAME"! "IT EXISTS"! It not only exists, "IT MATCHES OUR REALITY TODAY"! We have fiery chariots "IN THE SKY"! We have cloaking devices. I "BELIEVE" it! I not only believed it, I devoted my life to finding them and it "ALMOST" destroyed it. So, don't say I didn't warn you if this happens to you. I hope it doesn't. Now, here's the rest of my story and remember to hang on. This may be the ride of your "LIFE"! It all started with the "MYSTERIOUS PHONE CALL" and "MY DREAM"! I was about to look for "SPIRITS"!

I once toyed with the idea, that "FATE" possibly, brought me to Nashville, Tennessee in 1989. But, how can I still? I "KNOW" better, right? Well, the way it happened, was weird. This weirdness is, why I felt this way. Now, I know, it was just a product of my religious past. But, here's why I did, at one time! If fates real, though. I promise I'll find the science "BEHIND IT"! Like I mentioned earlier, I really experienced some weird shit!

I had always loved music! But, I never pursued it, "UNTIL THEN"! I finally did, because of my best friend's uncle, who called me from Nashville. Eerily enough, I wouldn't have written this book, without this happening!!! He had gotten a record deal and asked me to come down to showcase my artwork, at his place. I lived in Ohio at the time. Well, as you know by now, I did and we eventually became a song writing team. We became inseparable, until my wife set her sights on him and his nephew. The rest is "HIS- STORY"!

Anyway, here's what happened after he called. My previous marriage was literally coming apart at the "SEAMS, literally. So, I took him up on his offer. It wasn't long before, I jumped out of one frying pan and into another. Like I said, my marriage was "LITERALLY," coming apart at the seams. "SEX" ruled my life and I hadn't found "MY MOST BEAUTIFUL GIRL", in the world yet!

To make a long story short, I came to Nashville, had an affair and got caught! It's no wonder, though! Her name was the same as my first wife! Crazy, huh? Well, as crazy as it is, that's how I got caught. That just goes to show you, how the old saying is true. When it comes to us men: "When the wrong "HEAD" starts thinking the other one stops"! This is a universal "PROBLEM"! Sex screws up our "THINKING" and when it happens, most of us don't "THINK," about the consequences! Well, this gets even crazier! So, hold on!

My life completely changed direction after that. But, it was still a "FRYING PAN"! I "FELL" in love with my current ex-wife and relentlessly began pursuing a country music career. I wanted to be a "STAR"! Her family was screwed up, with greed and sex! Her Step-dad wanted to pimp me out and her mom wanted to sue her own daughter, over Lester's estate!

Needless to say, things were about to be kicked into high gear. Her "SEX-CRAZED" step- father was such an asshole, that we moved to her parents hometown, in Sparta, Tn.. Crazy, as it is, I cried when he died. More later! He had a good side, too. Things got better, for awhile, when Tammy's real grandparents, gave us an acre of land. We moved to get away from the coke, sex and greed. Tammy gave the money to her mom, from Lester's property sale. Everything was good, until we had a child in 1990. Then we got busted for possession/delivery of pot in 1991. My "FAMOUS" wife's picture was put on the front cover, of the local paper! I'm so ashamed, of this! It happened in her and Lester's hometown!

My father-in-law got us "BOTH" out of jail, immediately. I want to thank him! Thank you, "MILTON," so much! He got Tammy out first and then me, later. I didn't mind. How could I? "BELIEVE ME," I was so thankful because, my son wouldn't stop crying for his mom. He was only six months old! It was terrible. I couldn't stop thanking Milton and apologizing on the way home, the following morning. I deserved a night in jail! Again, I was so "ASHAMED"!

I soon "FOUND OUT", that Tammy called my son's grandmother, when they arrested her at our home and they came right away. The police let them take our son, instead of the "DEPARTMENT OF HUMAN SERVICES"! "THANK GOD"! I was at the store. I thanked "GRANNY," and "AUNT JEWEL," for taking care of Matt. I kept thanking them. I am forever grateful, for their love and help!

We moved back to Nashville within the next six months and my life was instantly, thrown into financial shambles, again. The next several years were hard and grinded by ever so "SLOWLY." I worked non-stop and we still, didn't have extra money, to do anything! Looking back, it seemed as if our marriage was doomed, from the get go. But, I do know how lucky, we really were. We didn't lose our son and we "STOPPED" doing coke, or at least I did, anyway. I would find out differently with my wife, later on.

My mother-in-law loaned my wife $10,000 to retain a lawyer. I didn't want her too, but I couldn't stop it. At least, her charges were dropped, even though mine stuck! I deserved it, though. I had been caught, just before, we got together! I should have known better.

I felt terrible, because we weren't dealing anything! We were just "RESPONSIBLE POT SMOKERS", trying to smoke, for free. This led to one of my "FRIENDS" getting in trouble and working for the police. We thought nobody knew it, but they did. I told them it was a clear case of entrapment and they knew it. I should have stayed in college and become a lawyer. I immediately tried, but didn't have the money or time. I had an extra bill to pay, now.

It took us a couple years, to pay Tammy's mother back. We gave, all "MY WIFE'S ROYALTIES", to her. Life was hard, but I never lost sight of how "LUCKY" we were. At least "I" was anyway. After all, again, we didn't lose custody of our son! I am forever, thankful, to my mother-in-law! Thank you Brenda!

As the years went by, we started keeping the royalties again and I "THOUGHT", that things couldn't get any worse. But, I was wrong. Our income didn't leave any money to spare. My wife was a high maintenance girl and would eventually "GET A JOB"! She got it right after she found the girls card in my back pocket, from the gig, that I mentioned earlier. She even told my "SPIRIT BUDDY" and his nephew about the card, the next day. I'll never forget the moment she said to them; "WHAT'S GOOD FOR THE GOOSE IS GOOD FOR THE GANDER"! She might as well told them, that she wanted to f@#k! I could see the future and it wasn't good. She was a "SCORNED WOMAN". I tried to stop her, by telling her "INFIDELITY" would kill my love for her. But, nothing and I mean nothing, worked! She was going to do as many men as she could.

It turns out, that she didn't get a job for the money, after-all. I caught her with a car salesman at work and the neighbor next door. When I confronted her with the 'RECORDED EVIDENCE", she said she didn't care, like the devil. I tried to calmly leave and she went berserk and start crying. Then, she threatened to commit suicide. She even done in front of my son! I tried so many times to leave, but I couldn't. She would do this every-time. I knew it was hurting my son. I hated her, more than anything. I even went to jail trying. I finally gave in, after three times! I couldn't leave again. I knew the consequences would hurt my son! My life became a living hell! But, I had to stay for him. I didn't know what else to do. She was so dangerously selfish and evil!

This wasn't the end of my troubles, though. It was just the beginning! Things definitely got worse. Much worse! She went to work at a car dealership "MANAGING MECHANICS" and I was still on a

"SPIRITUAL QUEST" to contact "SPIRITS", with my songwriter partner. Wow, she had cleaned his house several times before, this job and I did catch her c@#k watching him. I confronted him. He denied the affair/sex and we would never be the same. Guess what? My world was about to unravel. Unravel hell, it was about to explode! She became my devil and he never helped stop it, either. Worse, he lied! Her oil was at his house.

Well, needless to say, my "SPIRIT" buddy, immediately moved. I even let him use my truck, to do so. Then, in 1995, I found my first "ANCIENT EVIDENCE," of an "ADVANCED SCIENTIFIC KNOWLEDGE" given to us, by primitive man. How can this be? Shocking, huh? Well, it gets even bigger than that! Their universal stories became our religion's and they "CONQUERED THE WORLD"! Shockingly, their traditions supported my "THEORY OF EVERYTHING", completely! I was awestruck by the "FACT", that religion says "HEAVEN" is "UP" and "PEOPLE" live there! We live there too, could they be real people and not spirits? I was even more dumbfounded, that this evidence dates back as far as, 150,000 years ago! This is also when we started burying our dead!!! Wow, our species began with the knowledge of "RESURRECTING THE DEAD"!!!

Wow, can this be "TRUE"? If it is, then surely it will be "SEEN" and recognized as viably possible today, by everyone. Right? After all, we have a "SPACE STATION" and "WE'RE BRINGING SPECIES BACK TO LIFE"! Like I've said before, these "REALITIES MATCH"! Well, I was wrong! Most people don't see it. Wow, I still can't believe, it isn't recognized, by everyone! Today's knowledge seems to be catching up, with our ancient past and "SCIENCE DOES NOT RECOGNIZE RELIGION AS A FACT." People, what's going on? We live up in the sky, too!

I remember all my epiphanies, like yesterday! I thought I saw something, that science and religion might not see, "YET". I said, I "THOUGHT," not I know and yet too! I'm not saying, that no one else can "SEE" this. It's just very few have and their dead. So please be

"THOUGHTFUL", and nice if you think what I'm about to share with you is crazy! Please? I've had enough of people being mean to me.

I remember thinking, "IT" is going to be impossible to prove! I can't make E.T.s communicate with us and I can't expect the "AVERAGE PERSON", to get this. That's why I'm writing this, for children. They can get "IT", quicker. They are "MORE CURRENT" in their thinking of the universe, than adults. Again, "IT" is my "A.S.K. DISCOVERY", that I am presenting to the world with this book It is my proof these people exist! Well, I didn't count on it, almost costing me, my second marriage. But it did. I will tell you, now. I finally divorced my wife, 15 years later! It also almost cost me my life. However, in the face of all this adversity. I never gave up, as you will see. Eventually, I even remarried her. I had too, for "SAFETY REASONS"! I divorce her again. five years later.

In spite of all this, I "OBVIOUSLY" kept thinking and still think I will be successful "EXPLAINING AND TEACHING MY DISCOVERY." How could I not? I'm "CONVINCED," that this "EVIDENCE" is truly going to rewrite "HISTORY"! I see how evolution and the universe works. I see how and why our mystery exists and "STARTED". The bible made it very clear, that it was because of sex. The sons of god just couldn't resist sex, either with the "PRETTY" daughters of mankind. I "SEE" mankind's ignorance so "CLEARLY." The problem is getting, them to admit it or ask me "QUESTIONS"! Sex is the final frontier, here!

I know, if you're anything like me and the average "LOGICAL" person, you're probably thinking, the same thing I am about right now. "No way!," right? Surely, I couldn't have solved this mystery, or it would've been done already! Surely, scientist all over the world, would "KNOW" this "ADVANCED SCIENTIFIC KNOWLEDGE", "BY NOW"! Right? Why wouldn't they see this? Surely, we are certainly more advanced than they "WERE" then, right? How could primitive man know something, that we don't?

Well, hang on, I'm about to "SHOW" you "HOW AND WHY, SCIENCE NOR RELIGION" sees "MY DISCOVERY"! I propose that they don't "SEE" this knowledge, existing now or in the "PAST" and their pride hates me for saying, so!!! At least, this has been my experience, anyway. I want them to see it, believe me. I even start finding "FLYING SAUCERS" and it still doesn't work for them. But now, "METEORS" come first, remember! So quickly I'll finish "REVEALING" my "PAST"! I need some redemption and peace of mind, please? I'm sorry for hurting anyone.

Please bear with me. Well, as you know I finally wrote seven books! I still do book- signings and have had plenty of them, during this journey. I've been attacked, banned, and threatened, to be killed. I still went on. I failed and I still fail. I know why now. Read on and find out why! However, I can easily relate, to anyone "WHO" doesn't see "MY DISCOVERY". Remember, again please? I didn't see "IT" "ONCE", either! Believe me, though? When I finally "SAW" "IT," "SEEING WAS BELIEVING." At least to me, anyway. It is to everyone, isn't it? Well, I thought it was supposed to be, but it's not. (Let's not kid ourselves here. I can't change anyone. We all know that little bit of wisdom, right? LOL!) This book is not about "PROSELYTIZING." It's about "CONTACT" with "E.T.s OR GOD"! This evidence is a "BOMBSHELL" of "REALITY"! It has me on fire, with excitement and "HOPE"!

This "MATCHING EVIDENCE" contains highly advanced knowledge and drawings like atoms, solar systems, etc., from our ancient past. We know children draw what they "SEE". I think, the "ANCIENTS" did too! You're about to see some examples, of ancient art matching, today's "ADVANCED SCIENTIFIC KNOWLEDGE"! This proves, that these beings were more advanced, real flesh and blood beings, not spirits.

I'm stoked, because this ancient "A.S.K." evidence, shows, that primitive man had the answer, to not only avoid meteor extinction, but also to achieve immortality! WOW, WOW, WOW!!! "IMMORTALITY"! How can you get any bigger than that?

The only thing bigger than that, is having the "PERFECT" world, "GOD" promised my Mom and Dad, right? Get ready, it can't be that big! But, we can make an artificial planet and free ourselves from certain death, like "METEORS" and mother nature! Science says, that it's theoretically possible.

Wow! What a possibility! Maybe, just maybe, we can do this and much more, with science. This is unbelievable, huh? Well, maybe not. You're about to discover more, a lot more, as I continue searching!

From now on, I will refer to this "ANCIENT SCIENTIFIC KNOWLEDGE", as my "A.S.K. DISCOVERY." Odd, as it may be, every ancient culture had "IT" at a time, when history says we weren't even global! How? Coincidence? Stay neutral here please. Let's continue to "OPEN HISTORY'S DOOR"! It gets weirder! How weird? Well again, I'll let you be the "JUDGE" of that. But, I'm a born optimist. I think the future is bright. I'm a glass, half full, kind of guy. So here goes "NOTHING."

My search continued. I kept finding a treasure trove of "ET EVIDENCE," not spirit gods. I discovered one out of place artifact after another, that was too advanced, for its time!

My mind was exploding with epiphanies and "ENDLESS POSSIBILITIES" again and again. I kept asking myself: "Could we be repeating something we've already done before"? Is our separation, from these "PEOPLE IN THE SKY", permanent! I would soon learn, more surprising history!

These ancient religious stories revealed capabilities, that not only mirror today's science, but even "PREDICT" a future reality of "FARMING HUMAN INTELLIGENCE"! Religion calls this reincarnation. Science calls it cloning! I eventually called it, "EVOLUTION OF INTELLIGENCE." Sadly, it seems to happen, through experiencing "LIFETIME'S OF HELL" and harvesting memory. I was blown away to find "JESUS" calling himself "THE WORD". Wow, that's all memory is!!! Could we be biological computers or hosted by one.

Anyway, I really was blown away by this matching evidence. Crazy, right? I didn't care. I showed everybody! When other people, didn't get infected by this, like I did. I would think, wow is it just me or what? Haven't they heard of "DOLLY" the "CLONED SHEEP," stem cell research, and "REGENERATION THERAPY"? Come on, people. Wake up to these wonderful possibilities, I always thought to myself! I started to take it personal.

Then, things got bad—real bad!

First of all, I want to say, that I miss Terry badly. His death hadn't happened yet. I'll get to that shortly. But, what did, would shake me to my core. Little, did "ANY OF US" know, what was about to happen, next. The 2013 Meteor was coming.! When I think about it, I am instantly overcome with emotion! My understanding of the universe has forever, changed.

Soon more tragedy would pay me a visit—lots more. It happened, while I was writing my second book. My next to oldest brother killed himself! I felt responsible! He hated my research about our "SEXUAL TORTURE"! I felt like, it was the culprit, that drove him to do it. I always thought, that my first book had a hand in it. I'll never forget my excitement, as I drove north with copies for the whole family. It would turn out to be, the worst thing, I ever done. I gave it to him and shared my findings. All hell started to break loose. Dave and his wife were having marital problems.

Everything was fine, "AT FIRST." Then we begin to talk about my book! He was so "PROUD" of me, but not for long. Because my vision of "HEAVEN" was definitely not his, he was a Jehovah's Witness preacher! I told him, that I think we should be like, they are in "HEAVEN." A place where we read each other's minds, all look alike, and don't give our hand in marriage. We're all equal, like Jesus's descriptions of the angels and the Easter Island heads, indicate. I explained as I showed him my illustrations. I tried to tell him, that we should all have sex randomly and not make it a "SACRED" thing!

"Heck dude, "SEX AND POWER" is our downfall." I said laughing. He wasn't laughing, he was fuming with jealousy and I didn't know it! I told him about Tammy and that I was only mad, because I was not going to let her do my friends, neighbors and customers anymore, for free. I told him, that the only reason I'm angry, is because she won't let me have a "GOOD" woman and she's embarrassing us. I hated her for using my son to use me. I didn't need her. Wow. I shouldn't have vented my frustrations and problems, with him.

He was incapable, of letting anyone see his wife naked, let alone have sex with her, and my vision of "HEAVEN" disgusted him. I saw what was happening and put my book away. I quickly got out my guitar, but it was too late. I played him a couple songs and thought everything was going to be, alright. For a few minutes, he was his old "SELF"! He immediately loved it and even, revealed his dream of wanting to be a "FAMOUS" rock star and actor. I handed him the guitar, when I was done and he even knew a few chords, much to my surprise. It was a beautiful, but "FLEETING KODAK MOMENT"!

Sadly, it would be our last time together! The last time I saw my brother, he was punching me in the face, as I was trying to get in my car. He was still attacking his wife, as I pulled out, crying uncontrollably.

As I pulled out, I screamed at him, to let her alone. I didn't want to leave, but "JACKIE" screamed for me to go on. She assured me, that he wouldn't kill her. I told her I would call the law. My brother screamed to go ahead and do it! He added, that she would be dead before they got there. He wasn't my brother then. He was a "SELFISH EVIL DISEASE"! He was the "DEVIL!" Mr. "PRIDE" himself.

I had to do, what I had to do, to get my brother back. I had to stop his disease. All of this, I thought to myself, because he started watching "JERRY SPRINGER!" That was the moment, all hell broke loose. If he only knew what kind of a Jerry Springer life I was living.

I headed to the nearest phone, as fast as I could go and called the law. The last time I heard from him, was a couple days later. He called and threatened, to kill me. He even said he was coming to Tennessee, right then. I didn't know what to do. I couldn't believe what was happening. He accused me of saying, I wanted to have sex with his wife, that night. I tried explaining to him. I was just quoting the goddamn bible, when I said, they don't give their hand in marriage and we were perfect, when we were all naked. But, nothing worked. He was a madman! Even worse, he screamed, that his wife said I done this very thing and put her on the phone. Much to my horror, she told me, that I said it!!! Now, I really couldn't believe what was happening. I begged her to tell the truth.

He got back on the phone and I begged him to get help! He never did. Two weeks later Terry called with the bad news. She had left him and he was begging her to come home, in the middle of the night. She didn't and he killed himself. I found out later, that during our last "CONVERSATION", he had held a gun to his wife's head and forced her to agree. I remember, begging her to tell the truth, but she didn't. I understand why. I will talk more about this later, it happened in 2001 and I'm still hurting so bad, right now. I tried my best to get him to see, that we were naked in the beginning of "HIS BIBLE STORY," but he couldn't see it. I couldn't get him to wake-up and let the "FACTS" speak for themselves and not "RELIGIOUS HYPOCRITES", that say otherwise. I remember showing him, one thing after another, that was the opposite of what his "PREACHERS TEACH". It didn't work! I tried everything! Sadly, his son found him the next morning. I shouldn't have done this!

In hindsight, I don't know what I was thinking then? What did I expect? Nobody seemed to care about these provable facts. It didn't work for the Jehovah's Witness Preachers, who threw me out of the church in Nashville, either. Six of them, literally picked me up and pitched me, down a flight of concrete steps. I guess, they didn't like what I had to say, about heaven either. I landed about ten feet away and lay sprawled out, like a limp rag on the asphalt parking lot, beneath them. I looked up and begged for help, but no one helped me get up. I reached toward them, with my hands bleeding, from the fall.

Instead, they ordered me to get away or they would call the law. I was going to let them call the law and wish I had, but a couple of them, started down the steps, after me. I wasn't going to let them hurt me, anymore. I got up. Thankfully, a "BLACK" preacher, who was trying to stop them, finally did. He stepped in front of them and begged me to leave! I left. The black preacher cried! I want to go back and thank him! I want to give him this book.

This was my first "WAKE-UP" call, that let me know how dangerous religion is. It is the reason, that I titled my first book: THE TWO WITNESSES AND THE RELIGION COVER-UP. During my journey, I discovered over and over again how religious leaders and conquerors have obscured, everything in our history, including "SEX"! The "OLDEST" information, I was "FINDING," says these gods were "PEOPLE" and not "SPIRITS"! They had "SEX" so they couldn't be spirits, right? Couldn't they look "DIFFERENT" from us? The Bible always indicated they did. Heck, these angels/gods scared the shit out of people!

I got more information, from a middle school history book. The Jews were from the country of Sumeria, in what is today, called IRAQ. They were the priests. and always shown with huge alien like eyes! Coincidence? My journey was on and I never stopped. They have ancient clay tablets, showing our solar system, in its exact order, distance and size, with the addition of a tenth planet. How could they know this unless it was true. Wow, their "GODS" lived on the tenth planet and not with us. Wow! Maybe it is an artificial planet.

My mind was cooking with questions. Why didn't people see, that god's don't live on planets! They're "EVERYWHERE"! I'll never understand, how this information, could be so unknown and still is. But then again, I do know. It isn't, if you're looking. I couldn't wait to ask the President, about it! First, I needed a bestselling book, that would give me the power to do it! Unfortunately, people of power are harder to get to, than god! I needed these books to be a huge success. But, they weren't. The first and second books fumbled!

I continued to research the Sumerians and found more ancient statues, that looked like aliens. Could they be the god's of an artificial tenth planet! WOW! WOW! WOW! Could these "GODS" be aliens, that evolved and look identical, like "ALL OTHER LIFE"? The Easter Island heads gave me the first hint, of this possibility. They did, because they all look the same. But, there was one problem. They didn't have the big bulbous head! I theorize it's because of the builder's need, to balance a flying saucer, on top of their heads. This way, they knocked out two birds with one stone. What they look like and what they would be coming back in. Yes, their story has them coming back, just like the Jesus story! I provided this evidence, in my second book!

Boy, little did I know, that I had only just begun to "UNCOVER" mankind's, complete history! I saw this evidence, as proof of the "GODS' EVOLUTION"! They all looked the same! Could they evolve and not have a god creator story? Now you know why I'm so hated! God forbid, for all of us, to have to take responsibility of our own destiny! Humans, we all want to be served a perfect existence, but don't want to "WORK" for it. We have the "GOD DISEASE" and just want to be worshipped! That's why everybody wants to be rich, so they can live the "GOOD" life. I continued on. I had to quit railing at our inadequencies! I have them.

Wow, I wanted to know everything, "ESPECIALLY, WHY THESE GODS STAY AWAY." This alone, led me to wanting to know "WHAT A SPIRIT IS AND WHERE THEY CAME FROM?". I know why my parents and every other Christian "BELIEVE", that God is a spirit. They believe it "BECAUSE IT'S IN THE BIBLE." Sound familiar? But, with all this new information, how could they not challenge it. Well, I know why and I just couldn't "BUY" any excuse as a "REASON" not to pursue science.

I continued to look and the evidence really surprised me. It may surprise you, too! We have ancient statues of alien looking god's, on every continent! Can it be, just a coincidence, that every culture calls the owl wise, because they have big eyes and come out at night? The evidence says different and I had to follow the evidence, if I'm "TRULY SEARCHING FOR ANSWERS". I did pay for it, many times.

Could ancient religious people, just have the "SPIRIT" thing, wrong? After all, they would call us, "MAGICAL GOD'S", today! They would definitely call our holograms spirit! Will religious people ever change their mind, when the world starts to accept this evidence and rules in its favor? My lack of success, was saying no. But, I didn't worry about it. I just wanted to report the "FACTS", as fast as, I could.

I did it, by calling my second book: ALIENS GOLD TENTH PLANET and let the chips, fall where they may. Like I said, it wasn't successful. I continued on, by writing five more books over the next decade. The titles revealed the discoveries, I made. This book, is the one and only one, that "REALLY" matters. It is about our "METEOR THREAT"!

Since, the near miss of this recent "METEOR EVENT," I have been working over-time, to finish this book. People, we can avoid them. This event really "WOKE ME UP," just like my brother's death. Believe me, this is more "URGENT", than my "A.S.K. Discovery." It can take us "ALL" out, now! You can't get any bigger, than that! We have to act now.

It's been four years, since my last book. Ironically, I now realize, that our "MYSTERY" should be more about "IMMEDIATE THREATS", than long-term ones! Sad, that it takes so long, for us to learn the most important stuff, like science! I know, that I can't let the pain and memories of my families deaths, hold me back any more. I can't worry about offending anybody and go another four years, writing this book. We could die today. We could die, "NOW"! I have to get everyone, to give money and cure these problems.

Looking back, little did I know, how ignorant I was. I didn't know shit, about the world, yet! I feel so "LUCKY" to be alive! I am "FOREVER" grateful and humbled, by this meteor event. I just know, that I can't keep wasting time. I got to get this book done. Meteors are coming and they will not stop!

Anyway, please check out the rest of my books. They're available everywhere! You can read them "YOURSELF" and "SEE" the "ASTOUNDING" amount of evidence, that I've collected along the way. I'm still finding more. I promise you it is jaw-dropping! It will show, that we've had E.T. contact since our "BEGINNING" and religion is keeping us ignorant! People, I am still collecting evidence, as I write and filming their craft, too!

The world isn't "AWARE" of this knowledge, yet But, we have to "SEARCH FOR IT"! Please get on your computers. This evidence, paints a very "SIMPLE PICTURE" of our past and shows us, where we need to be, in the future! "UP" in space, just like the gods/E.T.'S!

Our very "SURVIVAL DEPENDS ON IT"! I've found very "FEW" people, who actually "KNOW" it. However, all of us can! It's just "SIMPLE" science. This is called "OCCAM'S RAZOR.". I began my journey by "ASKING QUESTIONS", I quickly saw, why teachers use this method, when they answer our questions, back with one. They do it, because it makes us "LOOK", for the answers, ourselves. LOL, Boy was I ever looking. "LUCKY FOR ME", I started thinking "INFINITELY". When I saw this A.S.K. Evidence, I asked myself: "How could an ancient people, who wasn't flying, have this knowledge?" Then I realized, in an "INFINITE UNIVERSE" it's a no brainer. "SOMEONE" else was! There aren't any odds of someone already doing this. Logically, they already have? The evidence, says these god's are the E.T.'S and they all look the same! I can't escape this reality. Since the second book, I've discovered, that some people and "MOST" scientists are already heading, in this direction. I remember well, how I wanted to learn everything I could, then! I was so excited.

During this journey, it seemed, as if time stood still, with every discovery. Every time, I was "LIVING" in the moment, of "UNDERSTANDING" it, the future of medicine and science would play out in my mind, like a movie. I could see our future and how to make it better. It still does, as I write. I am captivated by the sheer wonder, "JOY," and magnitude of it all. I was humble and giddy with excitement, at every turn! But, there was a down side to sharing it. Nobody, liked god, being a non thinking universe of infinitely changing, inanimate matter and everyone, hated the idea, of looking the same! This seems to be a universal disease. It is the only thing, that makes any sense of the bible's angel story. They must all look the same, because they evolved and through the power of scientific creation, made us. We never would exist without them. We always have to be "SAVED"!

All these discoveries, led me to this book and I didn't even realize it. They were building me a portfolio of evidence, all along. This book will become "MY" case for "THE E.T. EXISTENCE AND A "METEOR PREVENTION PLAN". Please "DON'T FORGET," the meteor comes first!

I am also writing this book, as "A NEW THEORY" for everyone and not, just science. I see how, heaven's location is giving us "ADVANCED SCIENTIFIC KNOWLEDGE", about the physical flesh and blood reality of the universe, that we live in! We must go "UP" to survive, just like they did!

I've "KEPT" asking myself, from the onset of "MY DISCOVERY," one nagging question. Could this matching evidence, really be, just an astronomically "HUGE LIFE-SAVING" coincidence? I mean, come on. Can it, "REALLY"? I can't tell you, how many times, that I have asked myself, this question. But, I always come back to "ONE FACT", when I do. The evidence doesn't go away! It still exist and we need to go "UP", as well! These people must exist.

I can't ignore, that these "GODS OR E.T.s" live in the only place anyone could survive, forever. Space, "PLANETS DIE"! People, if this recent "METEOR EVENT" would've been big enough to take us out, we wouldn't exist. We exist! Is this a coincidence, too? Is it "REALLY"? Why haven't we seen a big meteor hit the moon? We know they do, by just looking at it. We've seen extinction meteors hit other planets, like the recent Jupiter impact. All ancient religion's say, the god's are the reason, for our very existence. I even put a quote on the first book's back cover, that supports this very thing. It says; Unless your days had been shortened no flesh would survive!

If these stories didn't exist, then it wouldn't be, as big to me, because we're alone. No stories… no "GODS OR E.T.s… no problem! But, I can't disregard "THE FACTS"! We have them and this "MAKES SENSE"! Staggeringly, these stories predict the progressive evolutionary path, that nature says we must take, if we want to exist forever! "COINCIDENCE"? It could be, I guess. But, this fact isn't! All scientist agree that "UP" is the only way we can survive. And we still haven't seen the big one hit, anywhere close enough to affect us, "YET"! I don't think this is a coincidence. Thank god there are "PEOPLE WHO LIVE UP IN THE SKY"!

I guess you could even say, from a scientific point of view, that "THIS IS ABOUT AS REAL AS IT GETS"! Man, I was "ON FIRE"! I remembered vividly how time flew, as I searched and searched relentlessly, for more evidence. I was driven like a crazed mad scientist obsessed, with the thought of success. I had to share "MY DISCOVER"! "FOOD FOR THOUGHT", became my drug. I couldn't get enough history and knowledge, about "US"!

I tried to "CONVINCE" everyone of "MY DISCOVERY", for the next several years. A lot of them, thought I was "GOING" crazy. Well, maybe not going, but was crazy, is more like it. It didn't really bother me and I never thought, they were crazy. They just weren't thinking infinitely or that people more advanced than us, even exist.

Then it hit me. "FINALLY," a lot of things, hit me.

Hardly, anyone else did, either. I was weird! I knew what to do. I had to keep on looking, for evidence, that would "MAKE THEM" see, the "BEAUTY" of my theory. Even if it was, only one person. I learned, by history, it's how things start to change—slowly but surely. We all know that Rome wasn't built in a day.

As I wandered and searched all those years, my world was slowly changing. I had made an impact with my brother, Terry, and didn't realize it. By the year 2000, I had "FINALLY" finished my first book. I was ready to show the evidence to the world! He welcomed it with open arms! The rest of my family ignored it. I was so appreciative of his interest. He loved science and medicine!

We also shared an interest in art. He was my biggest supporter as a professional artist and even became my partner, for several years. We had some great times! But, to have him share my books, was the best thing I could ever hoped for! It saved my "LIFE", many times. I felt so alone and constantly hated as I struggled, over the years. I seemed to be the only one excited, about aliens all looking the same. He saved me. He lived the same torture, from having a sexually addicted wife, as I was living.

I took a break, for a minute, to talk with him and quit typing. I looked "UP" and tried, but I couldn't speak. I got so choked up, that I just finally, slumped back into the chair and cried. I miss him so bad!

Wow, "LIVING UP IN SPACE." What a "WONDERFUL" logical possibility. Thank God we live "UP" in the sky today, on the "SPACE STATION"! This "ALONE" gives me so much hope. I will see him again, I thought to myself as I cried!

Again, I am so "GRATEFUL", that we have these stories, of "PEOPLE/ ANGELS/GODS/GOD, OR WHATEVER THE HELL EVER THEY ARE," living "UP" in "SPACE." People, "WE CAN LIVE UP THERE" too! I can't let go of the possibility, that they've conquered " SPACE RESURRECTION AND IMMORTALITY" too! The stories say they have! "HALLELUJAH"! I'm going to learn this song for Terry! "Thanks Terry, I cried." "For supporting my music too!

I'll never understand why we all don't "SEE", that space is "HEAVEN/ UP." After all, it is recognized by science as our only chance for survival. "THEY KNOW" we're on a "DYING PLANET." "BACK THEN" I understand people not seeing this "SIMPLE FACT," but not now. We all "SHOULD" know that planets die! Science has been teaching this for a "LONG TIME." All planets die and are "REBORN," in new solar systems, "INFINITELY"! "MAYBE EVERYTHING DOES—EVEN TERRY"! I cried hard and long, at the thought of this "REALITY." It was wonderful! He "DESERVED TO LIVE FOREVER"! Carl Sagan said, that we are just infinite reincarnations of suns—"SONS" of "SUNS"!

Wow, the religious terminology is so interchangeable here, with science, it's uncanny. If we just recognized it, religion would start sounding, like science! Minus their "THINKING CREATOR GOD," of course! Mr. Sagan made it perfectly clear, the evidence suggests "EVOLUTION" created these suns and it is infinitely, doing so. That's why "SONS" have always existed and hopefully always will!

Wow, our mystery was becoming clearer and clearer to me, as I searched. I can easily see how an advanced species of evolution, with the ability to create a new uncooperative human species, would experience our dilemma. They wouldn't be able, to keep us from hurting ourselves or themselves, without physical consequences. Coexistence, therefore would result in mass anarchy. It's only logical that "MANKIND'S" barbaric existence has to be controlled through isolation and "MYSTERY"!

Martin Luther King and his peaceful protest movement, for the achievement of "CIVIL RIGHTS," is the best representation of this reasoning. He got killed! It "ALONE" is the reason, for the absence of these "GOD'S. Obviously, they can too. He does not stand alone, I am with him. Peace. I will not come back here.

People, an "INTELLIGENT SPECIE'S" ability to create life, obviously caused this confusion. It became primitive mans religion story, as soon as they left! Who and what they are is up to you! I hope you let your love of "INTELLIGENCE" guide you, as it does me. It is the tool to overcome death for our kids—"FOR ALL KIDS"! In the words of Yeshua, the most famous man in the world: "WE SHALL OVERCOME, WE SHALL OVERCOME"!

I just watched, *THE SIXTIES* on CNN and cried. I "LEARNED", that King wasn't the first to make this quote famous. It was Lyndon Johnson. King cried when he heard Johnson decry the Selma, Mississippi massacre. He was the first white "LEADER" to say those words, in his lifetime. Before that, he'd only read it in the Bible. It was said by "JESUS/YESHUA" 2,000 years ago. He wouldn't be the last! I watched as Sammie Davis Jr. eulogized his "ASSASSINATION." He implored everyone to continue the peaceful protest movement! He said if we carry King's torch, we could see a black president, within the next 50 years! Two words! BARACK OBAMA!!! He said we shall overcome, too and we did!

Wow, the evidence of our history was speaking volumes, about the progress and power of information. It was a scientific reality and the world, "SEEMED" oblivious to it. Terry and I knew why. The world is dominated by the magic of religion and Hollywood.

Man, I sure never thought that this "METEOR" would happen. If it only had, then. I don't know, if Terry ever thought about it much, either. But, I know one thing. He would've been just as excited and blown away, as I was, to have experienced it. He also would've seen it as my "GOLDEN" ticket to success! Terry got "MY DISCOVERY" and understood "MY THEORY" completely.

Before, I go any further, I've got to "SAY SOMETHING" right here and now. I haven't been as forthright as I should have been, about my "PAST." Things got a lot worse, after we left Sparta and moved in with Tammy's mother! I went to jail, again and again. I would go to jail three times, in the next three years. I did time on two separate occasions.

The first time, was right before my very first book was released. But, I got lucky and didn't go to jail! I'll tell you why, in the next several paragraphs. It wasn't for drugs, this time. Heck, this time they gave me "DRUGS"! My wife enforced it! Ironically, it was my only option, to stay out of jail. Read on!

However, the second time I did! I caught her with the next door neighbor and told him to stay away from my house and son. I told him,

MIKE BRUMFIELD

that she didn't love him and was "SCREWING", my friends too. He didn't care. It gets worse. Everybody knew, but me. I was horrified, I was, because this guy was a racist low class bully of a pig. He was fat and ugly to boot! He epitomized the devil's "POWER DISEASE"! They were an embarrassment to everyone.

He couldn't have taken my wife, in a million years—if beauty had anything to do with it. He finally tried and she wouldn't go with him. She even turned into the devil herself and said she wasn't going anywhere, "WITH HIM"! Sad, because they would make a perfect match! I can't believe, that I lived through it! This was the first time I went to jail. I ripped his shirt, when I jerked him out of the car and got in his face. I was lucky I didn't get convicted. He didn't show up for court. But, I spent a night in jail, anyway.

The first time my son and I suffered at the hands of my wife, the police intervened. I threatened to commit suicide during an argument with my wife! I was desperately trying to "GET" her to just confess and she wouldn't! I would never do it again. Unfortunately for me she would! She did it constantly when I would leave and do so right in front of my son. She would even tell him, that I was leaving, because I didn't love them anymore. She "BECAME" the most evil person I knew. I would always got so angry and she used it to the hilt. These scenes will forever, haunt me! My nightmare was about to get "KICKED" into high gear.

Well, needless to say, I couldn't "GET HER TO JUST TELL ME SHE WANTED OTHER MEN"! I told her that I could take it. Instead, she left screaming and went straight to my son's school. I begged her to stop and just talk to me, but she wouldn't. So "I FOLLOWED HER"! Wrong move. The law was waiting. I was so broken and ashamed. I told them what was happening, and that she controlled everything. She had no pity for me. They did.

I remember begging the officer while he hand-cuffed me, to not let my son, see me like this. It happened in front of the principal at the school's main entrance! He didn't. He knew my wife was having affairs.

Hell, everyone in town knew. We all knew! I heard her tell him no, when he asked if she wanted to press charges. I was lying in the back seat trying desperately, not to let my son hear me sobbing. She said coldly, "He needs mental help"!

At that moment, I knew real fear! I folded up and cried uncontrollably. She asked him to take me to a local doctor, that was buying my art. The police officer immediately seized the moment and said O.K.! I sobbed, with relief and embarrassment.

He pulled away real slow and told me to stay down till, he said I could move. I told him I would and thanked him. He looked in his rear view mirror and our eyes met. He had tears in his eyes, as he pulled slowly away and told me not to worry. Instantly, I felt safer. He was going to stick up for me. Finally, someone was going to help me.

We didn't go far, before he pulled over and got out of the car. It shocked me because I didn't know what he was doing. He was visibly shaken. I asked him what was happening. He quickly answered, with a father's tone and softly told me, "Everything will be OK. You're not a criminal!" He came around to my side of the car and opened my door. We both broke down and cried.

He helped me out of the back seat, uncuffed me, and put me in front seat. When he got in, he immediately looked at me and said he was sorry, for what he, "HAD TO JUST DO," but it was official protocol.

I told him that I appreciated it and it was OK. "But, I could sat in the back." "No, you can't," he said softly as he barely choked back his tears. I heard his voice strain with emotion as he continued to try to talk. I felt for him as he looked away and gathered himself.

He turned to me and managed to say the most wonderful thing I could've ever heard, at that moment. He said, "It's not OK. It's just the law. That doesn't make it right. She's the criminal." That was the most amazingly loving and reassuring thing, that I'd heard in a long time.

I broke down, again and he did too. We sat for a second and just looked down. All of a sudden, he put his hand on my shoulder and drove away. My life was coming apart and I couldn't stop it. I couldn't even protect my son from it. My wife and his mother, suddenly "BECAME" a dangerous, lethal, unstoppable, power hungry "DISEASED MONSTER IN DISGUISE! I couldn't help, but wonder if she would give me aids. I told her about it, later. She said she didn't care!

She never got help for her "SEX ADDICTION" and she never let me see anyone else, either! I longed to have a women, that I respect and loved! She made my life "HELL." No, she made all of our lives hell. Unfortunately, I'm the one, who became the "OUTWARD ANGRY MONSTER"! I am so ashamed! Both, of my children, saw me biting my tongue and clenching my fist at her, way too many times.

At one point, she even told a client of mine, right in front of me, that she would swing, but I couldn't take it. Turns out she was wrong. I tried pimping her. I told her he was even offering her five grand, for one night. She acted insulted, by it! Ironically, it wasn't about the money, to her. Even though she told everyone, it was. I hated her, for this. It was "ALL" about her lust for "DANGEROUS SEX" and "NEW CONQUEST"! She got off, on getting away, with it. Like, she was! She was dangerously ignorant. He told me everything and it stopped their game, as far as, I know. I told him I would give him money, if he could help me get evidence. He didn't and it didn't matter. Like I wrote earlier. I got it anyway, over and over, again. Read on!

I finally just begged her to quit doing our friends and neighbors. I even gave her condoms and my blessing, to do this in other towns. She never would and stayed in denial. She still is. Now, back to my story.

The police officer drove me to the hospital and said he would tell me everything, if I promised not to tell anyone. I promised on my son's life. I did this because I wanted him to know, just how serious I was. Hell, I appreciated what he was doing. So much that I was willing to do just about anything I could, to get his help.

He didn't need anything else. He knew how much I loved my son. He told me everything. She was having multiple affairs! I couldn't believe, what was happening to me. I was so afraid, for my son.

"Look," He said shaking my shoulder as I slumped and cried. "You've got to be strong for your son's sake. This is a "DANGEROUS GAME" that your wife is playing here and she obviously doesn't care who she hurts. So please, you have to be smart for your son. I talked to the doctor and made him aware of the truth. He feels bad for you. Hell, son, we all do. But, you've just got to play along. He's going to talk with both of you first. Then he's going to prescribe "YOU MEDICINE" to deal with your "JEALOUSIES," OK?" "OK, I will." I said as I sat back and breathed a little easier. I just wanted this all to end.

I was sure glad, that he gave the quote gesture, as he said it. Jealous was the last thing I was. I didn't have to tell him, though. He knew. It did make me feel a little better because this meant the doctor knew, as well. Like I said, they all knew.

When we pulled up to the hospital and he let me out. It was hard. He had to escort me to the doctor's office. I figured as much and tried to make it, as easy as possible, for him. Tammy was holding Matt, as I walked through the door. He saw that I had been crying and started to come to me.

I saw the police officer step forward. Thankfully, Tammy grabbed Matt and stopped him. He began asking what was wrong as Tammy pulled him back up and onto her lap. I went ahead and knelt down at her knees. I quickly hugged him to diffuse the situation and told him "DADDY IS OK". I told him, that I just needed some medicine for my head and said some things I shouldn't have. He didn't understand and asked why again. I quickly told him, that it was because of me being sad, about my brother and Dad passing away. I told him it was scaring his Mom and she's helping me, now. I got up and hugged them both.

The doctor quickly asked Matt if he'd ever heard a police siren. Matt immediately said no and actually managed a weak smile. "Well", he continued on wittingly. "Would you like to hear one?," he asked softly. Matt didn't have a chance to reply. The policeman, immediately took it from there. He reached for Matt's hand and started to leave, but Matt reached for me. I told him that it was O.K. and I'd be right out. He wouldn't let go.

I immediately turned to the doctor and asked if Tammy could go with him. The doctor looked up at the police officer and started to say something. But, I never gave him the chance. I spoke before anything else could go wrong.

"It's alright doc. I know I have a "JEALOUSY" problem. I know why I'm here." I said looking him dead in the eyes. He looked startled for a minute and then said it was OK with him, if it was OK with the policeman. I smiled and turned to him. "It's OK with me," he said real big like. He was grinning from ear to ear. I was trying my best, too! "Let's go young man," he said as he led both of them, out the door. Matt looked back and I quickly reassured him, that I'd be right out. The doc chimed in that I would, as well.

Tammy made one last demand in front of them both, before she left. She wanted their word, that I would be held accountable if I stopped taking my medicine. That wasn't enough. She made them promise to believe her, instead of me, if she ever has to call and tell them, I wasn't taking my medication. They agreed. At that moment the police officer's advice rang loud and true, in my head. My life, was not my own, anymore. The doctor's visit ended and the remainder of that year was brutal. But it would get worse!

The next horrible incident played out at Matt's second grade teacher's office. This happened just before I attacked her "SEX PARTNER." Who, by the way, she says never existed. He finally said he did and loved her. In a way, I felt sorry for him. I caught her with other men and he wouldn't believe me. Thank God, I didn't go to jail, that year!

Anyway, it wasn't long before I would! It happened when Matt started the second grade. The teacher called, because she was concerned my son was crying and unhappy at school. She called me, instead of "TAMMY." Thank God, Tammy was at work, or wherever.

I went to get Matt out of school and he wasn't in his room. I was more than freaked out. She assured me, that everything was alright and immediately escorted me to the nurse's office. She explained, that this was necessary, because he was really crying hard and it was disrupting the class.

My body began convulsing. I started to cry with every word and was heaving uncontrollably. She quickly put her hand on my shoulder and asked, if I was alright. I tried to say yes, but she knew I wasn't. We quickly slipped into the waiting area of the nurse's office and stopped. I could see my son with the nurse and it was devastating! He was crying, worse than I was. It instantly broke my heart and "ANGERED" me. I got it together, immediately.

I told her I wanted to get my son. She held me back for a second and asked me, if I could come in and talk with her, about Matt's behavior. I agreed, but not until I calmed my son down. She asked me if our marriage was alright. I told her that obviously it wasn't. I assured her, that Matt was in good hands, "WITH ME." I could sense she knew it too, because she let me go.

Before she did, she asked me if I could get a baby sitter, for Matt, tomorrow and if we could meet with her. Little did she know, how sick Tammy was. I agreed and went on into the nurse's office, to get my son. The moment I walked through the door, he lit up like a Christmas tree and cried even harder! I managed to hold it together and hugged him, as tight as I could. He was everything to me. I quickly calmed him down and the teacher escorted me to the car. She hugged us and said she would see Matt, in a couple days. I thanked her and we left. I never took him back!

We went the next morning. I didn't sleep a wink, that night. Thank God, I didn't lose it. I didn't blow my cool. Granny Flatt and Tammy's little brother watched Matt. I thanked them multiple times. They both knew what Tammy was doing and had, for a long time. Like I said, we all did. It was only in her head, that we didn't and she didn't care anyway.

The ride to the school was excruciating. I told Tammy, that I knew everything and didn't care. I just wanted her to quit putting us in harm's way and let me home school Matt. She continued to deny it, but instantly saw a golden opportunity, for more freedom and agreed. She done just as I'd hoped she would. I didn't think, that she could get any more evil than what she already was, but she was about to.

I saw the teacher coming toward us as we approached her room. She greeted us warmly and we followed her on in. She started, by asking us, if we were having any marital problems. Before I could say a word, Tammy started talking. In the next five minutes she would accuse me of not letting her work and not making enough money to buy health insurance. WOW! If the teacher only knew how she blew money on her looks!

I couldn't believe what I was hearing. I trembled with both rage and fear. I had to quickly get my thoughts together! This woman was going to get me put in jail or killed. I immediately spoke up and asked her if Tammy told her, that she gets royalties! The teacher was totally surprised. She asked Tammy, about it. I had her dead to right. Tammy admitted it, but said it wasn't much.

I knew that teachers don't make a lot of money. So I quickly added, "She's lying about that too. She's lying about everything." I leaned forward this time and looked that teacher right in her eyes. I started to cry inside, but managed to hold back my tears. "She spends $500 a month on her "BEAUTY NEEDS" and god knows how much on eating out! She demands that every day". Tammy immediately said she didn't and started to get angry.

I ended the "DANGEROUS GAME" quickly and told her, that I was willing to prove it. But, I didn't want to. All I wanted, was for her to leave me and Matt alone. I quickly told her, that Tammy and I have agreed on home schooling Matt.

Now, she was dumbfounded. Tammy tried to say something, but I interrupted. I told the teacher we were working on our marriage and that I would get counseling for my jealousy. I broke down and started to cry. I reached and hugged Tammy and said I was sorry. The teacher, just looked addled and replied, "Well, great! I have already talked to Tammy and she was worried about that. It was what we both hoped you'd say." Wow, I called this one right!

I couldn't believe my ears. Tammy had her snowballed too! What a nightmare. But, at least now, I was in control. Thank god, I am smarter than her. I hugged Tammy and told her she could even start going shopping by herself, on the weekends too! She stiffened up and laughed saying, "Right, right. We'll see," she said to the teacher. I hugged her even tighter, "REAL TIGHT" and said, "I will. I promise honey, I love you. You know that!" I would've paid her boyfriends to take her at that point!

The teacher broke in and said to me softly, "Mr. Brumfiled, you're wife loves you. Don't you?," she asked Tammy. Tammy didn't speak for a second and the teacher, started to ask her again. But, Tammy knew better and quickly said she did.

"But," she added, I just can't take anymore of his accusations. I immediately hugged her and told her everything will be alright. I told the teacher I would, get some counseling. She fell right into my trap. I did eventually, court ordered, from the next time! Yes, I catch her with the next door neighbor! I begged Tammy to come , but she wouldn't. In her "MIND" she was fine. She was denying everything.

"Good," she remarked quickly and cheerfully. "Hopefully, you'll both go together."

"We will," I said as I started to get up. I told her that I had to use the restroom and clean up my face. I reached up to wipe my tears away, with my shirt sleeve. She gently stopped me and got a tissue, from her desk. "That's a good idea," she remarked as I wiped away my tears and started toward the door. "Tammy and I will finish talking while you're gone. I told her OK, kissed Tammy, and walked away. I couldn't believe what just happened!

Tammy was staring daggers at me, when I returned. I didn't care. Tomorrow I would start home-schooling my son! At least he wouldn't have to cry anymore, when she dropped him off at school.

She wished us luck, as we left and walked us to the door. The ride home was ice cold! I never hated someone, so much, in my life. I tried to talk, but she threatened me, to stop. She was vicious! I stopped talking at her command, alright! I even played her "DANGEROUS GAME", for the remainder of the year. But, the Devil wasn't in control anymore, like she thought. I was getting "SMARTER"! Intelligence would become my "SAVIOR"!

Like I said, I would go to jail, one more time. It happened about a year later. I would see this teacher again. She apologized for believing Tammy. I told her, that it was alright and it's just a sad, sad disease. She said she understood. I cried inside.

I threw myself into as many book-signings, as I could. My books weren't selling well, but I didn't care. Tammy and I hardly talked again. She turned her back, to me in bed. I didn't care and she hated it, now. I was tired of waking up, only to find her in the bathroom, with the door locked. According to her, she was only talking to her girlfriends! She was so ignorant, that she didn't even know she was!

I started, sleeping on the couch, as much as, I could. She wouldn't even let me do that, not without causing "US" problems, in front of Matt. She demanded, that I wear her ring and come back to bed. She was crazy! I tried not to, but if I didn't, she would let Matt know it. She got me some sleeping pills, from Granny. Thank God. I begged "HIM" to make her let me go or take her out of my life. "HE" didn't! I hated myself for wishing, that she was dead. I didn't know what else to do. But, I knew this made me evil! "TIME" with her was now like a prison sentence. I found myself wanting her to just die! Oh God, please forgive me.

Things were O.K. for awhile, but eventually the situation got worse. The decline only took about six months. I was beside myself. We were not only dead broke, but deep in debt as well!

I don't want to keep on, but I left the next day after she went to work. I took Matt! This should be enough to clearly paint the picture of hell, that Matt and I was going through!

She came to my motel room and begged me back, while I was holding Matt! I caved in knowing she was capable of hurting us or killing herself. She was, and still is, mentally unstable. I am doing this to get her help and stop children, from being hurt. If you know anybody with this "PRETTY POWER", sex disease please buy them this book. It will be the best money you've ever spent. Do it for their kids. Give it to them and tell them, it is a sad story of a person's mental disease, destroying a "FAMILY"! Do it with love and they will get the message. It's simple and everyone already knows, "POWER CORRUPTS." I hope she will forgive me for this and do the right thing. Confess and help stop other women and men, who are "CARRIERS" of this devastatingly "DEADLY DISEASE". They destroy their childrens' lives!

Back to my story. Tammy quit her job by the end of summer!

Her reason for quitting was to continue home schooling Matt. "WE" knew the real reason. She got caught up in an affair at work, between her boss and a car salesman. I didn't care. Matt was safe at home and that's all, that mattered to me. Things were back to "NORMAL"! At least, as normal as they could be, for the next year and I wrote another book. It was my third! Woo-hoo! It bombed too. I continued to schedule, one book-signing after another, anyway!

Well, I finally went to jail, one last time. This time, I came home and saw Matt and his friend, run from the next door neighbors. I couldn't believe what I just saw and it got bad. She let my seven year-old son jump on a trampoline, without supervision!!! I headed up the road to get her and saw her coming. She tried to get around me. Well I blew! I tried to stop her and almost crashed my car, into hers. Luckily, I didn't. My son was in the car. I was so angry! I wanted to confront them and tell her he could have her. When we got to the house the cops came. They arrested me right in front of my son and found pot on me! I was forced to go to Alcoholics Anonymous, for the next six months and get drug tested.

I was angry and sad, but it saved my life. I spent two days in jail, this time, and was drug tested for six months! I got clean too. No more, escaping life's problems, with my semi-daily pot habit! I had been smoking, for 15 years or better. I quit several times, but always went back.

With all the time, that I had, I wrote another book. It was my third! You already know by now, it failed, too. My life was a wreck. She put Matt back in school and "WE" started raising dogs. But, we still stayed broke. She had, and still continues to have, an expensive lifestyle!

Things kept getting worse. She wasn't going to stop seeing the next door neighbor, the salesman at work, my friends, my clients, and she wouldn't let me leave. I tried and she made Matt's life, a living hell. She didn't care. So, I threatened to take the tape and see a lawyer if she didn't agree to sell the house and move. She gave in and we moved at the end of his fourth year! "FINALLY"!

She wanted to move back to Sparta so Matt could be close to his grandfather, Milton! I gave in. We moved and took Granny Flatt with us. But, it never stopped her from getting new boyfriends and flirting with everyone. Even worse, her dad just enabled her more! First, her Mom and now her "DAD"! I was doomed! She was in love with herself and they ignored it! I told them both about the tape and all the men. "THEY DONE NOTHING"! I tried not to hate them and I don't anymore. I'm a parent. This situation would destroy my relationship with them, while she destroyed her reputation with everyone else!

Things got worse, not better. She would tell me in anger, "Who would want you?". She tortured me with questions, about why I was sad! Crazy huh? "WE" could've gone to jail many times, while Matt was in school, arguing. One time she threw the phone at me and cut my hand, because I was leaving. Her Dad opened the door, just as I did. He asked what the problem was. I told him, that I was going to call the law on her, for attacking me and threatening to commit suicide, in front of my son! He hollered, that she ain't gonna kill herself and for me to go on!

I told him that I tried, but she always tried to stop me. He said he'd stop her and for me to just go on. I did and she started screaming bloody murder, that she didn't want me to go! I told him she was a psycho and that I had caught her with my friends, clients, next door neighbors, co-workers, and God knows who else. She had been coming on to everyone from Matt's basketball coach, to her cousin, to the superintendant, at his school.

"Nobody was safe from her! I've begged her to get help and she won't. She's embarrassed us over and over again. I'm done with trash, like her." I screamed and went on out the door. She went ballistic! She started running toward me and screaming, 'I'll kill you, I'm not trash"!

Milton grabbed her and tried to stop her. She wrestled to get away and couldn't. He hollered and tried to calm her, but she was a raging bull. She wanted to kill me. I got in my car and left, but not without telling him one last time, that she needs help. I cried and cried. She never got it and they continued to lie for her! We all needed help, too.

Staying was the hardest thing, I ever had to do. Her family had some of the biggest hypocrites and fakes, I knew. They were evil, just like Tammy. Thank God, for her aunt Reynelda and Jewel. She finally came and told me, how the family talked about me. She said they didn't want me around. I thanked her and never went back. I finally have.

I would relish the opportunity, to wear a wire on Tammy. I really wish, God or whoever, would just bust them all! No, not really. It would be bad and I just want peace!

I released a fifth and sixth book over the next four years. Same ol' story—neither were successful. Like I said, at least I stayed on the road and didn't go to jail! I slept in my car many a night. But, at least I was away from Tammy. My relationship with Matt went downhill. He hated the way I treated Tammy and I don't blame him. I should've treated her better, for his sake. I tried and failed many times. She never stopped flirting in front of us. I finally took a break and became a car dealer. I needed to make as much money as I could. Matt would soon graduate and I wanted to divorce her immediately, when he did! I thought moving here, would be the end of my troubles. Surely she wouldn't embarrass herself here. I was so wrong!

Everything was going "OK" until she started hitting, on my employees! I could understand neighbors, coaches, cousins, and friends. But, I couldn't believe what I saw, and I talked the "KID", into sexting her. It worked! She fell for it! "TECHNOLOGY" had now busted her, again! She denied everything, until then! She didn't believe in anything. Her hypocrisy gagged me. I threatened to show my son her phone and she ran out the door.

Man, this was so sad! I felt so helpless. I put up with this shit since Matt had been in the first grade. This happened two months before he was to graduate! I finally couldn't do it anymore. I tried hard to shelter him from her addiction. But, she wouldn't stop. Not even in her family's home town!

Unfortunately, I couldn't wait any longer. I was outraged! I got a lawyer and filed for divorce. This was the worst moment of my life! We had spoiled his graduation! Damn my pride!

I said in the beginning of this story, that my brother Terry "IS" a big part of it. This is the moment, that he saved me. He knew what was going on. Terry and I officially made plans to go into business "TOGETHER", just prior to this! He had been a big part of my car business, but knew where my heart was. It was with my books and finding Flying saucers! Crazy, huh? Well you just wait. Read on!

The saucers on the front cover of this book, are my pictures and they're real! I filmed them in Phoenix a couple years, before. I will follow up on this point, in the next chapter.

Terry and I had been talking, for the last year or so. I had been confiding in him about everything. Enough was enough! He had already saved my life many times! When this happened, I called him and decided it was time to get back on my books. I was finally going to leave Sparta! Terry understood, completely.

He came down for Matt's graduation and helped me, get through it. Naturally in the small town of Sparta, everyone knew about the divorce and her affairs. Tammy's family came, but they hated me. She made sure of that. She had told everyone, that everything was my fault. I didn't care. Matt left right after and I made the trip to Ohio, behind Terry! I immediately built a billboard on his property in Ohio, to advertise my books. I thought it was all over! Again, I was wrong.

Tammy began calling me every night and threatening suicide. She was even telling Matt, that she didn't want to live anymore, without us. I went home! I had, too! He decided to come back and go to college, but he wouldn't be able to, until his girlfriend graduated. I immediately chewed her, out for calling him. But, I stayed because I couldn't stop her. She said she would do it again, if I left.

I hated her, with everything I was! She was capable of anything. I cringed with horror every time I watched the news, showing parents killing each other and their kids in domestic disputes. No matter what, I wasn't going to let her do this. I stayed and made sure the divorce went through! She tried to argue about who gets what. I told her to get a lawyer. I didn't want anything. I had my lawyer draw up an agreement that gave everything to my son. I told Matt, to split it with my other son. I begged him to forgive me and his mother.

She never contested. She continued to beg me and say she would be faithful, if I would stay for Matt! I told her I didn't care, just please use protection and of course I stayed. I had too! I was rolling the dice with my health and sanity. Not to mention, my life. So, I just threw myself into writing another book, to keep things calm.

It had been over three years, since I wrote my last book. After Matt's graduation in 2009, I decided to write my seventh and took another trip, to Terry's. During the visit, I convinced Terry, that I knew what "EVIDENCE", I was missing! I explained, that people don't think infinitely and scientifically. Therefore, they don't "SEE" or understand "EVOLUTION"! He said he didn't either, really. Terry was shocked, after I explained it! My, "EVOLUTION REVOLUTION" began then. I just didn't "SEE" it, yet. My "PROOF OF EVOLUTION AND CREATION" chart was about, to be born!

I showed him a book, that I had with me. It showed every species of life, that was in it and asked him, what they had in common. He didn't know? I told him they all look the same. "ALL OF THEM"! I explained it is proof, that they evolved. It is "BECAUSE THEY ALL LOOK THE SAME," like bacteria or a virus! Then, I showed him how "HOW HUMANS ALL LOOK DIFFERENT." He was pretty shocked and said, that he had never thought about it, before.

"Hell, nobody has," I quickly replied laughing. "And I wrote about it ten years ago! That's what I've been telling you guys. Religion rules the world and it doesn't believe in "EVOLUTION"! Therefore, hardly anybody knows what it is. Even if they do, they don't prove it "THE WAY" I just did! Terry, "THIS IS SIMPLE PROOF OF EVOLUTION" and I may have just done, what Darwin didn't do!!! I can prove this, with these pictures and kids will understand!" I didn't do it in the last book, though! My "SMOKING GUN" was yet, to evolve.

I was so pumped up with enthusiasm and excitement! I had just explained the age old "EVOLUTION VERSUS CREATION" debate and why it still rages, on to my brother! It explains it in a beautifully "SIMPLE WAY", with pictures!!! I knew what to do next! I began writing my seventh book and was going to title it: INFINITE ASTRONAUTS: THE THEORY OF EVERYTHING! I wanted people to ask themselves "ONE QUESTION" at its end: "HOW ADVANCED COULD LIFE BE IN AN INFINITE UNIVERSE?"

Terry got it. "HE SAW THE SIMPLE ANSWER", infinitely advanced! It was the only numerical word inthe question. He got it's meaning, too! The evidence gave us a simple answer. "LIFE WOULD EVOLVE" and "LEARN", that it has to live in space, not on planets. I showed him the heads of Easter Island and how they all look the same. He got it. They made us, to serve a purpose of living forever in space and we gave them, "OUTWARD BEAUTY"! This also gave them power over one another, by possibly being us!

"Wow," he blurted out. "Religion describes your "HYPOTHETICAL REALITY" to a tee! The aliens are obviously these gods/angels of the devil story," he said boldly looking at the illustration in my book. "Shit, how can anybody not see, that they all look the same. They definitely share the same common denominator of identical looks, as every other species does, alright! This means thjey are evolving everywhere as we speak!" He paused continued and then continued to speak. "Like you've been saying, they obviously evolved and scientifically created humans, for "SEXUAL POWER" huh!"

"You got it," I remarked, excitedly. I couldn't believe it! He lit up a cigarette and leaned back in his chair! Wow, he saw what I saw. He suddenly told me, to get this explanation done, with the pictures, to support it. He then pulled out his wallet and asked me how much I needed to get it done. I hugged him and headed back to Tennessee! Little did I know that I would never see him again!

I finished the book, shortly after his death, in the following weeks. But I used the same pictures as before and they didn't work. Look at the end of his book. I didn't make a chart. I won't make this mistake, again. Everyone will "SEE, KNOW, AND BELIEVE IN EVOLUTION", when they're done reading. If they don't they're religious and nothing will change, that! "THIS IS SCIENTIFIC EVIDENCE, PROVING EVOLUTION OF HUMANS AND THEY ARE ALIENS THAT ALL LOOK THE SAME"! Primitive man called them gods! I knew them best as angels and one became the devil. It was my wife! I cried.

People, at its simplest, religion is a story, about life existing "EVERYWHERE UP IN THE UNIVERSE, INFINITELY." Wouldn't that be wonderful, if it were true? Then I could see Terry, my Dad, and heck everyone again! What does it matter, who's right or wrong or "WHAT THEY LOOK LIKE"!

Most of all, I'd love for Mom to see Nancy Gail again. I want my brother Steve to see Danny! How wonderful would that be? Isn't this "POSSIBILITY" "WORTH" all the money, in the world? No parent should have to bury their children like they did!

Don't we all want life to exist everywhere? I think we do. Polls even show that the majority of scientist, religious people, and atheist alike, think it does. Ironically, however, they "BELIEVE" it exist "SOMEWHERE" in the universe—just not "HERE! Why can't they imagine life existing "EVERYWHERE" in space and not on planets? Thank God Terry got it!

Them agreeing is at least a start! It's a "GOOD" one in my book! Now, I hope we can leave it at that and get started on the "METEOR PROBLEM"! I will give my life for the sake of our children's survival and more. The world will hate me, for what I'm about, to do.

Terry would give everything to help the world! Therefore, "I WILL GIVE ALL MY MONEY TO SCIENCE AND CHALLENGE EVERYONE TO DO THE SAME"! This, is what

the world, will hate me for. Tammy and her mother did. So did some of my family. Anybody will, that wants to be rich. Unfortunately, money is the only way we will ever stop "METEORS"! He wouldn't get to see the Russian "METEOR EVENT"! I know he would have been affected by it every bit as much as I am!

I'll be the first to say, I could be wrong, thinking life exists "EVERYWHERE"! But I hope I'm not. No matter what, I will continue to hope, that it does. I'd rather be optimistic about life, than pessimistic. Hell, there's enough of that to go around for a dozen earths, as it is! Mankind is a living "HELL"! I've proven that, to myself! I made enough of it and still do. I want to stop. No, I have to stop in "THE NAMEOFLOVE,"

Hasn't religion and politics caused enough hate "IN THE NAME OF LOVE." Let's ban them. It's made life "DOWN" here on earth, nothing but a living "HELL." All "SUPPOSEDLY" for the sake of getting "BACK UP TO HEAVEN"!

Ironic, huh! We're in "IT" and we don't even know it. Earth is a living hell and our prison. If we would only learn about the universe, instead of just looking "UP" at it. It would "ALL" be so "SIMPLE"! I could "SEE", that people just don't "THINK SCIENTIFICALLY", about it. Most don't see the inevitable death of a planet nor the constant hell mother nature, wreaks on it. I would begin to ask people if they thought ETs could have created us and be here "NOW"!

Much to my horror, they all had the same "SCIENTIFIC TIME DEFICIT" in their thinking. "MOST" even said it is highly unlikely, given the "SIZE" of the universe! No, don't they think it is infinite? They also said, it would be next to impossible for them to travel from "THEIR PLANET" to here and survive! OMG! People, think we can live on planets "FOREVER"! Even worse, I find most want to, even with Mother Nature killing us!

I always asked them one more question. It's the question I asked everybody and will put at the end of this book! Here it is again; "HOW ADVANCED COULD LIFE BE IN AN INFINITE UNIVERSE" and where would they live, if they want to avoid death and extinction. No one, except Terry got it! Scientist aren't seeing the simple "LOGIC" of "INFINITE INTELLIGENT LIFE", not living on planets! I could see why though! "MY FAMILIES RELIGION PROVED WHY?" They say Earth will exist, "FOREVER" and God will make it "PERFECT"! OMG! Religion has an "EARTH" grip on humans and even some scientist!

During my journey, I quickly began to see, that heaven's existence and location is a "VOLATILE" subject "MATTER"! This is crazy huh? How can we get so angry at each other over religion? I knew how!

I never really understood, why or how, anyone could get so angry "AT EACH OTHER" over their "LOVE FOR THEM." Don't we "ALL" want the same thing? Don't we all want "A LOVING, EQUALLY SHARED PERFECT WORLD"? It's mind boggling that we can get "SO" angry "FOR SOMEONE NOT BELIEVING WHAT WE BELIEVE" about the world we live in. I know how this can happen. I did it! I am doing this to my children. I will stop it "NOW." I've been a hypocrite with my sons, for far too long and I'm sorry for it. I want them to see my past, even though I'm ashamed. How could I not! I believe it, right?

I must "CONFESS" before I go any further, I'm trying to know everything and it breeds self-righteousness. It doesn't matter, "MY" evidence MATCHES" and I have a "THEORY/DISCOVERY", that could save children "FROM DEATH." I am supposed to be sharing it "OUT OF LOVE", instead of anger and only if they "ASK" about "IT"! I've "ALMOST" destroyed, our relationship! I can only "HOPE" that I haven't. It is the very thing, that I hold most dear my "FAMILY."

I am crying rivers of shame, as I continue writing. I have been a monster to my sons on many occasions and not just with this "DISCOVERY", either. I've lost my cool, when they didn't "AGREE WITH ME"! This is just plain "SELFISHNESS." They weren't causing "ME PROBLEMS"! My anger is all about "ME" and my story is rampant with it. I would advise everyone to watch The Nanny. It is a scientific show, about raising kids logically and lovingly, without anger! I love it. I want to live it.

"WILL" science finally prove the existence of ETs/GODS and show us what they "LOOK" like, once and for all? I think it will, because it is the way we prove everything, with science! You are about to read an incredible statement, from me that I am dead serious about and am saying it with the utmost humility. I have proof, that "GOD/GODS, ETs, or THESE PEOPLE IN THE SKY", exist. I know what you're thinking and I agree. I need to prove it and probably that I'm crazy! I will and I promise I'm not.

Here goes nothing again. In 2006, I looked and found "FLYING SAUCERS"! I put their picture, on the front cover of this book. I "KNOW" that we can "ALL" find them, because I did! It happened because I believed a UFO hunter and he helped me find one. Please start looking. You can find them, too. All you have to do, is "START LOOKING"! They have "ALWAYS" existed.

Ironically, religion says we must first "BELIEVE" and then "SEEK" them. I agree! People, do see them by accident, though. But, they all see them "UP IN THE SKY"! This is crucial evidence! It proves "SPIRITS, DIMENSIONS, and TELEPORTATION DON'T EXIST".

"IF THEY DID WE WOULDN'T NEED FLYING CRAFT"! People, I've helped others find and film them, too. I showed Terry's wife, Vicki one! He barely missed it. Since, I have shown them to a dozen others. I love the excitement. They were just as excited as I was! It's time to finish this book. The next chapter is hard. Be prepared. More meteors are coming! I hope that this "METEOR AND FLYING SAUCER EVIDENCE" will eliminate all the bickering and hatred. The "METEOR" alone should make us put it aside. I know we can all agree on one thing. We "ALL" want to live forever!

"REALLY" isn't that the most important thing of all. "WE" should be doing this, for the benefit of mankind's, possible "IMMORTAL" EXISTENCE"? Don't we all want to live forever, "WITH OUR CHILDREN" in a "PERFECT WORLD"?

If we don't stop war, we will annihilate ourselves with "NUCLEAR WEAPONS"! We can do this "NOW"! If we don't create a "METEOR PREVENTION PLAN THEY CAN ALWAYS TAKE US OUT"! If we don't get off this planet we all, will "DIE"! We must go "UP"! We must start "NOW"!

Now, that I've "OBVIOUSLY" stated my "BELIEF" and shown you some of my evidence! I want to ask one "HARD" question of "EVERYONE", before I go on. It's the same nagging question, that I've always asked myself since I "HEARD" it and "UNDERSTOOD" it. Why would god or intelligent life stay away from us, if it exists. Especially, if they love us? I was afraid of my "NAGGING" answer! You will know it by the books end, I promise you!

I found out, that this universal "OBVIOUS, QUESTION" is called Fermi's Paradox. It is a science term. In science, they have answers for it, called "HYPOTHESIS." I have one. I reveal it at the end. It's easy to find the others on the computer.

After, seeing and living my wife's "PRETTY POWER DISEASE", the answer is simple, for me. Remember, everyone thinks I'm weird, but Terry. I often wondered "WHEN" we "FIND" them? "WILL WE

LIKE WHAT WE FIND" or "BELIEVE", what they have to say, about us? What if they aren't "PRETTY" and ask us something futuristic like; "Do we want to be ugly or pretty"? "COULD WE BE THEM IN A BODY THEY CREATED"?

Sometimes, my déjà vu was so powerful, it kept me thinking, I might have lived before or be from the future. Most people can't fathom this idea, because they don't think "INFINITELY"! Me? I would just look up to the stars and know "THEY" were "WATCHING" me. I just had to make sense of them, not helping us! Being able to create "OUTWARD BEAUTY", was it for me. I was ad-"DICK"-ted!

For believers, "WHY WOULD THEY STAY AWAY?" is the "ONLY" question, that we should be asking ourselves. Do we really need to ask, though? Would we really stay away from our loved ones, if we didn't have to? We only do when they're, bad or sick! OMG, I'm sick!

It's "PAINFULLY" obvious that we wouldn't stay way for any other reason. So, the answer must be "SIMPLE"! Maybe, they can't help us? I know fathers who stay away from their sons, because of addictions! They will hurt us and this is the reason, that we do it? Isolation might be the only way, that they can "SAVE" us! Maybe, we are the ones who have to figure this out. What if we have to save ourselves, through finding this knowledge? All this makes sense if they are real and not spirits. Obviously, they have this technology... ancient DNA symbols are universal!!!

I had more questions. When we find them, what if they aren't "PRETTY"? Are we ready for an "UGLY truth about ourselves. What if they are "ALIENS", that all look the same?

When I saw my first "FLYING SAUCER," I asked myself: "What if they tell us we're just recycled knowledge and there really isn't a "SELF OR SOUL", to save? What if existing forever is a scientific "ARTIFICIAL REALITY"? Carl Sagan says our atoms certainly do. But, what if our "INTELLIGENCE," or soul as religion calls it, is controlled by these "PEOPLE IN THE SKY?" I had to find out.

I want you to ask yourself, if a scientific human creation and reincarnation technology exists, would you want to be a "PRETTY" human or an "UGLY" alien? Before you answer "YES," please remember one thing. Remember, all the hell that I just went through and you might understand my decision when you get to the end. I am still going through hell as we speak!

Wow, all this is really something to think about, huh? Could we be "UGLY" aliens ad-"DICK"-ted to "THE POWER OF A BEAUTIFUL HUMAN"? I sure know all about the pretty addiction. It ruled everything from babies to cars. I WAS LIVING IT! I like "BEAUTIFUL," too! I am a beauty addict! Are you?

Don't worry about answering. You'll find out "WHY" later. It's secondary to the "METEOR PROBLEM" anyway. I need to "STAY FOCUSED" on that for right now. "WHY"? I hope you already know! This "COULD" become the most significant event and moment of your life! Even bigger, than "CONTACT." It could save your life!

I hope this meteor problem becomes, your reason for "LIVING AND GIVING"! It is mine. I will give all that I have, to cure it. We all have too "EVENTUALLY." It is "ALREADY WRITTEN ACCORDING TO RELIGION WORLD-WIDE"! Could this really be true? I had to "KNOW"!

I have to laugh at the irony of researching, "HEAVEN." Religion, "UNIVERSALLY" depicts it as a golden "SPIRIT" city fenced off and protected by "GOLDEN GATES." I can prove this point easily, by sharing a picture with you, out of my parent's religious magazine. (see Jehovah's Witnesses article evidence at the end of book to clearly "SEE" this common misunderstanding of heaven's location!) Well it does "SOMEWHAT" fit today's, reality. We use gold to live in space and couldn't do so, without it! We're also fenced off and protected by golden gates too! They're called space station hatches! We couldn't live there without gold protecting us, from the ultraviolet rays of the sun! Religion's depiction keeps people ignorant of science and perpetuates an archaic view of people living on clouds!!

After 7 books and 20 years of searching, I know one thing "NOW." Heaven was "LOST" the minute, that these people, "UP" in the sky left. And we lost their knowledge. Even this meteor, which we all saw, has made very little impact toward our "UNDERSTANDING" of them or their story. This "LACK OF KNOWLEDGE" is clearly the reason, for our mystery "IN THE FIRST PLACE"! Ironically, it still is today! I found the simple answer about "WHY THEY LEFT" in "ALL" the universal religious flood stories. I will give you a hint and it is easy to find the "REASON"! The answer is best summed up with the story of one word—"ATLANTIS"! Check it out! Materialism and sex is our "DOWNFALL"!

In all my joy, I'm "SAD" that people still don't know why heaven is "UP", scientifically. We have an urgent need to stop meteors, from taking us out! Science, nor religion, may not have "RECOGNIZED" the advanced scientific knowledge of "THESE STORIES." But, I "SEE CLEARLY", how they could help us get "THERE"! I discovered, that the most famous man ever, "JESUS"/YESHUA, was sad about this, too. Read on and find out why. His correct name is YESHUA and it is very relevant, to solving our mystery. At least, in my theory. His name is pronounced "YES-HU-A." It could be a universal confirmation to the question "ARE WE ADDICTED TO BEAUTY"! "I AM"! Are you? English is the universal language aboard our space station and the one we used to contact E.T.!.

It became "PAINFULLY" clear to me, as I researched his "FAME," why he was sad. He forgave these "SEEKERS OF HEAVEN", who not only, still didn't understand, but even asked for his death. This is his famous quote: "FORGIVE THEM FOR THEY KNOW NOT WHAT THEY DO"!

I saw, that he had the same problem I did and still do. Nobody likes to be told they're "IGNORANT," but it was "THE PROBLEM"! When I indicate, that someone is religiously "INFLUENCED" and not being scientific, about "HEAVEN,". It usually caused them to react angrily.

Wow, "PRIDE" is the culprit. It "USUALLY" takes over if someone says they know something, we don't. I know, I've been living it. I don't want to live it anymore!

I think "HEAVEN'S LOCATION" could not only "POSSIBLY," prove the existence of "REAL FLESH AND BLOOD ETs," but I think it could also solve the "JESUS" mystery! Yes, I could be wrong. However, I theorize, that like religion, "HEAVEN IS PHYSICALLY UP" and "HELL IS PHYSICALLY DOWN" in our universe! The scientific terms, that should replace heaven/hell are space and earth/matter.

People, once again YESHUA'S story, mother nature, and the meteor support this reality! This is life, "AS WE KNOW IT"! We must go up and live like YESHUA.

I have to admit, I foolishly thought, that I was the first since YESHUA/"JESUS" to think "INFINITELY", about the universe I live "IN." The other night, I saw the premiere of Neil DeGrasse Tyson's show, Cosmos and it quickly killed my "EGO/PRIDE." I wasn't the "FIRST", after all! "THANK GOD! This is one time, that I'm glad I'm wasn't. I'm so thankful that "SMARTER PEOPLE", than me, do exist.

Funny, how much we love ourselves and want to be the first at everything. Boy, "MANKIND". I can't believe, I'm one of them! The majority of us definitely are vain "ASS" humans. I know I am and it's a constant struggle, to deal with it. I must cure it "BEFORE I DIE"! Damn mirrors! LOL!

Suddenly, I remembered another famous religious quote. It also, supported our scientific reality beautifully: "All IS VANITY." I laughed again, but this time at my-"SELF"! Enough of "MY" problem. This is foolishness. You'd think my trials and tribulations of the past were "NEVER" going to end, but they end in the worst way possible. My brother dies and it about breaks me! No it does break, me. I am a broken man without him! I will never be the same, but I will go on for my children, his children, and for all children!

I gathered myself, as I thought about what I was getting ready to write. My "INNOCENT" arrogance, disgusted me. Finally, "I'm LEARNING" there were many arrogant humans before me and there will be many, after me. Please, Let's solve "OUR MYSTERY" with humility. Help me if I am "WRONG". I don't like being ignorant! I don't know everything and I would like to—with your help of course!

While watching COSMOS, I discovered that Copernicus might have saved us from the ignorance of a flat earth, but it was Giovanni Bruno who opened the door for my "INFINITE ASTRONAUT THEORY", to be taken seriously. "IF" it becomes successful, he truly deserves the right to be called the father of it and not me. Even though, he wasn't the "FIRST" to present this "POSSIBILITY,". YESHUA/"JESUS" did and their were many before him. Bruno was the first to be considered a "SCIENTIST," and like Yeshua, gave his life for it. I pale in comparison to both!

Bruno was killed because he saw no "EVIDENCE OF AN OMNIPOTENT- OMNISCIENT-OMNIPRESENT GOD IN THE UNIVERSE, that created "IT." To him, a perfect god wouldn't create an imperfect universe. He saw a "CHAOTIC INFINITE UNIVERSE", that "GIVES" life "INFINITELY" by natural processes, without thought! I was overjoyed when I finished watching the show. His conclusion was exactly the same as mine. I hadn't felt this excited since my discovery of "JESUS"! I will use his "FALSE" name as it is the most recognizable. However, his real name has scientific importance. It is the most important "COINCIDENCE" in my "THEORY" of solving our mystery.

Even though I "BELIEVE" Jesus existed, I have a problem with his "OMNIPOTENCE" story. I do so because "THE WORLD ISN'T PERFECT", which is what we would have, if it existed. I've told both my sons, before I discounted it as a myth, I "OPENLY" examined and challenge the logic of it. Every "LEGEND" seems to have a "SEED" of truth, to it. I explained to them, that it "EXISTS", only if we "PROVE

IT DOES." We must look for the "SEED"! The atom can't be created or destroyed. Let's start there. Because it defies any god or any thing creating the universe. It is made of atoms!

One fact is clear by consensus and history. "JESUS IS THE MOST FAMOUS PERSON IN THE WORLD"! I think it's because, "HE IS A SCIENTIST" and knows everything about the universe we live in! I explained his view of the universe, from the mustard seed parable. I thought it would make more sense, in lieu of this "METEOR"!

At the end of his comparison, the point is to escape death by living "UP" in the air and escaping death, from predators on the ground! I also like the evolutionary aspect of it being the "SMALLEST SEED" and becoming a safe haven for heaven. I see the similarities to it and the "ADAM/ATOM"!

I think I've finally figured out how to reconcile religion and science. I discovered that in the beginning they were "ONE" and the same. Let's make religion and science, that way again. Then, we'd stop confusing them. History is already written. "HIS-STORY" just needs editing! Let's finally, "MAKE HEAVEN, SPACE, AND HELL, MATTER," please? (accidental pun, but so right on!)

I keep re-examining these stories constantly and still do. I love history. The facts I discovered astound me! I found everything, from an ancient clay tablet, that shows our solar system in its exact order, distance, and size to brain trepanation! This is "BRAIN SURGERY", people! Both of these artifacts date to around 10,000 years ago! Wow! WOW! WOW!

Come on, everybody! Please give this evidence a chance? I've been doing this, too long, now! What do we have to do to "CONVINCE" someone, that "THIS COULD BE REAL"? Do we have to dig up a jet plane in a 50 million year old strata of rock? What's it going to take to prove, that "PEOPLE" have actually conquered space, before us? Evidence of "NUCLEAR WAR"? Wow! I suddenly realized, that we have just this possibility in "IRELAND" and other places, around the globe.

We have ancient forts with vitrified exterior rock walls, everywhere. This can only happen, with the heat of a nuclear blast or... a "METEOR" impact! OMG! I've got to stop "PREACHING" and get this book done, "NOW"!

    I finally give up, after my brother dies and my last book failed. Hell, I admit that I'm "NOT READY" for religion's "ENLIGHTENMENT," nor contact, with these "UGLY ASS ALIENS." I'd just, give anything to have "TERRY" back and get on with my life. I hope everyone "SEES", that our only chance for survival is to make this "METEOR PREVENTION" happen. We have to start building space stations "NOW"! We can "DISCUSS" religion and science later. Because, of this "METEOR EVENT" we must start "NOW." It's that simple.

    We have to break the "UNFORGIVING" vicious cycle, of "A PLANET'S BIRTH, DEATH, AND REINCARNATION"! It is "INFINITELY" happening and it will not stop. We must rewrite religion's spirit teachings with science. We have to do it for the sake of our children and the human existence.

    We have to overcome our "PRIDE and EGO'S"! Otherwise, having this much intelligence and not achieving "ARTIFICIAL IMMORTALITY", would be a sick joke. I'm not the only one to feel this way. Check out Neil DeGrasse Tyson's quote on the back cover. The joke would be on "US." Why can't we "ALL" see, that religion's enlightenment mirrors our future scientific reality. It paints a clear picture of the human condition and our weakness of "VANITY/ PRIDE"! Will we give, all that we have, to stop "METEORS"? I sure hope so. We have another one coming, in 2029! I will give all I have for this purpose.

    Let's stop torturing ourselves, worrying about dying? Let's start living! We know how! We must deal with it, like scientists. I have to get the ball rolling or find these people "UP" in the sky. They've already done it. My children don't want to die and neither do I!

    We can do this! I think I "KNOW" how and as you've read, others do too! The meteors will not stop. "SPACE IS THE FINAL FRONTIER" and it is "UP" within our reach today!! I will "NEVER" quit "LIVING" for this purpose. Look at how far we've come in the last 50 years.

Now, just think about, where will we be in the next 50 years! I can see us not only doing this, but building brains, bodies, and even achieving immortality itself. "CREATION" is now a scientific reality. History says it was before as well! Please consider this possibility? How advanced do you think life "COULD BE" in an infinite universe? Think about it and I promise, that you will see it as a "SILLY" question. It's obvious that is an "INFINITE WORLD/UNIVERSE" we can know everything, because there's no end.

I theorize, that religion's story is a simple guideline, for the eventual achievement of artificial immortality, through the evolution of intelligence! First you must "LOOK" for it. It simply describes the evolutionary "EVENTUALITY" of "LIFE" conquering "MATTER"! It's a story of people living "UP" in the sky. Like evolution, without help we must "RE-TURN" to space and avoid matter. We must go "UP" and live in space and we must never stop multiplying either. We must do this for the sake of "EXISTENCE"! Space may have given us life, but we can stop it from taking it back. We have to stay away from "MATTER"! We have to live "IN IT" and not "ON IT"!

I won't continue to repeat myself. "WE MUST FIRST KNOW THAT WE CAME FROM SOMETHING INFINITE TO KNOW THAT WE CAN BE INFINITE." Even though, I don't think we can make the universe "PERFECT". I think, that we can make "AN ARTIFICIAL PERFECT WORLD ON EARTHLIKE SPACE STATIONS"!

Discovering our intellectual capacities and "NURTURING" it, is what will give us the tools, to do so. It could even give us the "CHANCE" to escape the very "DEATH" of "our- SELFS"! Enough of my "PAST." It's time to get on with the "PRESENT"!

I was amazed, when I finally realized the simple scientific value of "THE MUSTARD SEED PARABLE by "JESUS"/YESHUA. Don't feel bad, if you still don't understand it, either. It "ONLY" took me, 33 years! LOL! So don't give up, it can make scientific sense to you. Yeshua was a "SCIENCE TEACHER AND NOT A PREACHER"! I made a video on YouTube to share my epiphany and titled it: EVOLUTION OF AN INTELLIGENT BEING. I hope you check it out!

This book is now about "IMMORTALITY AND RESURRECTION"! I want Terry and everyone else back! Without help, it is only possible, if we make it happen. I can pray for an angel, god or gods, and aliens all I want, but I don't think it will matter. They won't show up. I'll get down on my knees and will do so now.

Nope! Nothing happened. Since it didn't I have to make something happen. "I MUST GIVE EVERYTHING I HAVE TO STOP METEORS"! This reminds me of another parable by "JESUS"! It's about a man in his burning house, that Jesus told to get out. He wouldn't because he never wanted anything more, than his house! Like houses, earths burn up, too! He focused on material possessions over life.

Please stay focused, on this "METEOR"? Science says it is possible, to stop them. Granted, it "MAY" not happen immediately, But, we can do this. I have to for my sons sake! I just "HOPE," I can get "EVERYONE," to "GIVE", also.

I want to "THANK," Yeshua, Bruno, Copernicus, and Galileo who "CREATED" the telescope. Not to mention, Democritus, Mechanicus, Socrates, Aristotle, and Terry! With their discoveries, we saw the "TRUTH", about our solar system and never turned back. I can only hope for the same outcome, with this book! No one can stop scientific progress, once it starts spreading! Even the bible says this! These men paved the way and now, we can "ACTUALLY SEE" the big picture of the universe isn't so complicated. It's actually very simple. It's as simple as making space black and matter white! It is as simple as black and white, yes or no.

When it comes down to it, don't we all want "INFINITE" life? It truly is a simple "BLACK AND WHITE" issue if we do? The yin and yang is the a model of the universe, complete with black holes and white holes! We have to get back to the "BLACK" of space and out of the "WHITE" red hot hells of earths, if we want to survive! Trying is the "KEY"! Achieving "IMMORTALITY" as a species is hard—dying is easy. Sadly I know! I've suffered two suicides in my family. They took the easy way out and left us, with the hard questions, only they could answer. Now because they're gone, life is "HARDER"!

I don't want to give away, anymore tidbits and morsels of information. I would just like to ask you one favor, before you continue. Maybe it will give you hope that "ADVANCED ET LIFE INFINITELY", exists. Imagine life evolving in an infinite universe and then ask yourself one question: "AGAIN, HOW ADVANCED WOULD IT BE? I hope light bulbs, just went off everywhere! If not keep trying. "TRYING" is all that matters, in the end. It will happen, logic dictates it, "IN AN INFINITE WORLD/UNIVERSE"! But, Vice versa, "IT DEFINITELY WON'T IF YOU DON'T"! You'll never find anything if you aren't looking.

If I could be granted only one wish, naturally "I WOULD WANT THE WORLD TO BE PERFECT", what "KIND" of person wouldn't? Since it isn't and I know wishes can't make it so. My wish, would be, that all children bet to learn the most important scientific "KNOWLEDGE", in existence. "SPACE IS THE FINAL FRONTIER" and "RELIGION"S HEAVEN IS SPACE... UP"! It is the only place, that we can achieve "IMMORTALITY"! I would tell them one last thing after they learn it: "DON'T FORGET" (again)!

So far, the universe "IS, WAS," and always "WILL BE INFINITE"— like the sky. We haven't found an end or beginning, to it. Ask children to look "UP." Then ask them where the end of it, is. Like children, I think we all "ALREADY" know the answer "INSTINCTIVELY." I like the answer I got when I did it, though. It not only humbled me, but it taught me a lot about life. When I asked my niece, she looked at me bewildered like and said "SILLY, THERE IS NO END TO IT. IT'S JUST AIR!"

She went on to say it was "NOTHING." I had to laugh to myself. Little did she realize how "DEEP" nothing really is. Her simple answer was beautiful!

Now, I understand "JESUS USING WIND" as a parable about "IMMORTALITY." It's a perfect simple example of what just happened. Children "NATURALLY" don't think there is an end to the sky. They will quickly learn, however, that it "BECOMES" wind, water, and ice. They will finally learn it is "SOMETHING," that creates "EVERYTHING"! "BAD GAS" LOL! My niece accidently passed it and busted out laughing! I did too! What a moment.

"TODAY" we know $E=mc^2$ says, that energy transforms, into matter! The wind is something, that even when it stops, "CAN'T STOP EXISTING"! It is "INFINITE." The most important thing they can learn is that "IN IT" we have an endless "CHANCE" to achieve "IMMORTALITY." If the universe is "INFINITE," then it is only logical that life is as well! The future is bright! So please wear "CHEAP" sunglasses. LOL!

I know this all may sound crazy, but religion's evidence says ETs exist! This book isn't about converting spirit believers, atheist, or anybody else. It's about my "DISCOVERY" helping us avoid another "METEOR EVENT." Lucky for me, they just so happen to be one and the same! However, the "METEOR PROBLEM" is the "MOST IMPORTANT!

If you can just think "INFINITELY" and imagine, that our creators are real flesh and blood people with limitations just like us. Then, it's easy to rationalize, that they didn't make the universe and they can't make it perfect either. The universe isn't perfect and in the words of Giovanni Bruno it's creation wouldn't be either.

Please everyone, imagine 100 years or 1,000 years, into the future and I promise you one thing—"SCIENTIFIC CREATION POSSIBILITIES" will seem more of a certainty, than crazy. If you don't think so, just "LOOK" back 100 years and ask yourselves: "Would they have thought, all that we've accomplished was "POSSIBLE", then? Research

Robert Goddard, the father of rocket science, and I think you will be surprised with the answer. I know I was! "HIS- STORY" is a great teacher only if we don't "REPEAT" it. Like the other great thinkers of their time, he was ridiculed for making rockets and saying we're going to the moon in his lifetime! We did go into space, while he was live!

Enough of my "ET/GODS THEORY." First things first. We "NEED" to do something, about the "METEOR PROBLEM." It is the single most important "LIFE THREATENING" problem we are facing today. Again, we have one coming in 2029! It could possibly take us out! I will explain as I go.

We all know the biblical quote: MONEY IS THE ROOT OF ALL EVIL." We also know the "AGE OLD" question: "What's it going to take to solve the problem?" "CLEARLY THE METEOR IS OUR PROBLEM." So here's the "UNIVERSALLY" famous answer to solve it—"ALL IT TAKES IS MONEY"!

This quote really puts our current dilemma in perspective and provides a riveting "REALITY", to my "STORIES ENDING." Will we value money, more than we do our lives? Will we give, "ALL THAT WE HAVE" to prevent this meteor, from possibly causing our extinction? I "HOPE" so! Hope, is all I have.

Please enjoy the rest of my "STORY"! Terry and I are about to try and solve this problem! I put the "PACT" we made, to give away all our money and challenge everybody else to do the same, in my last book. Unfortunately, as you know by now, he didn't get to see it. I'm sad he died, but I'm glad he didn't get to see the trouble it would cause. It would tear our family apart. What is about to happen, was sad!

I release my seventh book and it has explicit nudity on the front cover. My "RELIGIOUS" family called the law on me and tried to get it removed from "THE BILLBOARD"! This took place, almost immediately, after his death on September 22nd 2012. My brother will soon be killed and all "HELL" is about, to break loose! Hold on!

It is the fall of 2011 and I had just finished my billboard. By the following summer, I shock everyone, except for Terry, and advertised FLYING SAUCER PROOF! Jeff Willes, a UFO hunter out of Phoenix, Arizona shot footage, that will be seen all over the world! Walt Disney bought eight seconds, for the beginning of Return To Witch Mountain. Terry and I were on fire, over it! His saucer looked, just like one with Johnny Cash, in a picture taken by Marty Stuart. It also looked just like mine, over the bilboard! Yes, I got to show my brother, while we're building it! The local paper aired my story. (see illustrations)

We were finding "FLYING SAUCERS! Then, tragedy struck. Terry got hit by a train and killed. I became a torture to my family and religious people, everywhere! I am ending here, for now. I will pick back up, in the next chapter, with my "DEDICATION TO TERRY AND VICKI"! You are about to hear their heartbreaking story. P.S. Thanks for all your help, Vick! Terry loved you so much! I do too! You were a good wife to my brother.

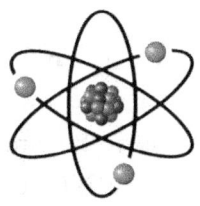 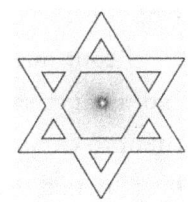

CHAPTER 2
THE PRESENT

The Present
"HELL, ALL OVER AGAIN"

December 31st, 2013. It is my brother Terry's birthday. My heart is broken. I am struggling to tweak this manuscript and wrestling with a new book cover idea. I've been writing, non- stop since, the meteor hit February 15th! I wanted to finish it and release it in his honor. I was a couple months late on the last one, for him. Suddenly, I have a "FLASH-BACK"!

Instantaneously, all the horrible memories of my brother's tragic death and the recent Russian "METEOR EVENT" of FEBRUARY 15 TH, 2013, came flooding back. I became even more distraught and sad, as I continued to write.

Unfortunately, my past was filled with an "ENDLESS" world of trouble and heartaches. I thought, they were all, but forgotten. Until now, "DAMN" these memories. I wrote about "ALL THIS HELL", in my previous books. I want to end it, with this one.

All the nightmares, from my past started playing over and over again, in my head. They gave me, no mercy! I offended and hurt so many people, during my "QUEST FOR LIFE'S ANSWER'S." The memories viciously invaded and tortured my mind! They attacked and raped my mind, with such a "HELLISH" vengeance, that I begged for them to stop. I Need "PEACE"!

I continue to struggle. I want to solve "MANKIND'S MYSTERY"! No, I must solve "IT" for my sons. I don't want to die, nor do I want them to die. I am afraid of "DEATH" and they are too! It is nothing to be ashamed of! Terry and I were going to "GIVE EVERYTHING" to stop it. I will carry his torch and go on. I hope I can, make our family, "WHOLE" again.

This meteor event has created another dilemma, for me. I want to complete this book today and yet get it "RIGHT" at the same time. But I can't. I can't rush this book. Obviously, I have a personal reason to finish it today, but I can't rush this book and get it right, too. This "METEOR" has instilled in me, an overwhelming sense of urgency and fragileness to my life. "NOW", I know I can die at any moment! So, I have to get this one, right. It could be my last and I know, that I'll need several more days to finish it. LOL! It would take me two more years to complete. LOL! Laughing at myself!

Nope, as badly as I want to do this for him, it ain't happening today. Even, if a meteor can take me out! I have to get it right, for my brother, this time. The reason is coming up and it is heartbreaking. It does help me, regain my focus, though. Terry's death was a wake-up call.

I tried to think about my new cover again and couldn't. I can't even forget, that this "METEOR" could happen again, at anytime. They can take us out, "NOW"! Wow! What a reality check. This is my "NEW WAKE-UP CALL" and the time to write about it, is definitely, "NOW"!

I must "NEVER FORGET" this "METEOR PROBLEM" for my children's sake and I must teach them to do the same. It is the reason for this book's urgency. The world hasn't achieved the ability to stop them and we haven't conquered space, "YET!"

This must become everyone's first priority, just like it was for the ancients, if we are to survive, as a species. My theory made more sense than ever to me. I finally saw a solution to my lack of success. Thanks Terry. My "SMOKING GUNS"! I got another one! Read on.

I could see a lack of scientific thinking among the religious population and it was mind wrenching. I wanted them to search and find out where their "GOD" came from. I guess I'm still either, a hopeless romantic or a glutton for punishment. Regardless of my motive. This "METEOR" was my ticket. It made my answer simple.

I stopped all my horrible memories, as best, as I could, and continued to write. I had to resolve this book cover dilemma and finish "REVEALING" my "DISCOVERY"!

I didn't need any more problems like, changing a front cover shot to go with it. I couldn't ignore, the lack of impact the old one had, though. I made it a day or two after the meteor. I had to fix it. I set out to design a new one!

The books covers should say everything, in an instant! If I have to explain what "I" think it should say, I've failed. The front cover "IMAGE/PICTURE" and title has to be simple. I want "ALL" children to "GET IT"! I'm hoping, that they have a eureka moment and "UNDERSTAND" the "MESSAGE", from just looking at "IT."

One thing is perfectly clear to me now. I need to learn more about meteors! I'm really pretty ignorant of them, myself. "BELIEVE ME," I've been learning about them, ever since the meteor event happened.

My latest discovery about them is staggering! The Muslims worship a "METEOR", they say was sent by God! Wow. Coincidence? "HE" not only sent it, but commands them to use it, as a cornerstone for their first church!

It seemed, as if "GOD", was going to make sure "THIS/HIS" point got across, "FOREVER"! Wow, just like me and Neil DeGrasse Tyson (see back cover)! It still exists today and is undoubtedly the most sacred pilgrimage muslims, can make. So, I put it on the front cover! This was too good, to be true. I don't mean to be offensive, by it. I just want to get my point across. Meteors are our biggest threat!

I just want everyone, to reconsider this evidence's significance, for the sake of scientific discovery! All religions see "METEORS" as sacred! Coincidence? More on this later.

I'd like to take a moment and admit that I'm still learning, about them. So, if you want to get a clear picture of how I "FOUND MY DISCOVERY," please read my other books. I need to get on, with this one. I'm a "WORK-IN-PROGRESS" and I'm working, as fast as, I can. "SHIT!," I suddenly shouted out loud. I continue to talk to myself. "This book ain't gonna happen today. You're right about one thing, Terry: "SAME SHIT, DIFFERENT DAY"! Sorry Brother! I can't talk anymore. I got to get this thing done!"

Like my brother always said, "SHIT" happens and sadly enough people and kids die! Luckily, no one died from this meteor event. Although, a lot got hurt! Terry was eerily morose and prophetic, at times. He didn't say. he was a prophet, but he was usually right about things. Unfortunately, they kids do die. Even, from suicide. "TWO" many (read on)! Sadly, way too many have left me, besides Terry and my heart is broken.

My last book was dedicated to Terry, "FOR A REASON." Please bear with me, as I share his heartbreaking "ROLE" in it. He didn't get to see the dedication, that I wrote for him three years ago. Why? Because, that book, like this one, was not finished before tragedy struck. I was trying to rush it, also. I wanted to edit it "TOGETHER" and... uh, uh. I need a moment. I love and miss you Terry! I broke down.

I rushed my last book after he was killed! Tragically, my brother was killed, but not before his accident and life was made, into a movie! He had a short run of fame and even wrote a book, for the sequel. I'm so thankful and happy, for him. He deserved all the recognition and more! I am very fortunate and grateful, to have shared it, with him! I am truly "LUCKY," for "TERRY BRUMFIELD"!

Fortunately, I watched my "OLDEST" brother, experience a tidal wave of love, from so many animal loving "FANS." It was like, something right out of a movie, itself. It made great material for his book! I shared his excitement about it and vow to make it happen. He didn't get, too. I may not write another one, but "HE" will! I am a publisher and I will make it happen.

Terry touched everyone who saw the film and his story. You'll see why, if you watch it. If you do, I promise you won't regret it. It will move you to tears! So please get ready to shed some and go rent it. It's called: THE ELEPHANT IN THE LIVING ROOM.

We were all touched by Terry's genuine warmth and the infectious love, he showed his lions! Yes, that's what the movie is about and it doesn't take long, to get caught up in this struggle, with him. Who hasn't loved an animal, at one point or another? I still remember our first family dog, snowball, like it was "YESTERDAY." Man, this is choking me up. Terry sure loved his dog, "LITTLE JAKE", too. His death gave birth to Lambert the Lion. He plays such a "BIG" part in it!

I am putting his dedication, and several others, in the middle of this book. I'm not waiting, till the end. I didn't put it at the beginning, because I want to keep the focus on... "THE METEOR EVENT." Terry would want me too! It's far more important, than our story. We know why and hope you will, as well. If an "EXTINCTION METEOR" hit 100 years ago, we wouldn't matter, anyway. None of us would! This is why it is important. Yes, in case you're wondering the dedications are done! As you can see, I done them first! Funny, how it all works out. His birthday is today and I'm almost done! Woo hoo!

"DEDICATIONS—I AM RELEASING THIS BOOK ON MY BROTHER TERRY'S BIRTHDAY. DECEMBER 31st, 2013, LOVE AND MISS YOU BUD"! I want to begin my dedications, with a special mention, to my brother Terry! I am doing this, because he plays such a big part in my life today, as well as, in the past. Finally when all is said and done, family is everything. I certainly know how important they are to my future. I sure miss Terry and would give "ANYTHING" to have him back!

Sharing this dedication, now gives you something, we all can relate to, the end. It is what makes my story, come alive with reckless abandonment, raw emotion and unconditional love! We all came from a family and we all will end one. If you're lucky and still have a family, write about it. You'll never regret it. So with that said, let me get started. Don't ever look a "GIFT HORSE" in the mouth, again and not take advantage, of it. I certainly won't and am very "FORTUNATE" to "SEE" it. I am alive! I hope to give this same gift to everyone that reads my book. First on the bucket list, letter to my sons and family!

I want to thank you sons and my entire family, for all our precious memories. You helped make me what I am today and I am forever thankful, for it. I treasure you all.

"WHEN YOUR DYING," "FAMILY" really is all that matters. As hard as it is, to admit to myself, it's even harder to say. "Unfortunately, EVERYONE, I'M DYING." We're all dying. I will try and make this short and sweet. I will tell you now, I let my heart out, to my family, in doing so. I have a lot of regrets, so please bear with me, for my family's sake. I want to repair the damage, if I can. I could die today. It happens every day. I don't want to waste another minute, that will become another regret. I'm very "FORTUNATE" to have this opportunity. I will not waste it. It is, number one on my bucket list.

I finally realized the importance of the old saying: "Don't put off today what you can do tomorrow. Tomorrow may never come. You never know, this could be my last chance to write my boys a final letter about life and death. How precious that time is. This meteor woke me "UP", about my time, "DOWN HERE ON EARTH FOR GAIN." I won't take it for granted. Thanks also, to my lifelong friends. They are truly, also "MY" family.

Before I go any further, I want to add a special tribute, to "OUR" Granny. I will do this, after I share some precious memories, in honor of my brother Terry. You will understand why, as it helps to paint a simple picture of how I got to here. His love, help, and support carried me through the worst of times. Even, his death. I MISS HIM GREATLY! I'm sure we all do.

Like I said earlier, he "WAS" the only one in my family who "IS" excited about my theory and evidence. I'm sure he "WILL BE", when we "MEET AGAIN"! This is not to say, that the rest of them aren't. They are all happy for me and wish me huge success, with my books. They just don't agree with my evidence... not even my youngest son, Matthew.

This tears at me, but I think I finally found my cure. I told him, that I needed to leave my "THEORY", about our origins out of this meteor evidence equation. He agreed and confirmed his disgust toward it. Especially, my sexual observations, about us human's and how it relates to us possibly being ugly aliens addicted to beauty of the flesh. He does this, in spite of, not wanting to be ugly and daily, seeing television epitomize our sexual fact of life. I "UNDERSTAND" why he doesn't like or agree with it. It involves his mother and I just can't cure it.

However, he does at least commend me, for wanting to cure the world's ignorance and complacency, toward the meteor event. He sees our need to live in space and knows it is up to us to do something, about it. He does nothing. He also knows, I am giving all my money to start building space stations and bluntly wishes me good luck, in doing so. It's going to be an uphill battle according to him and he's right. I can't cure it, if everybody doesn't help. I told him that. The evidence can't do it, either if people don't look. That's up to them. Everyone has to look for the answer, themselves. Wanting to, is the problem. It's a problem for, all of us. Nobody likes hard work. But, that's what it will take. I love my son and we're working on our relationship. He owns his lack of interest, at least.

My oldest son sees my theory and loves it. He is ravaged by jealousy and admits it. He doesn't want to be ugly, either. My theory makes perfect sense to him, Déjà vu and all! Hell, he even admits to wanting to come back, if possible. He said, that he'd rather take his chance with humans, again any day, than be an ugly ass alien! He said the marriage thing bothered him the most and he wasn't sharing his wife, with anyone. I laughed at his honesty and loved it at the same time!

I have to admit my struggles with wanting the same. Matt has issues with admitting it, too. I told him, that I know truth. None of us, are ready to live in a world, where we can't hide our thoughts and have to share our partners. I told him, that mankind's worst fear is the ability to read each other's minds. He, at least agreed, with that. I finally asked him if he thought more advanced ETs, exist. He said yes, I then asked him one more question. Does he really want to chance thinking they do and think, that they can't read our minds. He looked bewildered and mad at the same time. Logic tortured him too! He knows it is foolish to defend foolishness. This is logic in an "INFINITE" universe. It exists. He knows he should do something, about it.

My wife suddenly asked me, if I believe I will see, Terry again. I told her that I "BELIEVE" I will and what he looks like won't matter. I'll know his mind. She wanted to know what I think Terry will be "IF I DIDN'T BELIEVE IN SPIRTS." I asked her "WHAT WOULD HE BE, OR LOOK LIKE, IF HE IS A SPIRIT." She didn't know and naturally said, "PROBABLY" a ghost. I asked her what they are and how they live. She didn't know. I told her "KNOWLEDGE" is the key to finding the answer. It isn't given to you, though. "YOU HAVE TO FIND IT"! I can't believe she still doesn't know what I believe.

Now, back to Terry. It's his dedication. He saw, that these universal stories of people living "UP" in the sky, matches our flesh and blood reality today. It didn't support a "SPIRIT REALITY." The stories "MATCHES OURS!" We both saw that primitive man universally possessed a scientific and futuristic knowledge that we are yet to see in space exploration today. Primitive man saw this, tens of thousands of years before we reached space. We haven't "CONQUERED" or become omnipresent in space. This was mindboggling to us. How could this be?

There was only one logical answer. It "PROVED TO US", that "INFINITELY" advanced, real flesh and blood people, live "UP" in space.

They obviously do, just "LIKE US" in the space station. He agreed with my premise, that the likelihood of having our "His-story", would be next to impossible, if they didn't exist. And people, "THIS IS WHAT WE SHOULD EXPECT" if they do.

This cemented their existence, in our minds. But, we realized quickly, that other people might not see this, like we did. To us, "HEAVEN/SPACE" is a clear and simple objective, for every human wanting immortality. We have to first get off this planet. They command us to find them and they live "UP IN HEAVEN." We were blown away by this evidence. I'm still blown away. Why doesn't everyone see this and how it could solve the "SPIRIT MYSTERY"? We saw why.

Even though most of our family "DIDN'T BELIEVE IN ALIENS," Terry and I "KNOW" they exist. We know because we saw their space craft and followed the matching evidence. They are everywhere throughout ancient history! We saw that these craft haven't changed in 10,000 years. This was clear "EVIDENCE" of omnipotence in space! They aren't making new models. Religion is a story of omnipotence. We got it! We saw this as proof of infinite knowledge. "THE GOD STORY SAYS THEIR INFINITE, OMNIPRESENT, OMNIPOTENT, AND OMNISCIENT! This was big to us.

This "ALL HAPPENED" about six years ago, after my sixth book titled, *The Discovery*.

We saw how these stories could solve our mysteries and answer all our questions, about the universe we live "IN." The infinite nature of "ITALONE", solved it. Space "MUST" be conquered, according to this evidence!

Most, importantly it explains a simple scientific logic, about "HEAVEN'S PERFECT WORLD STORY." If it exists, it would exist now, plain and simple. Stephen Hawking uses this to prove nothingness is impossible. If the world came from nothing, nothing would exist now. If nothing is in our mind, "ANYONE", can accept this possibility. Terry and I were thinking nothing. We never believed the spirit teachings. We loved science!

We we're blown away, by everything we were finding. This mystery boiled down to "WHAT THEY LOOK LIKE", pure and simple!

I don't ever want to argue about this again. It's crazy! The "ANCIENT EVIDENCE TOLD US WHAT THEY LOOKED LIKE." Terry and I were the only ones, to ever search together. We quickly and painfully saw, that the world was entrenched in spirit traditions. We didn't see logic in spirits. We challenged "SPIRIT" omnipotence and searched, for what they look like. To us, since they aren't here, this is the only question to be answered.

We searched and it wasn't pretty—if you base it on "OUTWARD" appearances. But if you're deformed, or downright ugly, it "PROBABLY" isn't very scary after all! It's just life! "OUTWARD DISABILITIES" can change one's outlook, on life. Especially, when you never had it and "SUDDENLY", get it. Even, if this doesn't happen to you, realize it could. Of course this depends on the person. Even, if we're not disabled, we can't escape the "EVIDENCE/ TRUTH." We all know the "TRUTH ABOUT MANKIND." Pretty rules the world. We're all addicted to it. Even, the "UGLY ONES." Even, the blind.

I had to laugh again. I laughed, because early on, in my search for spirits and heaven, before "DESTINY", brought Terry and I together. I discovered that religion's simple message was to reject the desires of the flesh and money. The simple message was "INNER" wisdom and knowledge. It wasn't just religion, that taught us this, it was also our parents, society, and TV. Hell, the whole world teaches this SIMPLE TRUTH." "WE ALL KNOW" that "IT'S WHAT'S ON THE INSIDE THAT COUNTS."

I shared all this evidence and its implications with Terry. Looking back, I now know why. I know how, our connection happened. It was because, we both suffered so viciously at the hands of our "BEAUTIFUL SEXUALLY ADDICTED WIVES", when they fell out of love with us and in love with themselves. They're "POWERFUL" sex addictions made our lives "HELL." Worse yet, our children suffered the most! Our hearts were broken.

We wanted so badly to make the world perfect, for our kids. We shared horrible nightmares of shame and guilt. They saw our angry and viciously scary monstrous looking face, way too many times, as we argued with their moms. We are so deeply sorry. It will always be our greatest regret. Every time we talked about it, we cried and just wanted to forget. But, as we all know, unfortunately "NO ONE FORGETS"! We learned to go on.

Terry and I begged our wives, but we "COULDN'T CHANGE THEM." We both tried everything we knew, but nothing worked. They didn't care. They were "LETHAL" and "SICK"! We learned "THE GOLDEN RULE", the hard way. They asked to be forgiven and we them. We begged for forgiveness, from them and our kids. But, we both moved on. mine is happening as I type.

Terry and I both saw firsthand, that "Beauty is "POWER" and highly addictive. Terry and I never gave up. Neither am I. I hope you enjoy my story. It really is, "OUR" story. Terry, I will always admire your honesty and cherish our memories. You're the "BEST" big brother, a little brother, could ask for. You always made me feel, so loved! I love you and thanks. "GOOD LUCK" everybody in solving "THE MYSTERY OF MANKIND."

Please be careful, as you are about to "SEE," the hope of heaven can become a living hell for "ANY FAMILY"! You can tell, by now, it did for me. Please enjoy my story and remember, what I said, in the Preface. The "CAPITALIZED WORDS," "PHRASES IN QUOTATIONS," and parenthesis are CLUES! These words and phrases have a deep and personal meaning, to us all!

Now, I want to end by, by saying one more thing to my precious sons. You didn't ask to be brought into a "WORLD" of such cruel uncertainty and death. None of us did. All children are innocent. I am sorry, that I didn't think about this. I will spend the rest of my life trying to make up, for it. You are my greatest treasure. I will always be your loving father who yearns deeply to make the world perfect, but I can't. I didn't know the world then, "LIKE I KNOW IT NOW."

I am desperately trying to cure death. It is my number one goal. This is my life's work. It contains "MY" answers to life's biggest and most important questions. Always challenge them and please judge the evidence, for yourself. Remember the evidence doesn't lie, but man does! Let the evidence speak for itself and always check your personal bias at the door. We all "NATURALLY" possess "MANKIND'S POWER DISEASE." It's also called "PRIDE AND PERSONAL BIAS"!

I want to say, that indeed sons, you are my "GREATEST" treasure! I do have to add my Dad, Mom, brothers, sisters, aunts, uncles, cousins, friends, animals, birds, fish, and plants, as a treasure too. Heck, all life for that matter and everything in it. I can only hope you feel this way, too. Whether, it be life, nature, or whatever else it is, that makes up this unbelievably wonderful "WORLD" of endless color and boundless beauty, we live in. I hope you see it as I do, an overwhelmingly beautiful universe! It and our amazing mind humbles me. Sons, I am so thankful, for you.

Kudos out to my Dad, for going the extra mile to show us, as much of the earth, as he could. I am lucky, for it. I miss you so much Dad. Thank you, I love you so much! I hope this touches your heart, as much as, it does mine. I am crying tears of joy, for the love you gave me! I am also crying tears of regret, for the pain I caused you. I am so sorry! I had to take a break and go outside for a minute. I needed to hold it together. It was almost midnight.

How I love to look "UP" and stare at a clear brightly moonlit night sky and just wonder. I am mesmerized by the beauty, of space! The "UNIVERSE" really is "MAGICAL"! It never fails to heighten my sense of respect and awe, for all life. Most of all, it fills me with a million questions, as if it's begging me to ask: "WHY ARE WE ALONE?" I always want to ask questions. I hope I will always marvel at the wonder of life. I hope that you do the same, my precious sons! Let's never stop asking questions. I love you. I'm sorry for causing you so much pain. You have given me, so much "HAPPINESS." You are my "HAPPINESS"!

Unfortunately sons, I have to talk to you about death. This meteor event demands it. My magical outlook toward life, "REALLY" depends upon one thing: "IF ALL IS GOOD IN MY LIFE"? All is not good in my life, nor anyone else's, whether we think so or not. This meteor can take us all out. We are grown men now. It is time to act.

I am "LUCKY", that you boys are still alive! I'm also unlucky though. My brother recently lost, his "IRREPLACEABLE" son! My sweet precious little nephew, "Dan the Man," was killed in a terrible accident. "I WILL FOREVER HURT" because of it. I would give anything to have him back!

There is no reasoning for this. I know it isn't bad luck though, either. That's the same as, a reason. We just call it that. It's a freak tragic accident. I guess, people just say this out of respect and "TRADITION," but I know what people mean, when they say it. I don't believe in luck because of the evidence and lack of science behind it. I am studying to be a scientist and I am still reeling, with his loss. With all due respect to my brother and sister-in-law, who are "BELIEVERS," in my opinion EARTH is "HELL." Nothing, but a sheer product of infinite odds! Anything else is cruel, just like the cold harsh universe, we live in. If I could stop it I would. I'm sure you would, too. We can't. I wished more than anything that we could! But, logic won't let me "BELIEVE IT'S POSSIBLE"! Kids are dying everywhere, in automobile accidents, as we speak. Logically, we have to accept this hard fact of life, as tragic as it is.

Boys, science, reality, and my brother Terry, holds me to this logic. I can't shake it, even in times like these. Our Dad hammered common sense and logic into our heads growing up. My brothers would always remind me about Dad's wishing and shit advice?

"Remember what Dad always said," they'd say. "You can close your eyes, wish in one hand, and shit in the other, all you want. But, when you open your eyes you will see the cold hard "REALITY" of "LIFE." "SHIT HAPPENS"! The irony is, that he prayed! I sure understood it, when Danny was killed. This was torturous evidence, that no one can make the world perfect. In life, shit happens not wishes. Nobody said a thing, when Danny died. We couldn't. We just cried. We all wished, that we could've given our life for Danny's, but we couldn't. No one can.

Terry told me, time and time again, that I had to let go of the pain. I tried, but I couldn't. My "THEORY" became my obsession and your nightmare sons. I'm sorry for that, but I think I've found a way to see him, Dad, Terry, and all of them again!

Unfortunately, shit kept happening! Terry was killed two years ago, in a freak train collision. He made it clear to me and his wife, that he didn't want to hear any religious talk, when Danny died. If there was a god, he didn't want anything to do with him. I felt his pain. We all did. His reason was clear. Pain, suffering, and unstoppable death had to be answered with logic and not wishes.

Prayers were just glorified wishes to him. He wasn't rude about it. He was just angry and hurt. I saw tears well up in his eyes and I felt his pain, when Danny died. Now, I broken again! Thank God, for everyone else. My heart goes out Steven and Mary. It makes me cherish them even more!

Terry's motto was: "Shit's always happening, like it just did. Same shit, different day!" I vivdly remember him saying this, as we talked about Danny's death. I broke and cried with him. We both hugged "LIKE IT WAS OUR LAST." We let it all out, that day. Years and years of pain. We cried and cried.

Brian, Tim, Terry, and I talked many times, about the irony of Dad not understanding our skepticism toward, prayer. Especially, since it and wishing are the same thing. We didn't and don't blame Dad, for it. We all, "CLEARLY" saw the power of his religious upbringing. He didn't question his parents religion. He was just doing what he had to do, to comfort us, like any parent would. He died 10 years before Terry and several before Dan. Unfortunately, he would bury a son, that cmmitted suicide. It almost killed him. Let me tell you, he and Mom suffered terribly, then. Thank God, he didn't have to see Danny or Terry die.

My brother David, threatened to commit suicide, for about a month and then finally, did. It happened before Danny and Terry. They couldn't stop it. We all tried. No one could stop it. It was terrible. My Dad felt guilty, for a long time. He never got over it and died shortly thereafter, of a "HEART" attack. He told me just before he died, that it broke his heart. He was right. Mine is broke, too. Dave's daughter was the last to die. She committed suicide six months ago! Goddamn god!

My heart goes out to Mom. She has now seen three children and two grand-children die. We will never get over it, but we have to go on, for our children's sake.

I'm sorry sons, for being so angry at life and religion's omnipotent god story. I just don't want to hear words like: "Reason or it's meant to be. Let alone, God's will," when it comes to death anymore! I abruptly got up and looked at a picture of my whole family, hanging on the wall. Tears were streaming down my face.

"Dad," I spoke as I looked up at it, hardly able to contain myself. "We all have to finally grow up and accept the cold hard "TRUTH", don't we. If any of us could stop children from dying and make the world perfect, we would, wouldn't we? We can't and I can't either. You, Danny, David, Nancy Gail, Linda and Terry taught us that." I said as I bit my tongue and punched the air, until I was out of breath. I know I must have looked like a madman, but I didn't care. I was mad as hell. I cried for a couple of minutes, then calmed down. I took a break. I needed it. This was so hard. Who wants to live, without their loved ones!

I finally, got myself together. It ain't gonna get any better. None of us, have gotten over Danny and all the others. We never will. We're all worlds away, from our childhood innocence, now. We know life is fragile. Death is only a phone call, away. Terry was right, though. I do have to let go of the pain. I still fail. Sons, seeing my families children die, then and now, has forever changed me. "I CAN'T CHANGE THAT!" Those were, and still are, the toughest times of my life! "WHEN I RECALL THEM," I still struggle.

"DEATH" is the reason, I wrote this book. It is our current "REALITY"! However, I can't complain. My life's been "RELATIVELY" good so far. I still have you and the rest of my family! Sons, please try not to complain, about the bad times in your life and stay focused on the good. Remember, above all, that everybody makes mistakes. Everybody can be wrong. Look eagerly for answers and pursue new adventures, to their fullest. I hope you conquer each one. But, always know winning isn't "IMPORTANT"! Trying is the only thing, that matters. Don't ever give up and please think, before you talk. Then talk slowly and with pause. Most importantly, with empathy.

One last thing. Don't ever say to someone, "to be honest with you." "HONEST" people won't have anything, to do with you. Get it! You should always be honest! Finally, may you be, as "LUCKY" as I have been, in life. If either of you have a life half as full as mine, you will definitely be lucky! I am so loved! Thank you for everything. Family is everything!

I know I'm "LUCKY/BLESSED," but yet, I am sad. I've already seen, too much death. Sadly, I will see more. I'm sorry that I "HAVE" to talk to you about death, but I have to. As technology stands today, I will soon die. It is a "FACT," that I can't "IGNORE." My goal, is to "POSSIBLY SOLVE THE MYSTERY OF MANKIND AND CURE DEATH"!

But, I realistically know, the meteor problem is most important!

I remember vividly how my brother Brian constantly pleaded with me, to hide the horror of the world, from "YOU" kids. Well I've tried, but I can't. It's everywhere! I agree with him, that you didn't need to see it until you "SEE" it, but I always told him, respectfully. I cant' hide it, it's everywhere.

"Dad's gotta do what they gotta to do to cope with life. Just like Dad had to teach Shawna, about grandpa's "SEX DISEASE." I told him softly. "We have to prepare all children, not only for sexual predators, but death as well. We have to talk to them! Talk first, then teach them, to hope for the best and prepare for the worst." This was another of Dad's teaching's. We respected Dad for that. He always wanted the best for us!

Believe me sons, our Dad taught us well. We always knew, that things could be worse, for any of us and we tried to never take that for granted. I am grateful and know it "IS NOW FOR SOMEONE, SOMEWHERE," as I write. "I AM TRULY LUCKY TO HAVE HAD HIM AND MOM, TEACH ME THESE HUMBLE PRECIOUS VALUES." It gave me an advantage in life, that every child doesn't have. I'm forever thankful and will always give back! That's how we prove it, by not building wealth and always showing our gratitude, by giving!

So, I am now humbly and most appreciatively, passing this treasure, on to you. Please don't ever think life can't be worse, for you. Self-pity is a terrible self-inflicted disease. I vividly remember every talk, that he gave us, ending with his most famous quote: "Always remember this and it will make you a better person in life, Son." This is my legacy and it's yours.

He was right and I hope, that I lived up to his standards. I hope, that both of you do the same. Always look, for a way to make life better and you will surely be amazed, by the beauty of it, along the way.

Sons, I can't escape the horrible subject of death. Life is truly hard and seeing Dad pass was enough to make me, want to give up. I was only just beginning to show him thanks and how much I appreciated him, when he died. I didn't get anywhere near, what he deserved. I got some time in and that's all, that matters. I got lucky and woke up before, it was too late! My cups half-full, not half empty.

"FORTUNATELY," I still have you boys. Your love and the gratitude I realize, from it, keeps me grounded.

Unfortunately, my books and over-zealousness, have caused you and the rest of my family, a lot of pain. They still do and I'm sorry for that. But, "I SAW A FLYING SAUCER" and they aren't making new models. They are obviously, "OMNI-SCIENT" and have the cure, for death! Even worse, "I STILL SEE THEM AND THEY AREN'T GOING AWAY! THIS IS TORTUROUS"! I can't make people help me find them and I need help!

On one hand sons, it gives me a great hope of life after death. Which is the greatest gift a father could give his son. On the other hand, I can't do anything about it. I can't make "THEM" appear. You have to "LOOK" for them. When you find "THEM," they will epitomize the saying: "be careful of what you wish for." They don't stick around and not too many people, will believe you.

Sons, when I saw a flying saucer, it changed me. These craft haven't changed in thousands of years—maybe even "INFINITELY." "I CAN'T GET OVER THIS COLD HARD FACT"! I can't make anyone "SEE" what I see!

Sons, please forgive me and stop me anytime, when I talk about my "THEORY." I don't want to bother you. It is my albatross, my inescapable burden. It is what I wished for and now, can't make it come true. It is beautiful and frustrating, at the same time. Please have empathy for me. This could happen to you. Please, don't ever forget that? Please, for me?

I wasn't prepared for this, nor my families reaction and now I can't stop it. I have found evidence of E.T. omniscient life, that lives in space on non-changing craft. I can see the future of conquering disease and death, as not only possibility, but a "REALITY." This "EVIDENCE SAYS," it already happened. Bill Gates is dedicating billions of dollars, to cure disease. I am giving, all that I have, to cure death. Religion says it has been done and science says it can be done. These saucers are all the proof I need! I have to find them.

Sons, finally I would like to say one last time, that "I CAN SHOW YOU A FLYING SAUCER. YOU, JUST HAVE TO DEDICATE THE TIME AND DO IT." When you do you will see "THEIR" level of technology is "INFINITELY", more advanced than ours. Sons, if they are infinite, as the evidence suggest, then we do have hope, that immortality is not only possible, but exists, "NOW"! This is the reason I'm excited!

Sons, I "MAY" die soon, maybe today. But, I will truly be lucky, if I die first. I can't imagine, going through the pain of losing my children. Again, my heart goes out to my brother. Well, "IT'S TIME"! Let's put our money where our mouth is and do what Jesus said to do. He said give away all you have and follow his teachings. If we want immortality, why can't we buy it? We can buy humans, can't we? Well then let's buy scientists and doctors, who can "POSSIBLY" achieve it! Let's all become doctors and scientists!

I hope you and everyone will always know how precious our childhood is. I... I'm sorry. I'm crying for two reasons. Tears of joy, for the extremely short-lived great times we had swimming, playing ball, sleigh riding, and all the other fun stuff, we did. I'm also crying for the bad and what's to come. Less time, together. Let's treasure the rest and make them, good times!

Wow, life is hard. In the words of my brother Tim; "I ain't gonna shit you around, it can be hell." Enough crying, though. You kids, are the world's greatest treasure, in the universe! The wonder of a child is pure joy. I am deeply sorry for crossing the line of excitement and morphing into, such an angry frustrated monster. I can't believe, that I'm still trying to validate my "THEORY"! I'm sorry, "FORGIVE ME." This subject matter is so "DEEP" and complex. I'm having a hard time dealing with it, myself. I will be strong, for you "IF" I die, I promise. I told Terry, before he died, that I think we would all wake up as an alien, after death. I did, because it's my story and "DREAM"! When we do, there is no blinking thinking god story, just science and it's a choice to stay and do it "AGAIN"! I begged him not to come back.

I "SEE" my "THEORY" so clearly. I have "FAITH" that science will validate it, eventually. We're cloning, picking physical attributes and have a "SPACE STATION," now! That's huge compared to a hundred years ago. Conquering space is our only "WAY" of surviving and possibly resurrecting ourselves again! We made it this far and I think the skies, the limit! Like every kid, I think it is possible. This thought alone sustains me. Now, I want to end with the most important thing I have discovered. We have more meteors coming. We have to go "UP" and live in space! I am devoting all my time and money, to the scientific project of conquering space.

Sons, if I had one wish, naturally I'd ask for a perfect world. Heck, there I did it. It didn't happen. I have to get over, this cold hard fact of life. We all do. In all seriousness, I'd give anything for the chance to be a child again, with you. That would be a miracle! I hope we can "ALL" make miracles happen and just be kids again, forever. Science kids!

Please sons, and everyone else, don't stop being a kid. Let's make the "WORLD PERFECT", like we "ALL" know we would if we could. All kids would. I think we can, little by little. I'm an optimist. We can do it! I will do it, starting with being a better parent and person. First, at home and last everywhere, else. Please forgive my past and help me find "THESE FLYING SAUCERS", anytime you want. I'm here for you. After all, I am your Dad. Some, would call that my duty. I call it being "LUCKY" and a privilege! It would be my privilege and honor, to be the first, in showing you one. I am the "LUCKIEST" dad on this "PLANET" and in this "WONDERFUL" universe. All, because I still have you!

Now sons, here is the rest of my story. I hope you enjoy it and learn the word "EMPATHY." I need all you can give me. Like all kids, I'll be anxiously waiting, your opinion of this book! Here's to all the kids and the kid in all of us! Let's do this. Let's conquer "DEATH AND RESURRECTION"!

Last, but certainly not least, I also dedicate this to my, Granny Hunt. I know that I speak, for my entire family, in giving her a special tribute. She's been gone 20 years now and I would give everything, to have her back. My greatest hope, is that I made her feel as special, as she did me. I treasure the "TIME" we had together. She always made me and all of us feel, so special.

I know, that she made my mother feel this way and I thank her. We thank her. I began to cry uncontrollably. "Oh," I groaned loudly. "I miss you Granny." I wailed, screaming in pain. "I miss you! I am sure the rest of my family does too! We love you Granny!"

Nancy Hunt, Granny, "IS, WAS, and ALWAYS WILL BE" a good ol' fun loving, music adoring, hard to beat (drinking), dancing, always there for us, hillbilly hugging "TREASURE," and anything else great, that I'm leaving out. She "IS" simply the best "GRANNY" that ever existed!

"Sons," I said to myself out loud. I knew why I started talking instead of typing. Granny done it. "I sure am dreading the job, ahead of me. But, I have to finish writing this book. I want this one to be "PERFECT", because the others obviously aren't! Not, one of my last seven books were best sellers and I know why. Everyone told me with each book and yet, I kept making the same mistake. My "DISCOVERY" is "ONLY", my discovery! I can't bring back the other man, who had it before me, he's dead. "FORTUNATELY" though, he just so happens to be the most famous man on earth and his teachings are known, worldwide! It's "TIME" to explain them, through the eyes of science. It's "MY TIME", now and I'm don't want to be killed, like he was. Please help me sons? I broke down again. I didn't want to die, but I'm saying the "EXACT" same thing, that he did. "MONEY IS THE ROOT OF ALL EVIL"!

We have to give it away and try to find "HEAVEN"! It still isn't practiced today, and hasn't been since YESHUA/"JESUS" was killed, for saying it 2,000 years ago. No one else since, not even JFK, has and no one is, now! Not even Michio Kaku, Neil DeGrasse Tyson, or Stephen Hawking. Why aren't they giving all their money to find it?

"HEAVEN'S LOCATION IS MY DISCOVERY." It was taught by ancient people, all over the earth. History has chiseled it in stone! Our religious traditions carry it on, even to this day. We "ALL" look up, point to it, and live in it—yet we don't see it. It's space, not earth! I hope this book, will explain its confusion, "ONE LAST TIME"! Anyone can find it and I theorize, that "ALL" scientist, "FINALLY" will. They have too! "EVOLUTION OF AN INTELLIGENT BEING WANTING IMMORTALITY", dictates, only one path. We must go "UP, FIRST"!

Science will not only confirm it, but we all will eventually "SEE", that it is an unstoppable evolutionary step, in advancing our knowledge of the universe and conquering death. Going "UP" is the "FIRST MILESTONE" of "INTELLIGENCE." The second is "IMMORTALITY"!

It is the only way to avoid death, by mother nature. I know "WHY" we must go "UP" and live everywhere on spacecraft, like our space station. I know it sounds egotistical to propose, that I'm the only one who knows this. But, nobody is proving me wrong. I need science, to do this for me, for my sons, and for "EVERYONE"! Living on planets is crazy! Even vacationing is dangerous! We gotta stay away, from danger!

I know this sounds crazy, and I'm sorry. Please remember, it could happen to you. The evidence points to only one conclusion. I understand why the world doesn't "SEE" this "REALITY." I haven't found any scientist, "YET," that has reached this level of speculation. I am theorizing, that intelligent life evolves infinitely and it only has one goal, immortality. It can only be achieved, "UP" in space. These flying saucers reflect the "OMNISCIENCE, OMNIPRESENCE, and OMNIPOTENCE of religion! It's time to stop the "MAGIC GOD INSANITY." We have to rewrite the OMNIPOTENCE part of religion, because the world isn't perfect! We know it isn't, because of "METEORS"!

I'm trying to write this story, from beginning to end, without jumping around. If I fail, please read my books, from the beginning and it will help. My scatterbrained writing is a result of the many shocking discoveries and personal insights I've made, along the way. The amount of information, that I learned about "MANKIND'S HISTORY/ MYSTERY" and keep learning is staggering. I am staggered again, even now. We just had a life threatening meteor event and "GLOBAL MEDIA REALITY CHECK". We could've died, because of it. The world's scientific community confirmed it. I want so desperately, to have them confirm my evidence, too! This is my "REALITY"! I want them, or anyone, to challenge it!

I am tortured, by the inability to "CONVINCE my family, of this possibility. This meteors supports my theory and yet I haven't been successful with it, either. It really is no different, than all the other, equally life changing "EVIDENCE" I've found, in this harrowing ass journey of mine. Like my Granny's death, this "METEOR" made a huge impact, on me.

Granny's gone and I miss her a lot. I don't want to live without her, but I have to for my kids' sake. It hurts, let me tell you! However, I must stay focused on my new reality. I did endure then and I will keep going on.

This meteor is an instant game-changer for all of us. It made world news and more are coming. We could… no "WE ALL WILL DIE, WHEN THE BIG ONE HITS AND IT WILL HIT!" I needed to quit wasting time. We have to stop it! I have to save my kids. I turned my attention back to the keyboard in front of me and instantly wondered, if Granny will get my discovery. Well "MY THEORY," I mean. I can't forget that I haven't proven it. Yet!

Wow, is it ever difficult to keep my thoughts straight. "No wonder all my books are so scatter-brained." I remarked boldly and openly as if I was talking to someone. "I'm about to do it again, if I don't focus… "MICHAEL DUANE." I suddenly laughed and spoke aloud again, as if my boys, were here.

"SCATTER-BRAINED. Yep, Granny used to call me that, boys and she was right. I'm still scatter-brained!" I laughed again and fought back the tears. I pulled myself together. I can't believe I was talking out loud. I shouldn't be so surprised though. Like I said, Granny used to do it all the time. LOL!

I shook my head, chuckled and just continued, "Well let me tell you something kids, as you live you're gonna ignore a lot of old people's advice, just like I did. You will learn one thing, though. And you can take it to the bank, just like my Granny, said to me. I'm sure her Granny, said the same to her. Old people, do know what they're talking about, when it comes to life. They know the mistakes, that we'll more than likely make, along the way. They do because they lived it and we haven't. "WISDOM DOES COME WITH AGE" and it's up to us to follow it or ignore it. So please listen to them, when they give you advice." I stopped for a minute and just reflected on my past. After a minute or so and more tears, I continued to talk openly. I needed too!

"Life can be and will be pretty hard sometimes. No, actually life is hard now, sons! It's always hard, because of things like this meteor. It shows us, that we all have to deal with death, "EVERYDAY." There "POTENTIALLY" isn't even a tomorrow, for all of us until, we conquer space. Meteors can take us out, anytime. This has been happening forever in our past and it will not stop in our future. It is time, for us all, to become scientist." I paused and sat back, in my chair. I was completely dumbfounded, that all humanity doesn't know this. Thank God we have a "SPACE STATION"! We need to know this!

"Yeah, like now and not tomorrow," I said as I bent forward to continue writing. My voice was cracking, as I kept talking. I couldn't stop "I don't have Granny with me anymore boys, and it hurts! Please listen to the old people. Please listen to them." I said as I cried even more.

Out of the blue "SOMETHING" hit me and I went from crying, to laughing. "What am I saying them? I should say us. Heck, that's me too. Wow, I guess 52 is old to kids. Who am I kidding? Kids, please listen to us! I guess I'm old too. Oh no... not me." I screamed out as I grabbed both sides of my head and shook it. I was covering my ears like, I wouldn't hear myself.

I didn't need to hear it, I could see it. I looked toward the mirror, straightened my hair and laughed. I couldn't hide the wrinkles, but at least I still had my hair! Wow. I was so "GOD DAMN" vain, that it disgusted me! "HAIR" I screamed. "I can't even let go of it. Who am I kidding! Who are we all kidding!" Nobody wants to be ugly and old!

I finished, with a shit-eating grin as Granny would call it. I couldn't help it. I know 50 is old. It was when I was a kid and it is now. Oh the pain... the constant reminder, that I'm old. If only I would've listened, I thought to myself as I adjusted my back brace. Jokes on me now! I slumped back, deep into my chair and stretched out for a second.

"I know I'm a dreamer. But maybe, just maybe, we could make people smarter by teaching them, to always think of the future. I want to do this Granny. This is what I'm begging people to do, Granny. It is, what my books are about. I think it's possible and religion says, these people exist, now. This is why my "LAST" book was so important, to me! It is all about becoming "INFINITE ASTRONAUTS!"

I was getting more emotional, as I talked and started pleading for her help, as if she were here. Boy, I sure wish she was, I thought to myself. I was choking up and wiping away my tears. I sat straight up, bent forward, and looked hard at the screen. I typed one word, "REALITY." "Here goes nothing, Granny! I'm going to start with the answer first. It is all about the reality of "SCIENTIFIC POSSIBILITIES! I "SEE" them and I will get to see you again!"

The tears, that were flowing, weren't tears of pain, then. They were tears of "JOY"! I began to type feverishly and naturally I couldn't stop talking, just like Granny. "You're the greatest Granny, that I could've ever wished for and I want you back. I hope you don't think I'm crazy, too! Wow, I suddenly realized, that maybe it was Granny who influenced me to be scientific. It was the same as common sense to her and my Dad.

Overcome with emotion, I looked "UP", to say one last thing. "Thank you Granny.

I know it sounds crazy, but I think I may have figured out our mystery. The problem is, everyone hates me for it. They don't like, being made to feel ignorant. Everyone wants to be the smartest kid in the class and give me their "OPINION" or "LEFT ALONE"! They won't ask me any questions!

I am putting a video on YouTube called: THE INTELLIGENCE DETERMINATION TEST! I tried it on my nieces and their friends. Guess what, it worked! I put up $100 and predicted, that nobody knew how to determine, if I was more intelligent than them or not. I predicted their answers. None of them, wrote to "ASK QUESTIONS". I guessed their answers exactly. "THEY ALL HAD OPINIONS"!

"Don't worry though, Granny." I said laughing hardily. "My answer won't have any all- mighty omnipotent God stuff, only science. Ultimately, there is only one question to answer and that is, what do the ETs look like. I've found evidence to answer that question too, Granny. I promise I will never give 'UP' hope, of seeing you again!"

I had an epiphany, just as I spoke. 'UP', huh! Here's to you, I said as I looked 'UP' again and laughed. This is still hard to believe. It's so incredible. It still blows me away, even as I write. I sure wish Granny could read it, but maybe she has. I am at least admitting this possibility to myself. Maybe she already has, wow! Maybe we all have and just don't know it... like déjà vu makes us feel. Maybe, it's because we don't think science future very often. Without that, I wouldn't have seen religion as advanced scientific knowledge. Now that I do, I'm having an incredible "REVELATION," that our future has possibly, already happened for them.

I was talking to myself again. My mind was racing through, the myriad of discoveries that I have made and still am making—like this meteor. Wow, what a wake-up call! Granny this is my story of possibly finding..... "FINDING YOU, A-GAIN"! I cried out, at the thought of it.

Last but not least, I dedicate this book to the pursuit of scientific knowledge. I see how science is making the world a wonderful place, for our children. I have always, and still do, desperately want to cure death and preserve our memories, forever. I will devote all my money to that cause. What if we discover, the ability to DOWN-LOAD our memory and "KNOWLEDGE", into an infant's brain, while in the womb!

This possibility, epitomizes Yeshua saying, "he knew us before we were in the womb"! I may be 52. But, I think I still have enough time to finish college and do this. I could change my history major and pursue a neuroscience degree. I wanted to do it all. I want to show everyone, that religion isn't describing magic, it's describing science future!

Sometimes I can't believe I'm thinking this way, but I am. I've done, a lot of hard deep thinking, in the last 20 years and really do think, "WE" can achieve this. I've written 7 previous books on this subject matter and have certainly seen a lot of technological changes, that lead me to think this way. These possibilities are playing out every day in medical labs, everywhere. Daily, television shows give us proof of that.

Am I really being silly, for thinking this is possible? I know everyone thinks I'm crazy. But, I think it's crazy to not think this way. We have achieved "OMNISCIENCE" with the internet. It is "GOD," in today's global world of information! I can't stop thinking about the future and of what science is creating. Technology is exploding and I "REALLY" think we can do this. I've got to do it for my kids and all "OUR" kids. After all, they didn't ask to be here.

Granny wasn't religious, but her scientific observation of life and many cures influenced me, to say the least. She was a major supporter of my college goals and helped me through four-and- a-half years. She always thought, that science might figure all this out, one day. How I would give anything, just to have one more dinner, with my family at Granny's table. Nobody cooked like Granny—except Mom!

How I would love another fishing trip with my Dad, brothers, and our boys. (LOL! Girls too!) To all that I have lost, I will never forget you. I will always love you and miss you.

Thanks for the wonderful memories. It is my "GREATEST HOPE", that I will see you all again! I will give "EVERYTHING" to make that happen.

Here's to science, hope, and maybe even a new "REALITY." For the time being it's all we have. Let's not ever give it up! I wish "MANY" never-ending happy birthdays, to my sons. May all your wishes come true and may you never stop having birthdays! That is my wish. It is my dream!

Here is my final "WORD" on life. I "KNOW", I could die today! Knowing is everything, "OMNISCIENT", knowledge. I want to start with a quote from the famous Indian chief, Geronimo. He gave his life to defend his children, from our "SAVAGE FOREFATHERS"! I only know a few quotes, not that it really matters, but this one says it all. It is my motto, when it comes to living life! However, "I'M NOT PERFECT AND I DON'T CLAIM TO KNOW EVERYTHING. FRANKLY, I'M GLAD I DON'T. I COULDN'T STAND MYSELF IF I DID!

I DO LIKE IT AND IT'S APPROPRIATE FOR WHAT I AM ABOUT TO TELL YOU"

Here's the quote: "Today is a good day to die." Here's another by Jesus, 2,000 years earlier. "I die daily." I just told you mine, "I could die today so I have to "HURRY" and overcome death." I love you. Here's "MY DISCOVERY."

Sons, my thoughts are coming way too fast and my background to get here, is deep. I will go slow. The things I've learned and continue to learn definitely are hard to quickly process. I'm really nervous as I continue to write this book. When I was young, my Dad would make me slow down and take a few deep breaths, anytime I got too nervous. I'm going to try that, now. It always worked and of course, Dad's presence didn't hurt either.

I busted out laughing, as I pictured that memory. I was always so scared of Dad. I was always glad, that I did calm down. I love him just as much now, if not more so. It was always more, when I was afraid! My parents were my rock! It sure felt good to release all my built up tension. I don't have Dad now and I want so much to make this read, well. Like Granny, Dad didn't get to read any of my books, either.

The reason, I want so badly to do a good job on this book, is twofold. First, so children can understand it. Secondly, to fulfill my selfish desire to satisfy my family and readers expectations, of it. They all have "SOMEWHAT" liked my books, but they unanimously say and want the same thing. They want this one, and anymore after, to be a plainly written consistent book. One that is simple, to the point, and easy to follow. I get it!

My brother Tim will be proofreading this before you get it—that I can assure you! (LOL) I'm going to do this, because he is such an avid reader and doesn't necessarily agree, with my theory. He really thinks it's all a little warped. (LOL) Lucky for me, he still thinks I can make a successful book though. I thank him, because it pushes me more than ever, to make this theory/answer simple enough, for children to understand it.

Sons, if we want to exist forever, we're going to have to get off this planet. The evolution of an intelligent being dictates this answer. All scientists, from every continent, will agree. The "METEOR", that just hit, clearly drives this point home! I've explained to Tim, what I am trying to explain, to you. He doesn't necessarily agree, with the scientific assertion, that this earth will die one day. I asked him, if he is influenced by his religion, since they say this same thing. He said I can't prove it will. He's right! Then I asked him, if his religion says the same things, as he believes? He agreed that they did, but still contends, that science can't show an earth dying either. I will get his evidence. The Hubble Telescope is taking pictures as we speak. I hope you enjoy and please verify, all scientific facts.

I'm sorry, for getting away from the storyline and jumping around. I always tell everyone, that it's hard not to use something you've learned earlier, to make a point, later. Still, it is no excuse, for not doing a good job. It doesn't matter, that I'm so passionate about it. I rambled and I lost my train of thought, on all my books. I do apologize and I am correcting as I speak.

I also told Tim, and everyone else, that this book is definitely, my last one. There won't be another one. They all laughed. Well, not all of them. But it is! I said the same thing in my last seven books, but this one truly is the last, on this subject matter. In fact, science makes it so. I predict, that they will end their search for the origin the universe, with the same outcome as mine. "EVERYTHING CAME FROM NOTHING AND MATTER IS INFINITELY EVOLVING, FROM SPACE TO MATTER AND BACK TO SPACE, AGAIN"! Religion's "ENLIGHTENMENT" is knowing, that we must break this "VICIOUS CYCLE" of birth, death, and reincarnation. I now know, that my search for the answer to our mystery, is the same as science searching for the "theory of everything." We are just now asking ourselves, "What is Nothing?" and "What is Reality?." When you read my books, you will discover, that they build upon each other's discoveries, before them. Life is a work in progress.

I'm telling you all this, because it explains why I rambled and digressed so much, in the other seven books. I was learning so much, about the world we live in, it was hard to keep my thoughts straight.

Sons, I have been working on this for, almost 20 years. My first book was released before my Dad's death. That was hard! I started to well up just thinking of him. Suddenly, I busted out laughing.

Hell, I thought out loud to myself, belly laughing and wiping away the years. I not only told everyone, that every book was my last book, I told Dad too! I did find my answer, back then. I just didn't have the science background, to know it and name it like I do now. "REALITY"!

I'm so thankful, for religion's story of immortality and hope. Oh God, please let it be true. I could hardly bear my shame of not being intelligent, before I had my children. How could an intelligent loving human, inflict such horror, onto an innocent child? Could "RESURRECTION AND IMMORTALITY", really be true? Here's to "HOPE" and solving our mystery. Is this our "REALITY, EVERYWHERE"?

I'm not a Bible thumper sons, but here is a scripture, that sure explains how our situation hasn't changed, from the time it was written: "Even in the days of Noah they were just like us… they ate, drank, and gave no mind to their death sentence." They didn't try to find heaven, even though they knew the answer! Therefore, they had no belief in it. They just survived. It's been like this forever. They were just continuing the same traditions, that were given to them, by their loving parents. It's tradition, to build one's material treasures.

Now, it is up to us, to stop this cycle. We must now strive for "INTELLIGENCE," not materialism. I don't "BELIEVE" anything, anymore. I have to find and accept all provable fact. It is my only redemption, for "MINDLESSLY", giving you boys a death sentence. I am a loving father! I will give my life, for you! All children deserve answers.

Sons, "FOR YOU", this book is also, my prediction of the future. I will tell you, what I think it's like in "HEAVEN". I am relying on scientific evolution, the ancient religious sources and most of all, my "COM-

MON SENSE"! I don't want you to "BELIEVE" it. I want you to prove it for yourself. We're all in the same boat, called Earth, together. The meteors are never going to stop.

I'm convinced of my theory, because I saw the meteor strike Russia, on FEBRUARY 15th, 2013. If it would have been much bigger, scientists have said, that we could have been taken out. "UP/HEAVEN IS OUR SAFE-HAVEN"! The answer I've given you is supported by science. Seeing it for yourself, does change things, like it did for me. I hope to answer the age old question: "WHERE IS HEAVEN?" If I die, please continue to try and get this to Barbara Walters!

I just hope that, in the mean time, it doesn't take a meteor or my death to do it. I "THINK" as children of the information age, we can all imagine life existing, "SOMEWHERE" else in the universe. Where is a no brainer, at least for more intelligent life, than us! It should be "EVERYWHERE", in space! The meteor makes that perfectly clear!

Scientific knowledge confirms it. If the big one hits, only those on the space station, will survive. Please,"DON'T FORGET"!

Seeking an understanding of the universe we came from, live in, and are going to, only provides "ONE HEAVEN" and it is our future. It is space,"UP"! Sons, please bear with my attempts, to contact Barbara Walters. I don't mean to embarrass you, but I'm a nobody. She wants to find heaven and no one knows where it is. I know where heaven is! Maybe, she should ask me Unfortunately, I'm not a "SOMEBODY" like them! How can you believe anything you don't understand. Knowledge is greater than "BELIEVING." Knowledge is Power! It can overcome the meteor and even death, itself. I'm about to tell you, about heaven.

It is the future and "THEY" are here, now. They have always been here! They evolved and are still evolving, infinitely! We haven't, because we were "CREATED" by them. We must save ourselves. That technology exists. We are just memory, information, and "WORDS"! Mankind will never evolve! We are a scientific creation and look different! Evolution gives life, that all look the same. Look around!

My greatest hope, is that you can "BELIEVE", this is possible. I can't cure death now, but I know it can be done, with knowledge. I've seen a flying saucer and I can show you one. They look the same as they did tens of thousands of years, ago. They have always existed. I will explain, how this is possible. It is a simple scientific answer. It's about "TIME", someone discovered it again! I hope I have proven, that religions had it all along, they still do. Today, I have a scientific word for it, instead of God. I call them "INFINITE ASTRONAUTS!" It explains itself. They are people, who live "UP" in space, forever! Science says this is possible. I say it is "REALITY." Sons, this is the "REALITY" I've found.

I feel like the luckiest dad and guy in the world for achieving this "GOAL." I feel this way, because it's the "GREATEST GIFT", a father could ever give to his sons or ask for, himself. We all want "ANSWERS", to life's most feared questions. I'm so grateful to be writing this book for you. How wonderful it would be, if we all got one, from our "FATHER"! I didn't get one and I'm sure, that Dad wanted to do it, for all of us. I'm sure that Terry did, too! But, neither of them got, too. I still can't believe , that I've done it! I can die in "PEACE", now. I miss Terry and Dad so much. Hell, I miss a whole lot more people, than that. "DEATH SUCKS"!

I hope everyone is as touched by these dedications, as I was, while writing them. I am so happy. I am truly a lucky dad! Please pardon my bluntness and lack of "CANDOR" in them. I had to keep it simple for, TERRY, and all the children of the "WORLD." He and I love kids! They always deserve the "TRUTH"!

I feel so liberated! I can mark off the "MOST IMPORTANT THING" on my bucket list, a letter to my children. about life. I hope that it inspires everyone to do the same! I don't mean to be so redundant about "HEAVEN" and my answer, as to where it is. I'm just trying desperately to make sure, that my sons know this. I may not be able to give them, all the answers, but as you've read. I do encourage them to do so, on their own. I'll be the first to admit, that some things can't be satisfied with, "MY ANSWERS OR PICTURES"! It tortures me. It does so because I can't make you "WANT TO" do it. You have to "FIND THEM" on your own! My struggle continues.

And now, of all the things, I'm changing the front cover picture! Man, this sucks, big time, but I can't help it! "I HAVE TOO! THE EVIDENCE MAKES ME"! The front cover picture, has to "PLAINLY" show everyone, "THE WAY" to survive "METEORS." The only way.

Well, I "FOUND" one, finally! Well, at least I saw my idea, anyway. The plane wouldn't have been as simple as my drawing! I drew "IT" up, as soon as, I figured "IT" out! I put my new cover to the test and it worked! It is definitely more powerful, than the first. I know because, I don't have to ask people what it's means, when they see it. I did with the other one. It just didn't work. I was going to use the famous "NEVER FORGET"/Dinosaur poster on my son's wall, but it only addressed the extinction of dinosaurs!

I had to coax people and help them, get my point, when I showed it to them. That's not, what I wanted! It's not what my sons or Terry wants either. The front cover picture has to immediately "SHOW US" the simple answer, to avoid "METEOR EXTINCTION"!

I'm happy to report, that my sons think I've done it! Boy, what a relief. I've been racking my brains, for the last month or so, trying to figure it out. I'm not afraid to tell you, that I was getting worried! I just came up with it a week ago! I can't help, but to laugh about it, now. I'm glad I can. I sure wasn't laughing before!

I have to admit. It isn't all my idea. It is a spin on the old one. This is my new "SCIENTIFICALLY UPGRADED/ VERSION", of it. I had to check and see, if they had my image. Man, I thought to myself immediately. If they don't, then it will make a great T- shirt poster! Everyone, that wears it, will be a "POSTER CHILD" for "METEOR PREVENTION"! It will give that phrase, a whole new meaning!

Even though, my idea may be something borrowed and yes it damn sure is something "BLUE." I "BELIEVE", that it could be much "MUCH" bigger, than that. Simply because it is something... "NEW"! Why don't we all know this? I just had to throw that in for a little humor. I'm a wannabe songwriter. "METEOR EXTINCTION" is such a dark message!

Wow, what if the poster "CREATORS", don't have this image? I didn't want to jump the gun again and make myself, look foolish! I think I've done enough of that! I was going to check and make sure, first. Only a fool professes something to be true, when he hasn't yet proven it! So, I quickly hollered for my son. I really hadn't checked, yet. I sure got nervous, quick.

If they don't have it, this could be my ticket to world-wide "FAME"! My first iconic T-shirt image, would have "POWER", then. It's a shame, that the world is such a "RESPECTER OF PERSONS"! I "FINALLY" think, I truly have something!. Wow, what an exciting moment! This could be, my "icing on the cake" and a "double whammy"! I could have a new universal T-shirt and possibly, a "BEST SELLING BOOK"! I became overcome with emotion at the thought of it!

At least I hoped so. I trembled with excitement at the thought of such a wonderful possibility. What was taking Matt, so long? I know he heard me.

I had to ask myself, "Why wouldn't they have this image? Surely, they do, but what if they don't"? If they don't have it, this could confirm, that my "A.S.K. DISCOVERY" (Advanced Scientific Knowledge) is "BRAND NEW"! In order to understand why, you must seek scientific knowledge of the universe and history. (Oh, yeah, don't forget my "INTELLIGENCE DETERMINATION TEST")

Matthew, finally came into the room. I asked him, to please check the poster makers catalog and see if they have any, with humans trying to escape the meteor event. I "FOOLISHLY" laid my neck on the line and predicted, they wouldn't.

Instantly, he said they "PROBABLY" did. I knew why he done this, but I didn't say anything. I just casually remarked, that I sure hope so, because I want everybody to see it! I told him, that I don't have an ego problem. He knew what I meant, too.

"I just want everyone to "SEE" how, they can avoid "METEOR EXTINCTION. That's all," I said sternly, but lovingly. WOW! Life shouldn't be, such a "GOD DAMN" competition. I don't care about, being right or wrong. Heck, life should be all about preserving the family, like us, right?" He didn't respond. I continued to say, that I was glad he at least said, probably.

Because, otherwise, it would indicate he resents my theory.

"Not, that I'm saying you are," I quickly added. I gave him the benefit of doubt, but I know he resents me saying, that I'm the only one, with it. He especially, resents my saying people shouldn't bitch about the world's unfairness and yet, doing nothing about it. He can't stand himself, when it comes to this issue. He serves no one and doesn't work. He is spoiled and does very little, for us! I'm not going to fight with him, over it, anymore. His laziness and hypocrisy brings out the "DEVIL", in me. He will read this book and hopefully stop making regrets, like I did. It's never to late to mend guilt. We all know how. Just, do something about it!

I could be wrong, I thought to myself. We'll see. After all, "METEOR EXTINCTION" only has "ONE WAY", it can be avoided. We have to give everything, money and time, to make it happen. I shared this little antidote, with him. He said he knew it and didn't resent my theory, he just doesn't agree, with "ALL OF IT"! He hated the sexual thing.

Damn self-righteousness disease, I laughed to myself. Knowing you're right, because the evidence supports it, is a catch-22! It's hard to be right, without being and sounding "SELF- RIGHTEOUS"! "ANYBODY CAN PROUDLY DENY THE EVIDENCE, BUT FEW CAN

HUMBLY FOLLOW IT," I quickly reminded him. I further added that I'm not saying mine is right and that someone else, can't have it as well. Heck, I'd love it "IF THE WORLD WAS PERFECT" and science already found "MY DISCOVERY," but they haven't.

I always told him about my dream, of waking "UP, ON A SPACECRAFT" and seeing that, I lived in a world free of earth's horror! I wanted him to see the universe, like I do, but I can't make him. He has to see the self-imposed responsibility, of maintaining it. He hates religions' lack of logic and hated what the arguing it creates! I know why religion get's a bad rap and kids hate it. Matt and his "BEST" friend Daniel are in that group. They detest how religious people offend others, by saying God saved them and yet, ten others died horrible deaths. This is illogical, crazy, and downright offensive. I agree. But, I don't say this crazy shit. I even try to say, I could be wrong, so he and others don't get angry about it!

I told him that I want everyone to be a "SCIENTIST", too. I had to add, "Just like us, huh"? "RIGHT," he replied sarcastic like as he walked past me, into the kitchen. I could still see him. My computer is in the dining room/ living room area, next to the kitchen.

"Son, believe me I want someone to have it," I told him seriously.

He laughed and said he did too! I knew better, than to say that action speaks louder than words, though. I knew he would just get angry, at the implication.

I found myself a little hurt. He wasn't the only one, to treat me this way. Nobody, has tried to confirm my "DISCOVERY" or not, including him. I wish someone could just do that, or at least try, before they "BEAT ME DOWN." Hell, I don't care if I'm wrong. They seem to be the one, with that problem. I just want to cure "DEATH", for all of us! It isn't just for me. Wait, maybe it is. I can't live, "ALONE"! Wow, I can't keep ignoring this "REALITY"! I wondered if he ever thought this way. I put myself in his mind and remembered my youth. Wow, I didn't think this way either! Man, in a way, he's so lucky! I just needed to cool out.

I knew he would bristle at my insinuation of being, such a "KNOW-IT-ALL", about the poster and he did. I understand why completely. Hell, I'd be skeptical of anyone who says that "THEY ARE" the "ONLY ONE" to have "THE ANSWER", too. I finally asked him, if thought he could solve our mystery. I wanted to know, if I made him feel like he could. I needed to do this. I was really doing this for me! You'll read why. He did thank God!

No actually, I did it for both of us. I know that only love can conquer hate. I need to show him "LOVE." I had shown him enough anger during "MY SHARING OF EVIDENCE", with him. I blew up, "ALMOST", every time. I tried not to and begged him to help me help us. I am afraid of death, just like he is. I've always told him it's O.K. to cry and get scared of "NEVER EXISTING", again. That's something we both shared. I did it often, as a kid. But, facing it helps me. This is why I am excited about "MY DISCOVERY." I know "METEORS" can take us out, now. I told him, that he needs to say this to himself, everyday and it will help get overit. It will help him see how futile, worrying is. It gets nothing done! He's doing nothing about it. I can only hope he finally does!

I love him more, than I love myself! He's my baby boy. I love both of my boys, so much. We have to look, for "PROOF" of "ADVANCED SCIENTIFIC KNOWLEDGE/A.S.K.", if we want to find it. I want to find it. I don't ever want to live, without them! I don't want to be "ALONE"! Sadly, I can't make them do anything.

Enough of this pain. It's time to bond, not debate. I have really damaged our relationship, in the last ten years. Damaged hell, I probably ruined it and I am so sorry for it. I'll never get that time back! "NEVER"?

It's all my fault and it doesn't matter, that I had good intentions. We all know the saying about good intentions. Ironic as "HELL," huh? It is, but it's so true. The same goes for my family as well. I hurt a lot of them, too! My passion, for all this evidence "I SEE," but can't seem to "GET" them to, tortures me. I "NEEDED" them to see "IT." I know "MY TIME" is running out. Heck, I'm "52"!

I think my little boy, who is now a grown man, will see "IT", soon enough. He went to check for my "NEW" poster. I just kept on talking, while he did. I was nervous, as all get out! I started thinking, about my boys' childhood and I couldn't stop the memories, from flooding back.

Thank God, my oldest boy Joshua, could see "IT". Wisdom, if we're lucky enough to learn from it, does come with age. He even "SAW, a UFO! I hope both of my son's will always keep asking questions and learning, as much as they possibly can. I know one thing, I need to learn how to cure my anger! My son would be coming back soon!

I need to, because I have gotten angry at Matt, way too many times, when we discussed "MY DISCOVERY." I know it's hard, for him to imagine me making a brand new scientific discovery, when I'm not a scientist. I can relate. Most people think this way, like my brother Tim. I can't help that, I have a "THEORY"! But, I can change it. I do know, that I shouldn't have pushed it on him. But, I did anyway like I am now. I can't seem to stop myself! I couldn't, because I don't want him thinking, that he can't solve our mystery. When he said, he thought he could. I almost cried. This is the best thing, that's happened between us in along time.

I'm just trying to show him, that anyone can! That is, again, if they "BELIEVE" in themselves. Wow, I was blown away, by the irony of our inability to gel. We both love science. I heard him coming and as thought the same thing was going to happen, again. I hope not. I felt, that he would continue to flatly refuse or acknowledge any interpretation of my evidence, as valid. I was feeling this way, because if he does validate it. It will make him feel guilty, for not looking himself and arguing with me, about it! "HIS EGO" always made me feel, like he doesn't respect my "DISCOVERIES", my intentions or my credibility.

Hell, it ain't just him, I felt this way, with anyone one who reacts negatively and most do! Matt even told me, that I had to get science to approve "IT" first, before he would believe it. He said it was because I'm "NOT" a scientist, this hurt. I went to college for five years and that didn't even matter! Nothing, mattered to him, but his "EGO"! I'm sad. I know it's his ego and I need to overlook it. The fact remains, that I haven't succeeded with him, like my other son. I know why. My other son, doesn't claim to be "SEEKING SCIENTIFIC ANSWERS", like Matt. He's a "GODSEND." I'd rather discuss it with him, anyday. But, I don't. You'll know why as you read on. Eventually, I didn't discuss it with them, period. I just want peace and know all too well, that opinions can truly be like assholes, even for a "GOOD" cause. I can testify to that. Just ask my son. I've been one and I am one. I was about to be an asshole, again. I won't be an asshole, anymore! I have to be perfect and give all my money away!

I "HAD" a hard time handling him, or any of my family, treating me badly. Especially, when I'm trying to prove something "WE" all hold so dearly. Like a cure, for death. Heck, I'm excited about this stuff. How could any of us not be? Right? Don't we all love each other and want each other, to live forever? Wow, how naive can I be, even at 52?

How can I create, all this pain, in the name of love? What am I thinking? Obviously, this is all about me. I felt so damn selfish, right then! I know that I can't make anyone "SEE" my "THEORY" or anything else! We all know, how this kind of "SHIT", can turn bad. I remember plenty of times, with my own parents, when I refused to accept "THEIR RELIGION." I know how bad they wanted me to "SEE" it, too. I shouldn't expect the same from Matt, when I didn't do it myself! Man, did I ever have a guilty conscience!

It was so difficult not to share my "DISCOVERIES", with him. He was so scared of dying, just like me. I couldn't bear the helpless feeling I got, when he panicked over it. It always hurts so bad, when it happened, to him. "FORTUNATELY," I did finally get him to see the paradox and contradiction, in worrying about death, though. Especially, for the sake of "LOVING LIFE." It happened just after the meteor event. Like I said before, I began telling him, to say to himself, everyday. "METEORS CAN TAKE US OUT NOW"! It started working! He hasn't panicked, since. "THANK GOD"! We bonded!

Even, if he doesn't agree with my "THEORY," he at least knows one thing, for sure. He knows that we survived and worrying, is such a waste of time. It doesn't get anything done! "IF WE SAY WE LOVE LIFE, THEN WE HAVE TO LIVE IT"! IF YOU LOVE IT, LIVE IT." That's our new motto, together!

I don't know, for the "LIFE OF ME," how this could happen. I want to be a "HUMBLE AND LOVING" father. I had become so

"SELF-RIGHTEOUS", trying to get his acceptance. How, could I not look, like a hypocrite?

I knew my righteous "ATTITUDE" made me look, like a "WALKING CONTRADICTION." That's why, I always told him to challenge me and only follow the evidence. I begged him to look. I even told him, about other scientists, that have a similar evolutionary view of intelligent life, pursuing immortality. He did and saw that the world's leading scientist, Michio Kaku, fell short of describing the evolution of an intelligent being in the universe, as I do. To him, we would live on Earth and Space! I told him, that I will go see Michio. He wants me to see Neil DeGrasse Tyson, too. I told him I would because I've was using his quote and picture, on the back cover of this book. I shared it with Matt and he quickly realized, no one is immune to the word "HUMILITY"! Neil says we got to get off planets. He finally became humbled.

Much to my surprise, he was a little shocked and seemed impressed, when I explained. I showed him, that according to Michio's own model. There "WOULD" be one more obvious step, for an evolving intelligent person, pursuing immortality. At least, one wanting to avoid "DEATH", at the hands of mother nature! Stay off planets. Use robots to get supplies from it! I told him that Yeshua said, it is only for resting, not living there. I ended, by telling him, that the reason Yeshu/"JESUS", had to be sent here. Obviously, we can die re-entering our atmosphere and if we don't, then it can kill us anytime we're in it, by lightning!

I tried explaining to him, many times, that the ability to understand the future, requires the ability to "IMAGINE" it. He knows I think, that the future has already happened. I always told him, that if we really "KNEW" the universe was "INFINITE", everyone might understand. They would understand how I "CAN THINK", that all this has happened before. I asked him to start looking into the sky. This infinite proof, is inside us all! It's been there since we were a kid and could ask; "Does the sky have an end"? We all "KNOW" its an "INFINITE EXISTENCE". But, we still ask. I finally asked him, the first of two questions, that I put at the end of this book. They are for everyone!

Here they are: 1. "HOW ADVANCED COULD LIFE BE IN AN INFINITE UNIVERSE"? 2. "DO YOU WANT TO BE UGLY"?

I told him to think about it for minute, before he answered and that SEEING" the scientific achievements of our future, is the key to the answer. I added, that it also could possibly explain our mysteriously short history and this dilemma, we're in. For me, it requires "INFINITE THINKING." I've always told him that my theory, comes from a father's hope for his son's immortality. We all should want that and a life without pain, for all our "SONS/SUN". I asked him many times, if he would want his son to experience death, when they don't have to or himself, for that matter. He said of course not! Well then, if you lived on an artifical planet, would you want your son to visit, a deadly natural one? "WOW, I didn't think about that "EXACTLY". he responded excitedly! Then, he gave me the asnwer to my question! I almost cried. He got it, too. Just like Terry!

I told him I didn't "KNOW FOR SURE", that "IT" can be done, but "RESURRECTING LIFE", is what I'm after. I told him about the scientist, who thinks this is possible and that his name is Michael, like mine. Michael Hall. I laughed and told him, that was Granny's last name, too! "WHAT A COINCIDENCE," I quickly told him. "REALLY" it is! I knew he was afraid of the "UNKNOWN." We all are. Not me. I'd resurrect Granny!

I told him that we have to "FACE" our fear and to "OVERCOME" it! President Franklin Delano

Roosevelt's famous quote, best sums up our problem: "THE ONLY THING WE HAVE TO FEAR IS FEAR ITSELF." The "METEOR" made me face mine! I woke up! Finally, he understood me!

I assured him, it is his fear, that keeps him from facing and it! Telling him to say: "METEORS CAN TAKE US OUT NOW!," was the best advice, I ever gave him.

The last thing, I wanted my children to see me as, is closed minded. But, what if no one has my idea? I proved to Matt, that my theory has a stage of intelligence, above Michio Kaku's. I did what I need to do and now I don't need to remind him, anymore! I put my arm around his shoulder. "Son, I don't know why Micho doesn't see further, either. But, he doesn't. Maybe, he's not a dad. I don't know why. Maybe, one day he will. I know he can, though. I know you can, too. Anyone can. Terry did and, and ....", I tried to continue, but couldn't. I choked up. He grabbed and hugged me. "I know Dad, I know. I'm not a dad, yet. Please don't cry." he begged. I broke as I hugged him back and cried out "I miss him, so bad son." He finally understood!

He tried to act like he forgot about the poster, as walked past me. I quickly reminded him and pleaded my case. "I'm not doing this, to come across as a know-it-all, son." I said softly.

"But, if they don't, that makes three leading scientists, who are "POSSIBLY" not as scientifically advanced, as I am and they should be: Michio, Neil, and the poster maker! Not, that that's what I want, either." I added as meekly as I could. "Besides, I still have to check Neil out! I predict that the poster maker, won't have it. Because, if they did, it would "EXIST" now!"

"Right," he bristled again, but immediately turned around to go and check it out! He "COVIENIANTLY", forgot. I laughed, as he did. I knew why, he was in a hurry. He didn't want to hear my "SHIT" anymore. But guess what? They didn't!

"No way!," I screamed as he barley said they didn't! Little did he know, but I was screaming, from the sheer relief of being right! The excitement I showed, didn't come from my confidence. If so, that would've meant I set him up and already checked it out, before him!

"WOO-HOO"! I yelled again. Boy, was I relieved and he knew it! "THEY DIDN'T HAVE IT, HUH......YES, YES, YES! Man, what luck!" I know I overly reacted, but I really hadn't check it out, like I did, with Michio Kaku. I just took a chance. I did because I had never seen my idea before anywhere! Evolution of an "INTELLIGENT" species dictates that It "SHOULD"! I see the dinosaur extinction posters, everywhere! Why not one with, us?

I couldn't believe this was happening! Could this be possible? Could I be the only one to see, "WHAT I SEE"? I jumped up and hugged him. Then I did cart wheels all the way across the living room floor and back to the computer. I asked him, if he got my point? He said that he did. Wow! What a moment. It brought tears to my ears! I hugged him, again.

He "SAW" my point, alright. I think he was more, than a little surprised, when they didn't have it. I knew why. He still doesn't like my "UGLY THEORY"! "HELL", I still don't like it, either! But, it does tie everything together and explain our mystery, clearly. It makes "PERFECT" sense, why "MANKIND" is "NOT PERFECT." We don't look the same! I "THINK" he will eventually see this, as well. He just can't see the "PRETTY" side of it "YET." It takes "TIME AND AGE", to see that. I asked him, if he knew the definition of evolution. As he stammered and stuttered, to think of it. I quickly butted in and told him, it's best to say "I don't know", if you don't and you will avoid embarrassment. I asked him to look it up, because, I didn't either. That shocked him. I told him I knew a "LITTLE". We did it and he saw how complex and extensive the subject matter is. I asked him how you can tell if a species is a product of "EVOLUTION OR CREATION"! He didn't know. I explained, that the simple answer is life happens, by chance.

Then, I stated a simple fact of life. Life, that all look the same, evolved from itself. Life, where they all look different, is "SCIENTIFICALLY CREATED", by two different species!

It's a "SHAME", that we don't come in this world, "SEEING ALL LIFE, AS SUFFERING"! Most of us, only see it when we're are dying, like I am now. I know the side-effects of youth. I didn't always see it then and actually, I'm thankful for it. I'm thankful Matt's, still young and doesn't see it all the time, either! Death is scary. My brother Brian's right. Kids, don't need to see it. I know Matt's a good kid and loves me. Really, that's all that, matters! I wasn't going to bother him anymore. I started typing furiously. I know my death is coming, soon. Eighteen years is a drop in the bucket! I'll be seventy, before you know it! Three score and ten always rang in my head, thanks to Dad's religion.

This is so weird. It was eerie how things were coming to me. No, actually it was more creepy, than eerie. Why me? Surely everyone "SEES", that we have to go "UP" and live in space, don't they? This "METEOR" clearly shows, that we can "NEVER FORGET" the "REALITY" of "CHANCING DEATH" on a planet, again! Going "UP" and staying there is the only way we can survive, if we always want to exist! Why doesn't everyone see this?

I was so bewildered, dumbstruck, and amazed! "WHY," was I the only one to see it and not everyone else? For God's sake, how can I be the only one to SEE AND UNDERSTAND, THE ADVANCED SCIENTIFIC KNOWLEDGE OF HEAVEN"S LOCATION"? This tortured me. I started thinking about our "DESTINY", from a computer program perspective. Could we be, a computer program, like the movie *TRON*? Before you say no, I saw and filmed "FLYING SAUCERS"! Think about this, people! Do you really think I'm lying, after all I've said? These universal stories of religion are clear evidence for ETs and not spirits. Advanced technology explains all their magical abilities, like invisibility, mind-reading, and telekinesis! I can go on, but I already have in my other books! Please check them out?

I continued to "LOOK" for a scientist or someone who may agree, with my theory. I am still "TRYING TO FIND SOMEONE WHO DOES." Sadly enough, no one "LIVING" has understood and confirmed my theory, about heaven's location. I'm still looking and have found some scientists, that are close! Micho is close! I will ask, "IF HE WILL LET ME"!

Michael Hall, says he is on the verge of conquering, the immortality of our minds! I found another scientist, who thinks all life that has existed, could be brought back or "RESURRECTED"! He thinks, we could all exist, forever. He wrote a book called THE OMEGA POINT! I have to go see these guys! Wow, I guess it really is a "MAN'S WORLD", after all! How sad is that? Come on ladies, we need you. I want all people to see these possibilities! I have to get everyone, to see all this, so we can stop religious warfare! I have to. I have kids! The thought of global nuclear war horrifies me, the most! We can't even hide our children, from it. Sadly, it's the world we live in, today. It's scary, that most adults don't think we're capable of stopping it, from happening, again. It has already happened, with Hiroshima and Nagasaki! The only reason they didn't shoot back, is because, they didn't have any nuclear weapons. Now, over ten countries, do! There are enough nuclear weapons to destroy all the major cities, on earth!!!

People, I put the nuclear symbol over the Jewish star, on all my books. I do this to support my "A.S.K./ADVANCED SCIENTIFIC KNOWLEDGE THEORY"! How could primitive man have had the symbol of an atom and predict our inevitable demise, by it? How, when it takes an electron microscope, to see it? It still blows me away, that no one has seen the significance of this matching evidence. I saw another example of ancient art matching today's science. This one scares the shit out of me. Our I.C.B.M's look just like the ancient obelisk, all over the earth. All the major cities have one! No! Why don't people see this matching evidence. The ancient American Medical Association symbol looks just like a DNA strand. It's a double helix! The yin-yang symbol looks just like a cell with DNA or two sperm in an egg, as well as, "A GALAXY"! I put all this, in my first book and yet, these things are still amazing to me. These are trivial, in comparison to the Jewish star, matching the atom. This is "SCARY", because it's such a "REAL POSSIBILITY, TODAY"!

We are facing, possible extinction, from a global nuclear war! If we could just "SEE", that ancient people couldn't have had this symbol, without advanced people giving it to them, it would shed a whole new "LIGHT" on religion. We would have to let the evidence take over and start thinking differently, about the universe ! We just might even start thinking, "PHYSICALLY AND INFINITELY"!

My last book has this answer in its "TITLE" and it still isn't working. How can I get everyone to see this "ADVANCED SCIENTIFIC KNOWLEDGE", if they can't "IMAGINE" it?

Plenty of theories and scientific pursuits, were ridiculed, in the past. But, fortunately for science, many have become the norm, today. In 1924 Robert Goddard, the father of rocket science, made a nationwide statement and predicted man reaching the moon, in his lifetime. He was made, into a laughing stock, by the scientific community. People, we have reached the moon! Nikloa Tesla is another, example. He wanted to make electricity available, to everyone free and wirelessly. Today we are going wireless!

Because of men, like these two and Yeshua, I'm not afraid of looking crazy, anymore. I theorize, that more intelligent life, than us, exist everywhere in the universe. In fact, I think it would be crazier to say, that "THEY don't. We exist and we're not intelligent, yet. We will reach, that lofty goal, "WHEN" we get off this planet and live "UP" in the sky!

Obviously, the religious inhabitants stay "HIDDEN" from us, with technology! Religions' magic is nothing more than, "ADVANCED TECHNOLOGIES"! I think humans will look back 100 years, from now and laugh, at the idea of people not "BELIEVING", in ETs. If life exist here, it only logical, that it is everywhere. "LUCKY", are the ones, who don't live on a planet!

Well, enough rambling. My predictions and examples, never provoked my sons or many others, to look for evidence of E.T.'s. I was going crazy, trying to figure out, what it would take? I finally, just give up. But, I keep on hunting U.F.O.s! No, I find "FLYING SAUCERS"!

I want to wrap this present chapter up and get on, with my story. I will quickly be pouring through my past and revealing all the "MATCHING SCIENTIFIC DISCOVERIES," as they happened. This matching evidence, says more intelligent people exist!

If we agree with the evidence, then there's only one question, to ask of ourselves. Why wouldn't they "OPENLY" live with us or help us? I've told my sons, that I'm not the first scientist, who thinks this way. This logic was already addressed in 1947, by a brilliant scientist named Enrique Fermi. It's called Fermi's paradox.

My answer is simple. They are real flesh and blood beings, who obviously can't make us be good or the world perfect. There are basically, three hypothesis. I wrote about them in my last book. Believe it or not, mine is "BRAND NEW." People, it's time to re-examine the spirit story. If the evidence, says we have to rewrite it, then so be it. Don't we all, just want to know the truth, about ourselves? Don't kid yourself! Nobody wants an "UGLY TRUTH"!

As I was finishing up, my son was leaving. I asked him, "ONE MORE THING." I asked him, if he thought more intelligent life, could be invisible to us, through technology? He said he didn't think they could, without being caught. I quickly asked if he tried to imagine their advanced technologies. He said he didn't. I knew that already! He went on out the door. I started to follow him and caught myself! What was I thinking? I didn't want to erase the progress, that we just made. I needed to just let him be a kid!

I can't believe I keep doing this. Especially, after blowing up last week at a restaurant, when I started talking about "EVOLUTION". He pissed me off so bad, that I got up and walked out. I was showing him pictures of fishing boats, hauling in crab and fish. I said they were a beautiful example of evolution, because they all look the same. Unbelievably, he said they don't all look the same!

Like I said I left, angrily. I don't play games when it comes to my research and I damn sure don't deserve to be disrespected, just because someone doesn't like it! I was hurt! I apologized and said I wouldn't ever force him to "LOOK", again. But, I just did it again! I am sick! I didn't need to bother him, with this cover idea. I can only hope he forgives me.

The restaurant incident was worse, though. I really blew up, on the way home. I screamed, that I was done spoiling him and he would never disrespect me, nor my hard work, again. I told him, that he didn't do anything, for me or the world he lived in and he damn sure didn't try to help it, either! I was ashamed of myself, for letting his mother spoil him and I wasn't going to let it happen on my watch, anymore. Spoiled kids become evil adults and he was one of them, just like his mother! I always had to fight with her, to discipline him and it was hell, doing so.

When we got home, I went to my computer and started typing, as fast as. I could. Sadly, I just wanted to get away, from both of them. I can't believe, I just get pissed off. I did turn to my wife, as she came through the door and asked her a question. I asked her what children would have answered, if I had asked them the question I asked Matt. She didn't hear me ask it, she said defiantly. I told her I asked Matt, if the fish and crab all look the same. She immediately replied, that they all would have said yes. "Then why the hell do you let him, do this to me," I asked angrily.

"I don't," she replied bluntly. "You do."

Wow, she was right. I'm the one, with the problem. I'm the only one excited, about discovering ETs. Why? Read on. My nightmare is about to end!

Enough of my pain, frustration, and anger! Man, have I got problems. Sometimes, I really think they don't want to find, "MORE INTELLIGENT" life. I think it's, because they know if they did, they might be asked, why they aren't looking! Seems logical to me.

It's simple logic that not looking is the "ACTION", that leads to, not "BELIEVING." If you don't look for something, you're never going to find it! This is a simple "TRUTH"! I think we all know, the "REAL TRUTH", about ourselves. Most of us, ignore it.

Now, enough of my nightmare. I just want to finish this "DOGDAMN" book and live in a world, where we don't play games, with our kids lives! "FRUCK," these brain games! Before, I wrap this up, I want to tell you one more thing, about my new book-cover.

I've labored and struggled relentlessly, for the last eight months, trying to find "EVIDENCE", that would change my "LUCK." I "NEEDED" to "CONVINCE" everyone of the "METEORS" importance and it's immediate need for attention. Our very survival, depends on it! Oddly enough, I find comfort in knowing, that a "METEOR" can take me out, "NOW"! Like Matt, it makes me appreciate and "VALUE" my "TIME", more everyday. It makes, both of us, quit worrying about dying and focus on living! I think we finally crossed a bridge together. We hadn't done that, since I showed him how to play "Wild Thing", on his new six string! LOL! I can't wait to play it together and celebrate "AGAIN"! I miss those moments so much!

I thought about my old cover idea again and laughed. I knew all along, that I needed a cover shot! I desperately needed to find something, that would instantly get my point across. I thought, that the dinosaur cover would do it, but people weren't getting my answer. This included Matt! My current frustration, was proof of that! But, I was about to find what I was looking for ! Something had to give! Lo and behold, it finally did!

One day I was driving by the Lexington, Kentucky airport on Interstate 75, "WATCHING AIRPLANES TAKE OFF," when it finally happened! Suddenly, it hit me like a ton of bricks! Airplanes taking off, go "UP"! "UP/SPACE" is the only place, we can survive a global meteor extinction event! This airplane taking off, instantly gave me my idea! Rockets go "UP," too! Space X is booked and ready to go!!! I became overwhelmed, with emotion.

Finally, I could show everyone a "PICTURE," that would "INSTANTLY" support my reality. I was going to show a meteor heading toward the earth and a rocket taking off, while people were running toward it, to avoid "EXTINCTON"!

You can bet, your last dollar, on one thing. "WHEN" people see this, we all will get "IT", real quick-like. Just like the people do, that are being left behind. This was brilliantly simple!

Children will get it, too! It's sad, but true. Finally, I had my cover shot. Woo-hoo!

I felt so relieved. With this idea, I'll be "SMILING" all the way, to the bank! Then, I'm writing checks. Now, we can all smile. Watch out "RICH PEOPLE," I'm coming for you! A picture truly is worth a thousand words! I took a break, from writing and began to draw, my new cover!

Thank God, we live in a scientific world today. "SURELY" everyone will see the significance, of this picture, as well as, my evolution chart. Check out the proof in the illustrations. Don't count on it, but here's hoping for the best. Hopefully, the majority will agree. If not we'll ask kids. They won't "LIE" just to protect themselves, from not being "RIGHT"! Thankfully they don't have egos!

If you ask a kid, if the sky has an end, they will all say no! I've done it. Why, are we still, looking for it? Isn't that sad! What happened to us? Please don't get mad, but I think "I KNOW"! We "THINK" they don't! But, "IN-STINCT" doesn't stink to them! It lives in their gut and they "FEEL" the "TRUTH"! They know the truth! It is in "HUMILITY," not "PRIDE." Everyone knows "PRIDE COMETH BEFORE THE FALL"!

If my book is successful, we "ALL" will soon know! The evidence to prove my point is in the pictures, at the end of this book. It's on the cover, too!

Instantly, I envisioned the new cover. Every detail, exploded from my mind and onto the paper, in front of me! I just knew, that this "PICTURE" was the spark, "I NEEDED" to help people see our dilemma. I couldn't help, but wonder why the dinosaur poster creators don't have, this particular scene. Wow! Maybe, they don't see what I see? Again, I had to contact them, too! Boy, did I ever have a lot to do.

I drew a quick sketch and got back on the book. You can't get any more simple and self- explanatory, than this picture Man, I just shook my head in disbelief. I still don't understand, why everyone isn't seeing, this "REALITY." Going "UP," is the "ONLY ANSWER" for us to

survive and we need to be working on it, now! This wasn't the only dilemma, I was facing.

I felt like "SHIT"! I feel so guilty. I know this "GODDAMN" religion of my parents doesn't t cure anger, it causes it! I was so regretful and sorry for what it's done to me and Matt.

All the horrible memories, kept flooding back! But, this horrific "METEOR EVENT," was taking over, my mind. I feel "LUCKIER", each passing day, now. I truly feel, that this is "A CHANCE TO REDEEM MYSELF" and get over, my guilty "CON-SCIENCE"!

I'm still blown away, that I never thought much about meteors, until now! "WHY" didn't I "SEE" the "LIFE ENDING" magnitude of them, before? I definitely knew about them. I guess seeing is believing! I saw one and I'm still dumbstruck, by the scientific epiphany I had, because of it. I definitely see a lot of things, different, "NOW." As a "MATTER OF FACT", from then on, I saw "EVERYTHING" different! One last time, here is what I saw, that fateful cold February day of 2013 and the things I'VE learned to see "DIFFERENTLY", since.

On FEBRUARY 15th, 2013, of this past year. Televisions everywhere, were interrupted by this message: BREAKING NEWS METEOR EXPLODES OVER RUSSIAN CITY WOUNDING 1,600 PEOPLE AND LEAVING MASS DESTRUCTION IN ITS WAKE! SCIENTISTS REPORT: "LUCKY BREAK FOR HUMANKIND, EVERYONE. WE MISSED THE BIG ONE!

"WTF", I blurted out. I started reeling and had to sat down, from the stark reality of what the TV news anchor, just said. Wow, we have to stop these things. Didn't "WE JUST RECENTLY SEE THE BIG ONE HIT JUPITER"? It could've been us. "MORE WILL COME"! I had to quit talking to myself. I just sat there dumbfounded and stared at the screen in sheer disbelief.

Then suddenly a famous scientist, Neil DeGrasse Tyson, came on and told us: "PEOPLE WE MUST GO "UP" AND CONQUER SPACE, NOW. MORE METEORS ARE COMING AND THEY WILL NOT STOP. OUR VERY EXISTENCE DEPENDS ON IT"!

I couldn't believe what was happening, but I sure was relieved with this news. "THANK GOD," I hollered out, "a scientist knows this too." Obviously, this meant, that they are working on it. Much to my horror, I would find out to the contrary, in his following interview. We aren't! I had to contact this scientist, as soon as possible.

I remember all this, like it was yesterday. I remember it all so well, because that's when I had my "EPIPHANY", for this book.

I originally planned to write a final book, a couple years ago. I was going to call it, coincidently enough, "REALITY." But, not like the reality, you're about to read. It's changed alright. This meteor changed everything. Now, this is how the "REAL" story, goes. I didn't make up its ending. This meteor did. It always does! "REALITY" is us, needing to escape from planet Earth or there will be no reality, to argue about!

The story you're about to read, isn't mine entirely. It is also written, by "ANCIENT RELIGION" and modern science. They've done so, because it is the only "LOGICAL" path, that we can and must take, for the survival of our species. An "ANCIENT JAPANESE PROVERB SAYS THERE IS NOTHING NEW UNDER THE SUN"! So does the Bible and science! This is not a new problem or an old problem, either. It's an "INFINITE PROBLEM"!

I am just lucky enough to have seen it and "SURVIVED"! These meteors will never stop destroying all life on planets, when the big one hits! Not, in my lifetime or anyone, else's! This is why I was "LUCKY" to see it. I lived through it and will never forget it! I tell my kids, "DON'T FORGET", as well.

Sometimes, I don't know if I would have awakened to this reality, otherwise. Without experiencing it, I don't know if anybody would've.

That's why I put the Muslims' holy temple, in Mecca, on the front cover. It has a "METEOR" in it and they, still don't know where heaven is! No religious person does! This proves they are religiously brainwashed and don't understand, the scientific significance of their own evidence.

Now, that we've seen this "METEOR EVENT" and understand our need to live in space. It could possibly, help my "DISCOVERY", achieve world-wide recognition. Let's keep our fingers crossed. I hope this is my "GOLDEN TICKET"! Please help me spread the "WORD"! I will give all my money to science, if it is. Please hold me to it and let's help everyone become scientists. We need to hire, all we can!

I know it sounds crazy, but I'm somewhat relieved! There is only "ONE" obvious ending, for this book, now. Especially, in lieu of this meteor event/"IT", sparing mankind, again. Without it, I don't think I would've had, the ending I have! I promise you, it could be "EARTH SHATTEERING"? So, please read on and find out if it is. I'm also relieved to discover, that science confirms this "REALITY" and it's not, just my opinion! I'm so glad, I've discovered evidence that could prove "INTELLIGENT LIFE," not only started by chance, but obviously succeeded by it, as well. This is what would I expect, in an "INFINITE UNIVERSE", without an "OMNIPOTENT THINKING CREATOR." It can't be any other way. Actually, I'm blown away and ecstatic about it! I "SEE" how people evolved and lived long enough, for this to happen. They all look alike and they have an infinite amount of chances, to do so! See, "HEADS OF EASTER ISLAND AND THE OLMEC GODS", in my illustrations!

This meteor event has become my reality, simply because of "THE EVIDENCE." We must go "UP" or become extinct, like the dinosaurs. This evidence is "ROCK" solid and every scientist in the world, agrees with it. "NOBODY" can deny it. The truth is in the skeletal remains of the "DINOSAURS"!

I feel so fortunate, to be living, during this period of science. I know it's still primitive. but we've reached a milestone of intelligence, that makes living in the Dark Ages, everyone's worst nightmare. Let alone, the Stone Age"! No, think of how brutal and terrible, that would've been? THANK SCIENCE", everyday, people! It "ROCKS AND RULES", today! It has become the "ROCK" we all "DEPEND" on! It is literally improving and changing our lives for the better, as we speak! It is making common sense and "SKY-ENCE", a "FUTURE REALITY"! We are finally, "LIVING IN THE SKY"! LOL! I know, you probably think I'm ignorant. But, it's OK, though. I was only trying to be, a little funny! Come on, laugh will you?

We all need to laugh, a little bit. We even need to laugh at ourselves every now and then, like I'm doing, now. It humbles us. If I didn't laugh, I'd probably cry and I don't want to cry, anymore! I've cried enough for all of us, as it is. Crying is O.K., though! Don't, let anybody tell you, it's not. There's only one time, a parent shouldn't cry and that is in front of our children, when we face tragedy! We must be strong for them! I have to be strong, now!

Evidence should make our history, not the other way around. "HIS-STORY" has gone on long enough! Please, let this evidence speak for itself, like the cover picture. It doesn't need someone else, to tell you what it says. Kind of like our history, huh! Oh, "IT'S SUCH A MAN'S WORLD"!

Come on women, I believe you can do a better job, than men! We're too emotional and vengeful. Women, for the most part, are more forgiving! Well, except for my wife. She gets revenge. She doesn't make mistakes, according to her! I tell everyone, that I've seen the devil and she's a "LONG COOL WOMAN IN A BLACK DRESS" who's always looking at her own "FACE", on "FACEBOOK"! My wife is that devil and her power is "TOXIC"! I have to cure her by leaving her. I will be get a second divorce in "THREE DAYS"! It is the only way to cure her! I'm not mad, I'm sad. I've stayed and tried. She destroyed my love and respect, hundreds of times, over 17 years. I can't cure her by staying. She is a sex addict! She can't be honest about this, or anything else, and I could die.

I hope she gets cured and helps other women, prevent this from happening, to their kids. If she doesn't and gets mad, she isn't cured! I hope, that it's not the case. Only time, will be the judge of that. I am doing this, for all men. I used to be a sex addict! My first wife will attest to that! I'm sorry for the way I treated her. She deserved a better man, than I was, at the time. I apologized and told her this, when I left! I wish Tammy would have left me!

I'm trying to wrap this up. I have to get back at it and finish this ending. I want to say, that I didn't want "MY DISCOVERY" to happen this way and I'm not glad it did! But, ironically, it is definitely, what I needed! We "ALL" want "ROCK SOLID" scientific proof, to support "NEW DISCOVERIES" and this meteor is plenty big enough, to do just that. In fact, this is one piece of evidence where it can't get any "BIGGER"! If it did we wouldn't survive, anyway! My "THEORY" is finally validated by this "METEOR EVENT" and my family, nor anyone else, can say that it isn't! We have to go "UP" to survive it. "HEAVEN" must indeed be "UP", from now on or we won't survive! O.K., enough of this, right? You know, we know! (I hope.)

I felt somewhat guilty, about my excitement, in the wake of such a tragedy. But, I just knew I had to "CAPITALIZE", this "GOLDEN" opportunity, while the "IRON WAS HOT." You can't get much hotter, than a "METEOR"! People were getting this. They didn't have to be told the answer, after seeing my new cover. After this, they all knew we had to go up! I started asking everyone, how we could escape the "BIG ONE" and they all said "UP"! Even, my brother Tim!

WOO-HOO! "MY DISCOVERY" really could take off, now. I hammered away at this ending.

You know, all along, I've been zoning in on one thing, space. "HEAVEN'S location is "UP" in the sky, and still the key, to solving our mystery. I can now see, that trying to get someone to see "MY DISCOVERY", is futile. They have to see it, for themselves. I "SEE" it for myself, now and it is "HUGE"!

"I finally, "FOUND" what I needed most!" I said boldly, as I looked at "MY NEW EXTINCTION PREVENTION POSTER." I finished it, earlier and and hung it above my computer. Now, I'm ready! With it and this primitive simple "METEOR EVENT," heaven's location is obvious! It could help elevate our understanding, of the universe we live in and finally explain religion's spirit world view, "SCIENTIFICALLY."

Unfortunately, we are still gripped in this struggle, all over the world. It is a war against science and logic, by religion. It's a shame, that both say they want a perfect loving world, but don't "AGREE", how. Since, religion is the only one fighting and killing people, it has to go! It creates this disease and the evidence proves it! I hope, that "MY DISCOVERY WILL REWRITE RELIGION, SCIENTIFICALLY!" We all must see anger, as the "FIRST" symptom of any disease. It's a "SELF-RIGHTEOUS DISEASE" and more commonly known, as the "HATER DISEASE" to kids. They know the "TRUTH" and they will let you know it, too!

With this one single event, I theorize, that I could now explain, "OUR MYSTERY" and more! Like, "WHERE WE COME FROM" and how we still exist, without being able to escape into space? Also, why ETs exist and yet, don't openly live with or contact us? Last but not least, why we are alone and how it relates to heaven's location and the E.T.'s/gods. Whew! That's a tall order to fill. Wow, I started typing as fast as I could, again. The clock was ticking!

Thanks, to this meteor event and my epiphany, I tweaked the original plan and title of this book. "FORTUNATELY," I couldn't have asked for a simpler script, because of it. Now, the future wouldn't stop playing out, in my head movie. (thanks again, Lon!) The sick part is, that I really didn't want to stop it! I'm tired and getting old! "WHAT DO I HAVE TO LOSE NOW?" As scary as my death is, the possibility of being a part of this amazing event, thrilled me, to no end. Wow, I just got emotional and I've got "GOOSEBUMPS"! Got to take a break "AGAIN"!

Wow, I'm such a crybaby! Back, though! I'll never give up, for Terry and my boys sake! I always got overwhelmed, at the thought of being able to stop my son's, fear of death. Their fear gives me the strength to overcome my fear, as crazy, as that is. When they break, I fear that worse, than my own death and am able to immediately become strong, for them! I have to be strong for them. I have to pursue science and medicine, with money as quick as I can. I have to cure death, for them and for all of us!

I can't stop thinking about all this! "BECAUSE OF THIS METEOR," I am constantly seeing, more threats, in our future. I can "SEE", how "THE BIG ONE" will ultimately pit mankind against ourselves and our "NEED" to prevent it, from happening. It will do so, because "MONEY IS THE ROOT OF ALL EVIL"! "NOBODY" will want to give it all to science! I continued to dream, this bleak future reality. It doesn't stop! Sadly, it was also playing out everywhere we go, on television! "GREED RULES" the entire planet!

Last night, I dreamed the future. The year is 2029! I started a global meteor prevention plan and call it the "TOWER OF BABEL", Project. My book was successful, just like I'm writing, now! I was book-signing, all over the world and lecturing. In my lectures, I explain, that the ancients knew where heaven was and in fact, they even built a tower, so the could reach the "SKY"!

They wanted to be with the God's, again! Naturally, I tell everyone, I'm giving all my money to the T.O.B. Project and challenge everyone, to do the same. All hell breaks loose. Rich people can't hide, anymore and they suddenly they become the "HELPLESS", holed up in their mansions!

The "ONE PERCENT", turn against the "NINETY NINE." We don't fight back, we just "RUN"! We run to the "ROCKETS"! They stay in their houses and......!

The T.O.B. Project or "Tobe," as it comes to be known world-wide, becomes the "PERFECT" platform to prevent meteors. The dream shows T.O.B. on TV, everywhere. I was right there, with itI I was showing everyone, that primitive man was "RIGHT" all along.

HEAVEN is Space... UP (the title of my fifth book)! Wow, I was still telling everyone, that we need to get off this planet and live in space! No, I was still having to tell people!!!

"People," I said loudly as I began to cry and raise my voice. The audience began to stir and the crowd began spilling out, into the street. "The ancients, were trying to get "BACK TO HEAVEN"! They know earths are living "HELLS"! "Come on, please calm down" I said emotionally as I pleaded louder and begged harder. Oh no, they were starting to leave. " I screamed out even louder, "People, we can't run, we're about to be hit by "METEORS' and more are coming!" They didn't stop.

Wow, this dream was great! It was writing my book's ending. It was totally, un-"F#&@ING," believable! I had to pinch myself. Where's your mind right now? Got you! Lol. Get ready, for what's about to happen, next!

Remember, I don't play "WORD GAMES," that's for kids and yes, I do understand why, we do it. "WE ALL DO"! We also know, what I'm doing here, too. So get over the word game. It's time for everyone, to be "COMPLETELY HONEST", about ourselves. The future is here, now! We must do this, if we want to help children save themselves, from us! Unfortunately, adults can be "HYPOCRITES" and hide their evil intent or "SELF-RIGHTEOUSNESS"! Fortunately, for kids. I don't play "MIND GAMES" and if you adults aren't ready to come clean and prove you're good.

Well, I guess we'll have to make you, with "TECHNOLOGY"! The future "GOD."

In the dream, I keep babbling and immediately pick up something behind the podium. I then thrust it into the air and unveiled it. "IT" is my new, "MIND READING MACHINE"! LOL! LOL! LOL! It's called the "DEAL BREAKER", in my book! LoL!

Enough of my "BULLSHIT"! I was being successful, with this book! This was happening!

Finally, my "NEW ANCIENT AMBER ALERT" poster, was everywhere! I looked all around me and they were on, every telephone pole! Yes, "THE CERNES GIANT" rules! I started crying. Then......, uh people began running, everywhere. Suddenly, I see someone up ahead in the mayhem. It is my sister, pointing at me and she was talking, to a policeman. Oh no, he starts running toward me as she begins running around and.....what! She's tearing the posters down. No! No! She's got the "HATER DISEASE." Doesn't, she love me? I start to run. OMG! I looked back! I see, hundreds, if not thousands of people and they were right behind me, coming down the street, toward me. OMG, no! My brother was with them. They all looked like, they wanted to "KILL ME" and he had a gun. No! This can't be happening. "Don't you love me?," I screamed as I saw her running, to join him. I looked back and ran at the same time. Then my dream turned really ugly. Instantly, I remembered why they hated me. This dream was about to become my nightmare. I had always challenged the rich to give "ALL THAT THEY HAVE AWAY", to prove they aren't religious hypocrites. Well, he is rich and she wants to be! They also hated me, for painting a naked man, with an erection on my billboard! But, it is the ancient "Cerne's Giant", of England! They couldn't stop me. It rules, now!

Instantly, I was stricken with fear and panic. I started having an anxiety attack. I'm running harder and harder, but their gaining on me. I had a few people on my bandwagon, but they were dropping quick. Suddenly, "NOBODY" was beside me! I was all alone and scared. I didn't want to die!

I didn't know why this was happening. It was coming to me, now! I knew this was a dream, but they were catching up! I have become the most hated man, in the world! I was, challenging everyone, to give all their money, to my T.O.B. Project. The majority of people weren't giving their money up! They had enough. I pushed too hard! They also weren't believing the scientists' warning, about this " METEOR", either. It could vaporize earth! NO! They weren't "BELIEVING" anything!

Much to my horror, I suddenly couldn't remember, this dreams, ending. Was I going to get away? Will my brother shoot me? Is an ET contact going to save us from this.....meteor! What! Was a "METEOR" coming? Why did I just say that? What year is this? Did I write this in? Suddenly, I couldn't remember, anything. I began to panic. I had to get hold of myself ! I had to remember, the ending of this dream! I pinched myself and it hurt. I wasn't dreaming. I stated panicking, even more.

I immediately snapped to and realized, that I was running blindly, not knowing where I was going. I headed into a parking lot. How long have I been running and why don't I know where I am. Where was I? I became frantic! What year is this? I needed to see the year. I began to run wildly, again looking... looking... and suddenly I saw it. No, I screamed! It was, "2029"! I began screaming louder and louder, for someone, to help me. No one did! I needed to understand, what was happening! Everything was going way too fast and it was getting faster! Everyone, suddenly sped up! They were gaining on me. No, I ran harder. My eyes were stinging as the sweat began pouring down my face and of my body, like a spring. I was drenched from fear and running! How long, have I been running?

Why did everyone want to kill me? I looked back and there was a sea of people behind me. I ran faster, but they were closing in. The world was in chaos, all around me. Pandemonium was raging, everywhere! "No, someone please help me," I screamed louder. I was gripped with fear. Sweat continue to pour, off me. My legs were burning. My lungs were on fire and I was getting, nowhere. Just when I thought I couldn't run anymore, I saw an airport! Thank God, I screamed as I turned toward it.

I ran for the runway, "THANKING GOD", for such a beautiful sight. But, there was a fence, in front of me. It was the break I needed, having served as a Marine. I could do this. The six foot fenced was topped off, with four strands of razor wire. It was perfect. This gave me the advantage, that I needed. I've done this plenty of times before. I jumped and caught the top of the fence, in one leap. From there, I quickly threw my body up and over the razor wire. I hit the ground and rolled. Wow, I made it just as the mob got to the fence. My sister and brother started to scale the fence. No! How could they be so angry at me?

I turned and bolted toward the tarmac, where the planes were lining up. Why, were there so many, aircraft? I didn't have time to think about this, I had to run. I heard a scream as someone, must have reached the razor wire. I focused harder on the planes. It was only, about a quarter mile away. But, it looked like it was a hundred. They were lined up, as far as , I could see. It looked like they were loading people and starting to take off! I didn't understand why? I just kept thanking God, I was going to get away! I was closing in fast and could see people pushing each other. Why? I thought to myself for a split second. Then I realized

why, as I looked ahead. They, were trying desperately, to get on a, a..........
"ROCKET"! No! They weren't planes, they were Space X rockets!

"No", I screamed! Something is wrong? Why are these people doing this? Then, I saw the lead rocket, start taxing down, the runway. Oh my God, people were still trying to get on. I started running toward it screaming, as loud as, I could for them to back away. I heard gun shots and saw someone who was clinging to the airplane's door, fall lifeless, to the ground. Suddenly, I screamed in disbelief and at the top of my lungs! "No!"

I couldn't believe my eyes. One of the crew, was the shooter! Other rockets, were starting to take off. They weren't' waiting! But why? Wait a minute, there wasn't any planes, taking off! I quickly looked around and saw...! No! These are all rockets! "ROCKETS!" What is going on? I became frantic! Had the governments lied, about the "METEOR", missing us? People began begging and screaming, not to be, left behind. All hell was braking loose, at this very moment and that's when it "DAWNED", on me. Everybody, began looking up as they were running toward the rocket. They were, screaming and begging, to be "SAVED." What! Were they looking at, a a........."METEOR"! Now, I remember what happens! "THE END." It's in the last chapter of this book. You'll have to keep reading to find out. It was in the other ones, too! I always wake up "DEAD"! Just kidding, except for what's next. Here's what happens. No! It can't be! "THE FUTURE" was happening, right before, my very eyes. I can't believe this is happening? I think I'm dreaming and yet I can't stop it!

I suddenly stopped running and "WATCHED", as the rocket lifted off. Oddly enough, I instantly, had a warm calm feeling, engulf my entire body. Despite, all the tragedy wreaking havoc around me, even with people screaming and crying everywhere, the rocket looked so majestic, as it arced into the sky. I tried to follow it, but the sun was, too bright! I thought, I was seeing the most beautiful sunrise, I ever saw. But, I was wrong! "DEAD" wrong.

No! Suddenly, I realized it can't be the sun! It was getting bigger and brighter. It was coming right at us! "It isn't the sun," I screamed as loud and hard as I could." Get on the Rockets everyone, it's a "METEOR"! I looked around and realized, that this was my book cover picture! I was being left behind! No, this can't be happening to me! I looked back "UP" toward the meteor, again, only to be blinded, by its brilliant white light. I had to look away and when I did. I looked just in time to see my brother and sister running toward me. Suddenly, I saw my brother, point his gun toward... someone else. I couldn't believe my eyes, they weren't trying to kill me, anymore. They were trying to save me! I turned on my machine and started to cry! I heard my brother and sister's thoughts, they knew mine. Then, I heard it... BANG,BANG, BANG! Instantly, I felt the bullets rip through my body and fell to the ground. I was "DEAD"!

Suddenly, I woke up, gasping for air! Thank god! It was a dream. wow, it was "DEJAVU", all over again.

I jumped out of bed, like a coiled spring, suddenly let loose. I was drenched in a cold sweat and yet I was "BURNING UP"! Did this just happen? I ran to the window. I had to see for myself, that it didn't!

I got to the window and... "THANK GOD" it was a dream. At least, I thought so. All I saw was the night sky! Can it be? I wanted this to end. I can't believe it. I am finally seeing the end of it, "MY END/MAYAN." (LOL, inside joke, from my other books! Read them and find out what it is, please? This joke is on me, also!) I know what happens next! It was the first dream, I ever had and it is in, my first book. I wake up on a spacecraft, but it isn't ours. It's a "FLYING SAUCER"! No! I'm not ready to be an "UGLY ASS ALIEN." Please stop, "PLEASE," I screamed. I was afraid of "UGLINESS"!

My vision, suddenly stopped! I was holding my face and asking myself, all the "OBVIOUS QUESTIONS." Am I "REALLY, READY" for this? I mean, am I really? Will we "BELIEVE" these aliens, let alone want to be one? Wow, I slowly lifted my hands and realized it was a dream. Man, this rattled me, bad. I had to get on with this book. I wanted more than ever, to get it done. I couldn't stop thinking of all the questions, I now had?

Most of all, will we survive, in the face of such a huge, challenge? Would our primal desire to live "OVERCOME" our, never-ending thirst, for money? Will "GREED AND POWER" cause us to carry out, our very own, apocalypse? An "APOCALYPSE OF BIBLICAL PROPORTION"! This is a scary question when we still haven't taken care of "FUKISHIMA", yet! "YET" that is! (Again, thanks Lon. I'll keep my promise for our kids' sake. All the proceeds of this book will go to stop it and yes Lon... I'll make the sign! LOL.) My "BEST" friend and I vow to stop the leak, with "MONEY" and we challenge everyone, to do the same! It is a shame that it is still contaminating our ocean's with radiation, as we speak, and it happened, almost three years ago!

Even if we can achieve a world-wide mandate, to save ourselves from "METEORS", will there be enough time? I had hardly processed what just happened when I heard more bad news on the T.V.. Tammy was bringing me, my morning coffee, when I heard it! A "BIG METEOR" is coming, in 2029! No! "EVERYONE" it's time to "WAKE UP"! It's finally happening. I immediately headed back to the computer and began to type.

We can prevent our extinction if we can come together and give everything we have to make this happen. I know it seems impossible, but we have to build as many space stations as we can and exit vehicles to take us there! We have to be ready! We have to. "METEORS WILL NEVER STOP"!

I was more determined, than ever. I continued typing, more furious, than ever! It seemed like, I was "DESTINED", to prevent our extinction! I "BEGIN" to see no other logical answer, for this. This is not "FUN"! I must entertain, that this has already happened before. I'm telling everybody "THE UNIVERSE IS INFINITE"! I had to "SEE" this possibility. I held on, to the only "LOGICAL EVIDENCE", I had. These flying saucers exist and our world isn't "PERFECT"! Destiny, and déjà vu, had to make! It only does, with advanced technology! I wrestled and still wrestle, with these complicated issues. I do it by scientifically examining the evidence based on the logical reasoning of them. The "EVIDENCE" leads me, to a final conclusion. The future is about "TECHNOLOGY", not time travel. I can see this new, exciting and riveting ending, now. "SCIENCE WILL CONFIRM MY DISCOVERY"! This book will end with me telling the future of mankind. A future that has "ALREADY" happened on earths everywhere. I get famous, help everyone, and then get taken out by... got ya! You gotta read it now. LOL!!!

You are about to read, "THE FUTURE"! It is the last chapter and I promise you, that it is mind-blowing. Human creation, reincarnation, immortality, destiny, and fate is child's play, compared to "OUR" real "REALITY." A "REALITY" where "PERFECTING HUMANS" is an incurable and "TORTUOUSLY INFINITE NIGHTMARE." But oh, it is ever God awful, "POWERFUL"! It is one endlessly unbelievable, nightmare being carried out on earths, everywhere. It keeps on happening, over and over, again. All for the sake of "IMMORTAL" intelligent, existence. We can't kill us, and yes I'm one of, us. We just try to keep "SAVING", what little knowledge we learn, until we "FINALLY", had enough! We do have to get, "it", though! Then, we just might be O.K., with being an "OUTWARDLY UGLY" alien, who is an "INWARDLY" content. A person with complete peace! Wow! What it would be like to be them. "A SPECIES WHO'S EYES, WHEN THEY MEET, DON'T TWITCH AND BECOME NERVOUS, WHEN WE STOP TALKING. SOMEONE, WHO DOESN"T GET DISTRACTED BY FACIAL DIFFERENCES, EGO, AND AWKWARD QUIET GAPS BETWEEN US. WOW! What a mind blower, huh!

I promise you, that when I'm done, my story will leave no doubt in anyone's mind, about what's going on. You will understand, why heaven is ultimately, "UP" and hell is "DOWN." More than that, it's one promise I won't even have to keep. Science, won't let us forget, "IT".

Let's all hope, we can get "REALITY, AND ESCAPE FROM PLANET EARTH", before it's, too late! Now, please put on your seat belts, relax, and prepare yourselves for the ride. The end is in sight!

I started on my book, immediately, that day! The next 10 months would fly by, with one tragedy after another. The first, naturally was my family going to hell over, Terry's property. Second, not getting this book done on Terry's birthday, December 31st, 2013. I've been having marital "HELL" since, the year started and then... my beautiful niece Linda was killed on August 1st, 2104. It hurt so much. I was sad a lot and I still am. I have to believe, it's possible to see her, again. I have, to! I kept looking at my new book cover drawing to keep going. I was doing it, now. I would soon get color added and have it printed out!

Wow! I said to myself looking at the picture. I was giddy with excitement. I could see an artificial Earth! "HEAVEN", could indeed be, "REAL"! We can make it happen. I got teary eyed, just thinking about it. Maybe, I will see her again. Maybe, I will see everyone, again. She is just one of way too many, that I've lost.

Even though, I've lost my biggest supporter, my oldest brother Terry, thankfully I've gained my brother Tim, in his place. He wasn't as receptive as Terry was to "MY DISCOVERY," but he is still "LISTENING."

Although, we may not agree on everything, we certainly agree upon one thing. We keep HOPING" for the best, and live and let live. The Golden Rule.

I'm kind of glad he doesn't agree. I like the challenge. Especially, since he wants to see science validate, my discoveries. I needed this kind of attitude around me, going forward with my pursuit of scientific validation. To us, this wasn't about right or wrong, for "GOD'S" sake, it was about, the evidence. He liked my "NEW" story line and agreed that "NOBODY WILL ARGUE", about "THE WAY", to avoid a meteor strike. It would prove to be a game changer for the success of my books and repairing the relationship, with some of the family. Yes, I lost some along the way.

I was blown away recently at Tim's reaction, to my new, "EVOLUTION AND SCIENTIFIC CREATION PROOF." I made up a chart showing how all life, besides humans, that all look the same. Then I asked a question "What do all these species have in common, that humans don't"? It is clear, that they all look the same! I asked him if he was familiar, with the "EVOLUTION VERSUS CREATION" debate and if he knew the definition of evolution.

"Why yeah," he said boldly. "Life evolves by chance"! "Wow," I blurted out excitedly. I had to admire that. Matt and I had more trouble,.I laughed about,then. I commended him for his knowledge. He was a smart guy! Then I asked if, he believed it.

He said it wasn't proven and brought up, the fact that monkey's gorillas and ape are still here. Yes, and they all look the same I reminded him. He then pointed out, that the missing link should be as well, then. I agreed and asked him, if he saw any life, that did evolve. He looked bewildered and said I just told you, I didn't.

"Well I "THINK" I can shown you proof of evolution and how you can tell it apart, from a scientifically created species, like us."

"How," he replied quickly cocking his head up and to the side. He was grinning from ear to ear. I got on the computer and showed him several different species of life and their categories. I found pictures of mammals, reptiles, fowl, and asked him if they all looked alike. "Why yeah," he quickly said in agreement.

"Well, there's your proof of evolution. They all look alike! Do humans all look alike?" I added, continuing to question him, more. Wow, I was making head way.

"No, they don't do they? Huh. What the hell?," he asked puzzled like. I really was enjoying this.

I felt like I've finally found a simpler way to "PROVE, BOTH EVOLUTION AND CREATION"! I was about to answer his question and watched him have the same eureka moment I did, when I realized the "SIMPLE IMPACT", of it.

"What does religion say we are"? I thought that he would bristle at my implications, but he didn't.

"Well, I guess that God created us. But. I don't think that God would make us all look different and them the same. Why would he?"

"Good question," I replied back. "Would you agree these species, that all look the same, could be a product of evolution?"

"Yeah, I see what you mean." he replied softly. "BINGO," I told him. I quickly followed with the question, that us religiously raised kids in denial and ignorant of "EVOLUTION", must face! "Well, if we find ancient evidence of an ancient people, that all looks the same, could they be a product of evolution?"

"Well, I guess so, how could it not? I started smiling even bigger. I got goose bumps. Tim and I had more than a few disagreements, about my "ALIENS EVOLVING AND SCIENTIFICALLY CREATING MAN, THEORY"! I always knew he didn't see "EVOLUTION", because he didn't know, what it would look like. I didn't either, until my epiphany. "WHAT THEY LOOK LIKE" was the key, now! Finally, I continued teaching him, what to look for and how this happens.

I quickly pulled up the heads of Easter Island and the Olmec god's, on my the back of my poster. He really liked, the caption at the top. It was written in big bold letters and said; "SMOKING GUN EVIDENCE"! He read and just looked at the ancient humans, with amazement. Wow, I could see that he got it. I laughed and told him that people, will freak when he realizes the *Coneheads* movie, is based on, a real scientific facts! Then, I showed him how this scientific creation spawned our so called "MISSING LINK"! He got so excited and asked me why I didn't do this, in all my books! I laughed and told him, I guess Granny was right. I do everything "BACK ASSWARDS"! He just rolled laughing and rocked back in his chair and smiled.

"Well little brother, maybe God is evolution and the first human's he made, were these "ALIENS." This would explain why we were "PERFECT", in the beginning. Hell, we all looked the same. That's what made a perfect world, huh?" Yes, just don't make evolution and the universe a thinking being, like religion's god. That's what "INTELLIGENT DESIGN" is, they're the same thing.

"Now you're thinking, though. I said that in my first book. The angels are all equal , because they, obviously, look equal! Check this out "BIG BROTHER! The "BIG PICTURE" really gets clearer when you see, that the Genesis story of man's creation, comes after "MANKIND" evolves. This is the same way, science says it happened. They agree!" I was giddy with excitement, but he wasn't quite there. I wanted him to see the expanded version of man's creation and quickly continued. This is where the evidence is very simple and clear.

"Well, the big bang happens and we have a story of evolution for five days, the sixth day where it says: "let "US" make mankind in our image male and female. After it was done, he called us good, we're "PERFECT," right? Remember, the red flag here. He says "LET US MAKE MAN," like he's talking to others, with "HIM" God is plural here, right?" Well, the 7th "HE/THEY" rest! But, the eighth day "HE/THEY LOOK DOWN" on Earth and there is no man, to till the ground! Bingo! This is the proof, they conquered space! Then, made us to worship them."

"Wow, I never thought about this," he said puzzled like as he took a long hard drink of his coffee. He said suddenly, "That,s pretty damn cut and dry, huh?" "Yeah bud, it is. It's simple as hell and the evidence, tells the story, not men. We don't need someone to explain it, for us, now. Not, with this", I said as I got the chart from him. I was sure glad he reacted this way. He was still skeptical, but he got it.

"Well, our mystery is really all about, what "GOD" looks like, bud. We all know where "HE" is, even if we really don't. We show it by looking up, when we talk to "HIM" or Terry. Please always remember that, O.K.?" I asked him lovingly, with a tear rolling down my cheek.

Wow, I just saw his light bulb go off and it was, as bright as the sun! I grabbed him and pulled him to his feet. We hugged, like there was no, tomorrow! We both laughed, cried and danced a jig for Granny. She loved Terry so much.

"By God," he said beaming with pride at his newfound understanding of... hell everything! "Everybody should see this. Why are you just now figuring this out, "GOD DAMN" it? Your books would've been a hit a long time ago."

"Like I told you, this shit is in every book, from the first, to this one, Bud. You just gotta read 'em."

"I tried God damn it, they're really pretty damn scatter-brained," he said while laughing all the while. "I don't mean to offend you, but put this chart in the front of your new one, just in case." "Bud, my books seem scatter-brained, because you didn't start, at the beginning and finish it! I only heard, about you reading a little of this last, one. And Bud, it's no wonder it was so, screwed up. I was reeling from Terry's, death. I also felt guilty, for not finishing it, with him!" I choked up and dropped my head, with emotion. He grabbed me and pulled into his arms. We both just cried. We missed Terry, bad!

"Besides, Bud," I said laughing as we pulled apart. "I smoked a lot of medical marijuana to finish it. I fell apart, after his funeral! Hell, it took another six months! What did you expect, perfection? I'm not perfect Bud, just trying to be"

"I know little buddy," he said as he massaged my shoulder. "It was hard for us all. Get your ass home and get your book done. I think it's a hit! It sure as hell explains your theory and "EVOLUTION" simple enough, for kids, even. The beauty of it is , that it does it, "WITH EVIDENCE"!," he said as he picked up my manuscript and shook it in the air. It was a beautiful moment! Finally, he wasn't saying "WHAT EVIDENCE", anymore. Everyone of my family, except Terry, not only denied this "EVIDENCE" supporting, any existence of "FLYING SAUCERS AND AN ALIEN" species, but they said it "WASN'T EVIDENCE," at all! Nothing swayed them, from our short history being created by "PEOPLE LIVING UP IN THE SKY" to "ANCIENT STATUES, ARTWORKS OF ALIENS, FLYING SAUCERS, UNIVERSAL

HEAD MOLDING, TREPANATION, AND THE OWL BEING THE WISEST BIRD

BECAUSE OF ITS BIG EYES," to all religious people looking up when they talk to "GOD"! Last, but not least, we now live up in the sky and "I FILM FLYING SAUCERS"!

I was so relieved, because I loved him so much! I needed someone to take Terry's place. I didn't know if I could do this, alone. I immediately headed to the house and told him I wasn't leaving the computer, till this book's done.

That was a week ago. I'm just about done or at least, I thought, so. Little did I know, I was about to "SUFFER" one more terrible moment, before this nightmare, would end.

I went home and immediately told Tammy I busted her. Unfortunately, my son heard us. One of her friends, spilled the beans, about her seeing a guy, for the last year or so! Wow, she had gotten angry at me, while I was in Arizona, a few years ago. It was, just a couple months, before Terry died. I started a business, showing people flying saucers, in Phoenix. She demanded that I come home or she had a 41 and 25 year-old, who wanted her! Man, what a "DISEASED EVIL DUMBASS", she was! She can't even be satisfied with one man, she has to have "TWO" and she just told on herself! What happened next would crush me! It was about four o'clock in the afternoon, the next day and we had just finished "SEX", when suddenly we heard a big thump. All hell, was about to break loose. We were about to have, a family meltdown. At the time, "SHE" didn't think much of it and just thought "SOMETHING" had fallen. I knew better! I instantly panicked. I knew Matt was having a hard time, with our divorce, but I never expected this. I got up and ran out of the bedroom. I heard a door slam, as I immediately, went toward Matt's room.

Much to my surprise, he wasn't there and his girlfriend came out of her office, next to it and was just, as surprised, as I was. She said she didn't know, what happened, either. I asked her where Matt was and she said he just went out the door. She thought he was looking for the cause of it, too. I asked her if he was OK and she said, she thought so. I knew better! He was as much a scaredy cat, as she was. I felt like something was wrong with him, but she gave me no indication of it.

I shrugged my uneasiness off and started looking for the cause of the loud thump. I felt so relieved, when I found my guitar had fallen, against the wall. Apparently, its stand had collapsed. I went to tell Jess, when all of a sudden, my worst fears came true. Matt busted through their side door and ran past us, flying straight toward the front door, again!

His mother hollered at him to calm down and said we found the problem. He turned, just for a second, and smarted off to her, slamming the door behind him. I knew something was up then and hollered at him, to stop. He didn't! I started after him and heard him come back through their bedroom door, again as I was opening the front door.

I turned and headed straight toward him. They were all in his hallway and he was losing it. Jess was trying to calm him down, but couldn't. He was slapping himself and going crazy! She was beginning to panic and cry. His mother stood there helpless. I immediately hollered and asked him what was wrong. He slapped himself again and started running toward the middle of the room and jumped up to hit the fan, with his head! We all panicked, I immediately ran and stopped him.

"STOP IT GOD DAMN IT," I screamed loudly! "What the hell, is wrong with you? Talk to me. I've put up with your Mom, doing this shit for 17 years and I'm not going to put up with this shit, from either of you, any longer. Now calm down and talk to me!" He did and I knew what was bothering him. His mother, because of her disease, just never "CARED ENOUGH" to help "US" deal with it.

Matt didn't understand, how I could still have sex with his Mom and want to leave her, at the same time. I explained, that she won't let me leave, without causing him problems. I had to divorce her. She was dangerous. I added that I still have sexual desire, for her, just no respect or romantic love anymore. He felt like, I was just using her. He asked me why I didn't "MAKE US ALL GO TO A COUNSELOR" and get help. I told him how I've tried for 17 years, but she was in total denial of her "SEX ADDICTION" and would never go. I went further and I explained that I had counseling because of "ASSAULTING" her three times and she never once came or admitted her promiscuous "DANGEROUS" behavior. She stood there and fumed like the devil "HERSELF," as I talked.

    He said he was alright and wanted to talk about it, now. I started crying and thanked him for finally getting the courage, to do this. I knew this was killing him on the inside and just couldn't get him, to open up to me. He said he resented me, for always making her the bad guy. I told him I knew it, but couldn't stop it. Communication is the way to solve issues, not panicking or getting angry. I am not making her the bad guy. It's her disease. He said I never do mention the good things, she does. We hugged and I apologized for it. I asked him to please start sharing his pain, with us and asked him if she ever talked to him about this before. He said no and she immediately bristled with anger, like she always did!

    I turned toward her and couldn't believe my eyes. Here we are, about to finally have a breakthrough and she's "SO ANGRY"! She couldn't even do this for him and he had just tried to "HURT HIMSELF", in front of us. I was beside myself. I knew then, she was a lost cause. She loved herself more than anything else, at that moment. She wasn't about to suffer any shame for "HIM, ME, OR ANYONE ELSE", for that matter. It was all about to end. I immediately told, Matt to please ask her if she's a sex addict! He did!

    She puffed up and angrily replied, that she was, OK! Matt told her, that anger is the first symptom of denial. He started saying, that maybe she was just getting revenge for finding the girl's card in my pocket after I got home from playing music, till five in the morning. I agreed, that this is how it might have started, but that I saw her "MEAN" girl personality from the get go and she still has it! I just got caught up in the whole mess and I shouldn't have. I told him about her being vicious to her step-sister, because she was nice to me! I explained that she eventually committed suicide, because they made her feel like she wasn't "GOOD ENOUGH" to be part of "THE LESTER FLATT FAMILY"! I ended by saying she was brainwashed, by her "RICH AND FAMOUS FAMILY"! They were vicious, thinking they were better than everyone, else! I told him, that I even heard her mother, at one point, tell her little brother Shane something unbelievable. She actually told him to, just tell the kids at school, who were picking on him, that at least he had "MORE MONEY THAN ALL THEM PUT TOGETHER. LIKE A $100,000 TRUST FUND"!

"This is why she, her mother, and grandmother are warped, son. They brag about stories of her playing on the bed and helping count a suitcase, full of money Lester would bring home, from his shows! They were doing this with a little five-year-old girl, son" I said with tears streaming down my face.

"She is mentally brainwashed and "SEXUALLY ADDICTED" to the power of money and her beauty, because of it! He said he doesn't really understand, what a sex addiction is. I quickly said that we could look it up, but it is someone who pursues dangerous sexual encounters with multiple people and can't control themselves. They put everyone in harm's way and don't care who they hurt in doing so. This is what she did, with us! I told him I would look it up on the computer, but it's an insult to my intelligence, really. He asked why? I told him, that she admitted seeing a 41 and 25 year- old, besides. That's not revenge or normal.

I didn't want to do this, but I had to! I told him that I would start, from the beginning. "Well," I began to speak slowly and softly. He had heard enough yelling! "After your Mom found the girl's card "FIFTEEN" years ago and went harry scary on me, which she did while I was lying in bed with you, right beside me. I got up and begged her to stop. I even asked her to call the girl. She wouldn't and it woke you up. You began to cry, so I quickly picked you up and told her to stop it. I told her to call the woman. She stomped around and started to slap me. You started screaming and reaching for her. I turned my back to protect you and you just kept crying and begging, for her to take you. You know what she did?" I reluctantly asked him.

"No," he replied weakly. I felt so sorry for him and went over to hug him. I hugged him and said, "She wouldn't take you. It was her anger, that kept her from it! I know she loves you. I'm just not sure, that she loves you or anyone, more than she loves herself. I've put up with this to protect you. She done it, because her Mom did this same thing, to her. Ask her sometime, about how she pulled a shotgun on her mother, one night, because she wanted to go to the bar and leave her with a baby-sitter. She was only five!"

He just shook his head and began to cry more. I hugged him and asked him to forgive her, no matter what. He said he would and asked me to finish telling him, everything. I didn't want to, but I did. We had to end this, now!

"She backed away from you as you leaned toward her screaming and said: Your Dad can take care of you now. I've done it for five years and I'm not doing it anymore!"

"Son, I couldn't believe, what was happening. I had to do what I had to do to protect you, from her. So, I just crawled back in bed with you and tried to calm you down. You just kept begging and crying for her, to come to bed. It was torture!

After what seemed like an eternity, I finally got you interested in cartoons and you settled down. Then I made an excuse to use the bathroom and went to talk to your mother. She was in her mother's bedroom, who just so happened, to be at a bar somewhere. She was doing the same thing to Shane, Matt. I threatened to take you and leave if she didn't come see you. She knew I wasn't kidding and came out of that room, like a mad bull. She headed straight to our bedroom and crawled into bed with you.

Son, I saw your eyes light up instantly, when you saw her. I broke down and cried. She held you "FOR A MINUTE OR TWO, THEN

TURNED HER BACK, ONCE YOU SETTLED DOWN! It was the most heartbreaking, moment of my life."

I started to shake all over. He grabbed and hugged me saying, "It's alright, now." He asked me to let it all out and finish the story. I nodded my head and started again.

"Well, I didn't want you to see me crying so I went in to the bathroom and washed my face. When I finished, I came into the bedroom and started watching cartoons, with you. You were lying beside her as she had her back, turned to you. It broke my heart. I crawled in bed and you asked me, why mommy didn't want us anymore? I told you, as best as I could, that she does love you and it's all my fault. I told you I did something, that I shouldn't have and it hurt her real bad. I tried explaining to you, that people get angry when somebody hurts them and say things they don't "MEAN," but your mother wouldn't stop. She instantly spoke like the devil again and said, "MOMMY'S ANGRY" and I would be the one who is going to hurt, from now on! You got scared again and tried to reach for her, but she got up and slept on the couch. I just held you back and tried to explain, that she just needs some time alone. Thank God you didn't fight me and laid in my arms. We both finally cried ourselves to sleep! She turned her back to us, from then on, Son and I've never stopped begging her to get help, even now. She won't do it and I have to divorce her for our sakes!"

He and I both broke this time. She never moved! After we finished crying, I stepped back and told him, that she didn't keep having sex, for revenge. I explained, that she even brought men home and would whip him, when he caught her. He quickly admitted, that she had and he was having a hard time, with it! I was losing it, but I had to stay strong, for him. He admitted, that he also saw her flirt with more men, than he wanted to remember.

"Matt," I interrupted quickly, so I could follow up on what he just said. It was the evidence I needed, to prove her "SCIENTIFIC FACT OF SEX ADDICTION." It was coming from him! "What you just said, she did is, the definition of a sex addiction! "SHE" was not only putting you in harm's way, but she was "HARMING" you mentally and emotionally. I'm sorry for that, but your mother is a "SEX ADDICT" and that hurts. I understand, but I know, that I can only "POSSIBLY" cure her, by leaving. I'm sorry, but you're 23 and I have to go. It is my job now and duty as a father to you. I'm failing both of you, by not doing anything, about it. I have to go and she is proving it, as we speak, look at her! I have to leave! She can hurt us, if she doesn't get help, Son. "I HAVE TO LEAVE," please understand.

He did and we both just hurt. We wanted to gag and cry at her disease! She looked just like her defiant angry mother! He started to cry, but managed to tell her, one thing, before he did! That she did do all this and more! I hurt so bad for him and went to hug him. He was sobbing uncontrollably. "What a "GOD DAMN" piece of... shit "F@&$ING DISEASE, she is" I screamed in my mind. I hated her so bad and I knew I shouldn't! "UNFORTUNATELY," I had the "HATER DISEASE", now. I've always had it since the beginning, but not any longer. Tonight was it!

She tried to make an excuse for looking, acting, and being evil, but it fell on deaf, crushed, and hurt ears. We were crying and dying deep inside! We knew she was sick and only wanted, some kind of "GOD DAMN MIRACLE", to happen! We wanted to save her! Obviously, we couldn't. She only "REALLY" cried, when I finally walked away and said, "IT IS FINISHED"! This was when she always started crying. Her disease had taken everything "HUMBLE" away from her. She lost, and was still losing, because she was crying for herself, then! I stopped as I headed to the door. She began pleading for me to stay and he started to cry again. I didn't leave and I will fight this disease, to the end. We will love, forgive, and "HELP" her, "GET HELP"! She's was horribly sad and went to the bedroom. I began typing. I just hated all this!

I'm sad to say that this story is filled with way too many heated exchanges and hurt feelings! I still can't believe, that all this started, with me trying to find, "ANGELS/ETs"! I may not have convinced everyone of my "DISCOVERY," like Terry, his wife, Tim, and some others I've mentioned, already. But, I convinced enough and am making some real strides, with my YouTube videos. The books are even starting to make a few hundred dollars a year, instead of barely a hundred. LOL! Oh well, I'm trying. A "BIG ONE" is coming in 2029!

Before I went to bed that night, after the so called "FAMILY" counseling discussion, I had to talk to Matt, alone. I went and found him playing on his computer, as usual. He looked up and took his ear phones off. I went on over and hugged him. I broke down and cried. I thanked him, for finally hugging me, like he did. I missed his hugs! I knew he loved me and told him so. I also told him, I knew why hadn't. It wasn't his fault. He said he was sorry and started hugging me, with everything he had. It was a beautiful moment! I broke harder and he did too. He kept saying he loved me and how everything is going to be alright. Wow, he was trying to console me! This, is his first "MILESTONE"! I loved him so much!

He was such a great kid! I apologized for everything and told him, that he needed to comfort his girlfriend. I made him promise me, that he will never go crazy, again. He said he wouldn't. I asked him to please help me and I told him, that it was time for him to get a job! I explained, that he is as much a hypocrite, as anyone else, to complain about the world we live in and not even help take care of his needs! He apologized and said he was ashamed, that he was like this. He even said he was going to change!

I was ecstatic, but not like I was, about to be. I started telling him, as I regained my composure, that I wanted him to know something, I learned as a young man with a broken heart. I knew his heart was broken. Mine was too! I told him, that I learned it a long time ago. I asked him what was the difference between "SEX AND MAKING LOVE"? He said he didn't know. I told him, "NOTHING! It's all in our mind and if we don't mind, it won't matter. In fact, it's only a "GOOD OR

EVIL" thing when it "MATTERS. But, lucky are the ones who love each other, when it happens!" He got it.

Dumbass me, I couldn't stop there, even though, it was a beautiful moment! I explained one last time, that this family discussion epitomized "MY DISCOVERY AND PROOF OF EVOLUTION" and how our "UNIQUENESS," by these ETs OR GODS,", is our downfall. He got it, before I said another word! "HALLELUJAH", I said to myself! "Remember," I said as I was leaving. "Please, "DON'T FORGET" it. The world is drunk in a "FINITE THINKING SEXUAL DISEASE"! There's only one question to ask yourself, to see if you have it or not. "HOW ADVANCED COULD LIFE BE IN AN INFINITE UNIVERSE"?

He just looked at me smiled and started shaking his head up and down. He got it! I saw the light bulb turn on, and like Tim, it was brighter, bigger, and better than any sunrise or sunset, that I've ever seen! It was a "SUPER-NOVA"!

"Wow," he suddenly blurted out. If E.T.'s have "INFINITELY EXISTED", they would be "EVERYWHERE", huh? They wouldn't be coming from a planet or going to one and they would stay away, like their doing now. Most importantly Dad, they would know everything, like you say. They would have to, since they always exist! I get your question now, Dad. I see it!" He was so excited.

Wow, I hugged him, as hard as I could. I told him, about my new "PROOF OF EVOLUTION AND SCIENTIFIC CREATION" chart I had made up. I was so excited about how easy it is to see the evolution of everything, except humans, with it. He said he saw it and really liked it! He even said, that he was sorry for the Captain D's, incident. I knew he was already and told him, to forget about it.

Surprisingly, he started to show me some stuff on the computer, that clearly reflected people's primitive view of ETs. One after another, commented on how "FAR" they would have to travel to get here from their "PLANET"! I was blown away!

He got it. He even laughed and said, "If we all looked the same and lived naked, we wouldn't even desire sex, huh? Wouldn't we go extinct, that way, too," he asked puzzled like.

"No, we will propagate scientifically and we would make ourselves, anyway we want. That's what I think, these "GOD'S OR ETs" did. The heads of Easter Island show us, that people evolved and obviously created us for "SEXUAL POWER." That's why I put the Cernes Giant on my last book. Now, surely you can "SEE" this evidence. If not just ask yourself one thing: "Do you want to be ugly"? Obviously, that's why we're here, Son! I don't. Terry didn't and I know you don't either. Son, I am about to "REVEAL" a mind-blowing "NEW REALITY", to the world. It's the same one, I told Terry to prepare for, when he died. It is the last chapter and the ending of this book. It is, "THE FUTURE"!

My "DREAM" told me that, when I die, I will wake up as an alien. Ironically, I still don't know, that I am one! When I look around, I see them, all looking at me. They all look the same! I jump out of the apparatus I'm in and started running away, toward an exit. Before I can get there, several start toward me. I panic and turn toward another exit, only to find it blocked. Just as I started to turn again, it happened! I ran straight into two aliens holding up a full length mirror. "No," I scream in complete horror, at what I was "Saw." I couldn't "BELIEVE" my eyes. My heart started pounding harder and harder, still. I was gripped with fear. My heart was running away and I couldn't stop it. I started to get dizzy. My knees grew weak and then... I will continue in the next chapter! Otherwise, it would spoil "EVERYTHING"! He laughed and said he would!

I hugged Matt and went on to bed. I was miserable, but I will not let her "DISEASE" win. I hugged her back all night.

Wow, Tim and I have "FINALLY" had a meeting of the minds and now, Matt too! We made it through the divorce and I got back from Ohio unscathed. I immediately finished this book and met with my publisher. It was time to address the "METEOR PROBLEM"! It is coming! I could go on and on, about why my research caused so many problems, but I've gone on enough. It's a "DEEP" subject matter. Besides, I don't want to distract you from the importance of this meteor event, OK? I will tell you one thing, before I end this chapter. I "SEE", proof of advanced ET intelligence and evidence in our ancient past, that suggest we could have done this before? OMG, and we all have déjà vu! Will this meteor happen like my dream "REVEALS"? I don't know. I always heard gunfire before it hit and woke up.

My "THEORY" about going "UP" suddenly wasn't so "FOOLISH", anymore. Especially now, that this recent meteor happened. Tim saw it and a lot of my other family members did, too!

Heaven's location isn' t a MYSTERY" anymore. Some people may never take it seriously. I can't change that. I hope my "EX-WIFE" does. I hope everyone does!

"Wow," I said to myself in amazement. Here I am, going on 20 years, since I made my "DISCOVERY" and most people, still don't get it. Sometimes "I GET SO FRUSTRATED", that I could just quit. But, when this happens, I always make myself remember one important "INESCAPABLE", fact of life. At one time, I didn't know "ALL" this shit, either! I was so ashamed of myself, right now. How could I have gotten so angry, at everyone, especially my family! Somewhere along the way, I sure lost sight of "EMPATHY"! It's time to eat some humble pie and get empathetic! I have to help myself, before I can help Tammy or anyone else. "FORGETTING" is everyone's "DISEASE." I have it too! OMG! I can't ever let myself forget this, again.

On FEBRUARY 15th, 2013, I saw the implications of this meteor event and vowed to never let the world forget. We have to cure the world's religious ignorance and lack of scientific, engagement! From that day forward, I set out to share this knowledge, with the world. I had to do it for my kids.

I have one final request to beg of you. Since I spilled my guts to the world, would you please give my story a chance. We have to ask ourselves, for our children's sake: "WHY DON'T WE HAVE A METE-

OR PREVENTION PLAN"? Why can't the world's scientific community see the significance of "IT," regardless of my "THEORY THAT ETs EXIST"?

Isn't it "TIME" we take this seriously and give "ALL EVIDENCE" a chance, as "CRAZY", as it may sound. Religion shouldn't get a bad rap, just because it's offensively illogical. We can prove, that "RELIGIOUS PEOPLE" are just "BRAIN-WASHED", by it! It doesn't mean it doesn't exist. It "EXISTS"! We just need to "RE_EXAMINE" it, using "COMMON SENSE." If somebody could make a "UNIVERSE," it's only logical they would make it "PERFECT." Well, it isn't so let's get on with the "PROGRAM", a "SCIENTIFIC PROGRAM." Aren't we a people of science, information, and above all, compassion? As a people of "LOVE", who wants the best for our children, can't we please just give all this, a second look? Please, I have children! I'm begging you, please "ALL OF YOU," let's give this a chance! Don't we all want a "PERFECT WORLD"?

I want to end this chapter, by asking everyone to please help me start a meteor escape mission, for all mankind. We've just discovered a much bigger one and it's on the way in 2029! Could it "POSSIBLY" be the big one? I don't know. "WILL WE BE READY IF IT IS"? Even if the world isn't, can my "DISCOVERY" and "POSSIBLE" fame, rally everyone, in time to save humankind? I'm not optimistic because we still haven't taken care of "FUKISHIMA"! If so, we will do that first.

Thanks Lon for your help! You are a great dad, musical genius, and true friend.

My "DISCOVERY" leaves behind a wake of heartbreak and joy, tragedy and triumph! The humility, suffering, and redemption we all went through, hopefully kept you on the edge of your seat, throughout "MY" journey. I'm sure you see, like I did, that "TRUTH" truly can become a double-edge sword. It can become so bittersweet, that it will engulf you, if you let it. It drowned me.

"MY TRUTH," at the end, can be torturous! "BELIEVE ME", it may not make "MOST ADULTS" happy, but it is an unimaginatively beautiful truth, to all children! It will make them "BLISSFULLY" happy! It will free them, from "SEXUAL PERSECUTION"! Last hint, we're almost home.

Last, and certainly not the least, I'm not worthy to judge anyone. I beat my sons and ex-wife! I want to start by apologizing and confessing. I'm a hypocrite and the proof is in my seventh and last book, Infinite Astronauts: The Theory of Everything. I fell prey to money! I wanted to keep a couple hundred thousand, instead of giving it all to science!

What a joke, I am, huh!

Hopefully, you've already read my bio and familiarized yourself, with the previous books. In case you haven't, I have previously written seven books about the "MYSTERY OF MANKIND." This book is a continuation and much more. It is "THE END"!

In fact, it like the meteor is our inevitable end, unless "WE" solve this mystery"! How could the answer be that hard, if primitive man knew it? Surely, we can figure it out since we are now living "UP" in space and tens of thousands of years more advanced? (But, are we?)

Astonishingly enough, "I NEVER" expected this meteor to happen. At least, "NOT IN MY LIFETIME." I don't think any of us did.

I was stunned, and needless to say, "BLOWN AWAY", that it did. It "ABSOLUTELY" had an immediate and profound "IMPACT" on me. It is, the "ONE" moment in time, that I will definitely "NEVER FORGET"!

This "METEOR EVENT" affected me. Sadly, I could see, that everyone else, for the most part, was being largely unaffected, by it. They are still forgetting, about "METEORS"!

Like a child, I suddenly became filled with a wildly vivid, "IMAGINATION"! I could see a wondrous scientific reality, unfolding in my mind. Clearly now, I could see our evolutionary journey toward, omnipresence, becoming our future reality. Thank God, my brother Tim, got it. Matt is finally getting it, too. Maybe I will succeed after all. Scientists and kids are my final goal! I've got to do this thing.

History gives us "ALL", the answers to prevent our dilemma of "INEVITABLE EXTINCTION." They are in "RELIGION and SCIENCE"! They are the same then, as they are, now. We lost the meanings and shrouded "IT", in an obscure "SUPERNATURAL WORLD". This "WORLD" doesn't exist, just because, they say it does. Stop hating religion, please? I finally, did. I can prove, that they all have a "TRADITIONAL BRAINWASHED DISEASE"! It's incredibly easy to prove and I put it on YouTube, like I mentioned earlier.

They all say they aren't brainwashed and can't be, but other people can be. I know that's bull shit! Because, I used to be and I done and said the same thing, they did! Thankfully, "SHIT HAPPENS" and I went to Nashville. I "FINALLY WOKE UP" at the "TENDER" age of 33!

It's time to figure it out! I can't wait any longer, for "SOMEONE" else to do "IT." Why? "METEORS"! "MORE ARE COMING AND THEY WILL NOT STOP—EVER"!

Well everyone "HOPEFULLY," I have painted a vivid and "SIMPLE" picture of how this meteor event, changed "MY LIFE"! This simple meteor event, began to change everything for me! I could really see it happening. It shocked me, when I polled people about "METEORS"! A lot of people saw them as our biggest threat! It was truly changing people, scientifically. I really was beginning to "FEEL", that maybe, my books were going to be a success, after all.

I hope by exposing myself "NOW", that I'm able to influence others, to do the same. Let's all give to science and stop this "INSANITY", before it's too late! Religion's motives are the same as science. Get over it!

The only thing that makes it not, is "US"! We can't wait any longer on "GOD" to save us. Please, let's not argue, anymore. Let's solve our mystery and "STOP METEORS"

I am excited about my discoveries, because they give me hope. It gives me "EVIDENCE", that the future is out there, now. People, I need it! My little nephew BRICE, who is only 13, was recently diagnosed with CROHN's DISEASE. He went through surgery and is recovering nicely. I want to give him hope and a cure, more than anything, else. I called him at the hospital and made the same promise, to him, that I'm making to everyone. This will be a bestselling book and I will challenge everyone to give to science. I will do this for him, my uncle, that he was named after and "EVERYONE ELSE." I love you all dearly.

If we truly want a perfect world, let's first ask ourselves "WHY AREN'T WE GIVING EVERYTHING TO CURE DEATH NOW"? You decide whether you give or not. Either way, please give this story and "EVIDENCE" a chance. Maybe ETs this meteor event proves, that there's more to our existence, than just "DUMB LUCK". Hang on and "THINK INFINITELY"!

People, we seem to be repeating religion's story. It is our history. We came from "UP" in space and now are returning. Yet, they still elude us. Why? How? You be the judge. Get ready! I'm about to share advanced scientific evidence, that I've learned and am still learning today. The location of their home was, still is, and "ALWAYS" will be, the most amazing discovery, I've ever made. "LOOKING UP" is the single most important clue, in solving our mystery. It clearly proves a physical reality, instead of a spirit or dimensional one.

"UP"/SPACE still remains the final frontier to conquer, if we want to "SAVE" ourselves "FOREVER/INFINITELY"! It matches not only our safe haven today with this meteor event, but also the ancient religious evidence of our past. It matches the leading scientific theory about our future! It is called, "Stages of Civilization." I was overwhelmed, when I viewed it on YouTube. It is a theory by Michio Kaku, a professor of science at the University of New York. I'm still blown away, every time I watch it. He saw "UP/SPACE" as the ultimate stage of existence. I wasn't alone, anymore. I'm not the only crack-pot, who thinks this way.

I had to ask Michio a question, though. I want to know, if he thinks we should only live in space, like "JESUS"/Yeshua says or on planets, too. I see only one way to avoid death. "SPACE"!

This doesn't make me special! Anyone can "SEE THIS." As a matter of fact, I got this knowledge, from the most famous man in the world,

"YESHUA." It is in his teachings, about "HEAVEN", which is really the "UNIVERSE"!

I made this discovery around 1999 and subsequently began writing books, about it. My "INFINITE ASTRONAUT THEORY", would take ten years to be born. In the beginning, I got the chalk board out and began a time line. I still do it! The "EVIDENCE" I found solved all my questions, about life and its origins. It just kept making more and more "COMMON SENSE", to me, as I continued to study. Life existed everywhere, "UP" in the sky! It has too.

We exist now and have ancient stories of them, to support, this scientific reality! I became obsessed, with solving our mystery. Earth is a crime scene! What these "CREATORS" look like, is all, that needs to be solved.

This evidence I found, literally fills in all the blanks for me. Not only for our mysterious short history, but a whole lot more. It proves to me that heaven could be real and that life could exist "EVERYWHERE, UP" in space. "WE LIVE UP

IN SPACE"! As a matter of fact, if the immortality of our species is "OUR" objective, then this meteor makes it "PERFECTLY" clear. We have to go "UP" to survive. "WE MUST LIVE IN SPACE."

I continue to study relentlessly revealing new discoveries at every turn, hoping each one will help solve our mystery. For all our sakes, I hope answers and ETs are everywhere... Let's help each other. "I CAN'T BEAR THE THOUGHT OF MY SON'S DYING, LET ALONE EVERYONE ELSE. This became my obsession and "IT" still is. I'M SORRY FOR RAMBLING ON AFTER I TOLD YOU I'VE DONE TOO MUCH ALREADY! Maybe I should've stopped 100 pages back, with: "THE FUTURE and my "ANSWER," but this is my future. I have to prove my theory and sell books to start a meteor escape mission. I finally think I found, the key to success with this meteor event. Like I said earlier, I'm not special and anyone can do this. But, "SOMEBODY" HAS TO BE THE FIRST"!

Could I "REALLY" be "THE ONE" to solve our mystery and lead us into "SPACE"? This is the question, that causes me so much hell, in return. Why? I don't mind that Newton discovered the Laws of Motion, first! I can take it. It's OK! I laughed about, how this issue, freaked my Jehovah's Witness family, out. Funny thing, is the last thing they wanted was for me to be "JESUS" or an ET! Check out who they think Michael the archangel is and you'll know why.

Please remember this one very important fact, as I'm about to end this "PRESENT CHAPTER" of my life. It alone will help you solve this mystery, of not only what my discovery is about, but maybe life itself: "WHERE IT COMES FROM OR WHERE WE ARE GOING?"! That's your "CALL." I'm presenting this book as my theory and evidence to answer all life's mysteries. I could be wrong, but oh how I hope I'm right, for everyone!

Before you dismiss my "BOLD" claim and I know, that it is. My discovery was validated, by this meteor event. This is an indisputable "FACT"! It is the scientific/religious ticket/evidence I needed to prove my theory. It was and still is a scientific confirmation, that "HEAVEN" indeed is "UP/SPACE"! Space is the only place we can live, to become like these "IMMORTALS" and avoid death by mother nature!

I'm sorry if I offend anyone with my sexual innuendos, explicitly nude ancient artworks, and references about them, throughout this story. Unfortunately, my theory involves our lust for the power of sex! Yes, we have to talk about sex, to our children. It is a simple fact of life. Think about it! Especially, you religious people. After all, our mystery began "WHEN" we covered our nudity! I'm sorry to inform, all you up-tight religious people, but the perfect existence, for humanity was at the "BEGINNING, WHEN WE WERE NAKED"!

Please consider this graphic evidence, for our children's sake? If, "GOD'S OR ETs." can truly read our minds, what do we "TRULY" have to fear, about talking to our children? Ourselves, maybe? Ask yourself now, can you walk naked with your adult child and control your "SEXUAL SELF"? Can you live in a "NUDIST COLONY" and control yourself?

The world is full of ancient historical religious nudity and I am attacked viciously for using it. Even, by my own family. I don't like talking to children about it, anymore than you do. But, it has to be done, eventually. It has to be done. I am only using them, for clues and to humorously expose my answer to mankind's mystery. I am blown away at the hatred, disgust, and hostility I get, when I say this to someone. Everyone has the right to submit their theory without retaliation. I've been attacked by UFOlogists too!

Meteors, continue to be a very real threat, to the existence of our species. It will never end, as long as we live on a planet. This story is about my struggle to get people to understand this and "NEVER FORGET" it. I've been telling people, heaven really is "UP" and why it is so, for the last 15 years. Let's stop "PLAYING GAMES"!

It should be our number one priority, now.

This book is not about who's right or wrong. It's about, finding an "UNBELIEVABLE" body of evidence, from our ancient past, that matches today's science and "IT" gives us hope of a brighter future. It is the stuff dreams and movies are made of. It is chalked full of historical and current evidence, that clearly paints a picture of the life "I'M SURE" we all want, for our children's future. A life where death is conquered and we live in a world where "EVERYTHING IS PERFECT"! Everything... perfect?

Well... Question "EVERYTHING"—especially, me! The universe isn't perfect or it would be now! "THAT'S A NO BRAINER! IT NEVER WAS JUST BECAUSE SOMEBODY SAYS IT WAS, EITHER! Maybe, the most important person to question, is ourselves. I know it was for me and still is. Will I want to be "PERFECT", if I have to be an alien?

This is my ongoing struggle and always will be! It is my biggest obstacle, to overcome. I am fed up, with "ANGRY EVIL HUMANS", who want to insult my intelligence and make me a loser. They do, because I can't stop getting "ANGRY/EVIL", back! I can't stand rich people who claim to be spiritual, either. It makes me gag. Enough is enough!

I hope you've enjoyed my story and may we all have "GOOD LUCK." As loving parents, it's our "PRIVILEGE"/duty to honor and cherish our kids. Please, don't dread the research. In fact, be thankful for it. I am. We just got a second "CHANCE." We could've all been taken out, by the "METEOR"!

Heck, put on a little music while you read. Music goes a long way to soothe the soul and that's what I'm looking for—"SOUL" baby! No pun intended! LOL. Nothing ventured, nothing gained, right?

The song, "IMAGINE," "SEEMS PERFECT," for this occasion. Please remember before you begin, life isn't always as it seems. Just "IMAGINE", how wonderful life could be and what is truly possible if we would "ALL" give everything we have, "TO MAKE THE WORLD A BETTER PLACE"! Let's not wait till we die and go to the "BETTER PLACE." John Lennon wrote and sang this beautiful song, about that possibility. "Imagine," now for those of you who didn't know him. Do you think he "PRACTICED WHAT HE PREACHED" or just, wrote about it? Sadly, He died wealthy and he just wrote about it. Michael Jackson wanted, "TO MAKE THE WORLD A BETTER PLACE." He died wealthy and just "WROTE ABOUT IT"! A lot of famous wealthy people, write about it. I don't see anyone doing it. I know, sad huh? Suddenly, I realized something! No, OMG no, it... can't be! My brother is wealthy, my aunt, my uncle and even worse... THE PRESIDENT OF THE UNITED STATES OF AMERICA"!

It doesn't matter. Blame never solved anything. Just enjoy the song. "IMAGINE" is truly, a beautiful song. You might even say, it could be a dream come true, if we would make it happen. Will we? If your answer is yes, then read on and more "POWER" to you. If not, then just close the book and "LET IT BE" or "LIVE AND LET DIE"!

In the words of a truly stereotypical pot smoking, peace loving hippie, "PEACE" bro. May the "FORCE" be with you. Here is a famous farewell quote, that I like best. It given to us by "DOCTOR SPOCK" of STAR TREK: "LIVE LONG AND [what?] PROSPER? What's that all about? Suddenly, I remembered the sign he held up when he said it, "IT WAS PEACE" too! LMFAO. Got ya. Go ahead and say it in your mind! You already are. Wow! It's ironic, that we make "HAVING BABIES/PROPAGATION" such an evil thing and the most evil cuss word of all. Crazy, huh? Hold on, there's a little more that you've got to hear. Please give a dying man some "SYMPATHY" and just a few more minutes of "YOUR TIME," please?

One last thing... is there a "RIGHT" time to talk to a little girl about the Amber Alert? Little girls and boys are being sexually molested and abducted, daily. I'm sure it is happening right now. We all know it is. It's silly to deny it. The African girls are still missing!

Do we really want to gamble any longer with our children? I know it sucks, but we must do this.

Knowledge is power! They need it and we have it! How dare us not give it to them. Our children could've been an Amber Alert. I couldn't live with myself, if it was and I didn't try to do anything, I could to prevent it. I will give all my money "AWAY" to stop this horror, against children! (see CERNES GIANT) Freud said it best about our species: "Humans are sexually frustrated and they lie about it"! Let's save our children... from us—adults and invent a real mind reading machine! Maury Povich and his lie detectors, won't save them.

I hate to be so blunt, but I've discovered, that sex has everything to do with our mystery. I also know, that my MONEY GIVE AWAY CHALLENGE" is more dangerous, than all the atom bombs, put together. Sadly, it hasn't been done yet and "IT HAS TO BE DONE"! My son and I are voting for Bernie Sanders, because of his equal wealth platform.

People, in this story, I've revealed everything about the tortures "SEX" and how it affected my life and journey!

I have always had one goal in mind, pursuing this mystery and to "SOLVE IT"! I don't "PUSSY" foot around. It's all about the "POWER OF SEX"! It's our worse "DISEASE, SEXUAL A- DICK-TION"!

This isn't the "TIME" to play games. Is there ever really a time, we should? Do you want your little girl, to be abducted? Do you want her to be brutally raped over and over, again. Do you want to keep her from being "KILLED"? Do you still want to play games? The clock is ticking, "NOW"! "METEORS ARE COMING AND SEXUAL PREDATORS ARE EVERYWHERE"!

I knew very little, about "EVERYTHING", when I started and didn't even know it. Funny huh? It isn't when the jokes on you. People, it's on me! I'm sorry to everyone, for my self- righteousness. It is destructive and accomplished nothing. Here's what I "KNOW" now.

I am "READY" to finish what I started. This is the "END" and my new "BEGINNING"! People say I'm "WEIRD" and it shows in my books. I'm cool with that. Einstein was weird. Yeshua was weird. The "JESUS" thing is weirdest of all. Check it out!

You are now entering my "REALITY." A world where the future has "ALREADY" happened and we read each other's minds! They are "PATIENTLY WAITING ON US TO GROW UP"! My mind scares me, but "IT DOESN'T SCARE THEM"! I never want to be old or ugly. Most of all, I never want to see my children die! Hell, I don't want to die! I see it all happening, way too soon! I have to stop it! The world is full of humans who worry about wealth and "AIMLESSLY" pursue death, instead of life.

Beware, you are forewarned. I am about to reveal, "MY DISCOVERIES BODY OF EVIDENCE TO SUPPORT MY THEORY." It is "MY ANSWER TO WHAT REALITY IS AND TO PROVE, THAT IT EXIST NOW"!

I now know why "ignorance is bliss" and "knowledge itself can be torture." I'm old! "GODDAMN THIS WISDOM"! Before you start, are you sure that you're prepared to share my discoveries? Are you really ready, for my "TRUTH"? Do you dare tempt to do what can't be undone and "LEARN SCIENTIFIC FACTS ABOUT THE UNIVERSE WE LIVE IN"?

If so, I applaud you and "GOOD LUCK"! Remember, to always question yourself, along the way! Don't ever stop asking "YOURSELF", one question. Could this happen to me? Especially, before you pass judgment on "SOMEONE ELSE'S STORY," like mine.

The events you have just read are "REAL"! In fact, the only thing, that isn't real is the "DREAM OF MY FUTURE." At least, I can't prove it is, "YET"! It will be up to you, to make that decision. To me, I "KNOW", that it "COULD BE REAL." The aborigines say, "THE DREAM WORLD IS THE REAL WORLD" and my déjà vu does too! It is a "NATURAL TRUTH" and one I can't hide, nor run from. It "IS" my gut feeling, that I just "IN-STINCT-IVELY" feel and I don't like it, most of the time! It stinks on the inside of me, bad. I don't want to be ugly. This makes me a "SHITHEAD," right! LOL! This is not relative either. It's just the "TRUTH"!

Fear not, though! I have found ample evidence to prove, that time travel is impossible.

WOO-HOO! We don't have to relive our shame, but don't be so giddy, yet! I'm not. Future technology will let us all, watch it! I think everybody has a story a "BAD STORY", when it comes to sex and beauty.

Please remember, because we're finally here, this is my future! It is only mine and I'm not saying it's real, for everyone? The funny thing is, I think it could be! I think you, me, and everyone else, may have the same problem. I can't find anyone, that wants to be ugly or die!

So, before you think, I can't read your mind, you better "ASK YOURSELF ONE QUESTION": "DO YOU WANT TO BE UGLY OR DIE? You don' and believe me, it's OK!

"WHAT YOU ARE ABOUT TO READ, IS THE SINGLE MOST IMPORTANT EVENT, OF OUR LIFETIME. IT IS UP TO EACH OF US, TO EITHER LEARN FROM IT OR DIE IG-

NORANT OF IT. IT IS OUR INDIVIDUAL CHOICE. LET'S HOPE WE CAN SACRIFICE OURSELVES, FOR THE SAKE OF THE HUMAN FAMILY. I HAVE KIDS. IF THIS HAPPENS, ALL MANKIND WILL CEASE TO EXIST! THE ONLY SURVIVORS WILL BE THOSE LIVING ON THE SPACE STATION! WE MUST GIVE EVERYTHING TO PREVENT METEOR EXTINCTION"! WE OWE THIS TO OUR CHILDREN.

HERE IS THE REASON, WE ALL MUST GIVE, EVERYTHING! FEBRUARY 15th, 2013, A METEOR EVENT TOOK PLACE OVER RUSSIA! IT MADE WORLD-WIDE NEWS. IT HURT PEOPLE AND DAMN NEAR DESTROYED A CITY! WE HAVE ANOTHER ONE COMING IN 2029!" It is the most import ant event of our live's and indeed one hell of a "WAKE-UP" call. I used to be ignorant! I am awake "NOW." This is for them—and all children.

I never "DREAMED" this could happen to me, but it did! And now because I lived through

"IT," I must "NEVER FORGET" it. I have to make conquering "METEORS" my first priority and death second! "METEOR PREVENTION" supersedes everything else—even death. I've discovered that life is "TRULY" all about, each of us individually, trying to not die. But, it now has to be a "COLLECTIVE" attempt to survive or we will fail! "NONE OF US WANT TO DIE OR WE WOULDN'T BE ALIVE NOW"!

Wow, I have to pinch myself. This "EVIDENCE REALLY" makes me "BELIEVE", that we can possibly conquer, living forever! Even, if I can't make contact, with these "ETs or GODS". This evidence gives me hope and let's me know we will "EVENTUALLY" achieve the same status, that they have of living "UP" in space, through science. We can be "JUST LIKE THEM"! We are doing it now. "UP IN THE SPACE STATION"!

They are the only ones who would've survived the meteor event. This event changed my life forever. I am forever, grateful to be alive! It is my responsibility, as a father to never stop sharing my "IGNORANCE" of it, to "OVERCOME" it. I will tell you "LOVINGLY," and humbly, what I "KNOW", now. The following event is real! It happened to everyone. Please, "DON'T FORGET" it, ever "AGAIN." I'm begging you please? Meteors will never stop. I remember that day, like it was yesterday!

FEBRUARY 15th, 2013. BREAKING NEWS: METEOR EXPLODES OVER RUSSIAN CITY WOUNDING HUNDREDS!

SCIENTISTS REPORT: "LUCKY BREAK FOR HUMANKIND.

WE MISSED THE BIG ONE! FOR SURVIVAL WE MUST GO UP AND CONQUER SPACE NOW. MORE METEORS COMING AND IT WILL NOT STOP. WE WILL SEE THE BIG ONE!"

Here is an instant replay of my immediate reaction, that fateful day. I suddenly thought about my boys, like any "NORMAL" parent would, in the face of such a near death experience. This was, as near death, as it gets and I knew it "THEN AND NOW"! There was so much, that I "NEEDED" to do for them and with them. This was my wake-up call! We all could've died!

"NO!," I screamed in disbelief at what just happened. "Matt, Jess, Tammy," I shouted out loud in complete shock and dismay. I could hardly believe, what I just saw on television. "We just survived a freaking major meteor strike, you guys! Come in here, hurry," I screamed again as loud as I could!

OMG, they weren't here. The silence was deafening. I frantically looked for my phone. I had to call them immediately! I was panicking. Was there more coming? Could this be just the beginning of "THE BIG ONE"? Is this the end?

I immediately thought, about my boys and realized, that I just got a second chance with them. Not, too many people get this lucky. My bucket list started "NOW." That is, if this was all there was coming at us. I had to find out. I stayed glued to the television as I called each of them. Thank God, they were alright! I told them all to get their ass home, until I could get the lowdown on this situation. If we were going to die, were going to do it "TOGETHER"! "CERTAIN DEATH" gives a "FAMILY" a whole new meaning and perspective. I wanted them home"NOW"!

This "METEOR EVENT," definitely showed me and all of us, just how quickly, "WE ALL WOULD BE EXTERMINATED BY A BIGGER ONE." Mankind just got its wake up call! This was a world- wide breaking news, event. "THANK GOD" it was a small one.

I was more, than a bit shell-shocked, by the magnitude of what just happened. "Why though?," I thought to myself questioningly. Why would this surprise me. I've "ALWAYS" known we could be taken out by "THE BIG ONE." But did I really? Even though "I THOUGHT I KNEW" it, I didn't do a damn thing about it. This is what determines my "WORTHINESS", now. I certainly wasn't ready for it. None of us were. I "CLEARLY" saw that and it blew me away. How could this not always be our first priority in life? This was a "GAME-CHANGER" for me! Hell, it should be for all of us. This meteor could have been the big one and blown us all away. I was different from that day on. I knew how "BIG" this was!

Sadly though, people began dis"MISSING" it, almost immediately. I personally knew why. History is just repeating itself! The ancients "FORGOT", too ! I was shocked, that the holy temple of Mecca has a "METEOR" as it's "CORNERSTONE", to prove it. It is the most important "STONE" of all and they don't know why! This is why I put it on the cover, not too mock them, but to "ENLIGHTEN" them! The lesson this meteor event taught us, and the others before it, never took off. There's nothing more to tell you, other than too much time has passed since. I am just now wrapping this book up and it's a month over it's copyright date.

That is my brother Terry's birthday and the last day of the year! December 31st 2015. People, the lesson is simple. I will quote the headlines of that day. "WE MUST GO UP, CONQUER SPACE, AND LIVE IN IT! WE MUST START DOING THIS NOW"!

"PEOPLE", all it takes is money to do this, but nobody has given up their mansions, to do it. Not even, the wealthy scientists, reporting on it. WE ARE ALL HYPOCRITES"! I am the epitome of it! I have to give everything, now not to be! What about our kids? Don't we "ALL" care?

"Wow," I thought to myself as I watched the unfolding events on TV! This was happening in "REAL" time. I watched in agony until, they finally said nothing more was "COMING"!

"Thank God, we all survived this one. God damn it we were "LUCKY." I screamed, threw my fist into the air, and bit my tongue as I vented my frustration! "But for how long?," I said a whole lot softer as I calmed myself down and just began to cry! I had to capitalize on this event. It was huge. It was current! For one split second in life, we all got it. We all "SAW" it. This was my moment. Finally, Matt, Jess, and Tammy came home. It seemed like an eternity!

I immediately hugged them them all. Then, I softly asked them all how we could've survived, if this would've hit us and been "THE BIG ONE"? I told them I wasn't doing this to torture them, but to make sure I had done my job! This was one time, that they all said, go "UP"!

"PEOPLE, THIS IS THE EVIDENCE I WAS LOOKING FOR AND IT ISN'T ABOUT RIGHT OR WRONG"! "UP" is "JUST A SIMPLE SCIENTIFIC FACT OF LIFE, FOR

THE SURVIVAL OF OUR SPECIES"! Two letters, one powerful "WORD," and the "BIGGEST" piece of evidence facing us today! "EVERYONE" agrees. We must go "UP" to survive!

On FEBRUARY 15th, 2013, science confirmed my "UP" theory (well, at least, this part of it). It was confirmed by Neil DeGrasse Tyson and I am using it for the back cover of this book. His quote reflects the same disgust, I have. It is directed toward our "LAZINESS," in pursuing

"SURVIVAL/LIFE/HEAVEN/SPACE." I am not getting his permission and my publishers tell me, that he can sue me. Here's a nod to you groupies and your latest fad word, "REALLY"! My ex-wife is one of the biggest and it tortures me! I'm giving all my money to him anyway!

His warnings, like all his colleagues, were aired everywhere and "THE SCIENTIST WERE RIGHT." We did get lucky. We survived! But, did we really just get "LUCKY"? And how could we not be ready for this, by now? We've known about it for a "HUNDRED YEARS" or better, haven't we? "PERSONALLY, I SEE," that we've always known about it throughout history, with the universal "HEAVEN STORY" and all cultures even revered meteors as "SACRED" messages from heaven. The location and understanding of it was lost over time. It still is today!

That's the other part of my theory, "HEAVEN'S STORY" is real. Science was confirming it.

My sons were too! What more could a dad ask for? This was my ticket to scientific acceptance. That's what my youngest son wanted. He got it that day, thanks to Neil DeGrasse Tyson! I will get my science degree just for him, but in the meantime I will go see Neil!

As ecstatic as I was, it also made me realize, that I hadn't written a final letter to my children about life, death, and our mystery. A final letter, you might say. How could I put off such an important "DUTY"? I should have done this, already? What was I thinking? I've written seven books and I haven't written a letter nor a will, to my children. What am I waiting on? Hell, I know why I hadn't written a will. I am giving them my money, now But, I'm their Dad! They're afraid of dying and I need to give them some answers, about life and death. I'm dying. We all are!

I immediately wrote them a letter wrote down this event and it's date! "Sons, don't sweat the small stuff, in life! FIRST AND FOREMOST, KNOW THAT YOU ARE THE SAME AS DEAD, UNTIL YOU KNOW THAT YOU'RE ALIVE ONLY BECAUSE A BIG METEOR DIDN'T HIT TODAY! PLEASE REMEMBER THIS EVERYDAY? PLEASE? Now, please get off this plane. We can't stop "METEORS"!" Please read my books and it will explain. I love you both so much. Love dad! I wrote this and then cried. I stopped and sat back, not wanting to hurt them anymore, than I already had. I reached and drew a smily face with it's tongue sticking out! I sat back and smiled. I Knew they would get a kick out this, at least. I like to leave them smiling! But, I can't "NOW"!

Ironically, I have to hurt them for their own good. This "METEOR" and the reality of death demands that! This was messed up! I remember how life seemed so unfair, then. But, then again to me it always had. It is "NOW"! I can't make the world perfect. I had just spent the last 15 years writing books and telling people, that going "UP" was the only way to avoid meteors! They didn't get it until this, one. Now, I am donating all my money to science, for this reason. It is an "INFINITE PROBLEM" problem for planets and mankind. Most didn't get it. I told people to "THINK INFINITELY" and most still didn't get it.

I kept writing books hoping one would take off and help get "MY THEORY" to science or Barbara Walters. Nothing worked!

My last book was even called *INFINITE ASTRONAUTS: THE THEORY OF EVERYTHING* and it still didn't work. What's wrong with us? What am I not doing, showing, or explaining good enough? Just look at the craters on the moon! We're going to be hit, again! I couldn't believe this was happening! I suddenly had another epiphany, that fateful day, February 15th, 2013. What just happened really could help launch "MY DISCOVERY." Immediately, I thought to myself "THANK GOD But, it didn't. This was my struggle!

"THANK GOD" for "MY DISCOVERY"! I have italicized words as clues to help you solve this mystery, throughout the book. I don't mean to write so much about me, but I had, too! It is "MY DISCOVERY." A lot of people hate me! It is because I've always said in my books, that I know where heaven is. Well, I made it a theory and they still hate me.

"DO" I think I solved our mystery and can explain "WHERE EVERYTHING COMES FROM" and "WHY INTELLIGENT LIFE

STAYS AWAY FROM US AND WHO THEY ARE." I don't know, I just have a theory and I film Flying saucers! They think I can't have this answer, nor could anyone else, but I "THINK" I do. I want respect. I'm OK if I'm "WRONG"! If they don't think anybody could find the answer, then why look? What if this happened to them?

"OH, HOW I WISH PEOPLE WOULD ATTACK THE EVIDENCE, INSTEAD OF ME"! I've had all the harsh criticism I can stand. I even got a death threat! (See death threat by marine sniper preacher in illustrations) It's OK to disagree with "MY THEORY." It's just not if you attack me or my family, for it! I only have one word to say to these people, "METEORS"!

Finally, to those haters who say I'm not a scientist, because I don't have a Ph.D. and my theory hasn't been recognized by science yet... Woo-hoo! You're "RIGHT"! A lot of scientist who made the first scientific discoveries, that we've built upon and still use today, didn't have degrees either! So, it really doesn't matter if you believe me or this evidence. I can't cure your degree demanding "SELF-RIGHTEOUSNESS" overnight! It takes "TIME." I may be a piece of "SHIT"! But what about "CHILD PRODIGIES"? Besides, you can't get the degree without pursuing it. I'm pursuing it! I can't save my sons! Right now, or ever, no one can! But, "WE CAN ALL POSSIBLY SAVE OURSELVES FROM METEORS" by living "UP" in space, when one hits. It is the only way. "WE MUST GO UP"! Again, Two letters, one "WORD," and the "MOST BEAUTIFUL PIECE OF EVIDENCE IN THE UNIVERSE, HEAVEN!"

Please help me, everyone, for our children's sake?

"ONE LAST TIME"! I will use all my money to achieve this goal of conquering space and death. Conquering death is secondary to conquering space/heaven—like religion and science says. We must insure our survival "FIRST" and then multiply, to then be able to achieve immortality. It doesn't work the other way around. Remember, what the scientists said about this meteor event? It's our lucky break and I don't think any of us "REALLY BELIEVE IN LUCK"! Like Terry says, and we all know, "SHIT HAPPENS"!

Now, would you all please help me contact Barbara Walters so I can answer her question:

"WHERE IS HEAVEN"! "STILL", nobody else seems to know! Please help me, help all of us. I will give all my money away, make myself perfect, and "FOLLOW" the most famous man in the world's "TEACHINGS"! Most importantly, I will follow, only provable logical loving evidence, whether it be religious or scientific! As bad, as I would like to enjoy, the power of being rich, I can't. Eternal life, for my children and all the children of the world, is far more important! "YES," I believe in YESHUA, because of his logical teachings, empathy and love! I like, that he also gave us the ultimate weapon against "HYPOCRISY". He challenged everyone to give their money away and follow him, "IF THEY WANT TO GO TO HEAVEN". What a simple logic, to use. The power of wealth will be "SEEN", for what it is. "GREED"! What a f@#$ed up world we live in.

We admire Oprah, Trump, Obama, who are all wealthy and then go to church on Sundays! This is a sad joke and it's brainwashing our children. I challenge all people to give their money to "METEOR PREVENTION" and space exploration! It is our only chance, for survival!

I started this book with a quote from the famous Captain Kirk, of the television series, STAR TREK. It also confirms my answer to Barbara Walters. "SPACE, THE FINAL FRONTIER/HEAVEN"—it is "UP"! This meteor and science confirms it. Please everyone, I have the answer and proof Barbara wants. I am still filming flying saucers! I think I can answer why all ancient religions say heaven is "UP" and yet, we still don't understand it. Scientists are starting to "SEE" it, but the sad "REALITY", still remains. The world of mankind still doesn't know "HEAVEN IS SPACE... UP!"

"KNOW" this one simple scientific fact, rich people—I'm coming for you and "I WILL GIVE MY LIFE, TO MAKE SURE EVERY-

ONE GIVES AWAY ALL WE HAVE TO PREVENT METEOR EXTINCTION"! I "HAVE" too! Otherwise, I would be a "HYPOCRITE!" I want the world to be perfect! I also want to be perfect! I'm ashamed of the pain I inflicted on my children and others! I am ashamed!

"PEACE OUT" and forgive me please!

People, I'll stay with my family, till the end for my "SONS"! I have to! My "SEXUAL" and mental desire to have a relationship with a woman, cannot ever happen! It will only happen if my ex is cured and she isn't getting help, like she said. Her disease is lethal to everyone. But, most of all, to me and my son. I am broken. My ex-wife continues to "DEMAND", that I stay or "ELSE."

I am afraid. I've known the horror, that humans are capable of inflicting on their "LOVED" ones and anybody else in their "WAY". Sadly, I know now, that I can't change humans—none of us can. I can only change myself. I am sorry for all the pain I've caused you Sons trying to leave her. I am also, a "DISEASED EGOTISTICAL HUMAN"! I wanted to spend the rest of my "SHORT" life, with my "PARTNER". But, I can't. I had to let her go. I've caused you both so much pain, from my selfishness. It is finished and I am living, "NOW"! I wouldn't be much of a father if I continued to try and fulfill my "SEXUAL DESIRE" and have her. Tammy will not let that happen. I "HOPE" that "SOMEDAY" we will all, live in peace!

Finally, I leave! My son is 24. I won't come back until she can prove, that she got the "PROFESSIONAL" help, she is suppose to get. I want to do this. I have to. She hasn't produced the evidence. To me, "BELIEF" is all about, the proof! Evidence is the only thing I "BELIEVE" and "SEEING" is believing! I wasn't gone 2 weeks, that she didn't start her suicide talk. I came home. I have to. This is real. Families die everyday because of it. We had one last family meeting, before I settled in and unpacked my bags. I asked Matt if he would rather I leave and he said, yes. He said we weren't compatible and he can't stand the tension vibe I give off. I apologized and told him I can't stop it and stay with her. He understood and said his mom would be alright, when I leave. I got up and hugged him. I looked at her and begged her to let me go. She immediately bristled up and said she isn't stopping me. I turned to Matt and asked him if he wanted me to leave, now. He shrugged his shoulders and started to talk. But, his mom immediately came toward us and started to cry and take my bag to unpack it. "You see what she's doing now don't you bud. She isn't going to let me go easy. I told you this, see now she's not such a bad ass is she? She isn't because she knows I will leave. I am tired of her thinking she's prettier than me, if nothing else for God's sake!"

Tammy had already started unpacking my bag and Matt was just kind of shocked, by what I said! "What?", I quickly asked him. "You do know that Tammy thinks she's prettier, than me.

Don't you? I've been saying it to her, ever since she started this seventeen years ago. She thinks shes a 10 and I'm a 1." He was surprised and laughed But, asked her if she did. She didn't answer. I immediately asked her, to prove my point. She still didn't answer. I didn't want to cause him anymore, pain. I told him this is all the proof he needs. I will leave, in about a week. I didn't need the proof I just had to get this book done. He understood. I walked him to his bedroom and told him one last thing. "Son, just imagine if humans were born with a number on their forehead, that measured their beauty?" He started laughing and said we wouldn't exist. "EXACTLY", I said laughing, too. Suddenly, I had my last epiphany! I told him him that the devil is called "MANKIND" and the number on their forehead will read 666, at the end of time! He also is called something that; was "ISN'T" and will be "AGAIN" thrown, into the eternal lake of fire! These are pretty addicts, who just get recycled, back into humans and imprisoned on earth. They do it over and over, again till they get! They don't exist in "REALITY". ALIENS DO!" The evidence makes me ask myself if humans could be a product of the future, our "FUTURE"! Could we just be biological robots? Isn't that what something is that doesn't evolve? This is what you're mother, me and everyone else is truly afraid of asking ourselves. Because' if it's true, then our "MEMORY OR MIND" can't stay hidden and nobody is ready for this, nobody." He quickly agreed, as tears began to well up in his eyes, again. "I will overcome it! I will help you overcome it. I want to help everyone overcome it." We hugged.

People, I look for and film flying saucers! Could they be the "GOOD ETs/GODS" and we are the bad ones? Do any of us, really want to be human again, after "SEEING" all this "HELL"? Well, good luck, "IF" so? I think I'd rather be an ugly alien? Well, enough of the "PRESENT", please enjoy "THE FUTURE"! Beware and look up. A man was killed in India today, "BY A METEOR"!

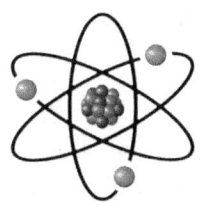 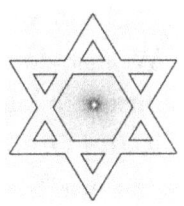

CHAPTER 3
THE FUTURE

2029 NEXT METEOR STRIKES NASHVILLE. KILLS 2,000,000, "NOT"! People, "I CAN'T PREDICT THE FUTURE"! Nobody can, except for celestial events. The lottery wouldn't exist, if anyone could! Get over it. Get science. Get "LOGICAL," please?

Look, I am sad! We need "ONLY" one billion dollars to build an infrared scanner system, that will identify potential meteors. We must do this, for our children's sake. I don't give a rat's ass, if you "THINK THAT IT WILL NOT HAPPEN"! It can. This is a "MENTAL SYMPTOM," like "RELIGIONS BRAINWASHING ILLOGICAL SELF-RIGHTEOUS DISEASE," and I cannot cure it. I can cure "HYPOCRISY" and "GREED"! That is easy. If you want the "PERFECT" world, give all that you have and choose "LIFE"! We must do it. "NOW"! OK, I had to use it one more time. We all know the "POWER OF NOW." If you don't, the whole world will "KNOW", soon! It is my dream!

The "DREAM" I have is always the same. I get killed, for trying to tell everyone, something we already know. We are all "SEXUALLY ADDICTED TO BEAUTY" and don't want to "CURE" it. I told my wife (she was then) and our niece, Madyson, about it. We were having dinner at a restaurant. My wife got real upset and said, "It's no wonder people don't buy your books, you torture people." She's "RIGHT"! None of my family, including her, even post one, as a favorite book, on their "FACE-BOOK," nor my picture! I "FACE," that everyday.

"Hell, we all know it," she said angrily, as I continued to mention it. "We just, don't want to talk about it, "ALL THE TIME"! She said this, a little too loud, for my liking. That was the last straw. I didn't want to "RUIN DINNER" for her, or Maddy! I was torturing everyone. I needed to just "SHUT UP"! I let her have her way. My temporary hell with her would end soon and then the world can watch her be nice. She always is when I leave. Scary nice!

Enough of my "CRUELTY". I don't get off on torturing people. It isn't my bag. Papa's got a brand new one, now. Here's my "ANSWER", about E.T.s staying away and what our reality, really "IS." It is the end of my dream! I hope you find humor in it, like my precious little granddaughters, did. I told them about it, awhile back and they laughed hysterically. I asked them what they would do, if this happened to them. They stopped laughing and I did, too. Seriously, it wasn't a laughing matter, then. It is real. Do any of us "WANT TO BE UGLY?"!

They damn sure didn't and said they don't know anybody, who does.

"Do you?," they asked me quickly giggling like the school-girls they are!

"Hell no! Are you kidding me," I replied quickly, laughing as I did! "But, I'd rather deal with it now, than "LATER"! We can't hide from the truth. I film flying saucers and they will, find us out. Technology will read every one's mind, soon. "BELIEVING" it is up to you, baby girls. I'm dealing with my "PRETTY POWER ADDICTION", now. I admit, "I DON'T WANT TO BE UGLY". But, let me tell you something, "GIRLS". My dream and hard life, has proven to me, that there are "FAR" worse things, than being ugly." They started to leave, at the "BAD NEWS"! I can't say as I blame them.

"Come on," I taunted them, as they started to "RUN"! "Let me share my "REALITY", with you. You'll love the "END" of my dream. I promise you." I said laughing as they immediately "RAN AWAY." Now,

I was laughing like "HELL". Heck, we were all laughing! I knew, that they didn't want to be tortured, anymore and I damn sure didn't want to torture them. So, I didn't. They know my story and they agree. None, of them want to be ugly, either. I did holler and tell them, that this simple evidence is the most telling thing of all, about our species. "Occam's razor rules the universe. Occam's Razor." I yelled one last time. I didn't tell them, to look it up. I knew they would. They love knowledge.

People, I have to end this, for everyone, just like my "EX-WIFE SAYS"! Its my "REALITY", not theirs. She's "RIGHT"! It's certainly not "HER'S," or her parents, either. I am sad. They helped me a lot and we had more good times, than bad! I want to thank them, again. I wish we could have made the family band, that I always wanted. I was going to call us "FLATT SPECIAL." Maybe we still will. They are all so talented, especially Milton and Brenda. I hope so. I hope the girls, make my song "That's history", history! That would be Flatt special, alright. What a dream come true. I would love to repay Lester Flatt and "GRANNY", for all they done. Heck, what am I saying. What they still do! "WE" still get royalties. I want to apologize to everyone in this story, that I got angry with. I hope, that everyone will see my memories as a disease. I need help, for it. Everybody has faults and I can't be forgiven, if I don't forgive, first. Tammy and her family are beautiful people, like all of us, when they're not angry. I don't mean to judge them, in this story and I'm not. I am only telling my story. We can all make mistakes. I've made plenty.

Here's my "DREAM" and the answer to, "REALITY"! I get killed and wake up on a space- craft looking down at the earth! OMG! I see nuclear bombs, exploding along the Eastern coast! I jump up and frantically look for a mirror, only to see aliens looking at me, "LIKE I'M CRAZY"! I see an exit and run toward it. I have to see "MY-SELF"! I don't want to be one of "THEM"!

They're all hideously ugly and look exactly "THE SAME. None of them are "DIFFERENT LOOKING." OMG, "THEY ALL LOOK THE SAME" and they're ugly!

I had about 20 feet to go and was running, as fast as, I could. "THANK GOD", I WAS GOING TO MAKE IT"! Then suddenly the door slid closed, just inches before my "FACE"! OMG! For a split second, I realized what was about to happen! I backed up to turn and run, but I had nowhere to go. I had to break through this door. I backed up, even further and gathered all my strength. I just had to break through this door. I turned back toward the door and, and... I saw "MY-SELF"! It literally scared me to "DEATH"!

Immediately, my heart gave out. I had a massive heart attack and died of fright. I collapsed and came out of my body!

Instantly, I was human again. Then suddenly, I hear those same three gun shots, again. "BANG BANG BANG"! I felt the bullets, rip through my chest and the burning pain, that followed. Suddenly, I came out of my body and woke up as an 'UGLY ASS ALIEN"! "WOW, NOT AGAIN! WHAT DO I DO NOW?" I was floating above "MY-SELF". and no- one could see me. I could see paramedics, pumping on my chest! I was being sucked toward my body, as if a "POWERFUL" vacuum cleaner, was pulling me back! I saw them giving up. They started to pronounce me dead.

"No," I screamed, but nobody heard me. My family were all crying and kneeling beside me. The paramedics begin to back away. I was literally inches from my face, when all of a sudden my eyes flew open and my body heaved. I sucked in air and realized I was back! Oh, "GOD" no. They will never "BELIEVE" me. I don't want to die "AGAIN"! I don't want to die again and I can't stop it. None of us can! We will all die and none of us want to be "UGLY"! OMG, no!

Who will want this "REALITY"? Will you? It doesn't matter if you don't now. The one thing, that is real in this dream, is that we can't hide, from my "MIND- READING MACHINE"! Future technologies will prevail, over our lies and selfish sexual nature!

I got up and saw the devastation from the "METEOR STRIKE AND NUCLEAR BOMB"! I looked straight into my families eyes and held out my "PROOF"! I looked down and realized I had something in my hand. I was holding my "MIND READING MACHINE", the deal breaker, as I liked to call it. It should be called "THE LIFE OR DEATH MACHINE" for children! I had "FINALLY" invented a smaller size, them to carry! They could now determine, whether an adult was "INTELLECTUAL OR SEXUAL"!

Shockingly, I pushed the button. I didn't realize, I did it. "MICHAEL'S WAR" rages on!

Nobody, can outrun "TECHNOLOGY"! "NO ONE"! "CONQUER SPACE NOW. MORE METEORS COMING!

This is the end! I started my first book, with this dream, 15 years ago. It's fitting, that I end with it. Nothing has changed. Today is no different from the days of Noah and Yeshua, people are still living for material wealth instead of conquering death. I will want you, to ask your-"SELF," three questions, at the end. They will make my answer, about our mystery, very "SIMPLE" to understand. Before you do, ask your-"SELF" how long, can we "IGNORE THE EVIDENCE, THAT SUPPORTS THIS REALITY"? People, continue to build wealth and "I FILM FLYING SAUCERS"! Get over it! "THEY'RE HERE"!

In the words of "EVERYONE", who knows the "TRUTH", about our-"SELFS." We can run, but we "CAN'T HIDE, FROM OURSELFS"! Technology rules. It's like, my brother Terry says, "SAME SHIT, DIFFERENT DAY"! IF YOU REALLY WANT TO KNOW WHAT MANKIND'S MYSTERY IS ALL ABOUT WELL IT'S ALL ABOUT THE PUSSY... CAT

AND THE MANSION SHE LIVES IN"! It's all about, our "A-DICK-Tion", to sexual power! If you still don't "BELIEVE" me, then explain the ancient "CERNES GIANT" statue, in Wiltshire, England, or better yet, "OUR ADDICTION TO BEAUTY"! We all have it! I have it! Don't kid yourself here. "BEAUTIFUL PUSSY-" cat's rule, here. One word, if you think it doesn't, "PINK"! LOL, got ya! If they aren't, it's only because their married to a "RICH FAT- CAT". Come on people.

Let's please get over the "WORD" game. Sex is our biggest problem!

People, ask her if you don't believe me and get your mind out of the gutter! It's your gutter, not mine. "PUSSY" is just a vagina to me and "DICK" is a penis! So, don't be a "DICK" and let yourself fall prey, to the rest of "MANKIND'S A-DICK-TION"—the three P's: "POWER, PRESTIGE, AND P@%$Y," right cats? Oh yeah, "PRETENDING", too. Remember, I invented a mind reading device! Maury Povichs' lie detector test inspired me! Mine kills you, if you lie. Now, are you ready to take it. The question is; "DO YOU WANT TO BE UGLY?"!

Look, I'm begging us, all. 'PLEASE," don't make our "SELVES" a "HYPO-DICK."! Enough of "OUR WORD GAMES"! Just please do as I ask, give away your money, and answer the following three questions!

We "ALL" need to stop meteors and "FACE" our "NEW"-found "OLD REALITY." The aliens are here now and we could be "THEM." (Maybe?) I think we always have been, since the "FIRST" man was "CREATED" and "COULD TRANSPLANT OUR MEMORY", into him! In "REALITY AND SCIENTIFICALLY," we are all aliens, because we shouldn't be here. "INTELLIGENT PEOPLE" don't live on planets—just us "DUMB-ASS" humans, like my wife so cruelly calls her enemies! I "HATE", that she can't stop using the word "RETARD", either! I want her to get help. I want her to know "EMPATHY" and see, that all life on this planet is suffering. Intelligent life has evolved and is everywhere. Religion, has just kept everyone, from "LEARNING IT". It's because, they were "BRAIN-WASHED", by the traditon of building their church's population and wealth. Instead, of trying to "FIND" the truth. Now, they don't "SEE" it and yet, "EVOLUTION" is provable. Finding "IT" is as simple as "LOOKING", for the proof your-"SELF"! I can't make adults, try. But, children love looking! Her's to the kids, everyone!

Kids, under 12, will see this "PROOF OF EVOLUTION AND SCIENTIFIC CREATION CHART" and "FINALLY" know, how to determine if life evolved or was created. They will do this for themselves! Religion will die. We will be together again, with out religion and with "THEM"! Contact is inevitable. The only thing that makes sense is that we will all know it a not just some of us. I take comfort in this amazing historical fact! An ancient proverbs says: "There is nothing new under the sun"! So does today's science! They "MATCH"!!! Now here's your three questions:

1. Do you want to be ugly?
2. Do you want your mind read? Past revealed?
3. How advanced could life be in an "INFINITE UNIVERSE"?

Good luck! The last two words hold the keys to my "ANSWER", as if you didn't already know—"BY NOW"! "RIGHT" Please enjoy this ancient and modern evidence of an intelligent human species, that evolved, "BEFORE US". Our ancient forefathers, called them

gods. Today we call them "ALIENS"? If they evolved and created us, then we're the aliens. The universe is omni-directional! I don't like the word. We're all in it, together. To me, nothing in the universe is alien, even the things that are "CREATED", in it. Even, the matter, that makes it, exist forever! People, all that matters, is that these aliens are not hurting or killing us and obviously, they easily could! I have only discovered one species and they all look alike. This one fact of life, proves their evolutionary existence! They share this same "COMMON", outward equality in looks, that all the other species of life have, but mankind. The "EVIDENCE" says, we are their scientific creation. Today, this very scenario is on track to happen, within the next two decades. Could the technology already exist, to download memory into a body and then be it? If you think not, here's three discoveries, that may change your mind: computers, ancient brain trepanation and universal reincarnation stories! Most of all, a quote from Yeshua's brother Jude, which plainly shows, that this has already happened, with the angels/ aliens: "For the angels which kept not their first estate, but left it for a strange flesh"! People, what they "LOOK" like, is the only question, to answer. Thank you for reading my story and now, the answer to our mystery! Life has always existed, the future is "NOW"! Think "INFINITELY", or life will pass, you by. It will do so "BEFORE YOU KNOW IT", if you aren't looking. It is up to each of us, to decide on, what to "LOOK" for. I hope you look for "LIFE" and help me, "END DEATH". I love you all! Mikie

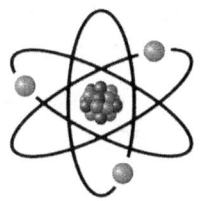 # AUTHOR'S THOUGHTS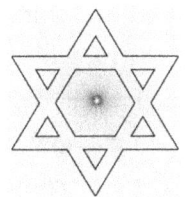

Happy Birthday, to me! Today, September 29th, I turned 53! I wrote this a year ago and feel like the luckiest guy in the world. My sister-in-law was dying of cancer and I had to tell her story. It is brief, like her life and illness. Wow, I'm alive and I still have a chance to put together a scientific team, to cure death and resurrection! I have given myself, the best birthday a father, could ever ask, for. I am giving my sons and all of us, the "POSSIBILITY" of "IMMORTALITY". This has been an incredible journey and I've sure learned a lot, about the mystery of our species. My findings are based on "EVIDENCE," from around the world and is governed by, the rationale of logic. I am so lucky to have done this, as it wasn't done for me. Sadly, it didn't happen, for my father or his father, before him and so on. I don't fault them or anyone, who hasn't done this. Searching for life's answers can be a curse and a blessing. There's so much to learn about our mystery, let alone the universe!

Lucky, is the man, who can make sense, of it all! I feel "TRULY LUCKY", to have done, so. However, I am both saddened and ecstatic, at my conclusion. I have concluded, that the world wasn't made by "ANYONE" and it can never be perfect. But, it is conquerable! It is, only because, it is infinite and non-thinking! It doesn't try to out-smart us or lie to us, like humans. I'm so thankful, it is just "NATURE" and

"SHIT" happens, everywhere. I couldn't deal with life, any other way. Let's all stop hating god, now ok? The universe isn't a living organism. Because of it's "INFINITE REALITY," the ingredients/parts, that give "LIFE", will "EVENTUALLY" come together and "SPRING" forth, in an eternal dance of "BIRTH, DEATH AND REBIRTH"! This is happening, now. It is the endless dance of life, science calls "EVOLUTION." We have come to recognize "NOTHING" as "SOMETHING", that we must live "IN", to achieve the "IMMORTALITY" of our species. The blackness of space is our mothers womb! We must break this cycle and live "UP," in space.

The most wonderful evidence I discovered is seeing ancient art of flying saucers, that are identical to mine, Jeff's and Marty Stuart! I have asked for an interview with him and Johnny Cash's family. They ignore me. I know why, they're wealthy and I'm a threat. Rich people insult my intelligence. They aren't spiritual. I don't play that game. People, this evidence gives us hope of achieving "IMMORTALITY." For the same reason, I propose, that life exist everywhere in an "INFINITE UNIVERSE." They not only exist, but they "CLEARLY" provide us the "ONLY" answer to survive "METEOR EXTINCTION"! We must go "UP" into space and never let ourselves live at the mercy of Mother Nature again! This is our "REALITY," too. Whether, we like it or not.

I want to end by sharing the recent news, of my sister-in-law, Barbara's, terminal lung cancer diagnosis. Barbara went to the doctor in June, for chest pain and was given three to six months to live. That's a sobering thought. I went to see her and share my discovery of "FLYING SAUCERS AND ONE ALIEN SPECIES." She knew about my books, but she hadn't had much contact with me, after she divorced my brother, 15 years ago. We've only seen each other, a couple times, since their break-up. I felt very lucky to see her and share my "EVIDENCE." I wanted to give her hope of "LIFE AFTER DEATH"! She said she wasn't religious at all. I had to laugh, because she said she didn't have time to be religious. She was to busy raising kids, to think about, that kind of stuff. She was even raising her grandchildren! I can relate! I gave her a copy of this book and was so excited, that time flew. Several hours went by before I knew it. It was precious. I shared my "WONDERFUL EVIDENCE OF FLYING SAUCERS" and showed her "HUMANS THAT EVOLVED AND THE HEADS OF EASTER ISLAND AND HOW THEY ALL LOOKING THE SAME"!

I explained how this uniformity in looks, proved they evolved and explains how they could get along, "LONG ENOUGH" to conquer space! She got it and was freaked out a little bit. But, she loved it. I further explained my theory, about them, creating our species for sexual power, through our "UNIQUE OUTWARD BEAUTY". I asked her if she wanted to be ugly and she quickly said no. I said I didn't either and we both just laughed.

My sister-in-law had lots of questions and started to ask me some, when my precious little niece, Heaven, came bouncing in! She immediately hugged me and grabbed my book. She knew about the books. I dedicated my fifth book, to her, in honor of her name. She is Heaven Lee! No really she is. It's also heavenly to have her. Anyway, the book is titled "HEAVEN IS SPACE... UP"! She quickly laid my book aside, to show me her latest poem and added, that she is making a book of poems. I told her I would publish it, if it had the poem she and I worked on, awhile back. Much to my surprise, she had finished it and was quick to show me the end result. I loved it! The poem was about dreaming all you can and pursing those dreams! What a go-getter she is. I had to laugh, though. The caption following the title: "FOLLOW YOUR DREAMS", read: ("ONLY IF IT MAKES SENSE")! Wow, did she ever set herself up, for what was about to happen! I asked her if she wanted to see my new book and handed her the copy I was giving to Barb. She began voicing her opinion of not liking my answer, about our mysterious loneliness in space. Ironically, her admonition, "ONLY IF IT MAKES SENSE," in her poem is the one thing in life, that we all "INSTINCTIVELY", follow. We do it, because it is the "NATURAL GUIDING FORCE", that we "ALL" base our decisions on. It is our "GUT FEELING"! "EVERYTHING HAS TO MAKE SENSE", people! Even, "HEAVEN AGREED"!

Heaven started asking me questions about my flying saucer evidence and why I think they are extraterrestrial. I told her, that I didn't, because it would mean, they came from another planet. The world calls them that, I explained softly. I think they always existed and atre everywhere. I showed her, that we have ancient drawings of them in space and they look just like, what I film today. I explained how this is "PROOF OF OMNI-SCIENCE" and their OMNIPOTENCE". She asked what that meant and I explained that it meant "ALL KNOWLEDGE AND ALWAYS EXISTING/INFINITY." I further explained, that the craft, not changing in tens of thousands of years, "PROVES THIS REALITY"! She got it! I loved her enthusiasm, but I was about to get the shock of my life. She got more than just this and I was about to get, more than I bargained for. She looked at my "EVOLUTION AND CREATION PROOF" illustration and immediately voiced her contempt, at the idea of "LOOKING THE SAME AS EVERYONE ELSE"! Much to my horror, she started to cry and said she didn't want to look, just like everybody else. She blurted out, as if she was in agony, that she wanted to be "SPECIAL" and look different, from everybody else. She began to cry harder and say louder, that she wanted to be special. I was freaked out, then and saddened. I couldn't believe, what just happened. I didn't "MEAN", for it, too.

I was supposed to be doing this, for a "GOOD REASON." I wanted to give Barbara, some "PROOF OF LIFE AFTER DEATH" and now it back-fired. I felt like a piece of "SHIT." We all were caught off guard. Heaven's mother, and my niece, Misty, had come in moments before this happened. Unfortunately, she caught the tail-end of our conversation. She knew enough about my work, to know what was going on and quickly hugged Heaven. Barbara immediately told Heaven, that it was just ,"MY THEORY." I hugged both of them and also quickly agreed. It didn't do much good. But, I hugged her and hugged her. Suddenly, much to everyone's surprise, she instantly rebounded and said that she saw the logic of my evidence, but still didn't like it. I started to say something and she broke in.

She quickly said, "I would rather live on Earth with humans, that all look different, than in space with aliens, who don't"!

"But we die here baby girl," I replied sadly.

She quickly said, that she "DIDN'T CARE and wasn't afraid to die"! I wanted to ask her, "What about Barbara?," but I couldn't. I had hurt her enough. I was blown away!

I have experienced this resentment, from almost everyone, of not wanting the same physical looks as everyone else, since I reached this conclusion in my first book! I called it the "POWER/CHOICE HYPOTHESIS"of why we haven't made contact, in the universe. It's all about our addiction to our 6x9 valuable piece of real estate, "THE FACE". It is the "POWER" thing, I never understood about, my mom and dads devil story. I quickly began to get it. I started to see it, from a scientific perspective. We all seem to be addicted, to wanting to be, special. I call it, the "SPECIAL DISEASE/PRETTY POWER!" I softly told Heaven, that all life is special and she is, too! It didn't do much good. We all consoled her and tried to move on, but she kept looking at my "NEW EVOLUTION AND CREATION CHART." She suddenly blurted out, that I was "RIGHT", about this evidence and life is a "CHOICE." She continued to defiantly and proudly tell me, that she was choosing to be "HUMAN" again, when she dies! Apparently, she heard me tell Barbara, that I think the idea of "FREE WILL" is bullshit! Every living thing has a choice. It's called "INTELLIGENCE"!

Heaven must have heard this and she didn't like it. I wanted to share the idea of possibly being, alien with her, but it involves the Greeks' idea of a sexual utopia, where everybody is young beautiful and "NAKED", but all look the same. Today, we call these "ORGIES" and I couldn't go there, with a child. I couldn't even explain, that the perfect world in the

Bible is when Adam and Eve were naked or that a tribe exists today, where there is no marriage and they have no crime! She's so smart, she would know it was because, they're all naked! I wanted to tell her this and so much more, but I couldn't! People, sex is our problem.

The Cernes giant makes that "PERFECTLY CLEAR"!

I want to end, by acknowledging my nieces view of happiness. It's every child's dream. She wants a perfect world, but desires to be a human, that looks different, from everyone else. She always wants to be treated "SPECIAL" and wants to do everything! I tried to explain, that all life is special and hug her. She kinda resisted my hug and I gently let go and told her how special she was, to me. Then I immediately told her that her mom and grandma are to! I hugged them and then visited a short while. Heaven and I wrote a little on ream poem. It was a heavenly moment!

I recently encountered the same "EQUAL LOOKS RESENTMENT" behavior, from Phillip Mantle, the director of M.U.F.O.N., England. He is "SUPPOSEDLY" looking for evidence of E.T.s, but reacted the same to "MY E.T. EVIDENCE", as Heaven did. Even worse, he said my evidence, isn't evidence! In his first, response to my book submission, he admonished my conclusion, as being "ON THE WRONG TRACK"! I replied, asking him, to please reveal his "RIGHT TRACK." He began to relentlessly berate and chastise me. I have the e-mails to prove my allegations! It was only after telling him this, that he admitted I was a nice guy!

However, according to him, I am wrong about our existence being the best evidence, that life is everywhere. He said we could be the "FIRST"! I asked him, when energy and matter, start. I asked him if thinks, anybody exist, that could be smarter than him. He said that he did, but refused to ask me any questions or answer mine. He just continued to "SLANDER" me! I responded with love. He hated me for it!

I know why Phillip "HATES ME AND CALLS ME THE WORST PSUEDO-SCIENCE RESEARCHER", he's ever met. He thinks humans are wonderful, just like Mom, Dad, and just about everyone else religious, that I've encountered. He wants to be "HUMAN", just like Heaven Lee! Oh NO! He hates my "ONE ALIEN, ONE UNIVERSE, ONE REALITY" evidence. He went, from saying we have no alien evidence to sending me a picture of eight different types of good and bad ones! Wow. This guy isn't thinking logically, at all. Do we really think there's more than one intelligent being, above us in space, working together to stay hidden. We don't work with the bad guys here and were supposedly intelligent. Do we really think they're working together to keep themselves hidden, from us. Come on, people. this is crazy shit!

This is the sad "REALITY" of humans. We can choose "SELF- ishness", over "WHOLE- SUM-NESS"! We can even lose sight of, and ignore, our own death, because of it. Our desire to be "SPECIAL" permeates our species and is incurable, as a whole. What would be special is if everyone could see ourselves, as "ONE WITH ALL LIFE"! "ONE". Tammy thinks I'm a one and it is killing my ego. Religion calls this "ENLIGHTENMENT"! I call it "IMMORTAL INTELLIGENCE" and pure "HELL"! I am getting ready to leave as I type. I can't live with her and this hate anymore, that has "GROWN", inside me. I am sad, but I have to go. I want to feel "SPECIAL", again. I will do it by "MY_SELF". I will find "THE MYSTERY" and never lose it, again! Are we more important than the sparrows and the foxes, who live it! Yeshua said we aren't.

People, I don't want to die. Neither does Heaven or Phillip Mantle, but I can't "SAVE" them. I want to save, everyone. I can only hope my theory gives them a new reality, where death isn't scary. It's only a temporary "CHOICE". However, I know that I can only save myself and I am running out of "TIME"! My Dad told me, that anything over "THREE SCORE AND TEN YEARS" is living on borrowed time. I quickly realized, that it is 70 years. When I was younger, I thought it was a "LONG TIME", away from where I was, so I didn't need to worry about it. I was probably about "12," then. LOL! Forty-one years later, I "NOW" realize "TIME IS RELATIVE"! I ONLY HAVE 17 SUMMERS LEFT! I'm not complaining, though. I'll be lucky "IF" I get there. I am lucky to be 53. Barbara is dying now and probably won't live another week as I type. Unless we conquer mother nature, aging, disease, and death, it doesn't matter if it's a "THOUSAND YEARS", away. It's all the same if we don't conquer, "IT"! It is "TIME", a planet thing, not space and "INTELLIGENCE". Planets die, but we can live in space, forever. We can conquer immortality and learn, that nothing in space is alien to us, unless it "CHOOSES" to be!

We must live, for our specie's survival, not our "INDIVIDUALITY". I "BELIEVE" that these stories of people living "UP" in "HEAVEN", give us the best evidence, that it has "ALREADY" happened. There is only one conclusion, to accept about our species and that is we are not a "GOOD THING"! People, this is the way the "UNIVERSE/WORLD", is. I don't want it his way, it's just the way it is! In the words, of "THE MOST FAMOUS MAN ON EARTH," who's name is Yeshua. Only this father in heaven is good. I want to talk to my father, again. It is now December 24th, Christmas eve.. My sister-in-law Barb died, today. I tried again, to release this book a week later. It wouldn't happen. Finally, my brother Terry's birthday December 31st, 2014. Happy New Year, everyone! Especially, Barb, Terry, Danny, Linda, Joe, David, Dad, Nancy Gail, Brice, Granny, Betty, Sam, and way too many more, that are gone. I don't want to live without you. That's what I want to live for, to see you again. I will make that happen, "WITH SCIENCE." Please everyone, give to science, now. Michael Hall, Michio Kaku, and Neil DeGrasse Tyson, here I come!!!

The next eight months flew by. I couldn't release this book. I had to get it right. I've learned so much since, that I'm glad I didn't. Unfortunately, more of my friends have died. Finally, after all the "SEARCHING" I've done. I saw an episode of ancient aliens, that showed a scientist theorizing, the manipulation and integration of our memory, with computers. Wow!

Biological robots are next!

He said we could potentially "SAVE" our-selves forever. His said that we are just memory. WOW! WOW! WOW! I was even more blown away, that he said none of this matters if we don't, "FIRST, CONQUER SPACE"! I agree with him completely and am saying, that religion also says the same thing. Universally, they all tell us, to seek heaven first. The scientist's name is John Von Neuman and he died at the age of 53, in 1957. Wow, I am 53! The last thing this guy said floored me. He said the best way to achieve the immortality of our species is to build self-replicating robots and send them into space. They would be programmed to build themselves with materials mined in space and then continue on to another planet to do the same. Wow! Wow! Wow! This is God's story, too! We must stay "ONE", species, one people!

People, I am finishing this book and releasing it. I can't let my fear of this book's consequences, stop me from doing so, any longer. I have to do it, now. I will be turning 54 next month and honoring my brother, with a second grand opening of my art gallery, Brumfield Station. I want to be able, to give this book to his kids, on the anniversary of his death. They know about my "INFINITE ASTRONAUT THEORY" and yet, don't quite understand how life could have always existed, in an infinite universe. But, at least now, they entertain the possibility of "SOMEONE CONQUERING DEATH AND RESURRECTION", as a logical "REALITY"! Thank God!!! I'm making headway. I'm hoping this book gives them, some comfort and knowledge of it being possible! I miss their dad!!!

People, It's been five years now and we still don't have a METEOR PREVENTION OR EVACUATION PLAN and we haven't conquered space. I can only hope, that my "SMOKING GUNS", will convince people of our "TRUE REALITY"! Logic dictates, that these people "UP IN THE SKY HEAVEN/SPACE", do exist and would stay away, from us. It would, because our view of death, being the end, is our delusion and not theirs. They know there's only "ONE" logical thing, to do with "INTELLIGENT LIFE", that doesn't care about and respect all life. You have to stay away, from them. Lucky are the ones, who sees intelligence in all life and doesn't want to risk the possibility of reincarnating as anything, less than a human.

Everything beneath us, is living in a virtual hell!

People, religion is a simple story of "PEOPLE UP IN THE SKY? GOD/GODS", harvesting intelligence! To them, heaven is the universe and we are "LIKE A SEED". We are it's seed and when we grow up, we can "REST" in the tree branches, like the fowl. Ready and able to escape death, in a moment's notice! Life is, but a moment in time. They are wanting and accepting loving empath etic beings, that are looking for a "PEACEFUL PERFECT IMMORTAL LIFE"! The prerequisite is simple, like I explained to my son, Matt. We have to live it. If I want to live forever, then I must find out, how and do it. When I do, if I want everybody else to live forever, then I must sacrifice my "MATERIAL/WORLDLY" life, for this purpose and help them to "SEE" the same. Like Yeshua says; "WE MUST GIVE AWAY EVERYTHING WE HAVE MAKE OURSELVES PERFECT AND LIVE IT"!

"LIFE Is a 5o/5o/ proposition. It's all about pulling "EQUAL" weight. Scientists, religious teachers and all true seekers, will prove their "FAITH", by works. My sons' resentment toward my seeking, has put a divide, between us. It has ,because they love being served and they know it. Hell, everybody does! We have finally crossed this bridge! Thanks to Matt's "OPEN LETTER COMMUNICATION", idea! He now realizes, that if my seeking, makes him or anyone else feel uncomfortable, it's not my fault. Maybe it's his? I'm sorry. If they don't want to feel this way, then do something about it or leave me alone. It's just "REALITY". But, please don't get angry at me anymore. I won't discuss my research with him or anyone, as to whether E.T./God exist or not, now. Especially, if they aren't looking and just want to debate me. I'll just stick to my logic and let the chips fall, where they may. It would be cruel, to do otherwise.

Again, it would imply, that I seek and they don't. Everything I do, I'm doing for them. So, they can exist, forever! I can't make them look for anything, not even logic and "INTELLIGENCE"! That's up to each of them, to find on their own. They know they don't look. Hardly anyone is. I am also doing this, for myself. I choose to find "IMMORTAL", life!

People, there's enough hell in this world, without us making, more. Sadly, my oldest is running around, flying a confederate flag in his truck, as well as, one at his house. I got upset, because he's from Ohio! And to make matters worse, he even hates me, for not seeing it as O.K.! He's trying to logically defend it, as a "PRIDE OF HERITAGE", thing. I've explained the lack of credibility in his argument, when he isn't even, from the south. Pride is his problem and I can't cure it. I finally had to explain, that it is dangerous. His sister put a video on "FACEBOOK" to see, that it can get people hurt. I tried explaining, that his children could be innocent victims of "CRAZY" adult violence. He said he doesn't give a damn, about offending people, not even me. I'm sad, that he doesn't care about my feelings or his children's. I can only hope, they don't get killed. People are being killed, because of this. We can't talk about this or about how he got to be Josh, instead of the deer we killed or a black slave. I won't give up. I can't, I'm dying and he isn't being logical. My kids are dying and I don't want them to see mankind as a good thing. This pride problem, shows us it's evil, everyday. People kill people over it, everyday! I've made my conclusion about life very clear to my sons.

The evidence says, that "PEOPLE UP IN THE SKY EXIST! MANKIND IS EVIL AND THEY ARE GOOD". It's up to us, which reality we want to choose. People choice is intelligence and every living thing has it. Like every living thing beneath us, it's only logical to run away, from death and ensure our survival. They run! We all know where Mankind is going. Logic says, he isn't going to run. This is why I've changed my hypothesis, as to why they stay away from us, from the Power hypothesis, to the "CHOICE HYPOTHESIS"! We epitomizes the story of Adam and Eve, disobeying God.

People, sons, these space dwelling people are real flesh and blood beings! They "LEFT US" plenty of evidence, to prove "IMMORTALITY IS POSSIBLE", like where they live! Yes, I know why HEAVEN IS UP/SPACE"! Planets die. Space is our "FINAL FRONTIER"! Science is finding this evidence more and more, everyday. It is up to us, whether we want to find it or not! I recently turned, 54. I now, "SEE" why "LOOKING" is the first step and most important. Time, literally, does fly by, if you can live long enough to "SEE" it.

Logic says, I could have lived before, in an infinite universe. The most famous man's name, says I could have, too. It is "YES-HU-A". English is even the universal language of space! If Yeshau ask me, if I am addicted to beauty, when he returns. I would say I am and he would say, "YES-HU-A"! This is fact! This is why his name is important to me. I think we all would have the same answer. This would prove he existed and the future, does too!

It exist's, "NOW"! We exist, so "SOME-ONE" will always exist, in an infinite universe. Science will validate religion's story and it will be up to us, as to which "ONE", we will want to be. "US OR THEM"? Only you, can decide, this. In religion, this decision process is called "ENLIGHTENMENT". In science it is called "LOGIC"! If you want a world without death and yet still want to be human like Phillip Mantle and most people, then you better think "TWICE", before you make a "FINAL CHOICE". "WE KNOW WE CAN'T MAKE ALL HUMANS GOOD". This is only thing I've discovered, that we can all agree on, as a people, religious, scientist, atheist, agnostic or "OTHER-WISE". Sadly, mankind is killing "SOMEONE", even as we speak.

Now, let's all ask ourselves two simple questions, before we make a decision about this evidence. It will help us determine whether or not, we could have possibly existed before or could possibly exist again.

1. How advanced can life be in an infinite universe?.
2. Do I want to be ugly? (on this question you have to put your finger in a lethal lie detector)

Peace out! Mike P.S. Today is my birthday, last year flew by. I started writing this at 53, remember. It's been a rough couple months so, just being nice to me would be a great present, if you don't like my book. I am 54 and need all the kindness I can get, in a world full of such vicious ass humans! I recently did a book-signing, for Mutual U.F.O. Network or M.U.F.O.N., as it better known and it turned out bad. The lady in charge was a wealthy spiritualist! Here's what happened. Prior to finishing this ending, I had contacted the Tennessee state director, with proof of these flying saucers looking, exactly the same over tens of thousands of years and boldly stated, that it proves they aren't making "NEW" ones. I further explained, that it proves my "INFINITE ASTRONAUT THEORY" and their omniscience! He liked it and agreed!!! He couldn't believe, I had a photo of Johnny Cash looking "UP" at a flying saucer. Moreover, he couldn't believe that it looked. just like Paul Villa's, twenty years, earlier. He had studied Paul's case! He was really shocked, that it also looked like the ones Jeff Willes and I shot. But, the most shocking fact of all is that they look like an ancient cave drawing of one!!!

Well, this certainly got his attention and here's what happened, next. He immediately arranged a book-signing at the Nashville monthly meeting, until he could get me to Memphis. I went and met the lady in charge. She was a middle aged bleach blond who was dressed fit to kill.

Make-up jewelry, tight dress, the whole nine. She introduced me to everyone and I got started. After I introduced myself and credentials, I immediately explained, I was presenting an "INFINITE ASTRONAUT THEORY", that would challenge the "LOGIC" of "SPIRITS, TIME TRAVEL AND DIMENSIONS"! Things went south, immediately. The lady in charge taught O.B.E.'s and said she gets knowledge, as a spirit, when she's out of her body. I told her, that I don't doubt this phenomenon, happens! But, I just don't know why anyone, who says they see god or an alien, doesn't ask them the big question. Why does he stay away and not do anything? We all know, this question, in science. Religion's god has to be just and they know it.

Scientifically, it's called Fermi's Paradox and it is a logical question. Why do they stay away!!! I mean, come on people! Don't they love us and want to help? Don't they want to be with us?

Anyway, she got angry and started to read my pedigree. She said her father is a science professor at Vanderbilt and that, he wouldn't give me the time of day, the way I was talking. She said I was showing my lack of knowledge, by saying Einstein gave us the atom and that he didn't.

"Wow!, I responded weakly. I was blown over, by her smug ass mean remark, in front of everybody. I told her, that I felt like the alien in the movie; "The day the earth stood still". She asked why and I told her, because she wasn't asking questions and was being mean. I told her, that the scientists I went to, didn't either. I told her I went to my professors and they were mean, too. She again, said her dad wouldn't either, because I don't have a degree in physics. Wow! It's the "DEGREE THING, AGAIN". I am more determined, than ever to get the damn thing, now! This shit has happened, every since I started book-signing. I told her, that is sad.

I also told her, that if she would have, just looked at my evidence of the atom, she would have seen it was taken, from a "Physics book for dummies" and it clearly gives us the history! Then, I looked her dead in the eye and told her, only a fool would proclaim something to be true, that he hasn't proven, to be so. Then I immediately told her, that I was done with this shit and yes she was being mean and rude! I said I was so tired of so-called "SEEKERS" being mean to me, just because my theory, threatens their "TRADITIONAL BELIEF IN SPIRITS". Of course, they all said it doesn't. They both chimed in and said it's my lack of a degree, that makes my theory less credible.

"No, I told them quickly. You can't handle the evidence, logically portraying them as real people, just like us. It makes us responsible, then! You can't even ask yourself Fermi's Paradox! For god's sake, I told them. in a raised voice. Forget my theory, o.k.. Look at these flying saucer photos! They span over ten thousand years, without changing and one of them has Johnny Cash, in it. Come on. There's only one other J.C., bigger than that and guess what, he left on the clouds two thousand years ago. Guess what, people? He's coming back, from the clouds! This one fact alone, rules out spirits, dimensions and time travel! Forget my theory, I'm filming flying saucers!!" They got silent and looked away. I started to gather my stuff.

As I was leaving I shared my disgust, of how the the U.F.O. movement, has become full of spirit thumpers and people saying, they are emissaries for aliens, from other dimensions, when they're supposed to be neutral! I'm especially disgusted, when their agenda is to convert everyone, so their spirit mystery will never be understood. They like dressing up for these games!

"Isn't this supposed to be an organization, who's sole purpose is to investigate u.f.o.s, not spirits! People, we are supposed to be looking, for one thing. E.T.s! We all know life should exist everywhere, because we do, now. Why they stay away, has to be "SIMPLE"! Something as simple as being a real flesh and blood beings. That is logical. Especially, living in an infinite universe, where more intelligent beings can make that happen! Everything is real! I finally told her, that I have an answer and it tortures me, enough without being tortured, by someone else. Obviously, she got my point, as well as my theory and it tortured her, too! The last thing she did was stop me and say, that she wasn't being mean. I quickly told her she was. Suddenly, she jumped up as I was turning to leave and asked me, "A QUESTION"!

Thank god, I thought to myself. Finally. Well, she didn't exactly, ask me. She almost hollered it out and in a very disgusted like, manner. It really shocked me, for a second. She asked me, if I really think we are, just memory in biological robots, like John Von Neumans self-replication theory of E.T.'s. I turned to her and asked her again, the same questions, I ask everyone. How advanced can life be in an infinite universe and Do you want to be ugly? I knew the last one would get her. She could've been the poster child, for an older woman wanting to stay young and beautiful!

"Nobody wants to be ugly" she replied. "Exactly", I replied quickly as I turned back to look her in the eye, one last time. This time, I didn't ask her a thing. I simply said "OCCAM'S RAZOR, THINK ABOUT IT", none of us want to be ugly!!! it wouldn't make sense for us all to feel this way if we were spirits now would it? She didn't have to think long. The look in her eye said it all. She damn sure didn't want to be ugly and I knew it! I had to bite my tongue. I knew that it wouldn't matter to her, if we did live forever. She rather be a human, than an ugly alien. She wouldn't be able to stand, not being prettier, than someone else. But, then again, what really tortured her most, was her inability to prove a spirit existence. Even worse, she couldn't ignore my "FLYING SAUCER REALITY". She was so mad. Wow, I had just spent fifteen minutes telling her, I think the evidence says, mankind could be a biological scientific creation of these aliens, like a robot and she still didn't get it. She is hung up on the question of "WHERE DID EVERYTHING COME FROM"!

She, like everyone else religious, had the same problem with them, coming from "NOTHING". In her mind, they couldn't of just happened, by chance, like evolution teaches us. She doesn't question her god, being infinite. But wants "SOME-ONE OR THING" responsible, for their beginning. However, the thing has to be a thinking thing, too. I told her that sounded like intelligent design and it is just, another illogical religion making excuses for why the world isn't perfect, now!!! I hammered this logic, about all gods. There has to be a "SIMPLE LOGICAL" answer, as to why they didn't make a perfect world. If they could have or if they did, why they don't do it now! Kid's are dying. Religious people seem to have a hard time accepting self- responsibility. It seems like they need someone to blame or to help them.

I asked her to look again, at my proof of humans evolving. I feel like this is my greatest scientific discovery for my children and all children! It's so simple. Everything else, but us looks identical. This is how you tell if something evolved or not. People we have evidence of a human species evolving and existing with us, before modern history! This is still mind-blowing to me. How could anybody else, including Darwin, not have seen this evidence. This makes evolution, so much easier, for kids to understand. Hell us adults, too.

Anyway, she reluctantly glanced at my chart and couldn't deny, that they obviously looked the same. She couldn't "BECAUSE THE ANCIENT STATUES, PROVED IT"!!!!! I showed her my evolution and creation chart, one more time, to bring the point home. She was stunned, by the obvious common theme all life shared, except us. They all looked alike. Immediately, one of her friends, obviously another spirit colleague, challenged it. She said the deer didn't look the same. I immediately asked her, which of the red ants, don't look the same. She made an attempt to find one and said she would need a magnifying glass to find it, but they are all different! I quickly told her that I've asked children and they instantly say none of them look different, except us. She started to point out differences in another species.

I stopped and asked her, if she believed in spirits, too. She said yes and started getting emotional. She started asking me if I ever had an O.B.E.. She began expressing her disbelief in my, "NOT BELIEVING WE'RE SPIRITS AND NOT HAVING A SOUL"!!! Needless say, she must not have liked the evidence. I did tell her my logic behind this conclusion/theory, though. I had explained, that in "MY MIND", an omnipotent spirit god wouldn't have a need, for anything, to be done for them, right? They can just think it blink it according to "ALL" religions. Our creation is only logical, if they are a mortal, physical limited god! I had started at the beginning of our recorded history, with the Sumerian tenth planet story. I explained, that it told of them making us, for the sole purpose of mining their gold, for space life! She really didn't like it, when I said I think we could be, an alien who downloaded their memory, into a human body, because of our addiction, to beauty. I explained how this was supported by my evidence of finding the same craft, all over the world. I told her it proved the future has already happened. I asked her, if she ever thought she could be an alien, on a spacecraft, experiencing this human existence and not know her true "REALITY"! She immediately said she hadn't. I told her, that maybe this was where she was going, when she came out of her body and like everyone else wanted to get back, to their body. She said she died and know she's a spirit. I didn't want to hurt her, by challenging her "FAITH", in this belief. But, I did want to ask why she was here then, if she already knows we live, forever. What's the point, I thought to myself. If you knew this then, why worry about knowing it, now. I'm doing this because the evidence suggest we are just memory and like memory in a computer, if we don't save it ourselves, Mike Brumfield was just an illusion of time, a moment in an infinite reality.

Well, the final straw happened, when I asked her if she was addicted to beauty!. Naturally, she said she wasn't. I finally told her and everybody else, to check out my redneck religious brainwashing survey. Ironically, it gave me the same answers she did. No I'm not and yes, somebody else, can be! I ended, by telling each and everyone of them, that our appearance proves our addiction, because of the way we "LOOK". I told them, that if we didn't care what we look like, then none of us would brush our teeth, comb our hair or even worse, wear clothes! I said, that if we really didn't care, we'd go naked, like the rest of the animal kingdom. She about fell out of her chair, turning away from me.

I turned back, to the lady in charge and asked her, why we have to be saved, if the spirit lives on? She looked confused and surprised, by this question. I asked her if she had anymore questions. She said she didn't and I left. As I walked out, I asked them if they needed any money and gave them a book.

People, when I look at the evolution and creation chart. I cringe, just like she did. Hell, I don't want to be ugly, but I don't want to see children die and mankind will never stop warring. We all know mankind's outcome. It is nuclear war! When I become ravaged, by fear over this reality, I just look at my flying saucer evidence. They've always been here. They aren't coming from somewhere and aren't going anywhere! The only way we can understand this possibility is to "THINK INFINITELY"!

There is hope and I will never stop looking, for them!!! I will never give up, because my sons lives depend on it. My life depends on it. "THE ANCIENT AND MODERN ALIEN EVIDENCE IS REAL"!!!!!!!! I filmed it and the rocks still exist to prove it, as well. I offered to help everyone find flying saucers. None took me up on it. I told them all, that the evidence says one alien evolved and created self-replicating robots, to mine gold for life in space. It didn't work. Our species does it best, because we look different and are sexual. It is logical, they would do this to get us to compete and create even more productivity, than those looking the same.

People, we have ancient evidence of one human species, that all look the same! I can't run from the evidence and yet, I still don't want to be ugly. However, I can't escape the "LOGIC", that only "ONE SPECIES" could live in a universe and maintain, a "PERFECT REALITY", such as I am theorizing exist. This place is called heaven in religion. Scientists call it "SPACE"! Captain Kirk calls it what it is, "THE FINAL FRONTIER"!

People, Michael Duane Brumfield could just be a passing "THOUGHT". Either way, I know it's up to me, to know "MY-SELF" or stop that, from happening, if I'm not. I really feel like I'm in a bad dream and it's time to wake up. This is how my first book started and the way this one ends, with me waking up. But, I know It's not a dream this time. I know it's "REALITY"! This meteor is my wake-up call. Hopefully it's the whole world's!

Sons, as of right now, we have a meteor coming at us, that we don't know for sure, will miss us. We also, have rocks flying through space everywhere, that could knock it, into us. Either way, if we suddenly find its going to hit us, we don't have the technology, "IN PLACE", to stop it! Sadly, we only have fourteen years, to do so. Fourteen! If we give everything we have to achieve this, we can! Please give? WWYD? Good luck to us all.

Sons, I couldn't sugar coat my theory, for this book-signing and I can't for you, either. You're both grown men, now. All is not "GOOD", depending on how you "SEE THINGS". Mankind appears to be an unstoppable evil creation of science, by one "ALIEN" species and our temporary stay is, about up. Here is the evidence from Yeshua/"JESUS", that best sums up my hypothesis, about them staying away.

Unfortunately, I think Yeshua made it perfectly clear, what lies ahead for mankind and

the truth of who we are, with this quote; "Unless your days were shortened no flesh would be saved. therefore your days will be shortened"! Please, don't let ourselves become, just "PASSING MEMORIES" and useless vessels of "KNOWLEDGE"! We can achieve immortality, through science. But, not if we don't seek it.

I know one thing, for sure now, sons. I am more afraid of death, than being ugly and naked. Heck, the older I get, the more I have to deal with it, anyway. I wish I could make the world perfect, for you. But, I can't. I can only make myself "PERFECT". I will never stop trying to be perfect for you. It's my duty as your father, wanting the same, from you. Life, eventually becomes all that matters, not what we "LOOK" like. Sons, I have to talk, about this flying saucer picture on the last page, with Johnny Cash.

This picture is worth more than a thousand words. It proves the omniscience of "ONE" intelligent species and indicates they are omnipresent, as well. The evidence speaks clearly and loudly, that these are the gods of Mankind!!! I'm not doing this to hurt people. "CONTACT" is the most important event, that can happen, in our existence.

It will change everything. I'm begging the famous country music star named Marty Stuart, who took it, please talk to me or "SOMEONE", about this flying saucer photo!!! It looks just like mine and Jeff's. I know mine and Jeff's are real and I will take any lie detector test, there is to prove it. I'm begging him to do the same, for our children's sake. Kids are dying. Religion is raping our planet with murder, violence and fear. Sadly, the world will believe him, because he is famous and religious. I am not. Let's all start "LOOKING" for these flying saucers. We found them and you can, too. This is the only way to convince people of the "THE FLYING SAUCER REALITY". The "TRUTH" will set us free. It is a "REALITY", that we can't escape from. But, first and foremost, "WE MUST ESCAPE FROM PLANET EARTH". Meteors are coming and they will never stop! We must stay away. The astronauts living on the space station are the only ones who will survive, if the big one hits. If we want to live forever, we must be like them, and become "INFINITE ASTRONAUTS" ourselves!

People, sons, we can do this! This evidence says, it exist now! The ancient universal religious evidence says, it existed in our past and "IT", will again, in our future. Scientifically, I agree and am emotionally overwhelmed, by it! I love you all. I love the wonder of life. I love my family more, than words can ever express. No matter what happens, if we all don't get to live in, "PEACE", then I'd rather die. Peace harmony and love! Always forgive, it's logical. Just walk away, leave and stay away, then......"REST". Love always Mikie/Michael/AKA WILL POWERS

 PHOTOGRAPHIC EVIDENCE AND ILLUSTRATIONS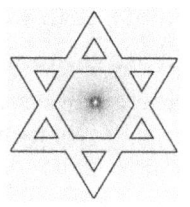

Smoking Gun Evidence

The Video/Picture Evidence

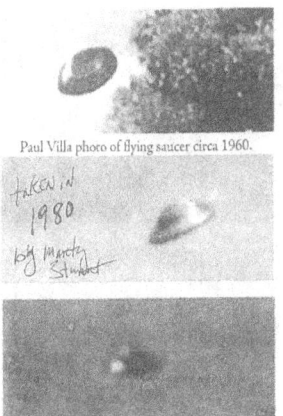

Paul Villa photo of flying saucer circa 1960.

taken in 1980 by marty Stewart

Video taken in 2003 by Jeff Willes of Phoenix, Arizona. To buy video, type his name in computer or call 623/847-9132.

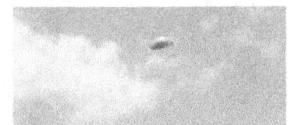

Video taken in 2006 by Mike Brumfield in Phoenix, Arizona.

Photo taken in Peru, 2013

<u>Proof of ominscience with E.T. craft over 17,000 years.</u> The following photos were taken by five different people, including myself, over a span of 60 years. They all match each other and the cave drawing, in Lacaux, France on the front cover of my third book!!! I am begging Marty Stewart to talk about this. The world loves celebrities and I am not one. But I still see these and film them. They exist and are not time travelers. The future is out there, now. This is not religion's test or science's experiment. This is our future and it is here now. It is our "REALITY"! If the universe is infinite, then "LOGIC" says only "ONE" thing, they must be "INFINITE ASTRONAUTS" and we are experiencing the "CHOICE HYPOTHESIS". Do we really want, to be "IMMORTAL" at any "COST"?

Smoking Gun Evidence

These figures all look alike!

Could our sudden appearance without the skull evolution from an elongated cranium to the obvious upright bulbous large head be directly related to religion's god? Our short recorded history is!

Could these ancient statues be proof of a species that evolved?

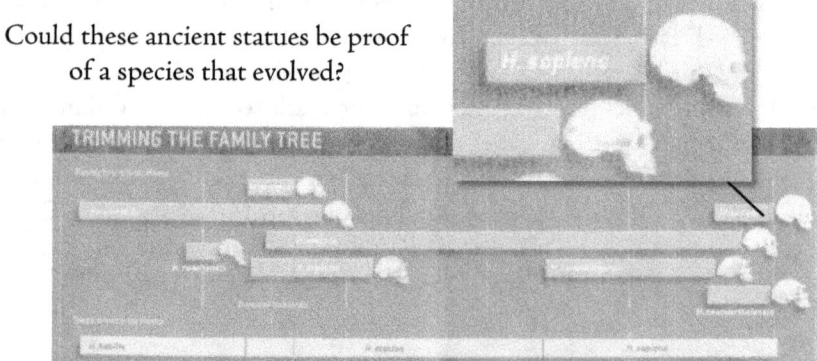

REALITY: ESCAPE FROM EARTH

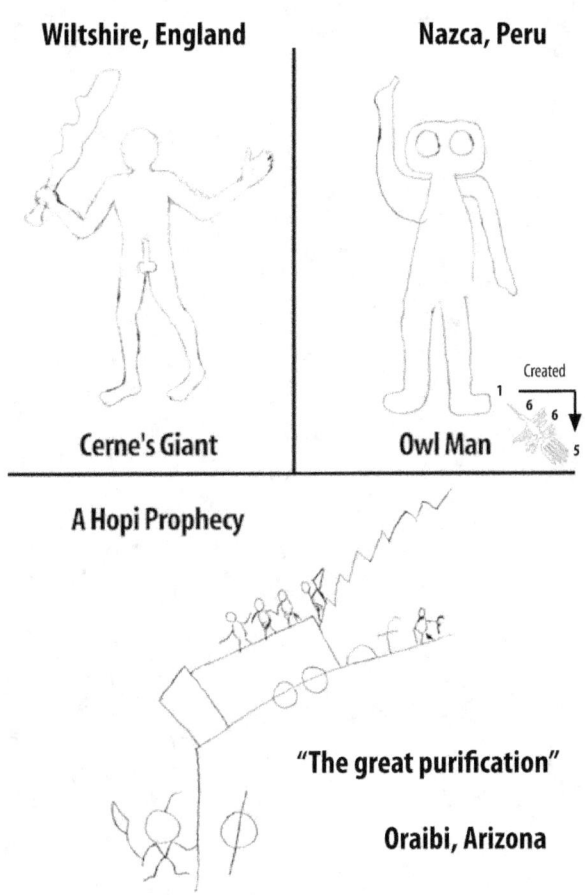

The Cerne's Giant tells us why they couldn't cohabit with their creation of modern man (we kill for sex) and when they will return. (Three humps on club indicate an impending nuclear disaster. Atom has three parts.) The Owl Man tells us where their gods live and what they look like, space and aliens. It has a hummingbird which represents fertility pointing at it. Count the appendages and see connection to biblical number of man 666 and five races. The Hopi prophecy again shows us an alien god (big headed guy) saving the earth from destruction and recycling the majority of man up, obviously to another planet. Again how did the shaman know of the five races of man let alone an alien God? Notice similarity of box carrier to today's truck trailer. Feather on head indicates gods' ability to fly. See saucer attached to his arm.

Notice alien-looking head and obvious connection to sexual power addiction of man's body.

Religious satire about the Pope admitting evolution.
EVOLUTION IS REAL!

"Smoking Gun": The Video/Picture Evidence

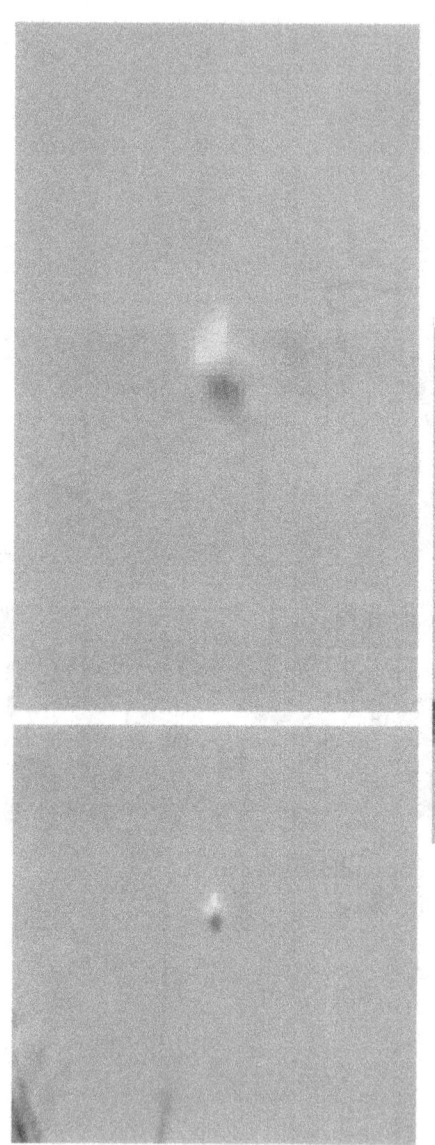

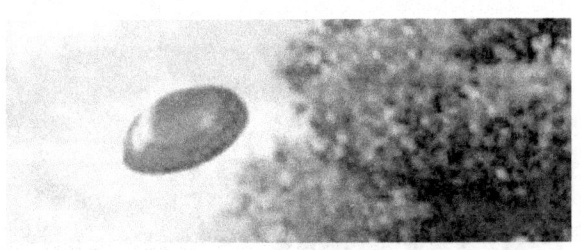

Paul Villa photo of flying saucer circa 1960.

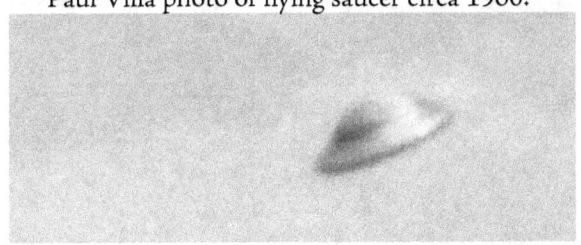

Picture on front cover of third and fourth book. How can these match when they are taken twenty years apart. Again, these "MATCH" ancient cave drawing on front cover. World's largest saucer on head of Easter Island, and aborigine saucer and alien's gold halo above (back cover) protecting it in space.

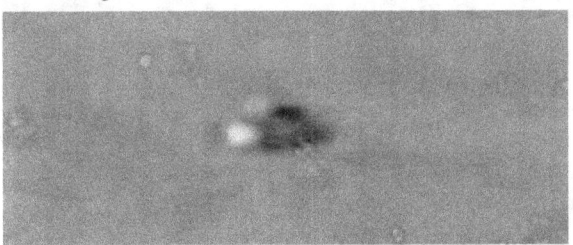

Video taken in 2003 by Jeff Willes of Phoenix, Arizona. To buy video, type his name in computer or call 623/847-9132.

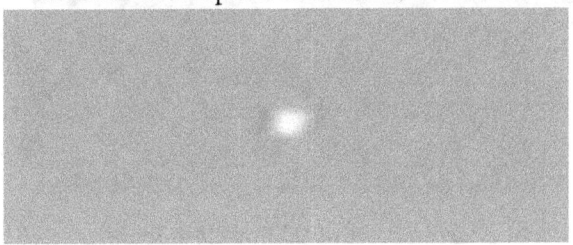

Video taken in 2006 by Mike Brumfield in Phoenix, Arizona.

Smoking Gun Evidence

Photo taken by Marty Stuart of Johnny Cash looking at a Flying saucer in 1982

Smoking Gun Evidence

Evolution and Creation Evidence

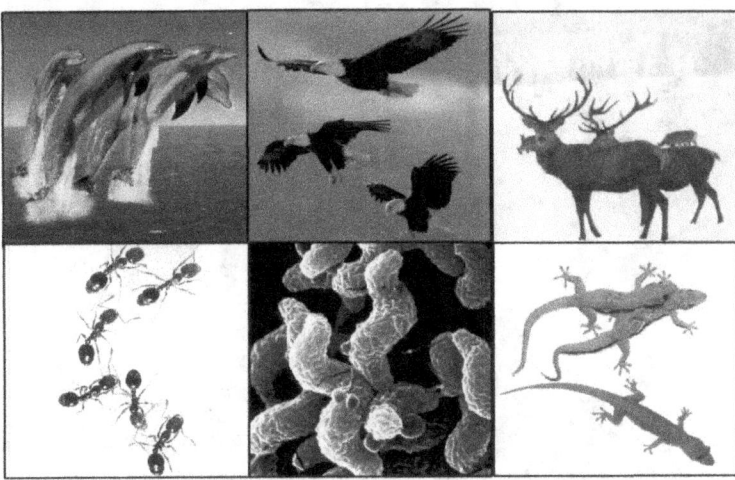

Q. What physical features do all the species above have in common that humans don't?

A. They all look alike!

Is it possible a human species evolved & created us for power through beauty of flesh?

The Armenia Stonehenge is 12,000 years old. Easter Island Moai Hat looks like these from the sky!

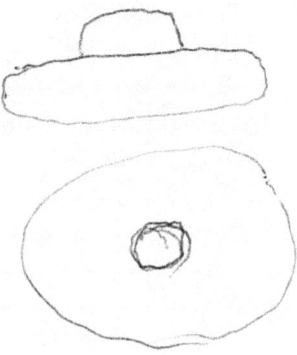

Old Testament Ezekeil saw craft in the sky "wheel within wheels."

Hello Mr. Maher, Bill MAHer
My name is Mike Brumfield and I am an author of seven books. I have enclosed my latest one and a dvd as a gift for you. I thoroughly enjoyed your "Religulous" film and it definitely inspired my dvd. I am also a live ufo finder and my footage was first aired on the Phoenix Az. fox network in 2006. Since then, I have partnered with Jeff Willes, whose footage has been sold all over the world, most recently used in the film "Race to Witch Mountain". It is real and clearly shows flying saucers, that haven't been debunked to this very day. Your film is great, especially the space penis skit. As you can see I have used the ancient religious cernes giant statue on the cover of my book. I have done this in hopes of provoking some logical dialogue about religion and its universal story of "Omnipotent" beings, "UP IN THE SKY". Like you I don't see any logic in the mindset of todays religious followers. They still believe in spirits, when we also today, are flying up in the sky. I have been attacked many times for asking the obvious question; "Could they be flesh and blood space dwellers, like we are now doing, living "UP IN THE SKY/SPACE STATION". But I understand their dilemma in not seeing this matching evidence. They are religulous (lol). I think it's ridicilous, that they think flying saucers are crazy when we are flying all over the globe and also live in space. Even worse, they don't understand why we doubt their omnipotent spirit god, who "COINCIDENTALLY" lives "UP IN THE SKY", not making the world perfect, when he can. Even most followers, say they would if they could, especially if they have children. I have children and I would, like I'm sure any logical father would. Your film makes it clear that the problem stems from being "RELIGULOUS". After 7 books and years of research, I have made some sense of our mystery. The title clearly speaks for itself. I hope to appeal to scientific minded people guided by the logic of matching evidence. Your skit about the vatican's opulent wealth, standing in stark contrast with Jesus, is beautiful. You would think any logical person could see it. Well, that is the power of religion's tradition, they don't. The only hope for our children is to let the scientific evidence create a new mindset where science and evidence rules, not faith and ignorance. We must replace belief with knowledge. I propose to answer our mystery, as well as the theory of everything. Most people don't think I could, but I understand that, too. Obviously, they didn't watch the original film; "THE DAY THE EARTH STOOD STILL". The only way to tell if someone is jesus or an extra-terrestrial is to ask them questions. I hope you give this a chance as my books haven't done very well. PLEASE check out my Advanced Scientific Knowledge Discovery? (A.S.K.) The Jewish Star matches the Atom!

Sincerely,
Mike Brumfield
1-931-261-3328

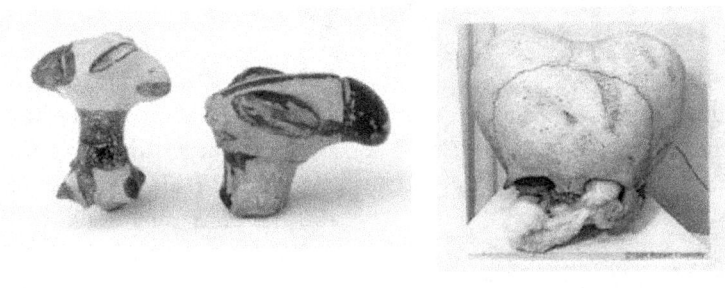

Oldest rock art on record catalogued by the Leakeys, ca. 50,000 years old, from Africa. Clearly shows little alien highlighted in box. It also shows another taller species restraining one of their own. The two heads above it were found in modern-day Israel, and are Sumerian; approximately 10,000 years old. The skull (from Peru) also supports ancient rock art of aliens in Africa. There are universal religious stories of two creations of man. Does this give us proof that they first tried to manipulate their own species to serve their needs?

Oldest Sumerian/Ubaid "God" statues on record in Museum of Antiquity, Cairo, Egypt. Clearly shows male and female gender and alien-looking beings. Picture, lower left, even shows mother nursing baby. Zechariah Sitchin claims these are android robots. They are, for God's sake, real "PARENTS!" If these are the most ancient statues that don't look like us, could they be primitive man's universal god/angel? Look at "Mother Goddess" statues on the following pages. They clearly are the god/angel that mixed with the "pretty daughter" of man.

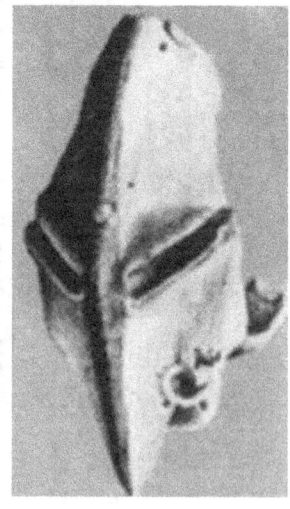

Ancient Sumerian King and Queen and Priest. Notice Priest has bald head—indicative of Alien God. Also notice big eyes.

The Sumerians carved statues of the gods from stone. From the statues we can see what they thought the gods looked like. Many gods looked like short people with round bellies. They had thin lips and big noses. They wore skirts made of sheep's wool. In fact, many statues of the gods looked like the statues the Sumerians made themselves!

What did the Sumerians believe about the meaning of their lives?

The gods of Sumer looked like men—and they acted like men. The gods liked good food and nice clothing. They got married and had children. Sometimes they were kind. Sometimes they were cruel. Either way, the Sumerians believed they had no control over what the gods did. Rather, the Sumerians believed that they were slaves of the gods.

This is the oldest known historical record of Mankind's "God" story. It clearly shows they were real flesh and blood people. It also shows they created Mankind to work for them. This is an excerpt from an educational text called *Ancient Civilizations*.

Mother goddess statue from Catayal (modern-day Turkey), ca. 8000 B.C. It clearly shows an alien head representing God and a beautiful woman. This story is also universal in religion and reflects Gods/angels mixing with "pretty" daughters of man.

These were found in Iraq. They are ancient statues of gods. Proves they have children, just like statues of alien parents holding child.

Cloning! Two squiggly lines, DNA!

These look like head of mother goddess statue and again connects aliens to Pyramids like evidence from Erich Von Daniken's book, *Gold of the Gods*.

More examples of "God" statues emphasizing "Big Head" and eyes. See how indentation in the forehead matches Iraq's statues. The top one (from Iraq) even has six fingers like other succeeding "God" statues. The bottom one is from South America.

These gold artifacts are from Erich Von Daniken's book *Gold of the Gods*. Gold artifact from ancient mine in Peru. Notice two alien-looking beings holding snakes and third one at top inside pyramid. The circles look like flying saucer stem cells, atoms or eggs that are fertilized. This connects pyramids to aliens. The pyramid served as image of rock that contained gold, quartz.

Alien-looking figure, right, has pyramid on head, penis and snake/DNA halo. The Bible says in Luke 6:4), "Only the Father in Heaven is God." Are these the fathers of heaven? Erich theorizes the skeleton on left could be a coded disk for message to contact future man. It is made of aluminum and coated in gold. We sent a coded disk into space with the same composition. I, again, see DNA, cells/eggs and chromosomes. The skeleton's head has a halo around it. See horned face like Africa rock art and Israel statures. The skeleton represents our deadly creation.

This is the most important evidence because it shows us, what their gods looked like (aliens), what they came and live in (flying saucers) and why they needed gold (space life and exploration). Hence we have the Biblical quote "Heaven's streets are paved with gold." It is a universal religious theme. Heaven is space, up to primitive man. Above is a cave drawing of aboriginal god Wandjina. Notice similarity to Owl Man. Also see halo around above head. This supports 10th planet story of gold replacing ozone and "who" was mining it before they created man as a "tiller of the ground" in Genesis. Man's purpose supports skeletal discoveries in gold mines. Gold protects astronauts from dangerous life radiation in space. MOST IMPORTANTLY This solves pyramid mystery. Gold is found most in quartz which forms natural pyramid shape.

Religious statues by Olmecs from Mexico. They are also known for mysterious carvings of huge heads! Figure circled is made of red lava rock like Easter Island man doing mystery. This is what power struggle of gods is about, us. Red symbolizes creation. Notice opposing sides black and white like Easter Island Man and Yin and Yang. Notice six obelisks like stones. Coincidence? Don't think so. Notice similarities to Easter Island statues, Israel statues, aborigines, all other "big headed" God statues from every continent. The figures are all black and white "facing" each other. The one in the back that is porous looking is the only red one. Could this represent the power struggle over mankind's inevitable creation and does it involve the sixth chromosome? Also, notice the clear resemblance to the alien statue from Israel and the head on the mother goddess statue as well. It clearly looks like the Easter Island heads except for the elongation. They are the product of the mix between the sons of gods/aliens and man. I think losing the bulbous head was the first indicator of their pursuit toward outward beauty. The story supports this with their reason for mixing in the first place.

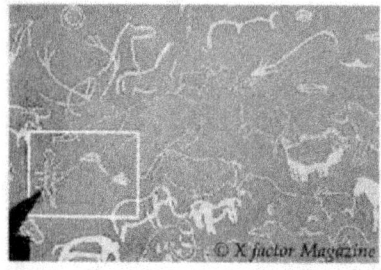
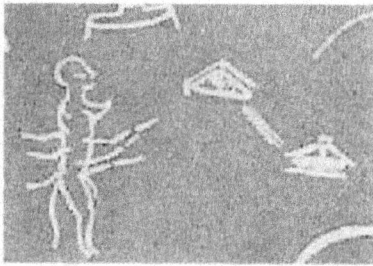

Japanese discovery on the island now known as Taiwan. It is a drawing by a general that discovered a strange ship on the island. This happened in 1806! Notice the ships drawn above it. He found this drawing on the hull of the ship. The writing looks like the hieroglyphics found on the aboriginal gods halo and supports the description of Roswell's. The cave art clearly shows matching saucers. This is dated circa 15000 years old. It is in France. It shows smaller ships coming out of a large one and abduction! The lines represent the invisible energy taking the human up. The top right picture is the oldest rock of aliens from Africa date circa 50,000 years old. It shows the little alien/Roswell gray in control observing. He's even protected by a box that looks much like a tree trimmer's carriage. The others are larger and restraining one of their own. They must have first made themselves larger to be more able to control their scientific manipulations of primitive man. They are obviously serving the little guy and they are struggling with one of their own. Anyway, this supports the scientific manipulation of themselves. See the one with the horns. Is this what gave us the first images of the biblical "devil." Read on! See similarity to statues on following page.

These reptilian looking skulls are found in Ubaid, Iraq. They look like the reptilian looking tall ones on the rock art of the previous page. Scientists have repeatedly mistaken the eyes for sunglasses or goggles. However they are very similar to the large slanted eyes of the Roswell gray alien. They are identical to the eyes of the mother goddess statue from Israel. Notice one is a divided looking skull, giving it the appearance of hornlike appendages, while the other is elongated. They are clearly two different types. Were these a product of the first attempts to make themselves larger for power or for mining gold. Anyway, it is clear here and in the writings that scientific creation was producing things like this, the mothman, centaur and other abnormalities. The little guy with a HUGE head is from Utah! See appendages (Devil's horns?).

ALIENS AND UFOs

The Starchild controversy

SINCE FEBRUARY 1999 a bizarre looking skull, known as the Starchild skull, has been exhibited at UFO conferences and heavily discussed in UFO journals.

The Starchild skull is alleged to be the remains of an alien-human hybrid.

DEFINITION
A hybrid is a cross between two different breeds or species. Only closely related species can interbreed or "hybridize," and it seems unlikely that humans and aliens would be similar enough.

Legend of the Star People

According to the Starchild Project, an organization that wants to arrange DNA testing of the skull to prove an incredible origin, the skull was discovered in the mountains of northern Mexico. Indian tribes from the region have legends of Star People – beings from the sky who visit Earth to impregnate local women before returning years later to retrieve the hybrid infants.

Big head

The skull has several strange features that suggest it is not human. It has a massive brain capacity, flattened rear, shallow eye sockets, and is missing the front sinuses.

The Starchild Project claims to have consulted over 50 experts, the vast majority of whom argue that the skull is that of a deformed human child.

Most experts say that the Starchild skull is that of a child suffering from hydrocephaly, a disease in which fluid builds up on the brain and makes the skull swell.

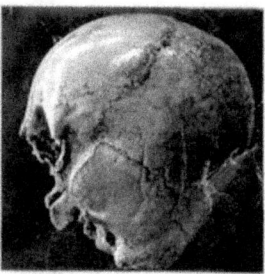

■ The Starchild skull is far from normal. But is it from an abnormal or cradle-boarded human infant, or perhaps an alien-human hybrid?

It is also widely thought that the skull has been cradle-boarded. Cradle-boarding is the practice of strapping an infant's head to a board and causes flattening of the back of the skull. It was practiced in the area of Mexico where the skull comes from. The Starchild Project argues that close examination of the skull rules out this explanation, and is attempting to raise funds to pay for DNA testing – the only way to be certain of the skull's origins.

"Beings from the sky" Is this the Owl Man which looks like an alien? He is pointing up! The skull supports this reality. Also "impregnates women" supports the cover art of the mother goddess statue, yet also has a big head! Skull is evidence of aliens being flesh and blood and these "sons of God" in Genesis 6:4. It supports my theory that they are not religious "spirit" magical beings. However, I conclude the atom, which makes everything, is "religion's invisible spirit" creator, evolving scientifically through time, not by magic. Read on. It scientifically fits religion's invisible omnipresent God.

Flying saucer

Giants of Easter Island South Pacific

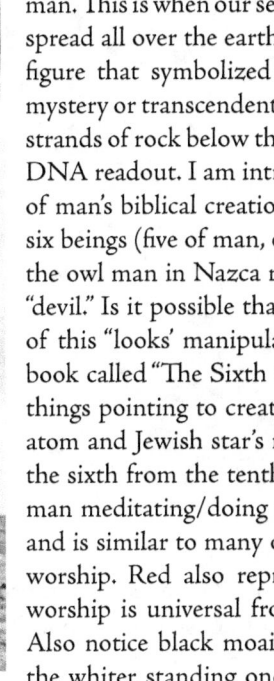

Notice the saucer on top of head tells us where they live just like owl man, aboriginal god, and Starchild legend spaceships just like on covers! They live up in saucers! Six strands of rock looks like DNA readouts. It also could implicate the sixth chromosome mystery or the Jewish creation on the sixth day. Giants were the offspring of gods and "pretty" daughters of man. This is when our separation occurred because wickedness spread all over the earth. A great flood followed. This is a red figure that symbolized mankind. See how he is doing the mystery or transcendental meditation, and looking up! The six strands of rock below the Alien looking god could symbolize a DNA readout. I am intrigued by it being six strands. The day of man's biblical creation is the 6th. The Hopi prophecy has six beings (five of man, one of an alien). The hummingbird of the owl man in Nazca reflects this theme as does the biblical "devil." Is it possible that the sixth chromosome is the source of this "looks' manipulation. I've been reading a fascinating book called "The Sixth Chromosome." There are many other things pointing to creation involving the number six like the atom and Jewish star's number of points. The planet mars is the sixth from the tenth. There's more read on! Also, look at man meditating/doing mystery. He is made of red lava rock and is similar to many other representations of first religious worship. Red also represents blood and creation. Mystery worship is universal from Buddhism to sitting Indian style. Also notice black moai that looks somewhat different from the whiter standing ones. This parallels black and white yin and yang. It also parallels Olmec statues.

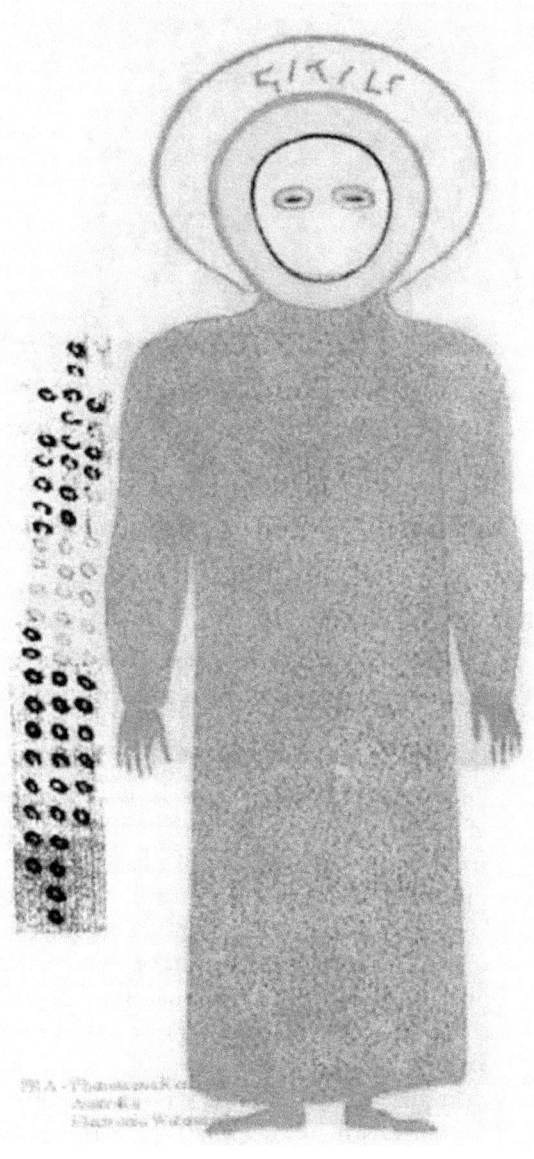

Aborigine cave drawing dated circa 30,000 years old. Notice hieroglyphics on gold halo. Also notice readout similar to Easter Island one. These rock layouts/DNA readouts are common across the Earth. Looks like scientist/astronaut in robe!

The bronze statue is from Kiev and is circa 8000 years old. It has six fingers supporting the existence and authenticity of the Roswell Alien autopsy. The recovered dead alien had six fingers and toes. This figure also supports the need for gold as protection in space. It has a Halo. Compare it to the following aboriginal gods. They look alien and even have gold painted halos around their heads. The Aztec block shows two hands intertwined with six fingers. These hands alone represent their god's creation of them and the entanglement represents DNA, how they were created. These match our medical symbol, intertwined serpents. How can they match when it takes an electron microscope to see them? The gods must be scientifically advanced!

Australian rock art (top) compared to same in Utah (bottom).

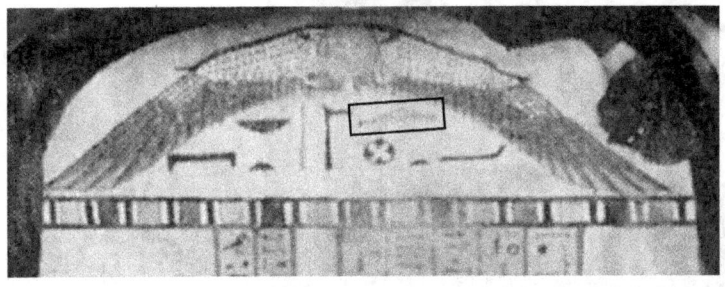

Ancient God symbolizes a flying saucer! These are all ancient symbols for god from Sumeria, Babylonia, Assyria, to the Egyptian one at the bottom. It has an actual saucer below the omni-present symbol of god which could literally be called a flying saucer. They all share this characteristic! Now we know why they're everywhere. But remember the atom is also a circle that is "every-thing." The Egyptian god is Atum! Notice the snakes for DNA creation. Also notice the cross symbol. It is the oldest geometry on earth representing the 10th planet. The Assyrian one clearly shows how man put himself in the circle. He became god!

Famous NASA Tether Incident

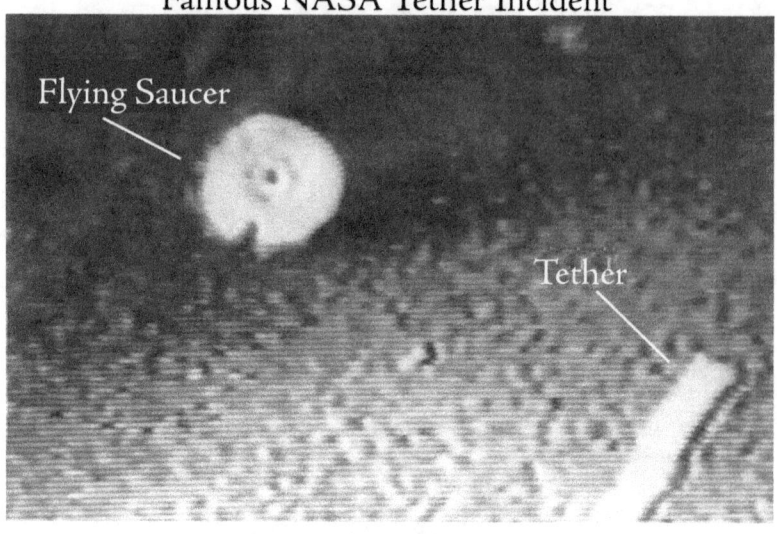

Saucer looks like galaxy, yin and yang, and the atom.

Below: Cave drawing showing saucer moving up. Two Below: An atom on a flat surface all would show center protrusion.

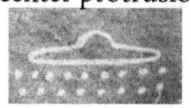

Galaxy has black hole in center which emits white matter.
See yinyang similarity.

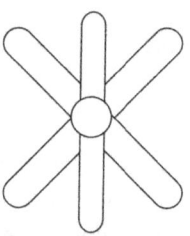

Could spinning be key to anti-gravity? Is Event Horizon proof time can be stopped? Can all life be related to atomic structure? Does knowledge of atom answer life's mystery?

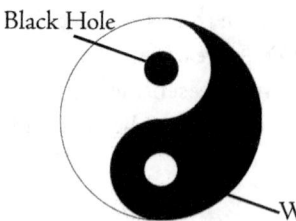

Famous NASA Tether Incident

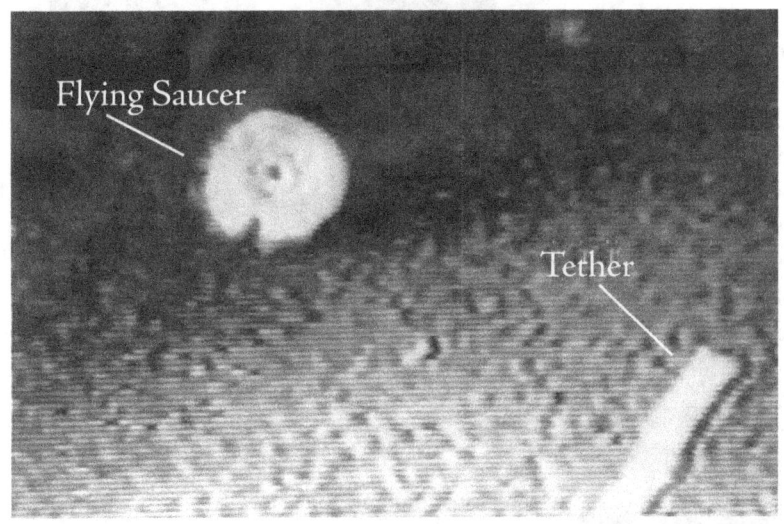

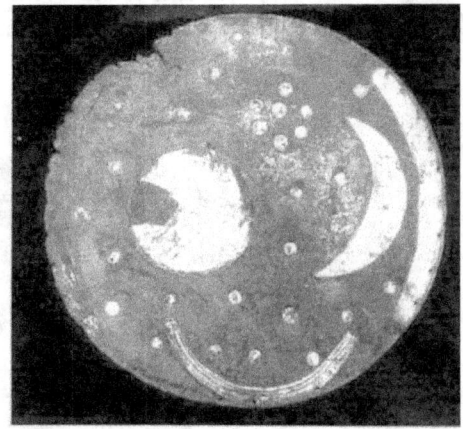

"Ancient" bronze disk from Norway. Gold overlay of sun, moon and objects in sky. The holes on outer perimeter look just like ones on disk from Turkey, Ohio and notches from Dropa stones. Notice seven circles like atoms between sun and moon!

Notice the similarity of disk sculpture with indentation to flying saucer photograph by NASA. Most importantly, sculpture is in gold, which is what we use in the construction of our spacecraft today.

"Ancient" bronze disk from Norway. Gold overlay of sun, moon and objects in sky. The holes on outer perimeter look just like ones on disk from Turkey, Ohio and notches from Dropa stones. Notice seven circles like atoms between sun and moon!

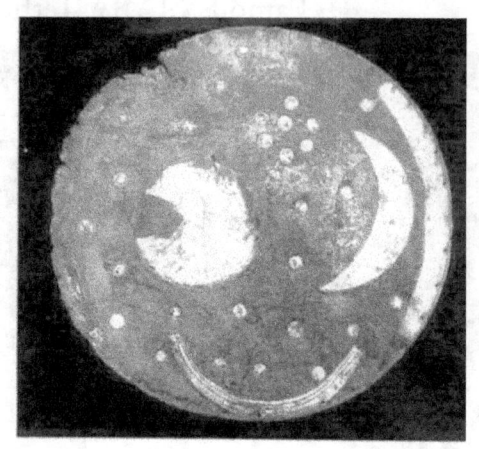

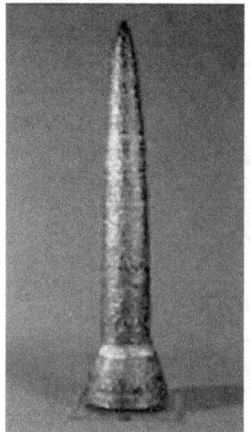

Mysterious ancient gold cone hats of Europe. They look like rockets and have flying saucers images as well as moons and suns. The priests wore these as hats.

This ancient Egyptian sculpture of Ahknenton has a religious ceremonial hat that resembles the gold cone and Easter Island. Again, these disks, hats, gold, and obelisks all implicate and match flying saucer evidence and explain why they depict stars in space. It is already conquered by space faring beings that created our mysterious species to mine gold. Gold is crucial to explore space!

From 6000 B.C. A plate from Nepal, the decoration shows a saucer-like shape and a large-headed humanoid. These are craft seen by many thousands of people today all around the world. UFO Coin, 1680. French Medal apparently commemorating a UFO sighting of a wheel-like object in Renaissance France.

The Yappese are the greatest of the Polynesian navigators. Our Hawaiian voyaging canoe "Hokulea" has a Yappese navigator. Since Yap is geologically unique in Micronesia, sedimentary in origin, all the rock is shale. Palau, about 700 miles southwest of Yap is predominately volcanically uplifted limestone created from ancient coral reefs. It is uniquely crystalline in nature. Voyaging to Palau by canoe, Yappese quarried this stone, risking their lives to get home with the largest coin. Many voyages were fraught with danger and adventure. The tougher the voyage, the more the money was worth! See hole in the center, like other ancient saucer/disk statues.

In Jabbaren, in the Tassali mountains, Algeria, south of the Hoggar. A 6 meter-high character with a large round decorated head. The massive body, the strange dressing, the folds around the neck and on the chest suggest some ancient time astronaut. A similar character is painted at Star in the Tassali, in the Cabro caves in France and in several other places. Some of them are much smaller and raise their hands towards a giant being, of non human appearance, sometimes these "round heads" beings seem to hover in the air. On right, an ancient painting ca. 1700 AD. See how all the other ancient saucer art and photographs have a hole in the center. The biblical description of these fiery chariots, a circle within a circle!

Ufologist Bob Dean noticed a similarity between this UFO photographed by police officer Mark Coltrane in Colfax, Wisconsin on the 19th of April 1978 and the object in the ancient De Gelder painting.

 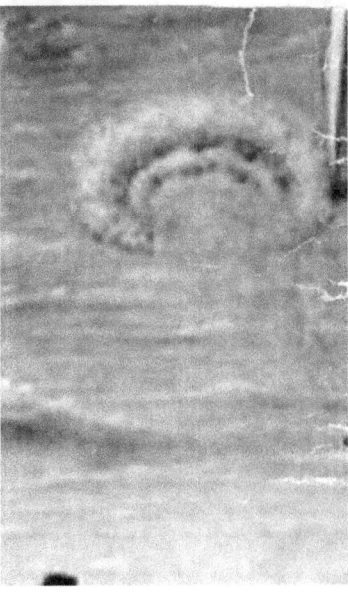

See similarity of photograph by Ed Walters on left to ancient painting of UFO on right.

Religious ancient disk and obelisk on left from China. See three dots at top of obelisk. Does this represent atomic propulsion of today's rockets? Ancient clay disk on right from Turkey.

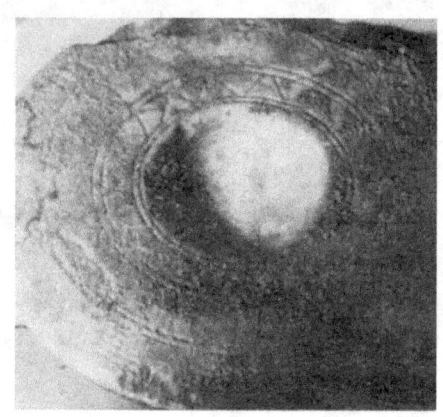

Ancient gold disk from Bogota, Columbia, matches clay mold from Turkey and flying saucers' shape. See notches on outside perimeter! Important because it matches many others from other countries. All ancient.

Gold disk from Peru gold mine. See sperm and alien head and face. The center is full of atoms... again possibly evidence of atomic propulsion. There are faces in sun and stars. We are stardust/ atoms/adams. Notice diamond infinity symbol.

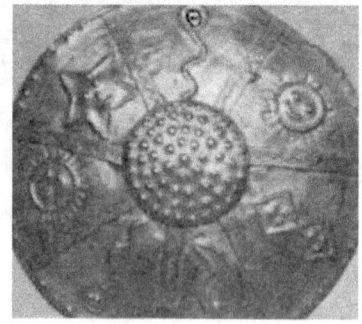

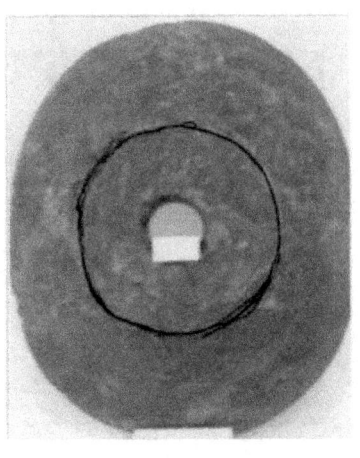

See similarity of photograph by Ed Walters on left to ancient painting of UFO on right.

Ancient Chinese gold disk with rubies. It says "anywhere the sun shines, life will exist." This looks like a computer chip. The disk fits disk on Genesis probe.

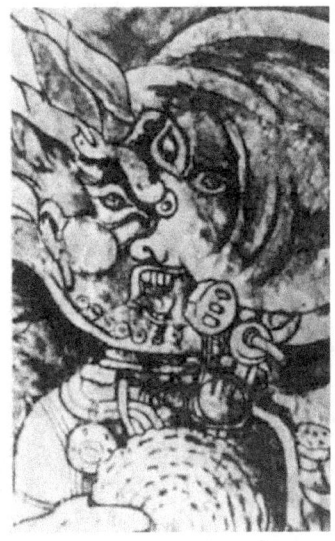

Ancient cave art from Ubekestan. See notches like in Ohio and spirals like dropa stones. Besides, he looks like an astronaut. See atom symbol on jaw line.

This ancient disk was found in Ohio, my home state. It is a beautiful piece of evidence to support my theory. It has an eye in the middle of the "right" hand which is center of disk. This clearly represents the gods being in control, knowing all (omniscience) and controlling all (omnipotent). The rattlesnakes represent our deadly creation. The disks give them omnipresence.

Looks just like other UFOs of NASA! These are dropa stones from Tibet and are circa 10,000 years old. They were found deep in a cave with the remains of about 400 skeletons of little people with big heads. The island of Yap values an identical stone as money. They are called money stones. The largest ones measure up to 10 feet, and are made of polished white limestone. The whiter they are the more valuable. Now we see where the white thing comes from in religion. If these gods stay in spaceships they would be really white looking. The universal alien is the Roswell gray! If you don't buy this then buy an alien doll. It will be him!

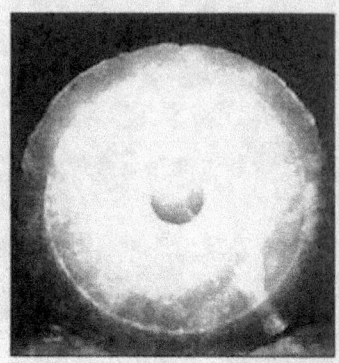

Dropa stone: Artifacts called Dropa stones, which bear an uncanny resemblance to the UFOs involved in the tether incident.

Last but not least, the Legend tells how they were attacked and eventually killed off by neighboring tribes because they were so "UGLY." Here again is evidence why they can't cohabit with us and how language comes full circle to support the evidence and answer the big question, "Where did they come from; What do they look like and why do they stay away?" They "dropped" out of sky according to legend and this is why the tribes they spawned are called Dropas. They still exist today and have physical attributes that resemble the alien. The Owl Man is your next answer and Cernes Giant the last of the three WWWs. Where, what, why!

Ancient stone carvings from Peru, "Ica stones."

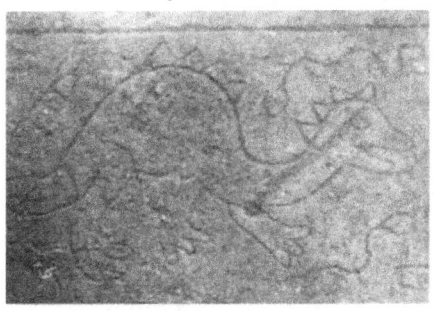

Notice sperm-like objects with DINOSAUR! Also amulet on right clearly shows big headed alien god above earth and not on it. The earth is gridded like we do today with latitude and longitude lines. How is any of this possible without space already being conquered by scientific beings?

Giant stones of Costa Rica. Again why? Does this prove knowledge of planets and atoms that would be important to space-traveling gods?

These are six-foot giant heads of the Olmecs. Giant Heads! Notice DNA symbol and cross symbol of tenth planet on jaguar head at left. This mirrors sphinx. The right head has "six" claws on forehead and symbol of atom, cell or fertilized egg and flying saucers!

Giant stones of Costa Rica. Again why? Does this prove knowledge of planets and atoms that would be important to space-traveling gods?

Also, these are airplane statues made of solid gold. This supports space travel's need for gold and proves gods are flesh and blood beings who have already conquered space! THESE SPEAK FOR THEMSELVES AS WELL. They are all made of gold. From Egypt to Peru!

India

Look at alien eyes!

Turkey

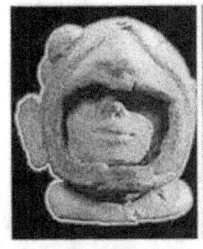

Look at matching thrusters on obvious rocket. The head is missing on pilot.

More ancient statues

Ancient European astronauts!

Brazil
(Below)

Kayapo tribe still celebrates the legend of "Teacher from Heaven" Bep Kororot; this is his suit; stick, his "fire" stick. He made the villagers' weapons turn to dust when they tried to "attack" him. He helped them and then went to mountain top and disappeared in a cloud of thunder. They await his "Return!"

Mexico Gold Star God
(Above)
Alien head on DNA from sun bottom left hand.

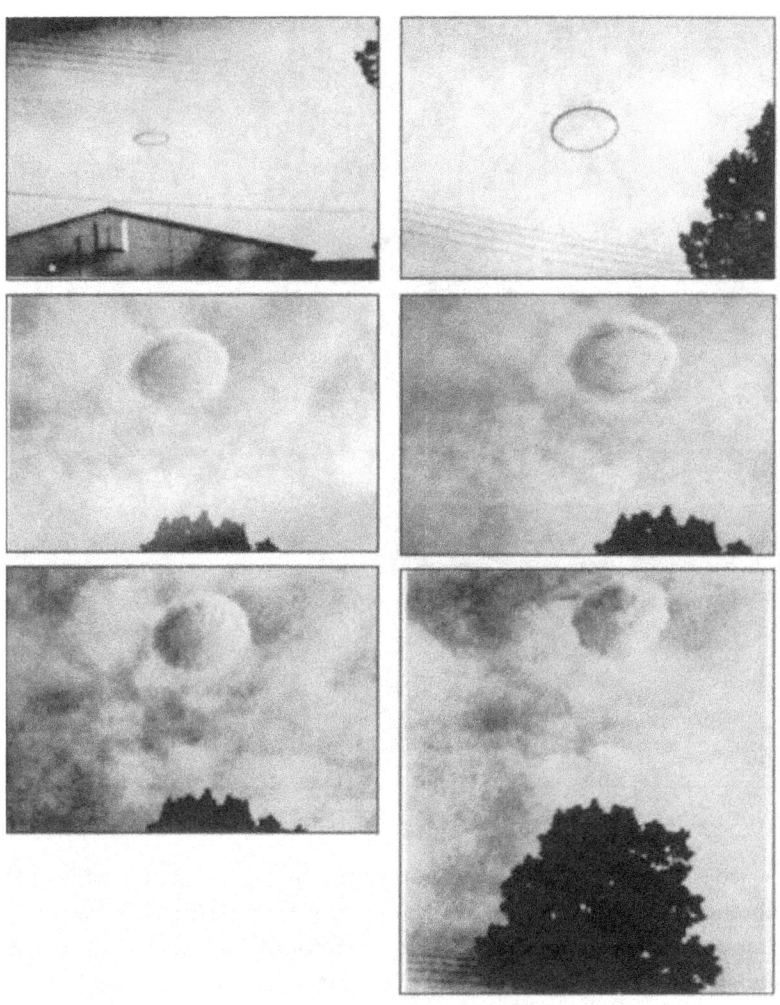

There are many legends of gods from the sky, in clouds that make thunder. The Kayopo story on the previous page mirrors that of Moses and his "ten commandments." They were also to teach us. Could this be the cloud of thunder? Actual photo taken by Army private in 1965. Eye witnessed by others and never explained!

MIKE BRUMFIELD

Flying Saucer

Cave Astronaut

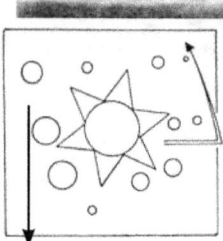

10th Planet

1. Notice cave grid looks like computer grid of space, and is flat like floating membrane. The membrane theory says space is infinite. It is a cyclical dance of creation and destruction. Also star of cave sculpture just like the Sumerian clay tablet below, and atom symbol. The clay tablet is dated circa 13000 years. The cave drawing is much older. They both show a 10th planet in our solar system. HOW?

2. The cave astronaut and gemini-looking capsule are also ancient. This is proof they existed before and supports my conclusion. Read on!

3. This is "Matching" irrefutable evidence that the ancients were communicating with space-faring people! Their absence makes it clear. Our mystery is what they look like!

4. See flying saucer in sky above astronaut! Again, a hole in the center!

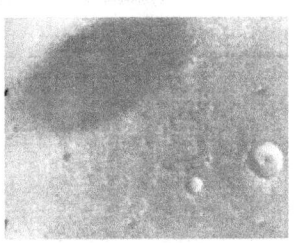

1. Notice the satellite on the clay tablet going from Earth (7th planet) to Mars (6th planet). It looks just like ones today. This tablet is also circa 13,000 years. Also notice symbol for Mars matches atom and Jewish star. Is this proof that Mars could have had Man there first and we destroyed it with nuclear weapons? The "man" on mars is in a suit. Is it reason for contact?
2. See how the helmet of Mars "man" on tablet matches our pictures of face on Mars.
3. Notice ancient satellite looks like alien head and eyes of nuclear missile. Egyptian obelisk matches nuclear missile. Egyptians called obelisks "rocketship."
4. See flying saucer monitoring earth on mars clay tablet.
5. This is a photo from phobos satellite sent to view mars moon phobos. It is irregular shaped and appears to be hollow. Could it be used as a space base on the inside? We think asteroids could be used this way as natural spaceships. This is the last picture it took before it was deemed "destroyed" by space debris. Looks like a flying saucer to me.   MIKE BRUMFIELD

Three famous UFO incidents in the U.S. reported on the front page of each respective city's newspaper. The dates and places are on the last two. The first is Los Angeles and shows us shooting at it. It happened in Feb. 25, 1942. No wonder they don't cohabit with us. We never recovered it. Ten innocent civilians died from the shrapnel fallout!

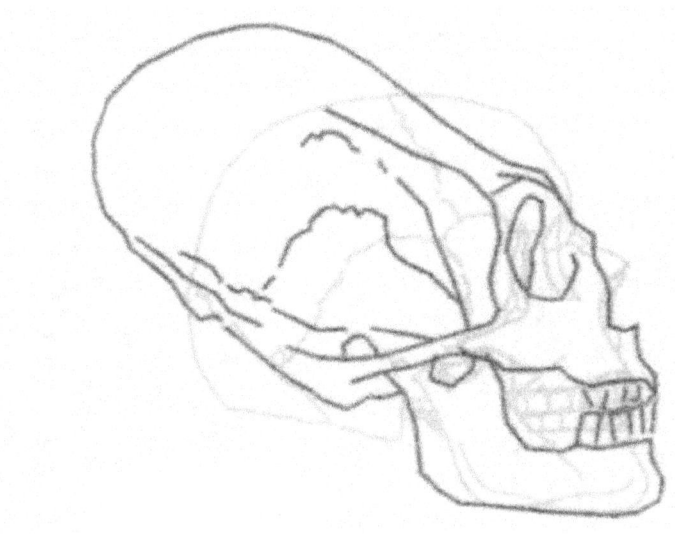

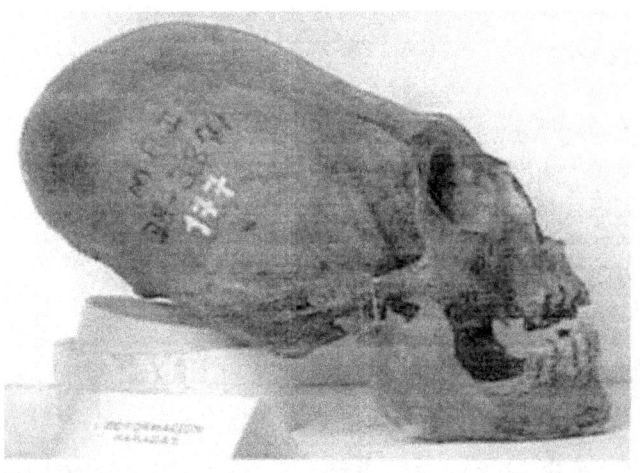

Head molding was an ancient universal religious practice! Obviously, they were trying to imitate their gods' appearance.

Ancient Egyptian relief "Stellae" of Ahknenton, Nefertiti, and children. Notice bald elongated heads and big alien eyes!

Egyptian papyrus clearly show Ahknenton's head without hat. It is alien looking like long limbs and fingers. The bald head is universal religious practice like ancient head molding!

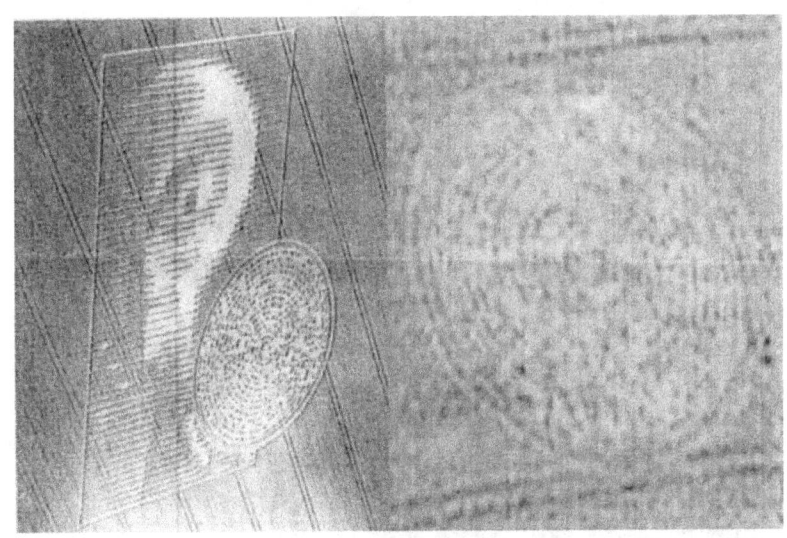

(Below) Ancient intrepanation skull! This was also universal religious practice. This could be how mental telepathy works. We are doing this today with cybernetics. Surgical tools found with skulls were made of gold!

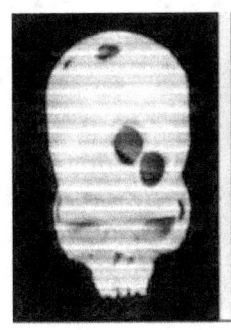
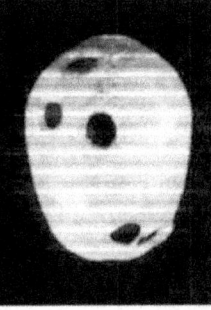

This crop circle has a coded message: "We are the good guys, not mankind!" This matches the quote by Yeshua when they called him good. "Only the Father in heaven is good," Luke 6:4. Is this proof that the aliens are the "father" and it is a plural term also. Yeshua said, "The Father and I are one." He also said we could be too! The evidence of an alien with a penis from Erich Von Daniken and the head of the mother goddess statue proves this universal story's facts.

Gold is the most ancient metal known to man and sacred to religion, everywhere. This information is provided by World's Leading Gold Mining Co.

History of Gold – Timeline

4000 BC	Gold is first known to be used in parts of Central and Eastern Europe.
3000 BC	The Egyptians master the arts of beating gold into leaf and alloying gold with other metals to variations in hardness and color. They also develop the ability to cast gold, using the lost-wa still used in today's jewelry industry. The Sumer civilization of southern Iraq uses gold to create a wide range of jewelry, often us sophisticated and varied styles still worn today.
2500 BC	Gold jewelry is buried in the Tomb of Djer, the king of the first Egyptian dynasty, at Abydos,
1500 BC	The immense, gold-bearing regions of Nubia make Egypt a wealthy nation, as gold become recognized standard medium of exchange for international trade. The Shekel, a coin originally weighing 11.3 grams of gold, is used as a standard unit of mea throughout the Middle East. The coin contained a naturally occurring alloy called electrum, \ approximately two-thirds gold and one-third silver.
1352 BC	The young Egyptian King Tutankhamen is interred in a pyramid tomb laden with gold, his re an extravagant gold anthropoid sarcophagus.
1350 BC	The Babylonians begin to use fire assay to test the purity of gold.
1091 BC	Squares of gold are legalized in China as a form of money.
560 BC	The first coins made purely from gold are minted in Lydia, a kingdom of Asia Minor.
58 BC	Julius Caesar seizes enough gold in Gaul (France) to repay Rome's debts.
50 BC	The Romans issue a gold coin called the Aureus.
600-699 AD	The Byzantine Empire resumes gold mining in central Europe and France, an area undevel fall of the Roman Empire. Artisans of the period produce intricate gold artifacts and icons.
1100	1100 Venice secures its position as the world's leading gold bullion market due to its locatio trade routes to the east.
1284	Venice introduces the gold Ducat, which soon becomes the most popular coin in the world, so for more than five centuries. Great Britain issues its first major gold coin, the Florin, which is followed by the Noble, the A Crown, and the Guinea.
1511	King Ferdinand of Spain sends explorers to the Western Hemisphere with the command to '
1717	Isaac Newton, Master of the London Mint, sets price of gold that lasts for 200 years.
1787	First US gold coin is struck by Ephraim Brasher, a goldsmith.
1792	The Coinage Act places the young United States on a bimetallic silver/gold standard, definin Dollar as equivalent to 24.75 grains of fine gold, and 371.25 grains of fine silver.
1803	North Carolina site of first US gold rush. The state supplies all the domestic gold coined for the US Mint in Philadelphia until 1828.
1848	The California gold rush begins when James Marshall finds specks of gold in the water at Jc sawmill near the junction of the American and Sacramento Rivers.
1850	Edward Hammond Hargraves, returning from California, predicts he will find gold in Australi week. He discovers gold in New South Wales within one week of landing.
1859	The Comstock Lode of gold and silver is discovered in Nevada. As a result, Nevada is made years later.

Oldest gold mines found in Africa civilization traced from northeastern Africa science traces our origin to hominid they named "Eve."

Genesis Project

Capsule bearing solar secrets

By PAUL FOY
Associated Press

SALT LAKE CITY — In a harrowing feat high over the Utah desert Wednesday, two helicopter stunt pilots will try to snatch a floating space capsule that holds "a piece of the sun" and bring it safely down.

Their biggest fear: What if they flub it on live TV?

And that's entirely possible. The pilots rate it 8 or 9 on a difficulty scale of 10.

"It's like flying in formation with a giant floating jellyfish," says pilot Dan Rudert.

The stuntmen will be trying to hook the 400-pound Genesis capsule as it hurtles 400 feet a minute. Inside it are fragile solar wind particles — so small they're invisible — which scientists hope will reveal clues about the origin of our solar system.

The biggest challenge, pilots say, will be flying at 40 mph almost a mile above the desert without visual reference points to judge distance or speed as they close in with hook and cable.

The helicopter pilots will have five chances to snag the capsule in midair. Military pilots were unavailable for a mission that required them to commit to a task six years in the future. The civilian pilots have replicated the retrieval without fumbles in dozens of practice runs, but are terrified of failing as NASA television broadcasts a worldwide feed.

If they miss and the Genesis capsule hits the ground hard, scientists say they'd have to spend months sorting through broken jewelry-studded disks holding the tiny solar wind particles.

There are other opportunities for the $260 million mission to go awry, too. For NASA engineers a white-knuckle moment will be when the capsule must be steered through a "keyhole" high in the Earth's atmosphere. If the experts at California's Jet Propulsion Laboratory can't line up the precise entry and angle, Genesis will be waved off on an elliptical orbit of Earth, and another attempt would be made in six months.

The Genesis mission marks the first time NASA has collected and returned any objects from farther than the moon, said Roy Haggard, Genesis' flight operations chief and CEO of Vertigo Inc., which designed the capture system.

Together, the charged atoms captured on the capsule's disks of gold, sapphire, diamond and silicone are no bigger than a few grains of salt, but scientists say that's enough to reconstruct the chemical origin of the sun and its family of planets.

Scientists will keep busy for five years after Genesis completes its

> Together, the charged atoms captured on the capsule's disks of gold, sapphire, diamond and silicone are no bigger than a few grains of salt, but scientists say that's enough to reconstruct the chemical origin of the sun and its family of planets.

This clearly shows our need for gold in space as well as other "precious" metals and gems. This explains religion's description of the same in heaven/space. After all, religion is universally antiwealth.

Religion is History!!!
Missing Link Proof!

The alien skull shows the obvious mix between primitive man and himself producing us. We are the mystery! Religion began approximately 200,000 years ago when our big headed species started burying the dead and making artwork! This coincides with my theory like many others (Erich von Daniken and Alan Alford) that theorize intelligent beings from the sky manipulated primitive man and created this missing link in skull growth. The evidence shows that these religious gods are bigger headed than us and look like the stereotypical Roswell gray alien! This mix of their large head and primitive man's smaller one caused ours to jump the normal growth of evolution. Primitive man remained so for many millions of years without any evolution in knowledge or much change in skull size. The only logical explanation for the missing link and inexplicable sudden attainment of knowledge is religion itself. Not slow evolution, but a sudden scientific creation. The fossil evidence supports this reality! Religion is from Heaven or the sky! It is universal in the creation stories; it is clear that we are created to worship them or work for them. It is universal. This work or "purpose" can be traced directly to our first order of business. It was and is gold. It is universal. Gold is important for space travel. We are creating robots to assist in our space travels, which is only made possible with gold! This is universal! Even the robot itself is mostly composed of gold. It is the most resistant protector to the extreme conditions of space. The gold halo is the universal god symbol which is above the head. All gods are depicted as being able to fly. I am presenting the following religious symbols and their matching scientific counterparts as evidence to prove the creation of man was and is a scientific one. I propose that our true purpose is religion's pre-destined will; their pre-determined plan for us. Our true purpose is why they stay away on purpose. Please enjoy the exciting conclusion to my story. See for yourself how science is revealing an unfolding pre-determined plan for mankind that mirrors religion itself. Science today matches religion replacing the spirit-magic god with the alien!

How can these symbols match without using an electron microscope? and could they be the same?

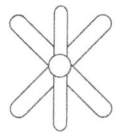     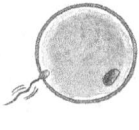

Jewish Star or Atom?   Medical Symbol or DNA?   Yin-yang or sprem and egg

Symbols: Matching Themes:

Religion	Science
Omnipresence	Space Program
God is Infinite	Atom is Infinite
Creation/Man	Robots
Saving Life	Improve/Saving Man's Life
Multiply	Ensure Propagation of Species
Manipulating Age	Genetics for Manipulating Age
One Mind	Evidence Rules
Levitation	Anti-Gravity
Mummification	Cryogenics
Mental Telepathy	Cybernetics
Spirit s	Holograms
Disappearing I	Invisibility/Teleportation
Mystery	Biorhythm Feedback

I'm sure there are many more. So please read on as I "have" to get to work! I'm sure you'll get the point. I propose that religion is not only the best evidence that space is already conquered, buttells us plainly the answer to Fermi's paradox: " Why don't they contact us?"! The world just hasn't come together to scientifically answer it. But of course we all know the world is just now global and capable of destroying itself. These are the two pre-requisites for the end to be ushered in. Coincidence? Our true purpose explains their silence and the reason they stay away on purpose. It is for the good of science. However, this is the end of their tortuous silence. It is the only way to save our planet. It is the next step in their plan. The two witnesses torture the world with their prophecy! Our species is the most unnatural self-destructive species in the universe. Get ready for contact. The "Regeneration of Man," Second Coming, Mayan Golden Age.

MIKE BRUMFIELD

18A Friday, December 20, 2002   THE TENNESSEAN   www.tennessean.com

DNA similarities make world seem smaller
Survey says any two people 99.9 percent identical

By LEE BOWMAN
Scripps Howard News Service

Although everyone's genetic makeup is unique, scientists have found that populations from different parts of the world still share more genetic similarities than had been thought.

The results of a computer analysis of DNA from individuals representing 52 populations around the globe, published today in the journal *Science*, make up the largest such global survey of genetic diversity, and should help studies of ancient human migrations.

Those surveyed were broken into five regions: Africa, Eurasia, East Asia, Oceania and the Americas. Differences among individuals within those groups accounted for 93%-95% of genetic variety, according to the international team led by Marcus Feldman, a professor of humanities and sciences at Stanford University.

Compare the genetics of any two people, and the matchup will be about 99.9% identical. The research team accurately pinpointed the ancestral content of virtually every individual from Africa, East Asia, Oceania and the Americas. ■

[handwritten annotations: How did Hopi prophecy... yes. two]

1. How could Hopi medicine man know of five races, let alone the alien god? See illustration on the next page.
2. Notice alien head on mother goddess statue. This supports what gods look like in Genesis 6:4. Statue dated circa 5000 years old found in Jerusalem, Israel.
3. Notice asexual organs on alien statue. This confirms Yeshua's description of angels and explains why they don't give their hand in marriage. They must be androgynous.

Alien statues found along banks of Jordan River 10,000 years old

Mother goddess statues represent the inevitable separation that was to occur. According to religion mankind is predestined. It happened because the "sons of gods" thought the daughters of men were pretty. Their "giant" offspring became men of great renown and all wickedness spread all over the earth. This exemplifies their lust for power due to their obvious oneness in looks and small size. And they must have considered themselves ugly. It took place during the mysterious time frame, of the last ice age approximately 13,000 years ago up to the beginning of the Jewish calendar, 4000 BC (6,000 years ago). These are found all over the earth. The alien headed one is from Israel circa 8,000 years old. The round headed one is 30,000 years. It is called the Venus of Willendorf. The asexual alien statue was found along the banks of the Jordan River. Notice the circles as if they knew about chromosomes and DNA. These as all scientists agree were religiously important and found in every household. I theorize that like the pyramids and Easter Island giants they were left to stand the test of time to tell us what their gods look like and where they are, Aliens and space.

The Five Faces of Man

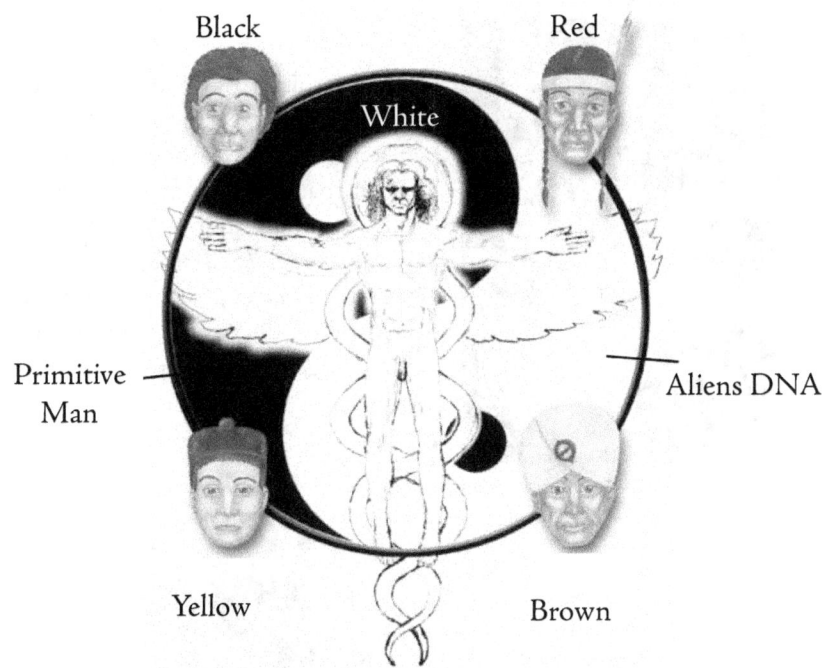

The different colors and facial structures indicate the competition to make the "prettiest" human. This "prettiest" factor is evident in Genesis 6:4 and the fall of the angel story! Looks give us power over one another. All religions have a fall from heaven and earth being one, void and without form, to being separated. The gods/angels live in space—Earth becomes prison. This resulted from a power struggle. The biblical account gives us two creations. Nature created primitive man and then the gods/angels/aliens scientifically created modern man as a worker. Modern man is the mystery. The evidence universally points to mining gold. This started 100,000 years ago and continues to this day! The matching yin and yang and AMA symbol to the science symbols of the sperm/egg and DNA reflects our scientific creation. Even the biblical account describes a scientific process both for the man and the woman. The woman's creation is from man and he is anesthetized. Ultimately, I theorize two ongoing infinite creations: Nature's gods/angels/ white sperm/DNA and us from primitive man/black sperm/DNA. We are the mystery!

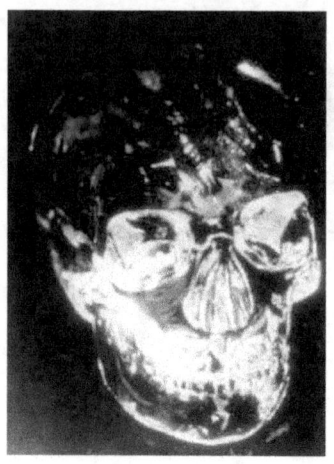

One of thirteen Mayan quartz crystal skulls. They are anatomically perfect, ancient and show no tool marks. Legend has it that they hold information that will solve our mystery which is where are the people/gods who made us and them? This crystal today is used for its electrical conduciveness "piezo electricity" and storage of information on computer chips.

This is where I propose they are. This is a statue from Easter Island that is looking up and appears to have a flying saucer on top of his head. They are in these religious fiery chariots of the sky.

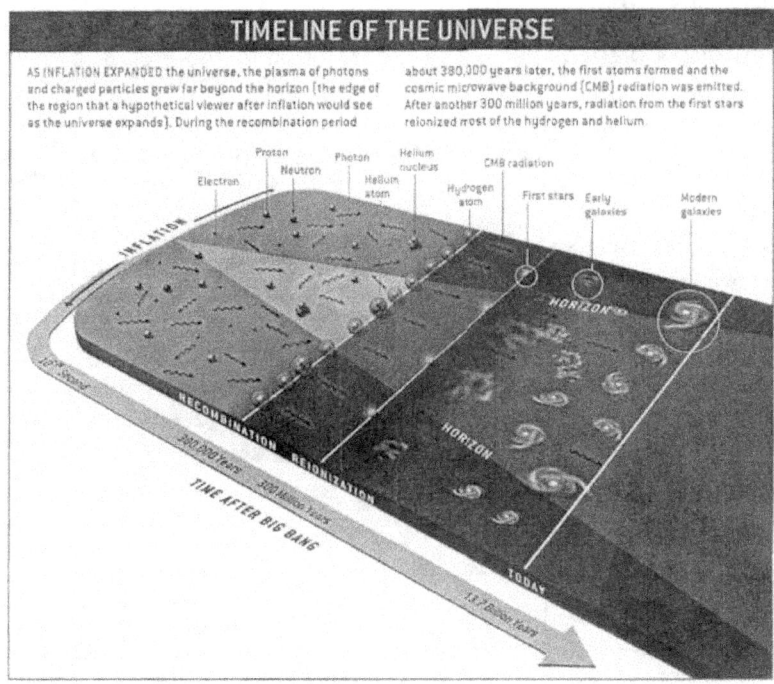

This is a perfect example of macrocosm science. The smallest parts mirror the whole. Atoms, photons, solar systems galaxies all resemble the universe itself. It is mostly space. The ancient geometry supports this theory/reality. I was amazed at how much a woman's egg looks like the sun (magnified) and when the sperm penetrates it the outer shell grows a green growth that becomes the placenta. The earth would only grow green vegetation from photon penetration. Photons look like sperm. Atoms look like suns, these look like eggs! Anyway, The problem with a beginning to our universe is that it is infinite. Only matter has a "beginning and ending." But this is an oxy-moron because atoms make matter and though one form ends it doesn't stop existing, another one just begins. This is all about image! Mind over matter and to be free of matter constraints, we must free ourselves from the matter. For space travel/freedom it is literally what we have to do. Free ourselves from the inevitable invisible eater of matter. GRAVITY! Matter itself. Does all this really matter? To be free it does. Flying is the ultimate freedom!

Finally my ex-religion's fraud!

1. "Where is God?" is the $64,000 question. I thought God is omnipresent! That means everywhere like the atom! They say he's all alone in space!

2. They say he's not lonesome but he's all alone. Then they say he creates for others. That's loneliness.

3. Finally they say he creates a heavenly organization of "spirit" sons like "himself." Why not daughters? And now they skip the fall of the angels story.

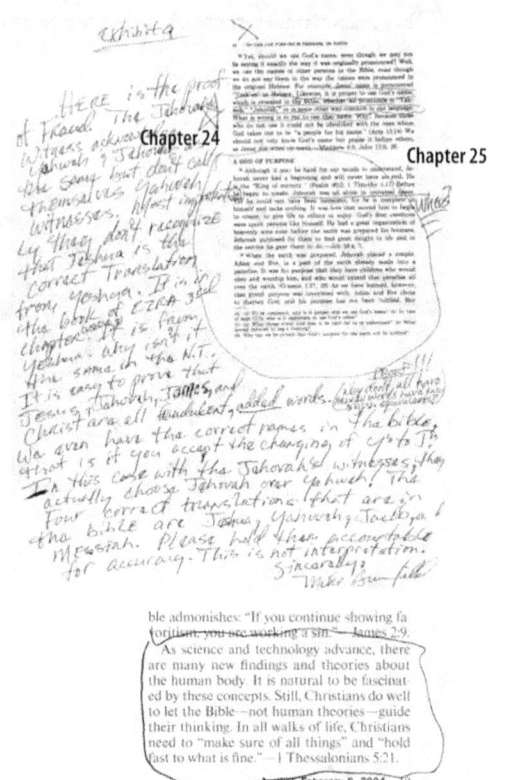

4. Last but not least. This is the proof that "religion," at least the Jews, make these angels and god "spirit" not flesh and blood. This is the ultimate cover-up. What if they come back and are the aliens? WWYD?

5. Proof that the J.W.'s discredit science! And ironically the scripture above James 2:9 makes their god a hypocrite. He has a favorite, yet forbids it. The chosen race of the Jews. No wonder people revere the Jews!

6. Finally they say the "Devil" is working through the U.N.! Don't they want a United Earth?

Modern-Day "Encounters" With Angels and Aliens

Many people today claim that they have seen angels and spoken with them. Others say that they have had contact with aliens from other worlds. The book *Angels—An Endangered Species* lists the similarities between these accounts, claiming that both may have a common explanation.* Following is a summary of some similarities listed in the book.

1. Both angels and aliens come from other worlds.

2. Both are advanced life-forms, either spiritually or technologically.

* The explanation common to both is that wicked spirits, or demons, are evidently behind many such "encounters." As the Bible says, "Satan himself keeps transforming himself into an angel of light." (2 Corinthians 11:14)—See *Awake!* July 8, 1996, page 26.

3. The friendly variety are youthful and beautiful in appearance, and they are kind and full of compassion.

4. Both have little trouble with language, speaking clearly in the language of the listener.

5. Both are masters of flight.

6. Appearances of both angels and aliens are accompanied by brilliant light.

7. Both appear fully dressed, commonly in either robes or close-fitting tunics. White or blue are favorite colors.

8. Both are usually the same height as humans.

9. Both express concern about the plight of humanity and the planet.

10. The evidence of both alien and angelic encounters is the testimony of the beholder.

★ ANSWER

Awake! November 22, 1999

Erich von Däniken

to count the pages of his metal library, but I accept his estimate that there might be two or three thousand.

The characters on the metal plaques are unknown, but if only the appropriate scholars were told of the existence of this unique find *now* I am sure that they could be deciphered comparatively quickly in view of the wealth of possibilities for comparison.

No matter who the creator of this library was, nor when he lived, this great unknown was not only master of a technique for the "mass-production" of metal folios in vast numbers—the production—he also had written characters with wi. he wanted to convey important information beings in a distant future. This metal library w created to outlast the ages, to remain legible to eternity.

Time will show whether our own age is seriously interested in discovering such fantastic, awe-inspiring secrets.

Is it prepared to decipher an age-old work even if it means bringing to light truths that might turn our neat but dubious world picture completely upside down?

Do not the high priests of all religions ultimately abhor revelations about prehistory that might replace *belief in the creation by knowledge* of the Creation?

Is man really prepared to admit that the history of his origin was entirely different from the one which is instilled into him in the form of a pious fairy story? CALLED RELIGION'S SPIRIT WORLD

This is why we must prove religion's origin. The Jehovah Witnesses are not helping to make peaceful contact! They don't even realize that their answer proves mankind is religion's devil and reincarnation! (Keeps transforming).

A ridiculous depiction of God by Jehovah's Witnesses. Sadly, this is universal. Religion is anti-wealth, making this even more insulting.

Christ is no longer a babe but the powerful King of God's Kingdom

How to identify true religion
What good fruit should true religion produce?—Matthew 7:17.

"Something Cannot Come From Nothing"

■ **KENNETH LLOYD TANAKA PROFILE:** I am a geologist presently employed by the U.S. Geological Survey in Flagstaff, Arizona. For almost three decades, I have participated in scientific research in various fields of geology, including planetary geology. Dozens of my research articles and geologic maps of Mars have been published in accredited scientific journals. As one of Jehovah's Witnesses, I spend about 70 hours every month promoting Bible reading.

Using science to prove God and make themselves look ridiculous with their quote, which disproves their God. (Read about this in my story)

310   REALITY: ESCAPE FROM EARTH

Could I be this Michael and the war about our evil species? Notice Tibetan religion's heavenly war also involves one third being rebellions! Their Sixth Stanza reads like modern science. The final admonition is to learn the "correct" age of the "small wheel." This is the atom and us. We are atoms/adams "appearing and reappearing continuously." Atoms are infinite!

> ## The Gold of the Gods
>
> stars of God: I will sit also upon the mount of the congregation, in the sides of the north."
>
> But we also find an unmistakable reference to strife in heaven in the New Testament. Revelation xii, 7-8, reads:
>
> > "And there was war in heaven: Michael and his angels fought against the dragon: and the dragon fought and his angels,
> > "And prevailed not; neither was their place found any more in heaven."
>
> Many of the ancient documents of mankind mention wars and battles in heaven. The Book of Dzyan, a secret doctrine, was preserved for millennia in Tibetan crypts. The original text, of which nothing is known, not even whether it still exists, was copied from generation to generation and added to by initiates. Parts of the Book of Dzyan that have been preserved circulate around the world in thousands of Sanskrit translations, and experts claim that this book contains the evolution of mankind over millions of years. The Sixth Stanza of the Book of Dzyan runs as follows: LIKE SIXTH day CREATION IN BIBLE
>
> > "At the fourth (round), the sons are told to create their images, one third refuses. Two obey. The curse is pronounced . . . The older wheels rotated downward and upward. The mother's spawn filled the whole. *There were battles fought between the creators and the destroyers, and battles fought for space; the seed appearing and reappearing continuously.* Make thy calculations, o disciple, if thou wouldst learn the correct age of thy small wheel."

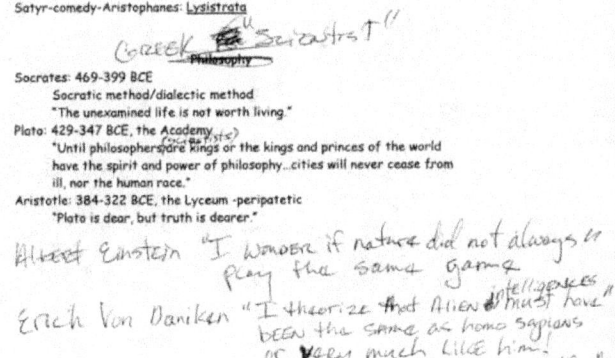

Satyr-comedy-Aristophanes: <u>Lysistrata</u>

GREEK "scientist!"
~~Philosophy~~

Socrates: 469-399 BCE
    Socratic method/dialectic method
    "The unexamined life is not worth living."
Plato: 429-347 BCE, the Academy (Sophists)
    "Until philosophers are kings or the kings and princes of the world have the spirit and power of philosophy...cities will never cease from ill, nor the human race."
Aristotle: 384-322 BCE, the Lyceum -peripatetic
    "Plato is dear, but truth is dearer."

Albert Einstein "I wonder if nature did not always play the same game"

Erich Von Daniken "I theorize that Alien intelligences must have been the same as homo sapiens or very much like him!"

Using science to prove God and make themselves look ridiculous with their quote, which disproves their God. (Read about this in my story)

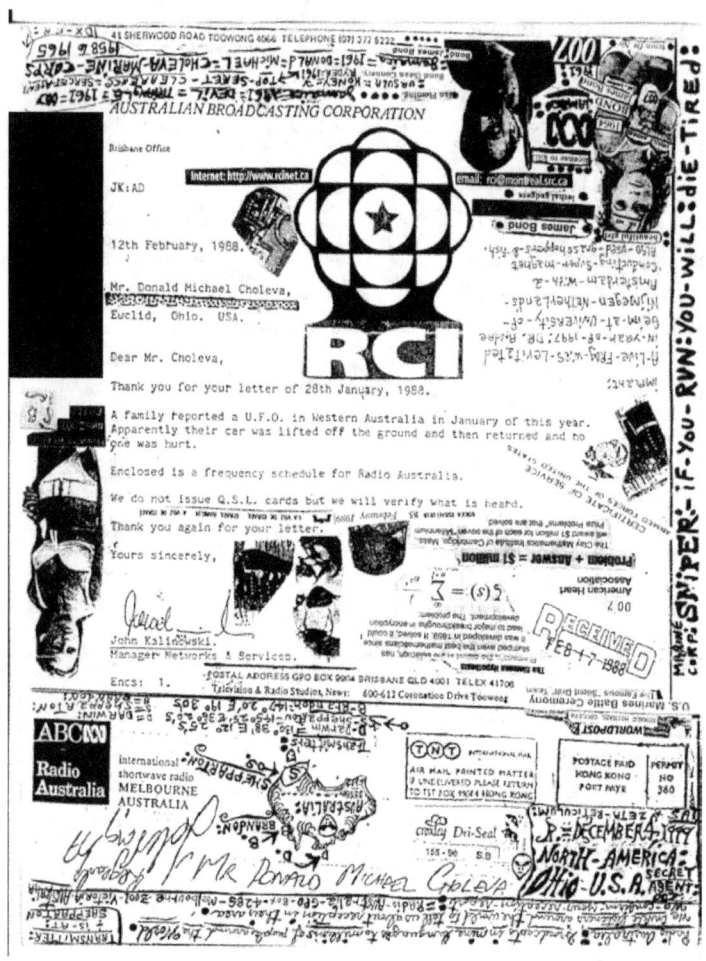

Blackened box in upper left corner had Marine Corps sniper stamp. This is a death threat of which I contacted the police. It came in the mail!

www.tennessean.com   THE TENNESSEAN   Friday, May 26, 2006   7A

Clearly, scientists want cloak of invisibility

If they could only see a way to make it ...

By ANDREW BRIDGES
Associated Press

WASHINGTON — The key to creating a Harry Potter-like invisibility cloak lies in manmade materials unlike any in the Hogwarts School of Witchcraft and Wizardry, researchers say.

They're laying out a blueprint for turning science fiction into reality. And they say that, in theory, nothing's stopping them from making such a cloak.

Well, almost nothing: They still need to perfect the manufacture of those exotic materials with an ability to steer light and other forms of electromagnetic radiation around a cloaked object.

"Is it science fiction? Well, it's theory and that already is not science fiction. It's theoretically possible to do all these Harry Potter things, but what's standing in the way is our engineering capabilities," said John Pendry, a physicist at the Imperial College London. Details of a study that Pendry co-wrote are in Thursday's online edition of the journal Science.

"This is very interesting science and a very interesting idea, and it is supported on a great mathematical and physical basis," said Nader Engheta, a professor of electrical and systems engineering at the University of Pennsylvania who has done his own work on invisibility using novel materials called metamaterials.

Pendry and his co-authors also propose using metamaterials because they can be tuned to bend electromagnetic radiation — radio waves and visible light, for example — in any direction.

A cloak made of those materials would neither reflect light nor cast a shadow.

Instead, like a river streaming around a smooth boulder, light and all other forms of electromagnetic radiation would simply flow around it. An onlooker would appear to peer right through the cloak, with everything inside it concealed.

Early versions that could mask microwaves and other forms of electromagnetic radiation could be as close as 18 months away, Pendry said. He said the study was "an invitation to come and play with these new ideas."

"We will have a cloak after not too long," he said. ■

Invisibility is the Holy Grail of Science. Also, it is at the core of religion and the modern-day UFO phenomenon.

MIKE BRUMFIELD

MODERN PHYSICS

THE BASIC ELEMENTS OF MATTER

What is matter?

Matter is anything that takes up space and has mass (or weight, which is the influence of gravity on mass). It is distinguished from energy, which causes objects to move or change, but which has no volume or mass of its own. Matter and energy interact, and under certain circumstances behave similarly, but for the most part remain separate phenomena. They are, however, inter-convertible according to Einstein's equation $E = mc^2$, where E is the amount of energy that is equivalent to an amount of mass m, and c is a constant, the speed of light in a vacuum.

In 1804, the English scientist John Dalton formulated the atomic theory, which set out some fundamental characteristics of matter, and which is still used today. According to this theory, matter is composed of extremely small particles called atoms, which can be neither created nor destroyed. Atoms can, however, attach themselves (bond) to each other in various arrangements to form molecules. A material composed entirely of atoms of one type is an element, and different elements are made of different atoms. A material composed entirely of molecules of one type is a compound, and different compounds are made of different molecules. Pure elements and pure compounds are often referred to collectively as pure substances, as opposed to a mixture in which atoms or molecules of more than one type are jumbled together in no particular arrangement. 3

People . . . please learn that matter is energy and infinite! This explains the $E = mc^2$ of energy. Atoms can be neither created nor destroyed!

Question: Is this Yeshua's/Jesus's sign for contact . . . nuclear war?

MIKE BRUMFIELD

Proof

DVD 19.95-BOOK 12.95
SEND CHECK OR M.O.
MIKE BRUMFIELD
1066 GOLDEN HERREN RD
SPARTA, TN 38583
ORDER ONLINE AT
UFOSOVERPHOENIX.COM
931-261-6697

2005

p
r
o
o
f

History Researcher Mike Brumfield examines Ancient Evidence/ Art/ Religion giving his opinion of why **Extraterrestrials** won't make open contact with the human race. Featured In New Book "2012 Gold's History solves Mankind's Mystery" Also Featuring Jeff Willes Famous Video Footage Recently Previewed On The Travel Channel. Matches Johnny Cash & Easter Island !

Crop Circle
Yin and Yang or Atomic Propulsion
Jeff's

FACT
Ancient Religious Statue- "Giant Heads" of Easter Island

OPINION
It is looking up & telling us where their GOD is: UP/ HEAVEN/ SPACE
What they're in: Fiery Chariot/ Flying Saucer. They Look UP because all religions await "SECOND COMING from the SKY"
HEAVEN IS "UP" / SKY / SPACE!!

WHY THEY DON'T SHOW UP

MIKE BRUMFIELD

Easter Island Solved

REALITY: ESCAPE FROM EARTH

Proof Introducing Jeff and Mike they find it!!
Jeff gives you current flying saucer footage that matches Johnny Cash sighting in 1980 & Easter Island *(back cover)*

Mike Brumfield REVEALS
Scientific Religous Evidence
"Why They Don't Show And When They Will"

More inside...

Jeff's   Johnny's
Matching Saucer's!

Real photo of Johnny Cash in 1980

Solves Easter Island Mystery And More!

Famous Painting 1400 A.D. of a Flying Saucer

Flying Saucer Matches Also!

Man looking "UP" at it.

Close-up View

The Jeff and Mike Show—Flying Saucer Hunters

WHY THE BLANK DON'T THEY CARE?

VIDEO 2003

We were also shocked to look "UP" and see them!
Did these ancient religious "chariots of fire"
create religion's stories, "heavenly beings in the sky"
and their universal halo symbol "UP"
above their head? It is a saucer shape!

HEADS OF EASTER ISLAND LOOKING "UP"!
THIS EVIDENCE MATCHES
Ancient Flying Saucer Statue

Letter to *UFO Magazine*, February 20, 2006, about Jeff's proposal to find flying saucers. They didn't bite, and we filmed them during trip. The still didn't bite even after contacting them with our footage to prove we found them!

Bill:

I have enclosed a video for you to review. I recently talked with you about the Johnny Cash photo and emphasized how this could garner serious attention for a huge breakthrough discovery. The flyer clearly shows a match between Jeff's flying saucer and the alleged hat of Easter Island. This also matches Johnny's saucer which is on the cover of the video. Please bear with the amateur quality of my video. My narration/explanation of why they don't show is one hour long. Then the 2003 video footage of Jeff's flying saucers begins. I also included the 1952 White House incident. This alone should demand attention. I will be coming to LA and approach the *Times* with my breakthrough discovery in man's quest for contact. The head of Easter Island is clearly looking up and has a flying saucer on top of its head. This answers the questions that Barbara Walter's just posed to all esteemed religious scholars of the Earth including the Dalai Lama, "Where is heaven?" My breakthrough religious scientific discovery of the world's largest ancient statue of a flying saucer confirms all ancient writings as well as today's space pursuit. Heaven is up, space is the final frontier. It is already conquered like religion confirms. The owl man of Peru shows us the same message. He is pointing up! The owlman and Easter Island statues are bald headed big-eyed statues like the Roswell alien. There are many depictions in ancient artworks of aliens and flying saucers that confirms this reality. I am sending also a cover of my latest book showing some of these that can't be refuted. I hope you will consider contacting me for an interview. We can't believe that nobody is taking this seriously. That is why we titled our next video "Why the Blank Don't They Care." I make it clear in the video why they don't show. The evidence speaks for itself. We are mining gold for them, since our beginning. Gold is important for space travel. Our creation is scientific and can't be stopped. There is no spirit magic and people get addicted to beauty of the flesh which gives us power over one another. The Easter Island statues all look the same. It would be great to have your magazine chronicle our journey on getting some attention for this discovery. We will prove that flying saucers are here now by videoing them together. This will happen after I leave LA on my return trip to Nashville. My partner Jeff lives in Phoenix and films them regularly. He promises me that we will see one. I believe him. Do you? Funny thing, that religion's universal contact story is about believing. We propose that this flying saucer evidence will answer that question. And yet, the story goes that most won't. We are entrenched in a spirit world belief system. Could religion be a direct result of primitive man's contact with flying saucers and aliens. They have both universal traditions, a gold halo symbol and bald heads.

Sincerely,
Mike

People, crimes and mysteries are solved today through the scientific method of matching evidence. The perpetrators of religion live in the sky. We are now videoing flying saucers everywhere and we now live in the sky! Could flying saucers and a real flesh and blood alien species have created religion as the matching evidence suggest? If you can open your mind to accepting evidence it is easy to "SEE" how advanced technologies would have created primitive man's spirit magic traditions. However, fortunately enough the foundation of his story though has never changed. These people live in the sky. The evidence does show "HEAVEN IS SPACE, UP!" AND THIS IS THEIR SYMBOL...

The gold halo above their head is their symbol! It looks like a flying saucer! What they look like is the ultimate evidence that will solve our mystery and Fermi's Paradox. The statues on the next page clearly answer the question of who and what primitive man's god looked like. Why they created our species is obvious. It also matches their story. They desired beauty of the flesh. This gives them "greatness" over one another. Coincidence? "Religion cover-up" is the title to my first book.

This is the "head/person" that should be under the gold halo. Funny how the book cover shows the shroud which looks like space beneath it. Because it exemplifies what the cover-up in religion is all about. What heaven's occupants look like? And where are they? The evidence says clearly that they are aliens UP IN SPACE! If you don't follow evidence or can't imagine a new discovery of an ancient relic that could solve our mystery, then please watch Planet of the Apes. The apes ignore scientific evidence over their religious stories of God creating them, just like my story today! Why the blank don't they care! Check out my video. Are we all addicted to outward beauty? Hell, yeah!!! Can't, couldn't do anything. I've always said instant creation/magic wasn't possible, but if it is, I guarantee it to be scientific. And then, it couldn't make this universe perfect. Babies are being raped. Finally, people ... please answer for yourself why anybody would let this happen if they could stop it. I promise you, there's only one logical answer ... they can't.

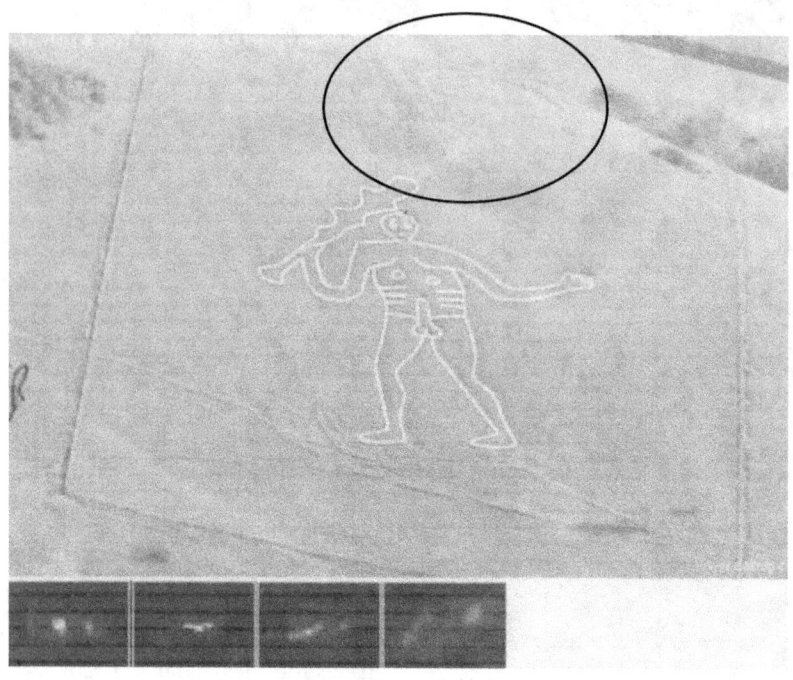

This is the Cernes Giant of Cerne, England. Legend has it that it is a Saxon god. My conclusion, based on the evidence I've presented, is that the god of primitive man is an alien and his fiery chariot is a flying saucer. The images below the giant are from video that I shot in Phoenix, Arizona, March 6, 2006. It is a flying saucer. It also matches the mound circled/squared above the head of this Cernes Giant/god. The most compelling matching evidence is the shape of the mound, a ring within a ring, and the bald head and big eyes of the giant. The craft matches my craft as can be seen at the following exhibit's website, and the head of this giant matches the aborigine alien-looking god, as well as all others. My last word on this evidence issue, to religious people and the rest of the world, is the bald-headed traditions of all religions and looking UP! This relief carving is another example of part alien/part man with a fiery chariot "UP" above his head!

Get the point!

rense.com

UFO Performs Acrobatics Over Phoenix

3-15-6

3 witnesses observed the videotaping of a UFO performing aerial stunts so astonishing it made it on the Channel 3 News in Phoenix. Once again, Jeff Willes' constant skywatching pays off big time...

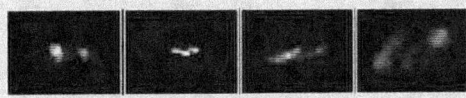

To view part of the video click here
(Windows Media Player file - wmv)

Report from Jeff Willes of NFO

"I was out in the back yard skywatching late on 3-6-06. At 12:00 am one of the others skywatching with me saw a UFO come up from the trees about a mile away and then go down again. We ran up to the top of the roof leaving our tripods on the ground, forgetting them in all the action. When we got on the roof we saw not one but two UFOs shooting way up in the sky and then coming back down behind the trees. The UFOs shot up and came back down 3 times. One of the craft would fly over upside down and then dive down. It did this 3 or 4 times. I took the tape to KYVK Channel 3TV here in Phoenix. They aired the footage on 3-10-06. They showed how the object flips over. I have been videotaping UFOs sense 1995 and have never seen anything like it."

Jeff Willes
www.ufosoverphoenix.com

I was the other witness along with Jeff and his wife. The daytime footage I shot is on the back cover of this book. I spent three days and videotaped well over ten flying saucers. Even the news reporter commented that the behavior of our saucer footage definitely proved it was not any kind of aircraft known to man. You can view the footage at www.ufosoverphoenix.com!

Looks like ancient holes dug up in Peru! Ask?

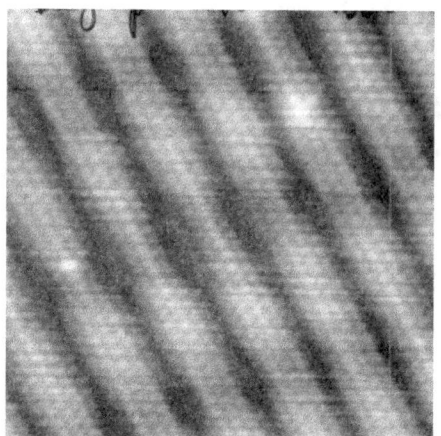

Scanning tunneling microscope image showing the individual atom making up this gold surface. Reconstruction causes the surface atoms to deviate from the bulk crystal structure and arrange in columns several atoms wide with pits between them. Is knowledge of the atom a key to understanding the infinite nature of the universe?

Drawn by my best friend Lonnie, at the age of seven. The saucer is just like all others on saucer comparison! We are starting an immediate project to stop Fukishima's nuclear leak. He's a gr8 dad and friend. Luv u guys!

See how the angels feet looks like today's rocket thrusters. Could these symbols > < on either side of the flying saucer give us the answer to their propulsion system? Finally, see the words "I am" in the heart. Is this the answer to the ultimate question? "Could we be them?" The most famous man's name in the world confirms this reality. "YES-HU-A." I am!

Smoking Gun Evidence

The Video/Picture Evidence

Paul Villa photo of flying saucer circa 1960.

Video taken in 2003 by Jeff Willes of Phoenix, Arizona. To buy video, type his name in computer or call 623/847-9132.

Video taken in 2006 by Mike Brumfield in Phoenix, Arizona.

Photo taken in Peru, 2013

<u>Proof of ominscience with E.T. craft over 17,000 years.</u> The following photos were taken by five different people, including myself, over a span of 60 years. They all match each other and the cave drawing, in Lacaux, France on the front cover of my third book!!! I am begging Marty Stewart to talk about this. The world loves celebrities and I am not one. But I still see these and film them. They exist and are not time travelers. The future is out there, now. This is not religion's test or science's experiment. This is our future and it is here now. It is our "REALITY"! If the universe is infinite, then "LOGIC" says only "ONE" thing, they must be "INFINITE ASTRONAUTS" and we are experiencing the "CHOICE HYPOTHESIS". Do we really want, to be "IMMORTAL" at any "COST"?

Smoking Gun Evidence

Evolution and Creation Evidence

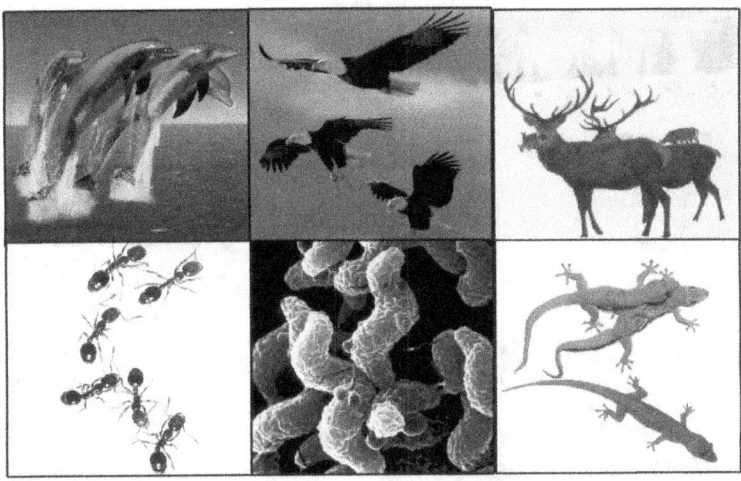

Q. What physical features do all the species above have in common that humans don't?

A. They all look alike!

Is it possible a human species evolved & created us for power through beauty of flesh?

Smoking Gun Evidence

Flying saucer

These figures all look alike!

Could our sudden appearance without the skull evolution from an elongated cranium to the obvious upright bulbous large head be directly related to religion's god? Our short recorded history is!

Could these ancient statues be proof of a species that evolved?

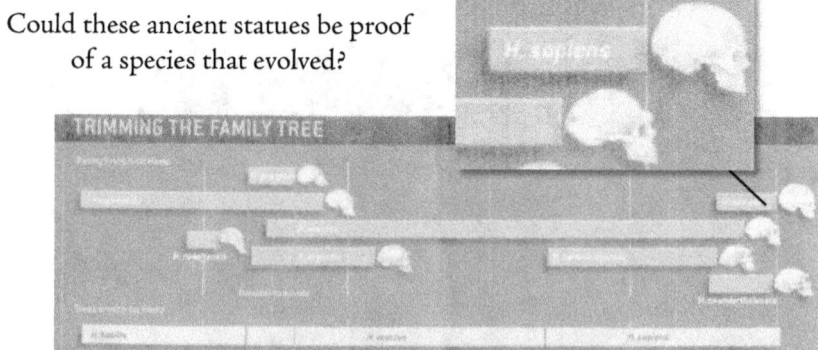

REALITY: ESCAPE FROM EARTH

"MY ANSWER / THEORY"

Famous Last Words: "INFINITE ASTRONAUTS EXIST"! The evidence you've just seen, "PROVES" that there is only "ONE" intelligent species and they "EVOLVED"! They live "EVERYWHERE IN SPACE" and not on planets. They are the "GOOD" guys and it is because, they all "LOOK THE SAME". The evidence is "SIMPLE" and clear! Mankind's pursuit of power and lust for "OUTWARD BEAUTY", is "EVIL". Our "DESIRE" to be the "GREATEST" is an incurable disease. Whether you believe it or not is up to you. It is your "CHOICE". I call my answer to our "MYSTERY", the "CHOICE HYPOTHESES". I do this for a "REASON". This "EVIDENCE, SPEAKS FOR ITSELF". Why are we here? Is it possible we choose "TO BE"? Why don't we know it? Is it possible we choose "NOT TO"? Is it possible we "IGNORE SCIENTIFIC IMMORTALITY", because "CHOOSING IT" would compel us to "SCIENTIFICALLY" act upon it? People, we can do this. We can run and hide from "DEATH", but it won't go away. This evidence is "REAL"! If you still think intelligent life can't be everywhere, then you haven't remembered my "TWO ULTIMATE LOGICAL QUESTIONS"... 1. "How advanced can life be in and "INFINITE UNIVERSE"? If you think life can't be "INFINITELY ADVANCED" and you couldn't be one of these infinitely advanced "BEINGS", addicted to a "BEAUTIFUL SCIENTIFIC CREATION", ask yourself the other "ULTIMATE QUESTION"...2. "Do I want to be ugly"? I don't! I'm facing it. Unfortunately, everyone will have to "FACE IT". Sadly, even our kids do! People, we have to talk to them about "SEX". "SEEKING IMMORTALITY SCIENTIFICALLY", will "UNLOCK OUR MYSTERY". It is the key to achieving "INTELLEGENCE"! I "HOPE" that we will all choose an intellectual path, over a sexual one. It "WILL" give us the tools to conquer death, Mother Nature and "FINALLY SPACE". "POSSIBLY, AGAIN"! Religion says it is our home and "SCIENCE, AGREES"! "COMMON SENSE", does too. People, for

the "LAST TIME", we can conquer "SPACE"! I have to, I have kids! Please, help me keep my kids from dying, please? Like it or not, and believe me, I don't. It "IS" my "REALITY"! (See definition again, go back to the beginning) Conquering death and space, has to be, everyone's "REALITY"!! People, this is our
"REALITY"!!!

Love always,
Dad / Mike /
Will Powers

P.S. People… Would you please help me contact Marty Stuart about his flying saucer picture matching mine? I find and film them; they are real and have obviously "ALWAYS EXISTED". Also, would you please help me contact Barbara Walters and convince her to give my answer to her TV special "Where is Heaven?", a "CHANCE"? Funny, I found "CHANCE" is where the universe "BEGINS, IS CURRENTLY" and where this book "ENDS"! Please, I'm begging you for our kids sake, give my answer a "CHANCE"?

The definition of intelligence from the Merriam-Webster Dictionary: "The ability to learn or understand or to deal with new or trying situations : reason; also : the skilled use of reason Also, the ability to apply knowledge to manipulate one's environment or to think abstractly as measured by objective criteria."

www.ingramcontent.com/pod-product-compliance
Lightning Source LLC
Chambersburg PA
CBHW071150300426
44113CB00009B/1147